Lecture Notes in Artificial Intelli

Edited by R. Goebel, J. Siekmann, and W. Wa

Subseries of Lecture Notes in Computer Science

Elisabeth André   Laila Dybkjær
Wolfgang Minker   Heiko Neumann
Roberto Pieraccini   Michael Weber (Eds.)

Perception in Multimodal Dialogue Systems

4th IEEE Tutorial and Research Workshop on Perception and
Interactive Technologies for Speech-Based Systems, PIT 2008
Kloster Irsee, Germany, June 16-18, 2008
Proceedings

 Springer

Volume Editors

Elisabeth André
Universität Augsburg, Institut für Informatik, Augsburg, Germany
E-mail: andre@informatik.uni-augsburg.de

Laila Dybkjær
Prolog Development Center A/S (PDC), Brøndby, Denmark
E-mail: laila@pdc.dk

Wolfgang Minker
Universität Ulm, Institut für Informationstechnologie und Dialogsysteme
Ulm, Germany
E-mail: wolfgang.minker@uni-ulm.de

Heiko Neumann
Universität Ulm, Abteilung Neuroinformatik, Ulm, Germany
E-mail: heiko.neumann@uni-ulm.de

Roberto Pieraccini
SpeechCycle, Inc., New York, NY, USA
E-mail: roberto@speechcycle.com

Michael Weber
Universität Ulm, Institut für Medieninformatik, Ulm, Germany
E-mail: michael.weber@uni-ulm.de

Library of Congress Control Number: 2008928841

CR Subject Classification (1998): H.5.2-3, H.5, I.2.6-7, I.2.10, I.2, K.4, I.4

LNCS Sublibrary: SL 7 – Artificial Intelligence

ISSN   0302-9743
ISBN-10   3-540-69368-8 Springer Berlin Heidelberg New York
ISBN-13   978-3-540-69368-0 Springer Berlin Heidelberg New York

Springer is a part of Springer Science+Business Media

springer.com

© Springer-Verlag Berlin Heidelberg 2008

Typesetting: Camera-ready by author, data conversion by Scientific Publishing Services, Chennai, India
Printed on acid-free paper   SPIN: 12322121   06/3180   5 4 3 2 1 0

Preface

The IEEE Tutorial and Research Workshop on Perception and Interactive Technologies for Multimodal Dialogue Systems (PIT 2008) is the continuation of a successful series of workshops that started with an ISCA Tutorial and Research Workshop on Multimodal Dialogue Systems in 1999. This workshop was followed by a second one focusing on mobile dialogue systems (IDS 2002), a third one exploring the role of affect in dialogue (ADS 2004), and a fourth one focusing on perceptive interfaces (PIT 2006). Like its predecessors, PIT 2008 took place at Kloster Irsee in Bavaria.

Due to the increasing interest in perceptive interfaces, we decided to hold a follow-up workshop on the themes discussed at PIT 2006, but encouraged above all papers with a focus on perception in multimodal dialogue systems. PIT 2008 received 37 papers covering the following topics (1) multimodal and spoken dialogue systems, (2) classification of dialogue acts and sound, (3) recognition of eye gaze, head poses, mimics and speech as well as combinations of modalities, (4) vocal emotion recognition, (5) human-like and social dialogue systems and (6) evaluation methods for multimodal dialogue systems.

Noteworthy was the strong participation from industry at PIT 2008. Indeed, 17 of the accepted 37 papers come from industrial organizations or were written in collaboration with them.

We would like to thank all authors for the effort they made with their submissions, and the Program Committee – nearly 50 distinguished researchers from industry and academia – who worked very hard to meet tight deadlines and selected the best contributions for the final program. Special thanks goes to our invited speaker, Anton Batliner from Friedrich-Alexander-Universität Erlangen-Nürnberg.

A number of organizations supported PIT 2008 including the IEEE Signal Processing Society, ACL Sigmedia and ACL/ISCA Sigdial. In particular, we are grateful to Springer for publishing the proceedings in their LNCS/LNAI series.

April 2008

Elisabeth André
Laila Dybkjær
Wolfgang Minker
Heiko Neumann
Roberto Pieraccini
Michael Weber

Organization

Organizing Committee

Elisabeth André (University of Augsburg, Germany)
Laila Dybkjær (PDC A/S, Denmark)
Wolfgang Minker (University of Ulm, Germany)
Roberto Pieraccini (SpeechCycle Inc., USA)
Heiko Neumann (University of Ulm, Germany)
Michael Weber (University of Ulm, Germany)

Scientific Committee

Jan Alexandersson	Paul Heisterkamp	Christopher Peters
Yacine Bellik	Dirk Heylen	Helmut Prendinger
André Berton	David House	Norbert Reithinger
Rolf Carlson	Christophe Jacquet	Thomas Rist
Cristina Conati	Ralf Kompe	Laurent Romary
Klaus Dorfmüller-Ulhaas	Rainer Lienhart	Fiorella de Rosis
Ellen Douglas-Cowie	Jackson Liscombe	Alex Rudnicky
Gabriel Cristobal	Joseph Mariani	Candy Sidner
Laurence Devillers	Jean-Claude Martin	Rainer Stiefelhagen
Sadaoki Furui	Dominic Massaro	Oliviero Stock
Jim Glass	Louis-Philippe Morency	David Suendermann
Silke Goronzy	Elmar Nöth	David Traum
Joakim Gustafson	Ana Paiva	Matthias Thomae
Eli Hagen	Tim Paek	Thurid Vogt
Hani Hagras	Patrick Paroubek	Wayne Ward
Udo Haiber	Catherine Pelachaud	
Gerhard Hanrieder	Alex Pentland	

Sponsoring Organizations

IEEE Signal Processing Society
ACL/ISCA Sigdial
ACL Sigmedia

Table of Contents

Recognition of Eye Gaze, Head Pose, Mimics and Lip Movements

Speech Recognition

Vocal Emotion Recognition and Annotation

Human-Like Social Dialogue

Evaluation Methods

Whence and Whither: The Automatic Recognition of Emotions in Speech (Invited Keynote)

Anton Batliner

Friedrich-Alexander-Universität Erlangen-Nürnberg, Lehrstuhl für Mustererkennung,
Martensstraße 3, D-91058 Erlangen, Germany
batliner@informatik.uni-erlangen.de

Abstract. In this talk, we first want to sketch the (short) history of the automatic recognition of emotions in speech: studies on the characteristics of emotions in speech were published as early as in the twenties and thirties of the last century; attempts to recognize them automatically began in the mid nineties, dealing with acted data which still are used often - too often if we consider the fact that drawing inferences from acted data onto realistic data is at least sub-optimal.

In a second part, we present the necessary 'basics': the design of the scenario, the recordings, the manual processing (transliteration, annotation), etc. These basics are to some extent 'generic' — for instance, each speech database has to be transliterated orthographically somehow. Other ones are specific such as the principles and the guidelines for emotion annotation, and the basic choices between, for example, dimensional and categorical approaches. The pros and cons of different annotation approaches have been discussed widely; however, the unit of analysis (utterance, turn, sentence, etc.?) has not yet been dealt with often; thus we will discuss this topic in more detail.

In a third part, we will present acoustic and linguistic features that have been used (or should be used) in this field, and touch on the topic of their different degree of relevance.

Classification and necessary ingredients such as feature reduction and selection, choice of classifier, and assessment of classification performance, will be addressed in the fourth part.

So far, we have been dealing with the 'whence' in our title, depicting the state-of-the-art; we will end up the talk with the 'whither' in the title — with promising applications and some speculations on dead end approaches.

E. André et al. (Eds.): PIT 2008, LNAI 5078, p. 1, 2008.
© Springer-Verlag Berlin Heidelberg 2008

A Generic Spoken Dialogue Manager Applied to an Interactive 2D Game

Andrea Corradini[1] and Christer Samuelsson[2]

[1] University of Southern Denmark
Institute of Business Communication and Information Science,
6000 Kolding, Denmark
andrea@sitkom.sdu.dk
[2] Umbria, Inc., 1655 Walnut St, Suite 300,
Boulder, CO 80302, USA
christer@umbrialistens.com

Abstract. A generic dialogue manager, previously used in real-world spoken language applications for databases and call-routing, was redeployed in an existing spoken language interface to a 2D game system, which required spatial reasoning, absent in previous applications. This was accomplished by separating general, domain, and application specific knowledge from the machinery, reusing the machinery and the general knowledge, and exploiting ergonomic specification languages for the remaining knowledge. The clear-cut agent-based architecture also contributed strongly to the success of the undertaking.

1 Introduction

Speech and natural language have been increasingly included as modalities to interactive systems. The rationale behind this trend is the assumption that these modes, being natural and common means of communication among humans, would facilitate the user interaction with the machine and simultaneously broaden its bandwidth. While some researchers criticize such an argument based on some evidence that people show different patterns of behavior when they interact with technology as when they interact with each other [Shneiderman, 1980], speech and natural language are of unquestionable benefit in certain domains and for people with special needs and disabilities [Rosenfeld et al, 2001]. Due to current technological limitations, robust and reliable treatment of natural spoken language remains a problem in large domains and even in restricted interactive applications, when recognition errors, misunderstanding and other sources of communication failures must be taken into account. This calls for a system capable to robustly deal with errors and guide users through the interaction process in a collaborative manner.

In state-of-the-art spoken dialogue systems, the dialogue manager is the component in charge of regulating the flow of the conversation between the user and the application. It interprets information gathered from the user and combines it with a number of contextual and internal knowledge sources (such as a dialogue and task history, a domain model and ontology, and a behavioral model of conversational competence)

E. André et al. (Eds.): PIT 2008, LNAI 5078, pp. 2–13, 2008.
© Springer-Verlag Berlin Heidelberg 2008

in the effort to resolve ambiguities that arise as a consequence of system failures, user mistakes, or under specifications. The dialogue manager eliminates uncertainty through clarification and confirmation requests, either explicitly or implicitly, provides assistance upon request and guides the user by directing the conversation towards a definite goal. In the ideal case, this results in a successful and effective interaction experience, but in practice, there is a trade-off between more user flexibility and better system understanding accuracy. Summarized to a minimum, the task of a dialogue manager consists in reasoning about external observations (such as the user input) in order to update its internal representation of the dialogue and determine what action to perform according to a certain dialogue management policy [Levin et al, 1999].

Several architectures for dialogue management have been proposed for this task. On the one hand, they have many similarities, as they all share a subset of basic core functional components. On the other hand, they exhibit conceptual differences in the way the dialogue state is modeled, and in the specification of the strategy that controls the dialogue flow. Based on these two features (and small variations thereof), architectures for dialogue management can be broadly classified into four main classes. Finite state systems represent dialogue structure in the form of a network, where every node models a question, and the transitions between nodes account for all the possible dialogues [Lemon et al, 2001; McTear, 1998]. The nodes of the network are sometime augmented with scores determined with machine learning techniques, to select optimal network paths [Hurtado et al, 2003]. Finite state systems are theoretically well-understood, and they can be deployed when the interaction constitutes a sequential pre-defined process. Another approach to dialogue management is based on frame structures. Typically, each frame consists of slot-value pairs that are filled in as the interaction proceeds and are also used to guide the user through the dialogue [Hardy et al, 2004; Hochberg et al, 2002; Pieraccini et al, 2001; Seneff and Polifroni, 2000; Ward and Pellom, 1999; Zue et al, 2000]. This strategy is typically deployed in task oriented systems. Its major drawback is scalability. In plan-based architectures [Allen et al, 2001; Bohus and Rudnicky, 2003; Chu-Carroll, 1999; Litman and Allen, 1987; Rudnicky and Xu, 1999] the interaction is driven by a planning process dedicated to achieving certain goals. To accomplish a goal, a sequence of actions (which may be sub-goals themselves) is carried out. The dialogue manager is thus simultaneously a reasoning, inference, and optimization engine, which employs its plans to achieve its goals, given the available information. The merit of such an approach is its ability to handle complex situations, but the drawback is that it quickly becomes computationally intractable. A different recent approach [Bos, 2003; Larsson and Traum, 2000; Lemon et al, 2006] introduces the concept of information state to model dialogues, explaining previous actions, and predicting future actions.

We here deploy an existing, generic, plan-based, slot-filling dialogue manager to an interactive game, where users play a board game using a GUI, as well as spoken and/or typed natural language. The structure of this article is as follows. Section 2 gives a general system overview, while Section 3 focuses on the dialogue manager and provides a worked example. Eventually, a short discussion concludes the paper.

2 System Overview

A sketch of the system architecture is given in Figure 1. It consists of a set of agents that communicate with each other by means of the OAA agent architecture [Cheyer and Martin, 2001].

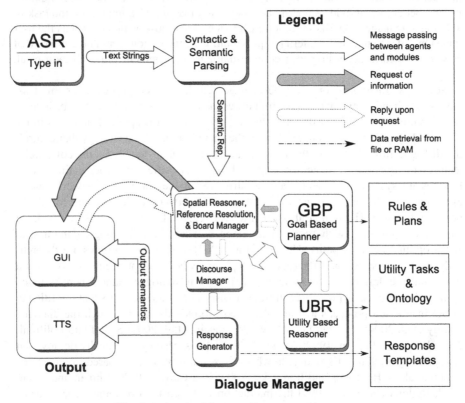

Fig. 1. A sketch of the overall system architecture

2.1 The Pentomino Game Domain

Pentomino is the popular board game of choice for our application. This puzzle game is named after the well-known Domino from which it differs only because its pieces are formed by joining five, instead of just two, equal sized squares together along complete edges. Excluding isomorphism (i.e. rotations, flipping and combinations of them), there are only twelve possible pieces. In Pentomino the player has to use up the set of pieces and land them into a predefined grid-shaped game board (see Figure 2). From a mathematical perspective, Pentomino is a particular type of Polyominos [Golomb, 1965] and as such it is considered an exact mathematical science.

Here, it was realized as a set of agents, controlled by a main GUI manager, which implemented the rules, logic, and presentation of the game, game position, and game history. It allows users to play the game through spoken and/or typed natural language or direct manipulation, i.e. via a mouse to click, drag, and drop. The user can choose to play in a slightly more challenging way by using the game timer and by attempting at producing a complete solution of the puzzle within the shortest time possible.

2.2 Syntax-Driven Semantic Parser

Players are shown a GUI version of Pentomino (see Figure 2) that they can play using either mouse or keyboard or speech or a combination of two or more of these modalities. In order to allow users play with the game GUI using speech, we use the Sphinx-4 [Walker et al, 2004] open source speech recognizer. Sphinx-4 is a flexible state-of-the-art decoder capable of performing many different types of recognition tasks. It supports all types of HMM-based acoustic models, all standard types of language models, and several search strategies. It can be used along with a JSGF grammar or with an N-gram language model in which case syntactic parsing is not performed by Sphinx-4. Currently, our parser can be used in case where either Sphinx is run using a JSGF[1] grammar or the decoder is bypassed and input is typed-in.

The spoken or typed user input is parsed into a term structure in several steps. The first step is done either by the ASR engine, using a recognition grammar, or by a separate syntactic parser, using the very same grammar. Both of these work as a recursive transition network, transducing the input speech or text into a flat semantic representation, consisting of a sequence of pairs and triples. The semantic parser then chunks this sequence, and each chunk is matched against a set of predicates to create one or more term-structured semantic forms. This output is similar to the predicate-argument structure produced by a syntactic parser using application-specific compositional semantics (see [Corradini et al, 2007] for more details). Such semantic forms constitute the input to the dialogue manager (DM).

2.3 Dialogue Manager Assistants

The dialogue manager itself, and its key components, are described in the next section. It does however have some assistants, from which it can request additional information. Among them, the spatial reasoner, which informs the dialog manager about spatial relations between given Pentomino pieces, and the board manager, which provides the location, shape, and color of all Pentomino pieces, are among these important components. They report to either the GUI module or the DM (in Figure 1 they are actually depicted within the DM module itself), but should be seen as independent contractors.

3 The Dialogue Manager Proper

The core dialogue manager is best viewed as a high-level corporate executive officer. It knows virtually nothing about what it's managing, and must constantly request information from its underlings. This analogy is also apt, in the sense that it employs greedy algorithms, but delegates all actual work. This has the advantages that less

---

[1] Java.sun.com/products/java-media/speech/forDevelopers/JSG

expensive resources can do most of the work; and that the dialog manager is highly portable, and readily redeployed elsewhere.

Key design features of the dialog manager include that it:

1. partitions knowledge three ways: general, domain-, and application-specific, reusing the first two when possible;
2. separates general dialog behavior from domain-specific behavior, handling the former with a goal-based planner and the latter with a utility-based reasoner;
3. formulates all application and domain knowledge in intuitive, high-level specification languages, which non-programmers can easily master;
4. keeps all data representation and interfaces generic and spotlessly clean, and the tasks of each component clear-cut and limited in scope;
5. recasts extra, specialized reasoning in existing terms, or relegates it to dedicated components;
6. and solicits information not only from the user, but interacts freely with other modules, especially with the client back-end system (typically a relational database or CGI-like transaction system)

This stern design austerity has paid off in terms of reusability, and in ease and speed of application development. In fact, the very same dialog manager, together with several of its components, has been used in spoken dialog front-ends to database query systems, call-routing applications, and transaction systems [Chu-Carroll, 1999; Chu-Carroll and Carpenter, 1999].

3.1 Dialogue Manager Internals

The dialog management machinery consists of:

- a goal-based planner;
- a utility-based reasoner;
- a discourse manager;
- a response generator;
- some agent wrapping.

The discourse manager maintains a summary of the dialogue this far. The response generator is responsible for producing text strings to be synthesized by the TTS and valid game commands for the GUI to carry out. The other relevant components are described below. Other supporting components to them can be added: here, for example, a reference resolution resolver to disambiguate references to objects and entities in the game world. The dialogue manager requires the following application-specific resources:

- a domain or application ontology;
- the set of possible back-end transactions;
- a set of plans and executable primitives;
- a set of response templates;
- a utility function;
- an interface to the other system modules.

The first four of these are created using ergonomic specification languages i.e. a specification language appropriate for the skill set of the developer that minimizes his or her cognitive load.

The first two vary little within a given domain and task type. For instance, building a transaction system for the next bank consists mostly in changing the actual names of low-level entities in the ontology and changing some back-end transactions. Clients however differ widely in how they want the system to behave and in the details of its responses, so both third and fourth item (and managing client expectations) outlined above can easily swell to encompass the lion share of all development effort.

The utility function for our current game system is based on arriving at a single transaction i.e. a complete valid (semantically and pragmatically) game command to send to the back-end system for the GUI to carry out. For a call-routing system, it would instead guide the user towards a unique destination. For a relational database, it could be much more complex, factoring in estimated or actual query response times and answer sizes. Although a fascinating area of inquiry, this falls beyond the scope of the current paper.

Interfacing with other modules is typically quite straightforward as it relies on Prolog-like message passing within the OAA framework. The particular interfaces to the semantic parser, the spatial reasoner, and the GUI manager are discussed below.

3.2 Semantics

A set of alternative hypotheses constitute a semantic form (SF). Each hypothesis consists of a set of slot-value pairs (as a matter of fact, we use quads of slot-operator-value-score rather than slot-value pairs; the score measures certainty; the operator handles local quantifiers, when interfacing with relational databases) interpreted as a conjunction. A hypothesis is inconsistent, if it contains multiple values for any key.

Semantic forms can be combined disjunctively, taking the union, and conjunctively, taking the cross product, of their hypotheses. Each back-end system call is formulated as a hypothesis; their disjunction constitutes a SF defining the set of possible transactions. No transaction may be a subset of another one.

The key goal is to find a unique game move, which is a subset of all consistent hypotheses of a particular SF, namely the resulting SF in Step 3 in the Dialogue Logic below, and where no other move is a subset of any of its consistent hypothesis.

3.3 Dialogue Logic

Here an outline of the deployed dialogue manager's logic:

1. The DM gets a user semantic form from the parser.
2. If it is a non-domain SF, it's handled by the goal-based planner. For example, if the user said "*What was that?*", the DM resubmits its latest utterance to the TTS system, possibly after rephrasing it, whichever the plans for achieving this goal under the prevailing dialogue circumstances call for. Or, if the user typed-in "*quit*", the DM will request an appropriate good-riddance message from the response generator, send it to the TTS component, and plunge into the overall system resource pool.

3. If it is a domain SF, the DM requests the current working SF from the discourse manager, combines the two with the transaction SF from the previous section, and delegates finding the best dialogue move, given the resulting SF, to the utility-based reasoner (unless that SF is compatible with a single transaction, see the previous section, in which case the move consists of the corresponding back-end system call).

4. The latter returns the dialogue move with the highest expected cost-benefit, in this case, either a call to the spatial reasoner (which is free of charge and has a non-negative expected benefit) or the user query minimizing the expectation value of the number of remaining possible back-end transactions. User queries and requests to other agents can be assigned different costs, probabilities of success, and prior distributions over the responses.

5. If the best dialogue move requests information from the spatial reasoner, the latter is invoked, the gathered facts are added to the discourse manager's current working semantic form, and off we go to Step 3.

6. If it is a user query, it is sent to the response generator, together with additional discourse information.

7. The response generator selects its highest ranked matching response template. Catch-all templates guarantee that some response, if awkward, is given; more specific templates create wordings of greater grace and clarity. Since users tend to adapt to their conversational partner [Pearson et al, 2006], all responses must be in vocabulary and covered by the recognition grammar.

8. Off we go to Step 1.

This logic resides in the set of plans, most of which can be recycled (modulo client interference) as they characterize the DM as an interlocutor. There must also be plans for when the current working SF allows no back-end transactions, plans to identify and correct user misconceptions, etc.

This is where the domain ontology comes in handy. If two attributes of an ontology entity conflict throughout the SF, e.g., shape and color, this is a golden opportunity for a system response like *"Sorry, there is no red cross. There is a blue cross and two red pieces: one L and the other W-shaped. Which one do you mean?"* to the user input *"Select the red cross"* given that there is no cross-like pieces of red color in the game.

The underlying discourse mechanism is the same as for other clarification requests.

4 Worked Example

A worked example borrowed from an interaction with a human user may clarify the dialogue manager's modus operandi. Let's consider the Pentomino board in Figure 2 and the following log of user and agent message passing.

During this dialogue fragment, these are the messages that are exchanged among the system components. For the sake of clarity, we omit the irrelevant ones. BM stands for board manager; ASR for speech recognizer (or type-in console) RG for response generator; UBR for utility-based reasoner; and DM INT is the parser semantic form, recast in the DM format.

DM to RG:	`greetUser`
RG to DM to TTS:	"Welcome to Pentomino!"
DM to RG:	`initPrompt`
RG to DM to TTS:	"What's your move?"
USER to ASR:	*"I wish to select the upper piece"*
PARSER to DM:	select(piece(col(upper,no,no), id(no),shape(no))
DM INT:	[[pieceAct=select,vert=upper]]
DM to BM:	`request(piecesOnboard)`
BM to DM:	piecesOnboard([
	piece(col(upper,left,red),id(3),shape(x)),
	piece(col(no,no,cyan),id(5),shape(z)),
	piece(col(lower,right,red),id(7),shape(p)),
	piece(col(no,no,purple),id(11),shape(l))])
DM INT:	[[color=red,hor=left,id=3,shape=x,vert=upper]
	:
	[color=purple,hor=no,id=11,shape=l,vert=no]]
DM to BM:	`request(piecesRestArea)`
BM to DM:	piecesRestArea([
	piece(col(no,no,red),id(0),shape(v)),
	piece(col(no,no,red),id(1),shape(t)),
	piece(col(no,left,red),id(2),shape(w)),
	piece(col(no,right,red),id(4),shape(u)),
	piece(col(no,no,red),id(6),shape(f)),
	piece(col(no,no,red),id(8),shape(i)),
	piece(col(upper,no,red),id(9),shape(n)),
	piece(col(lower,no,red),id(10),shape(y))])
DM INT:	[[color=red,hor=no,id=0,shape=v,vert=no]
	:
	[color=red,hor=no,id=10,shape=y,vert=lower]]
DM to UBR:	[[action=pieceAct,color=red,hor=left,id=3,
	pieceAct=select,shape=x,vert=upper],

[action=pieceAct,color=red,hor=no,id=9,

pieceAct=select,shape=n,vert=upper]]

UBR to DM to RG: `wh-question(shape,[n,x])`

RG to DM to TTS: "Is the piece n- or x-shaped?"

GUI: both pieces n and x get highlighted

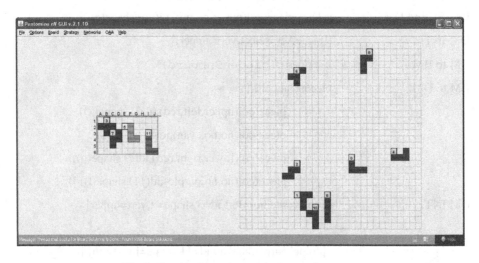

Fig. 2. Graphical interface of the interactive game

Upon quitting the game, the following typical situation occurs in terms of message passing.

DM INT: [[specReq=quit]]

DM to RG: `bidUserFarewell`

RG to DM to TTS: "Thanks for playing Pentomino!" input

The DM is clearly the brain of the system, issuing commands to the other agents. Here, the DM did not need to call on the spatial reasoner, as the semantic parser provided the required spatial information; if some user utterance had instead referred to piece locations relative to other pieces, this would have been necessary.

5 Conclusions

It is said that knowledge is power. Encapsulating knowledge, reusing what can be reused, and providing good specification languages for what remains, allows rapid application development. To stick to our corporate officer metaphor, we doubt that he can be effective without some understanding of what he is managing, but the described DM supports the claim that certain aspects of good management are universal.

There is another good reason for minimizing the DM's knowledge content: changes may go undetected by the DM (in this case, through the use of direct manipulation) and tracking any specific change should be the task of a single component, which, upon request, propagates this change to the rest of the system. Thus, the DM does not assume that the locations of the Pentomino pieces remain the same between turns; it asks the board manager for this info.

Note the three-tier knowledge division: general, domain, and application together with the separation of knowledge from problem solving machinery. The machinery and the general and domain-specific knowledge constitute the reusable resources. Investing in improving these assets yields large dividends.

Our system relies on a clean, standardized interface and agent architecture where each large task is broken down into several limited, clear-cut subtasks. Each component does one thing only, and does it fairly well. We demonstrated that a generic DM, also utilized in real-world spoken language applications for databases and call-routing systems, could be redeployed with little effort in a spoken language interface to a transaction system - in this case, to a board game that requires spatial reasoning, absent in previous applications.

Despite evaluating this kind of DM authoring convenience over multiple different applications is very difficult, preliminary on-going usability studies with human subjects seem to indicate a significant degree of user satisfaction. Dialogue management is still a relatively young science and at this stage of our development, we believe that our empirical experimental results should be weight heavier than any theoretical building. In other words, the DM built and deployed so far has proved its feasibility at all the tasks it has been applied to in our restricted domain.

Currently, we have to expand and elaborate on the templates for clarification requests and system feedback sentences.

Acknowledgments. The EU Marie Curie ToK Programme under grant #FP6-2002-Mobility-3014491 made it possible for the second author to spend a sabbatical period at the University of Potsdam where this research work was started.

References

1. Allen, J., Ferguson, G., Stent, A.: An Architecture for More Realistic Conversational Systems. In: Proc. of the International Conference on Intelligent User Interfaces, pp. 1–8 (2001)
2. Bohus, D., Rudnicky, A.: RavenClaw: Dialog Management Using Hierarchical Task Decomposition and an Expectation Agenda. In: Proceedings of Eurospeech, Geneva, Switzerland, pp. 597–600 (2003)
3. Bos, J., Klein, E., Lemon, O., Oka, T.: DIPPER: Description and Formalisation of an Information-State Update Dialogue System Architecture. In: Proceedings of the 4th SIGdial Workshop on Discourse and Dialogue, Sapporo, Japan, pp. 115–124 (2003)
4. Cheyer, A., Martin, D.: The open agent architecture. Autonomous Agents and Multi-Agent System 4(1-2), 143–148 (2001)

5. Chu-Carroll, J.: Form-Based Reasoning for Mixed-Initiative Dialogue Management in Information-Query Systems. In: Proc. of Eurospeech, Budapest, Hungary, pp. 1519–1522 (1999)
6. Chu-Carroll, J., Carpenter, B.: Vector-based natural language call routing'. Computational Linguistics 25(3), 361–388 (1999)
7. Corradini, A., Hanneforth, T., Bak, A.: A Robust Spoken Language Architecture to Control a 2D Game. In: Proc. of AAAI International FLAIRS Conference, pp. 199–204 (2007)
8. Golomb, S.W.: Polyominoes. Scribner's, New York (1965)
9. Hardy, H., Strzalkowski, T., Wu, M., Ursu, C., Webb, N., Biermann, A., Inouye, B., McKenzie, A.: Data-driven strategies for an automated dialogue system. In: Proceedings of the 42nd Meeting of the ACL, Barcelona, Spain, pp. 71–78 (2004)
10. Hochberg, J., Kambhatla, N., Roukos, S.: A flexible framework for developing mixed-initiative dialog systems. In: Proceedings of the 3rd SIGdial Workshop on Discourse and Dialogue, Philadelphia, PA, USA, pp. 60–63 (2002)
11. Hurtado, L.F., Griol, D., Sanchis, E., Segarra, E.: A stochastic approach to dialog management. In: Proceedings of the IEEE Automatic Speech Recognition and Understanding Workshop, U.S. Virgin Islands, pp. 226–231 (2003)
12. Larsson, S., Traum, D.R.: Information state and dialogue management in the TRINDI dialogue move engine toolkit Source. Natural Language Engineering 6(3-4), 323–340 (2000)
13. Lemon, O., Bracy, A., Gruenstein, A., Peters, S.: The WITAS multi-modal dialogue system I. In: Proceedings of Eurospeech, Aalborg, Denmark, pp. 1559–1562 (2001)
14. Lemon, O., Georgila, K., Henderson, J., Stuttle, M.: An ISU Dialogue System Exhibiting Reinforcement Learning of Dialogue Policies: Generic Slot-filling in the TALK In-car System. In: Proceedings of EACL, Trento, Italy (2006)
15. Levin, E., Pieraccini, R., Eckert, W., di Fabbrizio, G., Narayanan, S.: Spoken language dialogue: From theory to practice. In: Proceedings of IEEE Automatic Speech Recognition and Understanding Workshop, Keystone, CO, USA, pp. 12–15 (1999)
16. Litman, D.J., Allen, J.F.: A plan recognition model for subdialogues in conversations. Cognitive Science 11(2), 163–200 (1987)
17. McTear, M.: Modeling Spoken Dialogues with State Transition Diagrams: Experiences with the CSLU Toolkit. In: Proceedings of International Conference on Spoken Language Processing, Sidney, Australia, pp. 1223–1226 (1998)
18. Pearson, J., Hu, J., Branigan, H.P., Pickering, M.J., Nass, C.I.: Adaptive language behavior in HCI: how expectations and beliefs about a system affect users' word choice. In: Proceedings of the ACM CHI 2006 Conference on Human Factors in Computing Systems, Quebec, Canada, pp. 1177–1180 (2006)
19. Pieraccini, R., Caskey, S., Dayanidhi, K., Carpenter, B., Phillips, M.: ETUDE, A Recursive Dialogue Manager with Embedded User Interface Patterns. In: Proceedings of the IEEE Automatic Speech Recognition and Understanding Workshop, Madonna di Campiglio, Italy, pp. 244–247 (2001)
20. Rosenfeld, R., Olsen, D., Rudnicky, A.: Universal speech interfaces. Interactions 8(6), 34–44 (2001)
21. Rudnicky, A., Xu, W.: An Agenda-Based Dialogue Management Architecture for Spoken Language Systems. In: Proceedings of IEEE Automatic Speech Recognition and Understanding Workshop, Keystone, CO, USA, pp. 337–340 (1999)
22. Seneff, S., Polifroni, J.: Dialogue management in the Mercury flight reservation system. In: Proc. of the ANLP-NAACL Workshop on Conversational Systems, pp. 1–6 (2000)

23. Shneiderman, B.: Natural vs. precise concise languages for human operation of computers: research issues and experimental approaches. In: Proceedings of the 18th annual meeting of the Association for Computational Linguistics, pp. 139–141 (1980)
24. Walker, W., Lamere, P., Kwok, P., Raj, B., Singh, R., Gouvea, E., Wolf, P., Woelfel, J.: Sphinx-4: A Flexible Open Source Framework for Speech Recognition. Sun Microsystems, TR-2004-139 (2004)
25. Ward, W., Pellom, B.: The CU Communicator system. In: Proceedings of IEEE Automatic Speech Recognition and Understanding Workshop, Keystone, CO, USA, pp. 341–344 (1999)
26. Zue, V., Seneff, S., Glass, J., Polifroni, J., Pao, C., Hazen, T.J., Hetherington, L.: Jupiter: A telephone-based conversational interface for weather information. IEEE Transactions on Speech and Audio Processing 8(1), 85–95 (2000)

Adaptive Dialogue Management in the NIMITEK Prototype System

Milan Gnjatović and Dietmar Rösner

Otto-von-Guericke-University Magdeburg
Department of Knowledge Processing and Language Engineering
P.O. Box 4120, D-39016 Magdeburg, Germany
{gnjatovic,roesner}@iws.cs.uni-magdeburg.de
http://wdok.cs.uni-magdeburg.de/

Abstract. The primary aim of this paper is to present the implementation of adaptive dialogue management in the NIMITEK prototype spoken dialogue system for supporting users while they solve problems in a graphics system (e.g., the Tower-of-Hanoi puzzle). The central idea is that the system dynamically refines a dialogue strategy according to the current state of the interaction. We analyze a recorded dialogue between the user and the prototype system that took place during the testing of the system. It illustrates several points of the implemented dialogue strategy: processing of user's commands, supporting the user, and multilingual working mode.

1 Introduction

A possible explanation for the importance of dialogue strategies in human-machine interaction (HMI) lies on the fundamental level. One of the reasons relates to existing limitations of automatic speech recognition (ASR) technology. [Lee, 2007, p. 25] notes that state-of-the-art ASR approaches still cannot deal with flexible, unrestricted user's language. Therefore, problems caused by misunderstanding a user that refuses to follow a predefined, and usually restricting, set of communicational rules seems to be inevitable. A requirement for a *habitable language interface* that implies a need for dialogue strategies is related to generating a system response when a sentence uttered by the user cannot be parsed or understood. The response should be *informative enough to allow the linguistically naive user to immediately correct the faulty sentence appropriately* [Guindon, 1988, p. 191] and in a form that is *comprehensible for the user* [Carbonell, 1986, p. 162]. However, the limitations of technology are by no means the only reason. Problems in the communication may also be caused by affected behavior of the user or by lack of knowledge or interest in the user's attitude. In general, a dialogue strategy should support the user to overcome diverse problems that occur in the communication.

The primary aim of this paper is to present the implementation of adaptive dialogue management in the NIMITEK prototype spoken dialogue system for supporting users while they solve the Tower-of-Hanoi puzzle. The central idea is

E. André et al. (Eds.): PIT 2008, LNAI 5078, pp. 14–25, 2008.
© Springer-Verlag Berlin Heidelberg 2008

that the system dynamically refines a dialogue strategy according to the current *state of the interaction* (this includes also the emotional state of the user, as we discuss bellow). This paper presents further development and integration of three lines of our research: collecting and evaluating corpora of affected behavior in HMI [Gnjatović and Rösner, 2006], modeling attentional state on the level of a user's command [Gnjatović and Rösner, 007a] and designing adaptive dialogue strategies [Gnjatović and Rösner, 008a], [Gnjatović and Rösner, 007b].

2   What Should a Dialogue Strategy Address?

Before we design a dialogue strategy, it is necessary to define what it is aimed for. In our scenario, a dialogue strategy is aimed to address a negative emotional state of the user. We differentiate between three emotional states: *negative, neutral* and *positive*. However, to design and implement an appropriate dialogue strategy, it is necessary to define what the non-neutral user states exactly represent. More precisely, these states should be explained in light of the purpose for which the prototype system was planned in the first place. Therefore, we resort to the NIMITEK corpus [Gnjatović and Rösner, 2006] in order to get a better insight in emotion and emotion-related states of the users. There are two main reasons for this approach: (i) the application domain planned for the prototype system is also used in the WOZ simulation conducted to collect the corpus; and (ii) the WOZ simulation was especially designed to induce reactions to diverse problems that might occur in the communication.

The first phase of the evaluation process [Gnjatović and Rösner, 2006] had the primary aim to assess the level of ecological validity of the NIMITEK corpus. This phase demonstrated a satisfying level of ecological validity of the corpus. The subjects signaled genuine emotions overtly and there was a diversity of signaled emotions, emotion-related states and talking styles, as well as a diversity of their intensities. The important fact of the first evaluation phase is that the choice of annotation labels was data-driven—the evaluators were allowed to introduce labels according to their own perception, cf. [Batliner et al., 2006]. Thus, some of the introduced labels represent different but closely related emotions or emotion-related states. We mention a few of these relations between the labels, according to the explanations given by the evaluators:

– The labels *confused* and *insecure* are closely related to the label *fear* that was graded with low intensity of expressed emotion. This relation is even more obvious if we keep in mind that the label *fear* was never graded with high intensity during the evaluation process.
– The label *disappointed* is closely related to the label *sadness* graded with low intensity of expressed emotion.
– The label *pleased* is closely related to the labels *joy* (graded with low intensity) and *surprised*.

Therefore, there was a need to group labels that relate to similar or mixed emotions or emotion-related states. Following clarifications collected from the

Table 1. The ARISEN model of user states

Class	Mapped labels
Annoyed	anger, nervousness, stressed, impatient
Retiring	fear, insecure, confused
Indisposed	sadness, disappointed, accepting, boredom
Satisfied	joy, contentment, pleased
Engaged	thinking, surprised, interested
Neutral	neutral

evaluators, we mapped these labels onto six classes that form the ARISEN model of user states.

To prove the appropriateness of this mapping, we performed the second phase of the evaluation. The experimental sessions evaluated in the first phase were re-evaluated in the second phase by a new group of evaluators. There are two main differences in the second phase with respect to the process of evaluation:

- The set of annotation labels were predefined. The evaluators could use only labels from the ARISEN model.
- The re-evaluation was performed over smaller evaluation units. In the first phase, the evaluation unit was a dialogue turn or a group of several successive dialogue turns. Such units were selected to demonstrate that emotional expressions are extended in time. Also, a collection of larger units was also valuable, because they function more directly in the realization of higher-level patterns [Halliday, 1994, p. 19]. The evaluation material was divided in 424 evaluation units. In the second evaluation phase, we used finer selection of units—the same evaluation material is now divided in 2720 evaluation units.

Each evaluation unit was evaluated by four or five German-speaking evaluators. They performed the perception test independently from each other. To each evaluation unit evaluators assigned one or more labels from the ARISEN model. Similar as in the first evaluation phase, we used majority voting in order to attribute labels to evaluation units. If at least three evaluators agreed upon a label, it was attributed to the evaluation unit. The evaluation results are given in Table 2.

As mentioned above, for the purpose of defining a dialogue strategy we differentiate between two non-neutral user states: negative and positive. Using the ARISEN model, these states are defined as follows:

- negative state subsumes the states *Annoyed*, *Retiring* and *Indisposed*,
- positive state subsumes the states *Satisfied* and *Engaged*.

We comment this briefly. A distinction among the user states based on the valence of the signaled emotion is obviously an important one. The system should be capable to recognize negative user states as indicators for diverse problems that may occur in communication. Discussing the arousal, it should be kept in

Table 2. Results of the second evaluation phase

Evaluation units	Number
with no majority voting	315 (11.58%)
with one assigned label	1907 (70.11%)
with two assigned label	476 (17.5%)
with three assigned label	22 (0.81%)
total	2720 (100%)

Label	Nr. of eval. units attributed with the label
Annoyed	487 (17.9%)
Retiring	111 (4.08%)
Indisposed	156 (5.74%)
Satisfied	106 (3.9%)
Engaged	1548 (56.91%)
Neutral	517 (19.01%)

mind that it is not expected that a system like the NIMITEK prototype system would normally provoke emotional reactions of high intensity (at least, if it is not deliberately planned). It is much more likely that signalled emotions would relate to everyday emotions that are inherently less intensive (e.g., *nervousness, pleased, insecure*, etc.). However, the convincing fact that the most frequently marked state from the ARISEN model is *Engagement* points out that the level of engagement of the user towards a given task should be considered as important.

Now we can answer the question from the beginning of this section. A dialogue strategy designed to support the user in our prototype system should address the negative user state on the two tracks: (i) to help a frustrated user to overcome the problem occurred in the communication, and (ii) to motivate a discouraged or apathetic user.

3 The State of the Interaction

One of the underlying ideas of our dialogue model is to increase probability that a communication between the user and the system will not be interrupted, even with a limited understanding level, c.f., [Luzzati, 2000]. To achieve this, the system is given a kind of awareness of the state of the interaction in order to increase the understanding level. We model the *state of the interaction* as a composite of five interaction features:

(1) The state of the task in the Tower-of-Hanoi puzzle is defined by the current positions of the disks.

(2) The user's command in our scenario may fall in one of the following classes:

- valid command (i.e., the move is allowed according to the rules of the puzzle),
- illegal command (i.e., the move violates the rules of the puzzle),

Fig. 1. The focus tree for Tower-of-Hanoi puzzle

- semantically incorrect command (e.g., the user instructs a non-existing command, such as trying to move a peg instead of a disk, etc.),
- help command (i.e., the user explicitly asks for support),
- switching between interface languages (German or English),
- unrecognized command.

(3) The focus of attention is crucial for processing of user's utterances [Grosz and Sidner, 1986, p. 175]. In [Gnjatović and Rösner, 007a], we propose an approach to modeling the attentional information on the level of a user's command. The *focus tree* is a hierarchical representation of all instances of the focus of attention that may appear in users's utterances for a given scenario. Sub-focus relationships between those instances are encapsulated: each node, except the root node, represents a sub-focus of its parent node. In addition, we introduce the rules for mapping of user's commands onto the focus tree and for the transition of a current focus of attention. The focus tree for the 3-disk version of the Tower-of-Hanoi puzzle is given in Figure 1. At any given point, the current focus of attention is placed on exactly one node from the focus tree.

(4) The state of the user is introduced in Section 2.

(5) The history of interaction collects information about values of other interaction features, applied dialogue strategies and time stamps.

4   An Adaptive Dialogue Strategy

The NIMITEK prototype system dynamically refines a dialogue strategy according to the current state of the interaction. This includes three distinct but interrelating decision making processes:

Decision 1: When to provide support to the user? The system provides support when one of the following cases is detected:

- The user does not understand the rules of the puzzle or does not know how to solve the puzzle.
- The user's instruction cannot be recognized.
- The user explicitly asks for support.

Decision 2: What kind of support to provide? Two kinds of support can be provided to the user:

- *Task-Support*—explaining the rules of the puzzle and helping to find its solution.
- *Interface-Support*—helping to formulate a valid command.

For example, Task-Support is provided in cases when the user instructs an invalid command or when the history of interaction shows that the state of the task either draws back from the expected final state or does not make any significant progress towards the final state. Interface-Support is provided in cases when the user instructs a command that cannot be recognized or a semantically incorrect command, etc.

Decision 3: How to provide support? The manner of providing support is determined by the state of the user. The underlying idea is that the user in negative emotional state needs a more informative support than the user in positive or neutral emotional state. Thus, support is provided in two manners:

- ***Low intensity*** of support for users in positive or neutral emotional state.
- ***High intensity*** of support for users in negative emotional state.

Low intensity of Task-Support means to inform the user that her last move draws back the state of the task from the expected final state or violates the rules of the game. High intensity of Task-Support is to inform the user as well, but also to propose the next move.

Providing low intensity of Interface-Support, the system guides the user to complete the started command by stating iterative questions (e.g. which disk should be selected, where to move the selected disk, etc.). High intensity of Interface-Support is to check whether the started command can be completed in such a way that it pushes the state of the task towards the final solution. If so, the system proposes such an automatically completed command to the user. Otherwise, the system warns the user that the started command is not appropriate.

These decision making processes are discussed in [Gnjatović and Rösner, 008a] and [Gnjatović and Rösner, 007b] in more detail. In the next section, we analyze a dialogue between the user and the NIMITEK prototype system from the perspective of the approach to dialogue management being introduced.

5   An Example

To illustrate the functionality of the dialogue management module in the NIMITEK prototype system, we give an analysis of an actual dialogue between the user and the prototype system that took place during the testing of the system. The whole dialogue is given in Figures 2, 6 and 7. Utterances produced by the user and the system are written in *italic*, descriptions of non-verbal actions performed by the system (e.g., moving a disc, etc.) are <u>underlined</u>, and moments when the system detects a change of the state of the user are given in **bold**. The state of the user is provided by the emotion classifier. In this paper we do not discuss the recognition of emotions in more detail; we assume that the information about the state of the user is delivered to the dialogue management module. In the following subsections, we discuss processing of different types of user's commands, providing support to the user and the multilingual working mode.

5.1   Processing of User's Commands

User's commands may take different syntactic forms. Referring to the first part of the dialogue, shown in Figure 2, we discuss processing of *elliptical, complex* and *context dependent* user's commands. Processing of user's commands are closely related to the notion of the focus of attention and crucially supported by the focus tree structure introduced in [Gnjatović and Rösner, 007a]. Transitions of the focus of attention that are relevant for the observed dialogue fragment are represented in Figures 3, 4 and 5. Changes of a temporary focus of attention are marked with dashed arrows. Nodes representing temporary focus of attention are positioned in ovals, while nodes representing the focus of attention after processing a user's command are positioned in boxes.

$System_1$: **classifies the user state as neutral**
$User_2$:   *Den kleinsten Ring* ... (engl.: *The smallest ring* ...)
$System_3$: selects the smallest disk
$User_4$:   ... *auf die Drei.* (engl.: ... *on the three.*)
$System_5$: puts the selected disk on the third peg
$User_6$:   *Ich möchte gerne die mittlere Scheibe auf Position Zwei schieben.* (engl.: *I would like to move the middle disk to position two.*)
$System_7$: moves the middle disk to the second peg
$User_8$:   *Den nächsten Ring* ... (engl.: *The next ring* ...)
$System_9$: selects the biggest disk

Fig. 2. Dialogue between the user and the NIMITEK prototype system: Part 1

(1) Processing elliptical commands. The commands $User_2$ (*The smallest ring* ...) and $User_4$ (... *on the three*) are elliptical—in each of them the user gives only a part of the information that is expected to be contained in a fully formulated command. In the command $User_2$, the system recognizes a focus instance that relates to the smallest disk. Then it checks if this focus instance can be represented by some of the descendant nodes of the node representing the current focus of attention. For the given starting focus of attention (placed on the root node of the focus tree at the beginning of the dialogue), there is such a node—$disk_1$. The new focus of attention is placed on this node. The same discussion holds for the command $User_4$. A focus instance that relates to the third peg is recognized. This focus instance can be represented by three nodes in the focus tree: peg_{13}, peg_{23} and peg_{33}. However, only one of them is a descendant node of the node representing current focus of attention—peg_{13}. Thus, the new focus of attention is placed on this node. The transition of the focus of attention is illustrated in Figure 3.

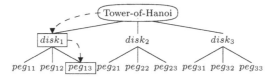

Fig. 3. Transition of the focus of attention for the commands User$_2$ and User$_4$

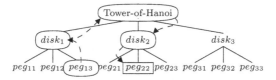

Fig. 4. Transition of the focus of attention for the command User$_6$

(2) Processing complex command. The command User$_6$ (*I would like to move the middle disk to position two*) is complex in the sense that it contains words that are not a part of the vocabulary recognized by the speech recognition module. The textual version of this command outputted from the speech recognizer may be represented as:

<*not recognized*> *the middle disk* <*not recognized*> *position two*

The system recognizes two focus instances. The first focus instance, *the middle disk*, can be represented by the node $disk_2$, the second focus instance, *position two*, by the nodes peg_{12}, peg_{22} and peg_{32}. However, none of these nodes are a descendant node of the node representing the current focus of attention (i.e., peg_{13}). Thus, a temporary focus of attention is degraded, in a bottom-up manner, to more general focus instances. It is iteratively transited to the closest antecedent node of the node peg_{13} that satisfies the condition that its descendant nodes can represent all focus instances from the command—in this case it is the root node. Then, similarly as already explained above, all changes of a temporary focus of attention are directed towards more specific focus instances. The focus of attention is first placed on the node $disk_2$ and then to its child node peg_{22}. The transition of the focus of attention is illustrated in Figure 4.

(3) Processing context dependent command. The command User$_8$ (*The next ring ...*) is elliptical, but it is also context dependent. Observing this command *in abstracto*, i.e., isolated from the surrounding dialogue context, it can be assumed that a disk should be selected, but it is not specified which actual disk. Therefore, the contextual information should be taken into account. The previously selected disk was the middle disk. Thus, the phrase *the next ring* relates to the biggest disk and the new focus of attention is placed on the node $disk_3$. The transition of the focus of attention is illustrated in Figure 5.

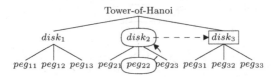

Fig. 5. Transition of the focus of attention for the command User$_8$

5.2 Supporting the User

Let us observe the continuation of the dialogue between the user and the system, given in Figure 6. In the command User$_{10}$ (... *on the three*) the user tries to instruct the system to place the (previously selected) biggest ring to the third peg. However, according to the rules of the puzzle, it is not possible to place a larger disk onto a smaller one. Instructing an illegal command is an indicator for the system that the user needs support. It should be kept in mind that the system classifies the emotional state of the user as neutral, so it decides only to inform the user that the instructed move is not possible (System$_{11}$).

In the command User$_{12}$ (*Help*), the user explicitly asks for support. This is another indicator for the system. The current focus of attention is still on node $disk_3$ (it has not been changed since the user's command User$_8$). Since it is an inner node of the focus tree, the system concludes that the user has a problem to finish the formulation of a command. In addition, it assumes that the user wants to formulate such a command that would place the focus of attention on one of the terminal nodes from the sub-tree determined by the node in the current focus of attention as its root node. Therefore, in System$_{13}$, the system asks the user on which peg does he want to place the selected ring. The user refuses to answer the system's question and repeats the request for support in User$_{14}$ (*I said Help!*) It should be noted that now the system classifies the emotional state of the user as negative, so its response to the user's demand is not the same as in the previous case. The system decides to provide support of higher intensity—it informs the user that the moving of the already selected disk would draw her back from the correct solution of the puzzle and propose the user to select another disk.

The user responds on the system demand. In the command User$_{17}$ (*The smallest ring ...*), she instructs the system to select the smallest ring. The system performs this instruction (System$_{18}$), and the user then again asks for support (User$_{19}$). The emotional state of the user is still classified as negative, so again support of higher intensity is given. However, in this case, the selected ring was the correct choice. Therefore, in System$_{20}$, the system proposes to place the selected ring on the second peg, and asks the user to confirm that she agrees with the proposal (in System$_{21}$). The user approves the proposal in User$_{22}$. A similar discussion holds for the rest of the observed dialogue fragment. In User$_{24}$, the user instructs a command that draws her back from the correct solution of the puzzle. The system reacts and proposes the user to undo this move (System$_{25}$).

User₁₀: ... auf die Drei. (engl.: ... on the three.)

User$_{10}$:   ... auf die Drei. (engl.: ... on the three.)

System$_{11}$: Dieser Schritt ist nicht möglich. Sie können nur einen oben liegenden Ring wählen. Sie dürfen keinen Ring auf einen kleineren legen. (engl.: This move is not possible. You can only move a disc from the top. You cannot place a larger disc onto a smaller one.)

User$_{12}$:   Hilfe. (engl.: Help.)

System$_{13}$: Welchen Stab möchten Sie auswählen? (engl.: Which peg do you want to select?)

User$_{14}$:   Ich sagte Hilfe! (engl.: I said help!)

System$_{15}$: **classifies the user state as negative**

System$_{16}$: Der letzte Schritt führte von der Lösung weg. Ich schlage vor, dass Sie einen anderen Ring auswählen. (engl.: The last move drew you back from the solution. I propose that you select another disc.)

User$_{17}$:   Den kleinsten Ring ... (engl.: The smallest ring ...)

System$_{18}$: selects the smallest disk

User$_{19}$:   Hilfe. (engl.: Help.)

System$_{20}$: Ich möchte diesen Schritt vorschlagen. (engl.: Let me propose the following move.)
              moves the smallest disk to the second peg

System$_{21}$: Sind Sie einverstanden? (engl.: Is this ok?)

User$_{22}$:   Ja. (engl.: Yes.)

System$_{23}$: **classifies the user state as positive**

User$_{24}$:   Den kleinsten Ring auf die Eins. (engl.: The smallest disk on the one.)

System$_{25}$: Ich möchte diesen Schritt vorschlagen. (engl.: Let me propose the following move.)
              returns the smallest disk again to the second peg

System$_{26}$: Sind Sie einverstanden? (engl.: Is this ok?)

User$_{27}$:   Ja. (engl.: Yes.)

Fig. 6. Dialogue between the user and the NIMITEK prototype system: Part 2

User$_{28}$:   Englisch. (engl.: English.)

System$_{29}$: switches to English language

User$_{30}$:   The big ring to the column number three.

System$_{31}$: moves the biggest ring to the third peg

User$_{32}$:   German.

System$_{33}$: switches to German language

User$_{34}$:   Den kleinsten Ring auf die Eins. (engl.: The smallest disk on the one.)

System$_{35}$: moves the smallest disk to the first peg

Fig. 7. Dialogue between the user and the NIMITEK prototype system: Part 3

5.3   Multilingual Working Mode

Verbal interaction with the NIMITEK prototype system is supported in two languages: German and English. This is illustrated in the final fragment of the observed dialogue given in Figure 7. In the commands User$_{28}$: *English* and User$_{32}$: *German*, the user instruct the system to switch to English and German language, respectively.

6   Conclusion

This paper presented the implementation of adaptive dialogue management in the NIMITEK prototype spoken dialogue system for supporting users while they solve the Tower-of-Hanoi puzzle. The central idea is that the system dynamically refines a dialogue strategy according to the current state of the interaction. We introduced the state of the interaction—a composite of five interaction features: the state of the task, the user's command, the focus of attention, the state of the user and the history of interaction. The appropriate attention was devoted to the discussion about the meaning of the non-neutral user's states in our scenario. The dialogue strategy is defined by three distinct but interrelated decision making processes: When to provide support? What kind of support to provide? How to provide support?

We analyzed an actual dialogue between the user and the prototype system that took place during the testing of the system to illustrate important points of the implemented dialogue strategy: processing user's commands of different syntactic forms, supporting the user and multilingual working mode.

The final observation is related to the direction of our future research. The implemented dialogue strategy provides a kind of support that we refer to as *immediate*. We intend to research in the direction of developing dialogue strategies that address the user's attitude towards a given task on the long-term. For example, if the user does not know how to solve the puzzle, it may be more appropriate to bring the user to a concept of the puzzle by facing her with a less complex version of the puzzle (e.g., with only two disks), instead of just proposing the next correct move. In addition, the problem of recognition errors, both for speech recognition and emotion classification, will be taken into account, and appropriate repair strategies will be investigated.

Acknowledgements. The presented study is performed as part of the NIMITEK project (http:// wdok.cs.uni-magdeburg.de/nimitek), within the framework of the Excellence Program "Neurowissenschaften" of the federal state of Sachsen-Anhalt, Germany (FKZ: XN3621A/1005M). The responsibility for the content of this paper lies with the authors.

References

[Batliner et al., 2006] Batliner, A., Biersack, S., Steidl, S.: The Prosody of Pet Robot Directed Speech: Evidence from Children. In: Proceedings of the 3rd International Conference on Speech Prosody 2006, Dresden, Germany (2006)

[Carbonell, 1986] Carbonell, J.: Requirements for robust natural language interfaces: the LanguageCraft (TM) and XCALIBUR experiences. In: Proceedings of the COLING 1986, Washington, D.C., USA, pp. 162–163 (1986)

[Gnjatović and Rösner, 2006] Gnjatović, M., Rösner, D.: Gathering Corpora of Affected Speech in Human-Machine Interaction: Refinement of the Wizard-of-Oz Technique. In: Proceedings of the International Symposium on Linguistic Patterns in Spontaneous Speech (LPSS 2006), pp. 55–66. Academia Sinica, Taipei (2006)

[Gnjatović and Rösner, 007a] Gnjatović, M., Rösner, D.: An approach to processing of user' s commands in human-machine interaction. In: Proceedings of the 3rd Language and Technology Conference (LTC 2007), Adam Mickiewicz University, Poznan, Poland, pp. 152–156 (2007a)

[Gnjatović and Rösner, 007b] Gnjatović, M., Rösner, D.: A Dialogue Strategy for Supporting the User in Spoken Human-Machine Interaction. In: Proceedings of the XII International Conference Speech and Computer (SPECOM 2007), pp. 708–713. Moscow State Linguistic University, Moscow (2007b)

[Gnjatović and Rösner, 008a] Gnjatović, M., Rösner, D.: Emotion Adaptive Dialogue Management in Human-Machine Interaction. In: Proceedings of the 19th European Meetings on Cybernetics and Systems Research (EMCSR 2008), Austrian Society for Cybernetic Studies, Vienna, Austria, pp. 567–572 (2008a)

[Grosz and Sidner, 1986] Grosz, B., Sidner, C.: Attention, Intentions, and the Structure of Discourse. Computational Linguistics 12(3), 175–204 (1986)

[Guindon, 1988] Guindon, R.: How to Interface to Advisory Systems? Users Request Help With a Very Simple Language. In: Proceedings of ACM Conf. on Computer Human Interaction (CHI 1988), Washington, D.C., USA, pp. 191–196 (1988)

[Halliday, 1994] Halliday, M.: An Introduction to Functional Grammar, 2nd edn. Edward Arnold, London (1994)

[Lee, 2007] Lee, C.-H.: Fundamentals and Technical Challenges in Automatic Speech Recognition. In: Proceedings of the XII International Conference Speech and Computer (SPECOM 2007), Moscow State Linguistic University, Moscow, Russia, pp. 25–44 (2007)

[Luzzati, 2000] Luzzati, D.: A Dynamic Dialogue Model for Human-Machine Communication. In: Taylor, M., Néel, F., Bouwhuis, D. (eds.) The Structure of Multimodal Dialoque II, pp. 207–221. John Benjamins Publishing Company, Philadelphia/Amsterdam (2000)

Adaptive Search Results Personalized by a Fuzzy Recommendation Approach

Philipp Fischer[1], André Berton[1], and Andreas Nürnberger[2]

[1] Daimler AG, Research and Development,
Infotainment & Telematics, Berlin, Ulm, Germany
philipp.fischer@daimler.com, andre.berton@daimler.com
[2] Otto-von-Guericke University Magdeburg, Faculty of Computer Science,
Data and Knowledge Engineering Group, Magdeburg, Germany
andreas.nuernberger@ovgu.de

Abstract. The cognitive load of the driver in future vehicles will be increased by a larger number of integrated or connected devices and by a higher complexity of applications covering various vehicle-related tasks and other information. Aspects of perception relevant to inter-action design of adaptive and multimodal interfaces are discussed. We propose an extension of a system architecture for user-adaptive information presentation in order to cope with high information load in a multimodal interface. Visual information and speech are used as output channels, and manual input and speech as input channels. In the system, current information from the Internet can be queried by natural language question-answering dialogs using frame-based dialog management. A fuzzy recommendation approach is described in detail and used in the system for structuring content items according to the user preferences. In addition to such a personalized visual list of topic areas for an initial choice, an adaptive ranking is applied to acoustical speech output. The item that relates best to the driver's preferences is read out first by text-to-speech. Therefore, the first items presented to the user are ought to be of high interest. Cognitive load can potentially be decreased by our approach for the task of choosing one item out of a sequence of alternatives in working memory. The choice can be immediately performed by using the barge-in feature.

1 Introduction

Minimizing the cognitive load for drivers is still an open issue due to the increasing number of information and entertainment services in premium vehicles. A number of reasons can be identified: the higher traffic density, a rising number of customer devices in the car, a stronger wish of the community for reliable mobile information and emotional entertainment services. In telematic environments, many of these features are becoming more and more available on the road.

In this paper, we focus on the goal of providing adaptive and personalized Internet information by a multimodal user interface. Information is presented

E. André et al. (Eds.): PIT 2008, LNAI 5078, pp. 26–36, 2008.
© Springer-Verlag Berlin Heidelberg 2008

on the head unit, which is the main human machine interface and interaction device in modern cars. Prompts and even entire speech dialogs are automatically generated from query result data and downloaded to the client system in the car. We specialize on search results for restaurants which are matched as among the most relevant for a given query. The list of results is read to the user by a text-to-speech component and gets ranked according to the user's preferences. An architecture is implemented to access Internet information in the car and allow the user to perform natural language question-answering almost without looking at the screen. We argue that multimodal interaction and the ranking of visual lists as well as the results on the auditory channel could reduce the distracting visual glances to the results on the screen.

1.1 Application Scenario

In the SmartWeb car scenario [Wahlster, 2007], information from the Internet gets occasionally downloaded to the car. The driver is notified when new information becomes available. In a first step, the user might request Internet information from the main menu and in succession a list of dialogs is presented by the system. It contains up to 5 topic areas (figure 1). After having chosen the item of interest from the list by saying the number or the title, the driver can put natural language queries related to the topic area. For example, the driver could ask something like "Where can I find Indian food nearby" or "What's playing at the movies" in the topic area "City information". In some cases the system will ask further questions, for example about the date or place. The driver can barge into the system prompts to shorten the reading out of the result lists. The user can ask other, more specific questions, for example about a particular cinema or director (e.g. "List all the movies by Quentin Tarantino").

The results which are found as relevant for the driver's query, are sequentially read out to the driver by using a text-to-speech module, e.g. "I found the following theatres: CinemaxX Potsdamer Platz, Cubix Alexanderplatz, Alhambra, ...". Lists are personalized using the recommendation approach described in this paper both for the visual channel (list of topics areas on the screen) as well as the acoustical channel (the result lists of restaurants, which are read to the driver).

2   State of the Art and Related Work

2.1   Perception on Multimodal and Personalized Interfaces

In cognitive load theory, the central "bottleneck" of the cognitive system is the learner's working memory. The conceptual base of cognitive load theory has been explored and refined by several empirical studies, but some generalizations have to be reconsidered, because they allow different and contradicting interpretations [Schnotz and Kürschner, 2007]. Working memory is limited in capacity and in duration. Only four information elements can be compared simultaneously under special circumstances [Miller, 1956] and items get lost within about 20s [Peterson and Peterson, 1959]. This is critical for understanding information

Fig. 1. The SmartWeb driver interface: buttons are structured into two areas "Favorite items" and "New information"; Labels are assigned to each headline; a profile button on the right activates a personalization screen

that is read by a text-to-speech component in a car environment, where even other tasks further reduce the capacity of the working memory.

On the positive side, the modality effect is known as reducing the cognitive load for understanding information items, if information, which is provided on the visual output channel only, required the user to split attention. Capacity of the working memory can be increased by the use of two modalities. [Tindall-Ford et al., 1997]

A central question for adaptive and adaptable systems is how to design and present the ranking and how to personalize the user interface. Brusilovsky discuss a number of techniques for adaptive presentation and adaptive navigation support, such as hiding, sorting or annotations [Brusilovsky, 1998]. Annotations are very powerful, but they do not restrict cognitive overload as much as hiding does, though hiding can be simulated by "dimming" for not relevant links on bigger interfaces.

A transparent personalization process is critical for the user. Recommendations will more likely be perceived as reliable, positive and something that he/she can be confident in [Sinha and Swearingen, 2002]. Hiding information or changing the user interface with no visual reason and documentation will confuse the user if he is not familiar with the system and does not want to spend time in understanding it. If the user does not understand the system, he will neither trust its answers nor accept its usefulness. In that case the user would most likely disable personalization or even stop using the system soon.

Explanations transport the rational behind the ranking of the system for a single item and the relationship between items. Pu has shown that "... explanation interfaces have the greatest potential to build a competence-inspired trust relationship with its users..." in a product recommendation scenario (see [Pu and Chen, 2006] and [Tintarev and Masthoff, 2007]). Furthermore, structuring and organization of the user interface in several parts can significantly increase users' perception of competence [Pu and Chen, 2006].

Space for presenting information on the driver interface in the car is very limited. The display can hold only about 5 items depending on their size whereas a complete list of applications can easily scale to hundreds of items. In order to achieve the user's acceptance and appreciation, we structure information into two categories. Headlines in the "Favorite" section remain unchanged for a longer time since they are of high interest to the user. The "New information" section of the display contains recent information that might be of interest, so its contents change more frequently.

Up to two related topic labels are appended to the right of each item to explain the relationship between items and the categories on the profile screen. The process of reordering items is visualized by having the buttons move to their new positions. Buttons being removed from the screen are faded out and new buttons are faded in. The user may disable and freeze personalization at any time.

One other important research aspect for personalization and recommendation are issues such as shilling attacks and trust in multi-user environments [Mobasher et al., 2007]. This is critical for telematics environments, where ranking in one car might be based on surrounding cars for specific applications.

2.2   Hybrid Recommender Systems

Three general categories of recommendation approaches can be distinguished: collaborative systems, content-based systems, and hybrid approaches [Adomavicius and Tuzhilin, 2005].

Some authors also describe knowledge-based / rule-based systems as separate categories (see [Mobasher, 2007] and [Burke, 2002]). In collaborative approaches, recommendations are calculated by comparing users with each other and finding similarities in taste [Schafer et al., 2007]. Those content items, which are preferred by similar users, are then recommended to the active user.

In content-based approaches, features or annotations are used to compare content items, which the user has preferred in the past, to other content items. Similar items are recommended to the user. Knowledge-based approaches and rule-based systems rely on explicit knowledge about the content or static knowledge about the users. Decision rules are often created by experts. Hybrid approaches aim to overcome the shortcomings of content-based systems (over specialization, "machine-driven" calculation of taste) and collaborative systems (lack of scalability for memory-based approaches, data sparsity and cold start problem) (see [Balabanovic and Shoham, 1997] and [Degemmis et al., 2007]).

Some systems store single absolute values ("ratings") for each single content item (rating based). Other approaches use relative preference relations between two alternatives (preference based) [Adomavicius and Tuzhilin, 2005]. In practice, ratings for rating-based approaches are easier to be learned from user interaction, while mathematical consistency of preference-based approaches (e.g. fuzzy preference relations [Fodor and de Baets, 2008]) is better understood.

In the work of Perny and Zucker [Perny and Zucker, 1999] and Cornelis et al. [Cornelis et al., 2005], a rating-based fuzzy recommendation approach is proposed. It is used to scale between fuzzy content-based approach and fuzzy collaborative filtering.

3 Architecture and Method

Technically, each topic area on the main screen represents one single speech dialog assembly, consisting of prompts and grammars. The prompts texts and even entire speech dialogs are automatically generated from structured parts of web sites (tables) [Berton et al., 2007]. Some dialogs use web services to query up-to-date information, for example the date and time of future events in a given city. The goal of the recommender system is to rank the list of items on the screen visually to minimize the effort of finding new and interesting items. In addition, the cognitive load, which is required to remember the items is an acoustical list, is reduced.

3.1 Hybrid Fuzzy Approach for Recommendations

We understand personalization as the adaptive process of filtering and prioritizing information based on the user's preferences and context, both changing over time. The user's preferences for unseen items are generalized from those that he/she has rated in the past. Customization is referred to the manual adaptation of the interface by the user.

The goal of the recommendation task is to order a number of items $I' \subseteq I$ from a set $I = \{i_j \mid 1 \leq j \leq n\}$ (Fig. 2, middle layer) for the active user u_{active} under one or more criteria. In a multi-user case, u_{active} might be one user out of a set of users $U = \{u_k \mid 1 \leq k \leq m\}$ (Fig. 2, bottom layer). The recommendation process is based on 3 basic steps: mapping the driver's multimodal input to the preference model, recommendation, and updating the preference model whenever the user interacts with the system.

Categories for Content-based Similarity. For performing content-based filtering, a method for determining similarity of content items has to be defined. Each new item, which gets downloaded to the client module in the car, is matched to one or many ontology categories $C = \{c_l \mid 1 \leq l \leq o\}$ (see Fig. 2, top layer and similarity relations $M(x, y)$). Textual data representing the content of each item are searched for the occurrence of a number of key terms for each ontology category. The frequency is normalized by computing the maximum frequency

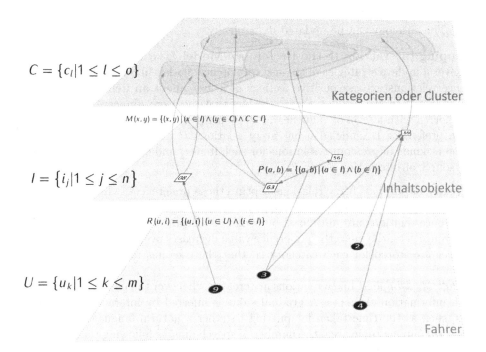

$C = \{c_l | 1 \leq l \leq o\}$

Kategorien oder Cluster

$M(x,y) = \{(x,y) | (x \in I) \wedge (y \in C) \wedge C \subseteq I\}$

$I = \{i_j | 1 \leq j \leq n\}$

$P(a,b) = \{(a,b) | (a \in I) \wedge (b \in I)\}$

Inhaltsobjekte

$R(u,i) = \{(u,i) | (u \in U) \wedge (i \in I)\}$

$U = \{u_k | 1 \leq k \leq m\}$

Fahrer

Fig. 2. Visualization of the preference model. several content items (middle layer) are gradually mapped to one or more concepts / clusters (top layer). In the multi-user case, many users exist (bottom layer).

over all keywords. Two document sources are used: the item's headline representing the item in the list and a short description about the content of the dialog. Headlines are weighted higher than other information. The value of the weighted term frequency is used as the membership relation between any item i and any category c.

$$M(i,c) = \{(i,c) | (i \in I) \wedge (c \in C)\}$$

By using those membership values $M(i,c)$, a similarity relation between two items is defined through aggregation. A T-Norm $T(M(i_x,c), M(i_y,c))$ can be used for "pessimistically" combining two membership relations M of two items i_x an i_y. The value describes to which extend each of those items belongs to a common category c. With a $max - min$ composition the following content-based similarity measure is used for each pair of content items i_x and i_y:

$$S(i_x, i_y) = \underset{\forall l}{\mathrm{argmax}}(T(M(i_x, c_l), M(i_y, c_l)))$$

This similarity measure is used for content-based recommendation. We built a domain ontology with 9 main topics and a total of 115 topics in a tree with up to 4 levels. This ontology is used to match dialogs to topics. In addition, the ontology is enhanced to restaurant categories to match restaurants for the result lists. The ontology can be updated dynamically.

Mapping Interaction to the Preference Model. The user input is mapped to several update strategies of the user preference model. In our approach, preference relations express positive feelings of a user about an item. Uncertainty has to be taken into account, due to the fact that the user's aim can usually only be inferred with a level of vagueness, e.g. by using a speech recognition process. Each preference is modeled using fuzzy relations $P : UxI \rightarrow [0,1]$. We store different kinds of preference relations for each item i_j and each user u_k based on the source of interaction data:

Individual-explicit fuzzy relations capture those preferences, which the driver has indicated on a profile screen (e.g. "cars", "sports") as preferred. Explicit preference relations are initialized by a maximum value of 1.0. The older each preference gets, the more the preference value decreases over time. Explicit preferences are stored for each category c_l, that the user has rated on the profile screen.

Individual-implicit fuzzy relations are created whenever the user is interacting with information elements. A gradual value is inferred by interaction parameters, such as the time taken for putting together a natural language question-answering in one topic area, the number of speech queries following the selection of an item, and events such as interrupting the system for a new query. By those scores, the interest for every content item is approximated and stored as a preference relation for any content item the user interacted with.

Global preference relations are manually initialized for each category. The interest scores for the topics were found during a user evaluation with 20 subjects. A proof-of-concept using 50 speech applications for our personalization approach was delivered. Subjects were asked to successively access speech applications according to their own personal choice while pretending to be driving a car. In a telematics environment, the global preferences are influenced by the preferences of the drivers in other cars. They are calculated by comparing the preference model with the preference model of surrounding cars. Collaborative filtering [Schafer et al., 2007] provides a method to find similar drivers based on preferences in their preference model. These preferences are necessary, if the user did not yet interact with the system and did not provide any ratings. Furthermore, those preferences are used to influence local recommendations by global knowledge, which could be relevant, e.g. for prioritizing warning messages.

Recommendation. On request of the driver, items get prioritized for presentation on the screen. Each following interaction causes the recommendation algorithm to update the preference model. In the update step, explicit preferences can also be decreased with time because they might get out of interest for the user and he/she might forget to update them.

The overall preference score for each item is calculated by aggregating individual and global preferences. Individual preferences of a particular user are calculated from explicit user ratings and implicit indicators by content-based filtering. For a given item i_q each other content item resulting in k best similarity scores $S(i_q, i_k)$. As we described above, the similarity score is based on similar relations of both items to similar categories. An algebraic product operator is used as implicator, to combine the similarity measures with the corresponding preference value of the item $R(u_{active}, i_k)$ for each content item i_k. Each output value is then aggregated by the max-operator for each content item.

The influence of global preferences is calculated by a collaborative filtering algorithm. It calculates the k most influential users by comparing the preference model of users with each other. The framework uses the Pearson correlation coefficient. The individual preferences for the k most influential users is then weighted by the correlation coefficient and propagated to the active user.

After the calculation, three values are known for each content item: an explicit value, an implicit value and a global value. A certainty measure weights the values for aggregation. The certainty measure is dependent on rules about the information density and applicability of each recommendation strategy in the current situation. For example, if there are new explicit values given by the user, then explicit values are mainly used. If there were many user interactions recently, implicit preferences are used preferably. The three preferences are accumulated by a maximum-operator (T-conorm).

3.2   Enhanced Speech Dialogue Architecture

The personalization module is part of an extended speech dialog architecture for processing natural language dialogs as well as Command & Control dialogs [Berton et al., 2007]. A common architecture for multimodal interaction is described in [Cohen et al., 2004]. Command & Control dialogs are processed by several modules of a classical architecture for speech dialog systems:

- Automatic Speech Recognition (ASR)
- Text-To-Speech Synthesis (TTS)
- Command & Control Dialog Manager (C&C-DM)
- Synchronization interface between various input and output modalities
- Graphical user interface and interaction module (widgets, state transitions)

This architecture is extended for integrating new speech dialogs and data from the Internet. Natural language queries are handled by additional modules:

- a Dialog Manager for natural language question-answering (NL-DM)
- a Meta Dialog Manager to coordinate activities between C&C-DM and NL-DM
- a module for receiving dialogs and data and compiling and integrating vocabulary and language model
- a personalization module for ranking and structuring visual and acoustic output

Any word of the new application grammar, that is not yet part of the vocabulary, is converted by G2P which is part of the TTS module in order to compile the phonetic transcriptions for the complete vocabulary. The personalization module is triggered by the Meta Dialog Manager whenever the user interacts with the system. The personalization module is structured into several parts: a component for matching new content items to an internal ontology, a data model for storing the user preferences, the recommender for calculating the ranking of content items, and an abstract representation of the user interface. This representation is used for mapping one or more model update strategies to input events.

4   Conclusions

We discussed a car scenario and a system for multimodal interaction and mobile access to Internet information. Up-to-date information, e.g. movies, restaurants, weather, petrol prices and speed monitoring, can be queried by the driver. We need to be more and more aware of the sophisticated effects on multimodal interaction and aspects on adaptive and personalized systems. An intelligent interaction design with attention to detail is important for building a robust and a successful system from the user point of view. Fuzzy technologies can handle the vagueness and uncertainty of sensorial input through automatic speech recognition as well as fuzzy human concepts and gradual truth when dealing with preferences and categories. A hybrid fuzzy recommendation approach with user preference data from 3 sources (explicit, implicit, global) and two recommendation strategies (content-based. collaborative) was applied to the results of speech queries for restaurant information Those items, which are expected to be the most relevant for the user, are read out first, which enables shorter dialog completion time. The user might also shorten the time by just barging-in.

In future work, we would like to improve the integration of the visual channel and acoustical lists. Result lists should also be synchronized to the visual information on screen while they are read out by the system. Furthermore, the ranking of the items should be dependent on multiple criteria and on the current context. For example, the preferences for restaurants might change depending on the current city and several criteria (price, distance, type of food). Each of those criteria might be of a different importance to the user in a particular contextual setting .Several approaches will be investigated to include fuzzy multi-criteria optimization and preference modeling [Fodor and de Baets, 2008] and to bridge rating-based and preference-based approaches.

Acknowledgments

This work was partially funded by the German Ministry of Education and Research (BMBF) in the framework of the SmartWeb project (01IMD01K). We would like to thank Craig Wootton for proofreading this paper.

References

[Adomavicius and Tuzhilin, 2005] Adomavicius, G., Tuzhilin, A.: Toward the next generation of recommender systems: A survey of the state-of-the-art and possible extensions. IEEE Transactions on Knowledge and Data Engineering 17(6), 734–749 (2005)

[Balabanovic and Shoham, 1997] Balabanovic, M., Shoham, Y.: Fab: content-based, collaborative recommendation. Commun. ACM 40(3), 66–72 (1997)

[Berton et al., 2007] Berton, A., Regel-Brietzmann, P., Block, H.-U., Schacht, S., Gehrke, M.: How to integrate speech-operated internet information dialogs into a car. In: Proc. of Interspeech (8th Annual Conference of the Int. Speech Communication Association) (2007)

[Brusilovsky, 1998] Brusilovsky, P.: Methods and techniques of adaptive hypermedia. In: Brusilovsky, P., Alfred Kobsa, J.V. (eds.) Adaptive Hypertext and Hypermedia, pp. 1–44. Kluwer Academic Publishers, Dordrecht (1998)

[Burke, 2002] Burke, R.: Hybrid recommender systems: Survey and experiments. User Modeling and User-Adapted Interaction 12(4), 331–370 (2002)

[Cohen et al., 2004] Cohen, M.H., Giangola, J.P., Balogh, J.: Voice User Interface Design. Addison-Wesley Professional, Reading (2004)

[Cornelis et al., 2005] Cornelis, C., Guo, X., Lu, J., Zhang, G.: A fuzzy relational approach to event recommendation. In: Proc. of 2nd Indian Int. Conf. on Artificial Intelligence (IICAI 2005), pp. 2231–2242 (2005)

[Degemmis et al., 2007] Degemmis, M., Lops, P., Semeraro, G.: A content-collaborative recommender that exploits wordnet-based user profiles for neighborhood formation. User Modeling and User-Adapted Interaction 17(3), 217–255 (2007)

[Fodor and de Baets, 2008] Fodor, J., de Baets, B.: Fuzzy preference modelling: Fundamentals and recent advances. Fuzzy Sets and Their Extensions: Representation, Aggregation and Models, 207–217 (2008)

[Miller, 1956] Miller, G.A.: The magical number seven, plus or minus two: Some limits on our apacity for processing information. Psychological Review 63, 81–97 (1956)

[Mobasher, 2007] Mobasher, B.: Recommender systems. Kunstliche Intelligenz, Special Issue on Web Mining 3, 41–43 (2007)

[Mobasher et al., 2007] Mobasher, B., Burke, R., Bhaumik, R., Williams, C.: Toward trustworthy recommender systems: An analysis of attack models and algorithm robustness. ACM Trans. Inter. Tech. 7(4), 23 (2007)

[Perny and Zucker, 1999] Perny, P., Zucker, J.-D.: Collaborative filtering methods based on fuzzy preference relations. In: Proc. of the EUROFUSE-SIC 1999, pp. 279–285 (1999)

[Peterson and Peterson, 1959] Peterson, L., Peterson, M.: Shortterm retention of individual verbal items. Journal of Experimental Psychology 58, 193–198 (1959)

[Pu and Chen, 2006] Pu, P., Chen, L.: Trust building with explanation interfaces. In: IUI 2006: Proceedings of the 11th international conference on Intelligent user interfaces, pp. 93–100. ACM Press, New York (2006)

[Schafer et al., 2007] Schafer, J., Frankowski, D., Herlocker, J., Sen, S.: Collaborative filtering recommender systems. The Adaptive Web, 291–324 (2007)

[Schnotz and Kürschner, 2007] Schnotz, W., Kürschner, C.: A reconsideration of cognitive load theory. Educational Psychology Review 19(4), 469–508 (2007)

[Sinha and Swearingen, 2002] Sinha, R., Swearingen, K.: The role of transparency in recommender systems. In: Extended Abstracts of Conference on Human Factors in Computing Systems (CHI 2002) (2002)

[Tindall-Ford et al., 1997] Tindall-Ford, S., Chandler, P., Sweller, J.: When two sensory modes are better than one. Journal of Experimental Psychology: Applied 3, 257–287 (1997)

[Tintarev and Masthoff, 2007] Tintarev, N., Masthoff, J.: A survey of explanations in recommender systems. In: Uchyigit, G. (ed.) Workshop on Recommender Systems and Intelligent User Interfaces associated with ICDE 2007, Istanbul, Turkey. IEEE, Los Alamitos (2007)

[Wahlster, 2007] Wahlster, W.: Smartweb: multimodal web services on the road. In: Proc. of the 15th Int. Conf. on Multimedia p.16 (2007)

Factors Influencing Modality Choice in Multimodal Applications

Anja B. Naumann, Ina Wechsung, and Sebastian Möller

Deutsche Telekom Laboratories, TU Berlin, Ernst-Reuter-Platz 7
10587 Berlin, Germany
anja.naumann@telekom.de
http://www.qu.tlabs.tu-berlin.de

Abstract. This paper describes initial results from an evaluation study on the use of different modalities. The application, a web-based media recommender and management system called MediaScout, was installed on two multimodal devices, and on one unimodal device as a control condition. The study aims to investigate whether users make use of multimodality if it is offered and under which circumstances they do so. Moreover, it was studied whether users' stated modality preferences match their actual use of the modalities. The results show that users do not make use of all modalities for all tasks. Modality usage is determined by the task to be performed, as well as the efficiency of the modality for achieving the task goal. Both modality usage and the range of offered modalities seem to influence subjective user ratings.

1 Introduction

Multimodal interfaces have been investigated since the early nineties. Since human-human-communication usually involves more than one modality, multimodal interfaces, especially those including speech, are assumed to be more natural (see [Kallinen and Ravaja, 2005]) than unimodal interfaces. Furthermore, multimodal interfaces are expected to be more flexible, efficient, and robust than unimodal ones (see [Hedicke, 2000] and [Oviatt, 1999]). One the other hand, multimodality may increase the workload since the selection of the appropriate modality requires additional cognitive resources (see [Schomaker, et al., 1995]). Moreover, the different modalities may interfere with each other (see [Schomaker et al., 1995]). Even though users prefer multimodal interaction for spatial tasks and have strong modality preferences depending on the task (see [Oviatt, 1999] and [Ren et al., 2000]) it remains unclear if these results also apply to other tasks. The potential benefit of multimodality therefore depends at least on the following factors: the task, the situation and the offered modalities. The current study aims to investigate whether users make use of multimodality if it is offered, and under which circumstances they do so. Moreover, it was studied if modality preferences stated by the user match their actual use of these modalities.

E. André et al. (Eds.): PIT 2008, LNAI 5078, pp. 37–43, 2008.

2 Method

2.1 Participants

The participants were twenty-one German-speaking individuals (11 male, 10 female) between the age of 19 and 69 (M = 31.2). Eleven of them were experienced Information and Communication Technology (ICT) users and nine were inexperienced ICT users. The ICT experience was measured via a screening questionnaire during the recruitment. For one participant the screener data was missing and therefore only twenty cases were analyzed for comparisons regarding the ICT experience. All users participated in return for a book token.

2.2 Tested Applications

The multimodal devices adopted for the test were a PDA (Fujitsu-Siemens Pocket LOOX T830) and a tablet PC (Samsung Q1-Pro 900 Casomii). Both devices had a voice control as well as a graphical user interface with touch screen. Additionally, the PDA could be operated with motion control, i.e. menu options could be selected by tilting the device. To find out if users rate multimodal systems better than unimodal systems, a unimodal device (a conventional PC controllable with mouse and keyboard) was used as the control condition.

The application, a web-based media recommender and management system called MediaScout was the same for all devices.

The users performed five different types of tasks: seven navigation tasks, six tasks where checkboxes had to be marked or unmarked, four tasks were an option from a drop-down list had to be selected, three tasks where a button had to be pressed, and one task where a phone number had to be entered.

Several questionnaires were used to cover different aspects of the users' opinions, like the AttrakDiff questionnaire by [Hassenzahl et al., 2003], adapted SUS-Scales by [Brooke, 1996], and the SUMI questionnaire by [Kirakowski and Corbett, 1993]. Furthermore, log data from the application, psycho-physiological data, and video and audio data were recorded during the whole experiment. This paper mainly reports the results of the SUMI, the final questionnaire collecting the modality preferences and overall impressions, and the log data analysis.

To analyze which modality the participants wanted to use, log data of the test block in which the users could freely choose modalities was annotated. For every task, the modality used first to perform the task was selected for further analysis. This way, the percentages of modality usage per task type have been computed.

2.3 Procedure

Each test session took approximately three hours. It was conducted in a usability lab. Cameras captured the participants and their interaction with the devices during the whole experiment. Each participant had to perform a series of tasks with each device. In the beginning, participants read a first instruction, signed a consent form and filled out a demographic questionnaire. Since psycho-physiological data was measured, electrodes were attached. In order to measure the baseline of the psychophysiological parameters, the participants watched neutral pictures on a PC screen for five minutes. After that, the MediaScout and the first device were explained by the experimenter. Then, participants were verbally instructed to perform the tasks with a given modality. This was repeated for every modality supported by that specific device. After that, the tasks were presented again and the participants could freely choose the interaction modality. Finally, they were asked to fill out the questionnaires to rate the previously tested device. This procedure was repeated for each of the three devices. The order of the devices was randomized for each subject. After the third device, a final questionnaire regarding the overall impressions and preferences had to be filled out by the participants.

3 Results

3.1 Modality Usage by Task

Figure 1 shows the used modalities averaged over all tasks for each of the multimodal devices. For both devices, the majority of tasks were performed via touch screen with the graphical user interface (GUI). These differences are significant for the tablet PC (Wilcoxon: Z = -2.83, p = 0.003) as well as for the PDA (Friedman: $\chi^2(2) = 18.88$, p = 0.000).

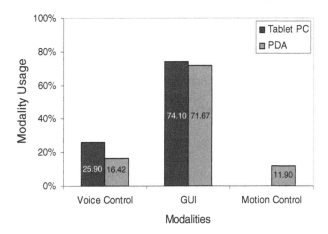

Fig. 1. Modality usage over all tasks when interacting with tablet PC and PDA (motion control option only implemented on the PDA)

A detailed analysis revealed that when interacting with the tablet PC, the only task for which voice control and GUI were used equally frequently was entering a phone number. For all other tasks, GUI was significantly more often selected as the first choice to perform a task (s. Table 1).

Table 1. Used modalities (percentages) by task for tablet PC

Task	Modality	Mean	SD	Wilcoxon test: Z	p
Buttons	GUI	73.02	44.25	-2.22	.041
	Voice	26.98	44.25		
Drop down lists	GUI	73.80	42.92	-2.46	.019
	Voice	26.19	42.92		
Phone number	GUI	47.61	51.18	-0.22	1.00
	Voice	52.38	51.18		
Check boxes	GUI	81.75	35.71	-3.24	.001
	Voice	18.25	35.71		
Navigation	GUI	72.11	38.72	-2.67	.006
	Voice	27.89	38.72		

When interacting with the PDA, the phone number entering task could only be performed with voice control or GUI. The modality usage is similar to the one on the tablet PC: When entering the phone number only voice control (M = 33.33, SD = 48.30) was used quite as frequently as the GUI (M = 66.66, SD = 48.30, Wilcoxon: Z = 1.53, p = 0.189). For all other tasks, the GUI was used significantly more often than the other modalities (s. Table 2).

Mean differences between voice control and motion control were not significant neither for confirming buttons (M = 9.52, SD = 39.64, Wilcoxon: Z = -0.965, p = 0.344) nor for marking check boxes (M = 10.32, SD = 42.97, Wilcoxon: Z = -0.850, p = 0.398).

Differences between experienced and inexperienced users and between female and male participants were only observed for the PDA's motion control: Experienced users (M = 6.36; SD = 10.51) used motion control less often than inexperienced users (M = 20.00, SD = 16.77, Mann-Whitney U = 22.00, p = 0.032). Women used motion control for 17.00 percent of the tasks (SD = 12.23), men only for 7.27 percent (SD = 16.03; Mann-Whitney U = 27.50, p = 0.045).

3.2 Stated Modality Preferences

In the final questionnaire the participants were asked about their preferred modality. They could choose between all individual modalities as well as the combinations of them. It was also possible to state that none of the modalities was preferred. Consistent with the results of the log data analysis, most of the participants preferred the GUI over the combination of GUI and speech control, and over speech control only,

Table 2. Modality usage (percentages) by task for PDA

Task	Modality	Mean	SD	Friedman test: χ^2	p
	GUI	80.95	35.86		
Buttons	Voice	14.29	35.86	24.82	.000
	Motion	4.76	11.96		
	GUI	80.95	26.11		
Drop down list	Voice	9.52	24.33	28.29	.000
	Motion	9.52	16.73		
	GUI	73.80	35.19		
Check boxes	Voice	18.25	36.48	20.90	.000
	Motion	7.94	14.55		
	GUI	60.54	36.39		
Navigation	Voice	19.73	32.73	11.03	.003
	Motion	19.73	26.13		

$\chi^2(2) = 10.90$, p = 0.004. Figure 2 displays the stated preferences. For the PDA, the majority preferred the GUI over all possible combinations and over speech and motion control, $\chi^2(4) = 10.50$, p = 0.031). Two participants had no preference (s. Figure 2). The most preferred combination was motion control and GUI (4 cases). Two participants preferred voice control in combination with GUI. The combination of voice and motion control was the preference of only one participant.

No differences regarding the stated preferences were observed between the experienced and inexperienced users. Slight differences between female and male users were shown for the PDA (Pearsons $\chi^2(4) = 8.29$, p = 0.057). The majority of the male users (6 cases) preferred GUI, most female users (5 cases) preferred a combination of modalities: Three of them preferred GUI combined with motion control, one preferred GUI combined with voice control and one preferred voice control combined with motion control.

3.3   Subjective Ratings of Multimodal and Unimodal Systems

The analysis of the SUMI questionnaire raw data (all items poled in one direction but not transformed to the T-Scale) of the global scale showed significant differences, $F(2,40) = 6.56$, p = .003; partial eta² = .247: The PDA, the device with the most modalities, was rated best (M = 45.29, SD = 10.14), the tablet PC was rated second (M = 40.19, SD = 7.87), and the unimodal PC got the worst rating (M = 38.04, SD = 7.06). Differences between experienced and inexperienced users as well as between female and male participants were not significant.

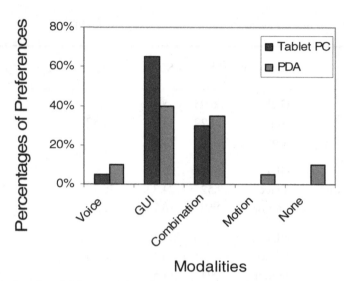

Modalities

Fig. 2. Preferred modalities for tablet PC and PDA (motion control option only implemented on the PDA)

For the subscales, significant differences between devices were found for affect, efficiency, control and learnability. The unimodal PC was rated worst on all subscales, except the learnability scale. No effect was found for helpfulness. The detailed results are shown in Table 3.

Table 3. Ratings on SUMI sub-scales (raw scores) for each device

Scale	Device	Mean	SD	F (2,40)	p (partial eta²)
Efficiency	Tablet PC	19.00	3.39	6.19	.005 (.236)
	PDA	19.90	3.48		
	Unimodal	16.67	3.15		
Affect	Tablet PC	19.33	2.13	10.02	.000 (.334)
	PDA	19.95	2.13		
	Unimodal	17.38	2.73		
Helpfulness	Tablet PC	22.05	1.96	1.46	.244 (.068)
	PDA	22.19	2.09		
	Unimodal	21.48	1.89		
Control	Tablet PC	22.67	2.27	3.33	.046 (.143)
	PDA	22.24	2.21		
	Unimodal	21.38	2.22		
Learnability	Tablet PC	15.57	3.23	5.98	.005 (.230)
	PDA	14.57	3.47		
	Unimodal	16.90	4.40		

4 Discussion

One of our goals was to investigate under which circumstances which modality is used. The presented results show that users do not use all possible modalities for all tasks. The majority of tasks were performed with the GUI, which was also stated as the preferred modality. Task characteristics seem to determine whether the offered modalities are used or not. Users seem to use modalities which are most efficient for reaching the task goal: For example, the phone number task could be solved more efficiently (i.e. with less interaction steps) via voice control than via GUI. In fact, this task was the only one for which GUI and voice usage was approximately equally frequent. But the GUI as the most common and therefore most familiar modality was used quite as often even though it was not as efficient as voice control. Possibly the usage of voice control would increase as a function of practice.

Individual differences like age and experience had only a minor influence on the choice of modality. But even if the offered modalities are rarely used, they seem to affect the subjective ratings: Modality usage was consistent with modality preference, and the ratings on the SUMI scales tended to be better for the PDA, the device with the widest choice of modalities.

In the next steps, parameters like task completion time and task error rate for each modality and each device will be analyzed. The aim is to investigate the influence these parameters might have on modality choice.

References

[Brooke, 1996] Brooke, J.: SUS: A 'quick and dirty' usability scale. In: Jordan, P.W., Thomas, B., Weerdmeester, B.A., McClelland, I.L. (eds.) Usability Evaluation in Industry, pp. 189–194. Taylor & Francis, London (1996)

[Hassenzahl et al., 2003] Hassenzahl, M., Burmester, M., Koller, F.: AttrakDiff: Ein Fragebogen zur Messung wahrgenommener hedonischer und pragmatischer Qualität. In: Ziegler, J., Szwillus, G. (eds.) Mensch & Computer 2003. Interaktion in Bewegung, pp. 187–196. B.G. Teubner, Stuttgart (2003)

[Hedicke, 2000] Hedicke, V.: Multimodalität in Mensch-Maschine-Schnittstellen. In: Timpe, K.-P., Jürgensohn, T., Kolrep, H. (eds.) Mensch-Maschine-Systemtechnik, pp. 203–230. Symposion publishing, Düsseldorf (2000)

[Kallinen and Ravaja, 2005] Kallinen, K., Ravaja, N.: Effects of the Rate of Computer-Mediated Speech on Emotion-related Subjective and Physiological Responses. Behaviour & Information Technology 24, 365–373 (2005)

[Kirakowski and Corbett, 1993] Kirakowski, J., Corbett, M.: SUMI: The software usability measurement inventory. British Journal of Educational Technology 24(3), 210–212 (1993)

[Oviatt, 1999] Oviatt, S.L.: Ten myths of multimodal interaction. Communications of the ACM 42(11), 576–583 (1999)

[Ren et al., 2000] Ren, X., Zhang, G., Dai, G.: An Experimental Study of Input Modes for Multimodal Human-Computer Interaction. In: Tan, T., Shi, Y., Gao, W. (eds.) ICMI 2000. LNCS, vol. 1948, pp. 49–56. Springer, Heidelberg (2000)

[Schomaker et al., 1995] Schomaker, L., Nijtmans, J., Camurri, A., Lavagetto, F., Morasso, P., Benoît, C., Guiard-Marigny, T., Le Goff, B., Robert-Ribes, J., Adjoudani, A., Defée, I., Münch, S., Hartung, K., Blauert, J.A.: Taxonomy of Multimodal Interaction in the Human Information Processing System. A Report of the ESPRIT Project 8579 MIAMI. NICI, Nijmegen (1995)

Codebook Design for Speech Guided Car Infotainment Systems

Martin Raab[1,2], Rainer Gruhn[1,3], and Elmar Noeth[2]

[1] Harman Becker Automotive Systems, Speech Dialog Systems, Ulm, Germany
mraab@harmanbecker.com
http://www.harmanbecker.de
[2] University of Erlangen, Dept. of Pattern Recognition, Erlangen, Germany
[3] University of Ulm, Dept. of Information Technology, Ulm, Germany

Abstract. In car infotainment systems commands and other words in the user's main language must be recognized with maximum accuracy, but it should be possible to use foreign names as they frequently occur in music titles or city names. Previous approaches did not address the constraint of conserving the main language performance when they extended their systems to cover multilingual input.

In this paper we present an approach for speech recognition of multiple languages with constrained resources on embedded devices. Speech recognizers on such systems are typically to-date semi-continuous speech recognizers, which are based on vector quantization.

We provide evidence that common vector quantization algorithms are not optimal for such systems when they have to cope with input from multiple languages. Our new method combines information from multiple languages and creates a new codebook that can be used for efficient vector quantization in multilingual scenarios. Experiments show significant improved speech recognition results.

1   Introduction

Imagine a German tourist looking forward to a wonderful holiday in Marseille, France. Imagine he is driving there with his new car with the latest, speech driven car infotainment system. Of course, he will most of the time interact with the system in German. On his way, however, he will drive through Italy and France. His holiday is long enough, so he wants to explore some cities on his way.

So, apart from Milano and Cannes, he wants to tell his navigation system to drive to Rozzano, Italy and to Roquebrune-Sur-Argens, France. As these city names do not belong to the language of the user interface, current systems are not able to recognize such names when they are spoken. Therefore a multilingual system is needed, that can recognize the German commands the user will utter as well as the foreign city names.

But there are further reasons why the user would want to have a multilingual speech recognizer on his journey. For example, he prefers to listen to his own

E. André et al. (Eds.): PIT 2008, LNAI 5078, pp. 44–51, 2008.

music collection rather than to radio stations in foreign languages. Even the most convenient haptic music selection systems however will distract the tourist on his long way. It would be much better if it would be possible just to say the name of the artist, instead. But as for the city names above, many artists names are not German. Again, without multilingual speech recognition such a system is not possible.

By now, we have motivated why multilingual speech recognition is a essential feature of future car infotainment systems. But, it should not be forgotten, that the user lives in most cases in one country and speaks one language. Thus, he will most of the time travel within his country, and the commands he uses will always belong to one language. Therefore, while we want multilingual recognition, we can not allow multilingual recognition to degrade performance on the user main language, as this is the language he will most of the time use to interact with the system.

To recapitulate, we want to built a Man-Machine Interface (MMI) for car infotainment that

* recognizes commands and other words in the user's main language with maximum accuracy
* but it should be possible to recognize foreign names as well as possible, because they frequently occur in music titles or city names

Previous approaches did not address the constraint of conserving the main language performance when they extended their systems to cover multilingual input [Koehler, 2001, Gruhn et al., 2004, Schultz and Waibel, 2001]. In one case improved performance on non-native speech was achieved without loosing performance on the main language, but only for the limited task of digit recognition [Fischer et al., 2003].

In theory it is hardly a problem to use recognizers for each language and all problems are solved. However, in practice this is currently a rather unrealistic approach. Car systems are still very restricted regarding computing power. Therefore, we build one recognizer that has trained HMMs for each language, but otherwise uses the same small set of Gaussians for all languages. This reduces both computing demands and memory consumption drastically. Using a small set of Gaussians is not new, and generally referred to as semi continuous speech recognition. There are also established methods (LBG algorithm, [Linde et al., 1980]) for the creation of such collections of Gaussians. Such collections are usually called codebook.

For our aims, we believe traditional vector quantization algorithms to be suboptimal. Either only main language training data is provided to the LBG algorithm, or data from all languages is provided. In the first case the codebook is only optimized for the main language, not considering the performance on the additional languages. In the second case the codebook is optimized for all languages without prioritizing the main language. For the car infotainment scenario, neither of these options is optimal.

Therefore we propose a new algorithm for the construction of a multilingual codebook. The first step is the construction of a codebook for each language with soft vector quantization based on the LBG approach. From these initial codebooks a new codebook is created. This new codebook should still achieve monolingual performance on the main language, but at the same time improve performance on the additional languages. As the new codebook is based on codebooks from many languages, we call it multilingual, and as the influence of each original codebook can be adjusted, we call it Multilingual Weighted Codebook (MWC).

The remainder of this paper is organized as follows. Section 2 describes the baseline architecture that we use to train recognizers for multiple languages. Section 3 explains how MWCs are constructed from initial codebooks. Section 4 and 5 describe our experimental setup and show the results. Finally, a conclusion is drawn and suggestions for future work are made.

2   Baseline System

We start with a well trained monolingual semi-continuous HMM speech recognizer. While keeping the main language generated codebook constant, for each additional language we do the following.

* Add all additional language HMMs to the recognizer
* Train these additional HMMs with training data from the corresponding language, not changing the codebook

Finally, the HMMs for all languages are trained. In the introduction we already stated why we believe that the main language codebook is not optimal for our scenario.

3   Extended System

To improve the performance on the additional languages, we replace the monolingual codebook with an MWC. The MWC is basically the main language codebook plus some additional Gaussians. Figure 1 depicts an example for the extension of a codebook to cover an additional language. From left to right one iteration of the generation of MWCs is represented.

The picture to the left shows the initial situation. The Xs are mean vectors from the main language codebook, and the area that is roughly covered by them is indicated by the dotted line. Additionally, the numbered Os are mean vectors from the second language codebook. Supposing that both Xs and Os are optimal for the language they were created for, it is clear that the second language contains sound patterns that are not typical for the first language (Os 1,2 and 3).

The middle picture shows the distance calculation. For each of the second language codebook vectors, the nearest neighbor among the main language Gaussians is determined. These nearest neighbor connections are indicated by the dotted lines. We use the Mahalanobis distance as distance measure.

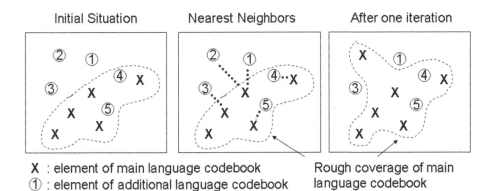

X : element of main language codebook
① : element of additional language codebook

Rough coverage of main
language codebook

Fig. 1. Basic Idea of Multilingual Weighted Codebooks

The right picture presents the outcome of one iteration. From each of the nearest neighbor connections, the largest one (O number 2) was chosen as this is obviously the mean vector which causes the largest vector quantization error. Thus, the Gaussian O number 2 was added to the main language codebook.

4   Experimental Setup

Our experiments base on 11 MFCCs with their first and second derivatives per frame and LDA for feature space transformation. All recognizers are trained on 200 hours of Speecon data for each language [Iskra et al., 2002]. The HMMs are context dependent.

We used five languages for the training of our recognizer (US English, French, German, Spanish and Italian). For each training language a codebook with 1024 Gaussians was created by the LBG algorithm. Information about test sets for native speech of all languages is given in Table 1. The first row contains the number of test utterances, the second row the number of different entries in the grammar used. All utterances are city names.

The non-native tests in Section 5.2 are conducted on the HIWIRE data [Segura et al., 2007]. The HIWIRE database contains human input in a command and control aeronautics application by 81 speakers (31 French, 20 Greek, 20 Italian, 10 Spanish). The spoken language is always English. Each speaker produced 100 utterances which were recorded as clean speech with a close talking microphone. The database provides the clean speech signal, as well as three further signals that are convolved with cockpit noise. We test on the clean speech test which is provided with the data (50% of the HIWIRE data). The non-native adaptation data provided with the database is not used. For a comparison of the HIWIRE corpus to other non-native corpora we refer to [Raab et al., 2007].

To reduce the number of experiments, German is always the main language when we build MWCs.

Table 1. Testset description (Utterances/Grammar)

	German	English	Italian	French	Spanish
#Utterances	2005	852	2000	3308	5143
#Grammar Size	2498	500	2000	2000	3672

5 Results

In [Raab et al., 2008] we describe preparatory several experiments to get setups for creating MWCs. For example, experiments with different distance measures and varying codebook sizes. The first part of this section presents results on five languages (German, English, Italian, French, Spanish).

The second part of this section deals with a problem that we have not introduced yet, but which is commonly known: non-native speech recognition. While it is one aspect to produce a better codebook for the recognition of multiple languages, this does not need to actually improve the performance in our target scenario. The reason is that speech by non-native speakers differs significantly from native speakers. Due to the unpredictable deviations, non-native speech is well known to degrade speech recognition performance severely [Witt, 1999, Tomokiyo, 2001]. Therefore the second parts presents results on several non-native accents of English.

5.1 Multilingual Evaluation

When 5 languages at once are considered in the MWC generation, it is likely that the four codebooks of the additional languages will contain some similar entries, as there will be sound patterns that occur in all languages. To remove these multiple representations of one sound pattern, the following is done. At first all additional language codebooks are thrown together, resulting in a codebook with 4096 Gaussians. Then very similar Gaussians in this 4096 codebook are merged until the codebook has 2048 Gaussians. By merging we mean replacing these two by one Gaussian that would have been estimated from all the training samples that led to the estimation of the two original Gaussians. It is not necessary to know all the training samples to perform the merging, a formula can be found in [Steidl, 2002]. This 2048 Codebook (the additional languages codebook) is the input to the MWC algorithm, together with the unmodified German codebook.

The top row of Table 2 is the baseline experiment which uses only the German codebook. The other recognizers contain a full German codebook with 1024 Gaussians and 200, 400 and 800 Gaussians from the additional languages. The total codebook sizes are 1224, 1424 and 1824, respectively.

The first column with word accuracies shows that the performance on the German test set varies insignificantly. This is due to the fact that the LBG already produces an optimal codebook for German. Thus, the extensions to the codebook can not improve performance on German, but they do not hurt.

Table 2. Word Accuracies on five languages

Total Gaussians	Added Gaussians	German	English	Italian	French	Spanish
1024	0	84.1	65.6	85.2	68.7	88.3
1224	200	83.8	68.4	88.3	69.0	90.2
1424	400	84.0	70.9	87.9	71.3	**91.5**
1824	800	**84.3**	**72.0**	**89.7**	**72.9**	91.0

However, for the additional languages the results show significant improvements. In general, the performance increase is correlated to the amount of Gaussians that were added to the codebook. The MWCs contain relatively few additional Gaussians and can cover all five languages significantly better.

Performance on Italian and Spanish improves significantly as soon as some additional Gaussians are added to the German codebook. Improvements in English and French are less pronounced at first. When further Gaussians are added, however, improvements in English and French are stronger than in Spanish or Italian. This might be due to similarities and differences between languages.

5.2 Results on Non-native Accents

In the previous experiments native speech of several languages was evaluated. In this section accented English is evaluated, i.e. uttered by Spanish, French, Italian and Greek speakers. Basically, the same systems as before are tested. As the MWCs base on the German codebook, we can actually regard two systems as baseline. Our first baseline is a system that uses a standard English codebook. This system will be optimal for native English speech, but the performance on non-native speech is not clear. The system with the German codebook is our second baseline. These two baselines are given in the top rows of Table 3. As a reference the first column gives again the performance of each system on the native English cities test.

Table 3. Word Accuracies with MWCs on HIWIRE

Codebook	US City	Hiwire SP	Hiwire FR	Hiwire IT	Hiwire GR
English 1024	**75.5**	82.5	83.9	81.6	83.1
German 1024	65.6	85.4	**86.9**	82.8	85.5
5ling_1224	68.6	86.2	86.6	84.6	85.3
5ling_1424	68.4	86.4	86.7	**85.7**	85.8
5ling_1824	70.9	**86.9**	86.2	84.2	**86.3**

At first the focus is on the performance relative to the system with the English codebook. Compared to this system, the MWCs steadily improve the performance, the larger the codebook is, the better the performance.

Now the focus is on the performance relative to the system with German codebook. Oddly, even the system using only the German codebook outperforms the system with English codebook in the recognition of non-native English. This shows how strong non-native speech differs from native English. For most accents, however, MWCs perform better than systems with only the German codebook.

While future work is needed to explain why a German codebook can outperform a native English codebook, one conclusion can already be made from these results. MWCs consistently provide good performance for all tested accents and are always significantly better than the native English codebook. One assumption why the German codebook is better as the English codebook could be that the German language is phonetically richer, thus better suited to cover the sound deviations non-native speakers produce.

6   Conclusion

With our algorithm for the creation of multilingual codebooks, we have successfully introduced a vector quantization that can satisfy the aims of our car infotainment scenario. We can fix the performance of a system on a given main language, but at the same time improve performance on additional languages.

The results show clearly significant improvements on native speech from five different languages. While open questions remain for the recognition of non-native speech, we can show that MWCs can produce significant better performance on non-native accents of English. A task left to future experiments is to analyze more closely why a German codebook can outperform a native English codebook for non-native English tests.

Regarding non-native speech, our results show the strong acoustic differences, but there are also differences in the choice of words. Thus, language modeling approaches like in [Fuegen, 2003] could be used with special treatment for non-native speech. A more recent review of language model techniques an be found in [Raab, 2007].

Acknowledgments

We thank the HIWIRE (Human Input That Works In Real Environments) project from the EC 6th Framework IST Programme for the non-native test data [Segura et al., 2007].

References

[Fischer et al., 2003] Fischer, V., Janke, E., Kunzmann, S.: Recent progress in the decoding of non-native speech with multilingual acoustic models. In: Proc. Eurospeech, pp. 3105–3108 (2003)
[Fuegen, 2003] Fuegen, C.: Efficient handling of multilingual language models. In: Proc. ASRU, pp. 441–446 (2003)

[Gruhn et al., 2004] Gruhn, R., Markov, K., Nakamura, S.: A statistical lexicon for non-native speech recognition. In: Proc. Interspeech, Jeju Island, Korea, pp. 1497–1500 (2004)

[Iskra et al., 2002] Iskra, D., Grosskopf, B., Marasek, K., van den Huevel, H., Diehl, F., Kiessling, A.: Speecon - speech databases for consumer devices: Database specification and validation. In: Proc. LREC (2002)

[Koehler, 2001] Koehler, J.: Multilingual phone models for vocabulary-independent speech recognition tasks. Speech Communication Journal 35(1-2), 21–30 (2001)

[Linde et al., 1980] Linde, Y., Buzo, A., Gray, R.: An algorithm for vector quantization design. IEEE Transactions on Communications 28(1), 84–95 (1980)

[Raab, 2007] Raab, M.: Language Modeling for Machine Translation. Vdm Verlag, Saarbruecken (2007)

[Raab et al., 2007] Raab, M., Gruhn, R., Noeth, E.: Non-native speech databases. In: Proc. ASRU, Kyoto, Japan, pp. 413–418 (2007)

[Raab et al., 2008] Raab, M., Gruhn, R., Noeth, E.: Multilingual weighted codebooks. In: Proc. ICASSP, Las Vegas, USA (2008)

[Schultz and Waibel, 2001] Schultz, T., Waibel, A.: Language-independent and language-adaptive acoustic modeling for speech recognition. Speech Communication 35, 31–51 (2001)

[Segura et al., 2007] Segura, J., et al.: The HIWIRE database, a noisy and non-native English speech corpus for cockpit communication (2007), http://www.hiwire.org/

[Steidl, 2002] Steidl, S.: Interpolation von Hidden Markov Modellen. Master's thesis, University Erlangen-Nuremberg (2002)

[Tomokiyo, 2001] Tomokiyo, L.: Recognizing Non-native Speech: Characterizing and Adapting to Non-native Usage in Speech Recognition. PhD thesis, Carnegie Mellon University, Pennsylvania (2001)

[Witt, 1999] Witt, S.: Use of Speech Recognition in Computer-Assisted Language Learning. PhD thesis, Cambridge University Engineering Department, UK (1999)

Evaluating Text Normalization for Speech-Based Media Selection

Martin Pfeil[1,2], Dirk Buehler[1,2], Rainer Gruhn[1,2], and Wolfgang Minker[2]

[1] Harman/Becker Automotive Systems, Ulm, Germany
[2] Information Technology Institute, Ulm University, Germany
martin.pfeil@uni-ulm.de

Abstract. In this paper, we present an approach how to evaluate text normalization for multi-lingual speech-based dialogue systems. The application of text normalization occurs within the task of music selection, which imposes several important and novel requirements on its performance. The main idea is that text normalization should determine likely user utterances from metadata that is available within a user's music collection. This is substantially different from the text preprocessing applied, for instance, in text-to-speech systems, because a) more than one normalization hypothesis may be generated, b) for media selection the information content may be reduced, which is not desirable for Text-to-speech (TTS). These factors also have an impact on evaluation.

We describe an data collection effort that was carried out with the purpose of building an initial corpus of text normalization references and scorings, as well as experiments with well-known evaluation metrics from different areas of language research aiming at identifying an adequate evaluation measure.

1 Introduction

Selecting music via automatic speech recognition (ASR) is currently one of the "hot" topics in language research in the automotive area. The goal is to allow users to listen to their digital music content as they bring it along on personal devices like the iPod. Especially in the automotive area, speech is seen as the most desirable interface modality for this task for a number of reasons, including efficiency and safety considerations [Minker et al., 2005].

However, a couple of factors pose interesting challenges to this approach: First of all, the size of the user's music collection may range from tens to thousands of tracks, including album and artist names. In addition, the music collection is not known beforehand (in contrast to, for instance, the list of city or street names to be used in destination address selection). The "quality" and stylistic peculiarities of the metadata provided as part of the music collection is rather unpredictable: Rather good quality may be expected from online stores, whereas user-generated content may or may not be poorly structured and/or inconsistent. Metadata information services like FreeDB (CDDB), which are commonly used for older CDs without own metadata, tend to have this problem. In any case, there is no

E. André et al. (Eds.): PIT 2008, LNAI 5078, pp. 52–59, 2008.
© Springer-Verlag Berlin Heidelberg 2008

widely accepted standard for music metadata. Another source of complexity is multilinguality, i.e. the fact that track and artist names are likely to originate from various languages. In many cases, the language used changes within the text. In addition to that, modifications and misinterpretations between original language and creator of the metadata are possible, such as the distorted German Umlauts in "Traumes Wirren - AuBerst Lebhaft". Finally, hardware restrictions in terms of processing power and memory capacity impose severe limits on the number of items and the way they are to be recognized.

In that context, text normalization is to be used in the interface system at run-time to extract from the information that is available within the music collection (metadata, ID3 tags) parts of a language model to be used for ASR. The task is quite different to text normalization and preprocessing known from TTS synthesis in that it may generate multiple hypothesis, while a TTS system normally opts for the best hypothesis. Further, some part of the information content may be "neglectable" or "inadequate" as the information found in metadata tags are often intended for visual displays and may include background or reference information, such as ordering information (cf. Table 1).

Table 1. Music metadata examples

Content	Type
Christmas Carols, Sacred And Liturgical Works, Songs For Children & Patriotic Songs And Marches	Album
The Choir of Trinity College, Cambridge,His Majesties Sagbutts and Cornetts	Artist
Marc Seales, composer. New Stories. Ernie Watts, saxophone.	Artist
House of Virginism, I'll Be There For You (Doya Dododo Doya) (Stone's Glamarama Club Mix)	Title
We Want You - Megamix; Ymca,In The Navy,Go West,Macho Man	Title

The main task of a text normalization procedure would be to identify these portions of the data and remove it from the language model, because it is unlikely to be used in a spoken selection command; for example *Christmas Carols, Feuchtgrubers 23 neue Großstadtspektakel, The Choir of Trinity College, Marc Seales and Ernie Watts, I'll Be There For You* and *We want you Megamix*. Such a normalization procedure may be realized by using a set of hand-crafted rules or a statistical model, but is out of the scope of this work.

These differences have an impact on the question of how to evaluate a text normalization procedure. Thus, our approach was to first perform a data collection and an evaluation by human judges. Based on that, different metrics known from different areas of language research were considered as evaluation measures.

2   Building an Initial Evaluation Corpus

The setup should be as realistic and similar to the later application as possible. Here, this would mean to ask people to select items from their personal music

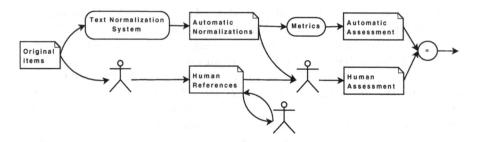

Fig. 1. Overview of evaluation process

library by speech and record the spoken utterances. The recordings may also be carried out within a Wizard-of-Oz scenario, which may take further considerations like dialogue flow issues into account. But we think both are not suitable for building an (initial) evaluation corpus as it is difficult to obtain recordings from different persons for the same item, which is essential for an evaluation corpus, if each participant contributes his individual music library. A Wizard-of-Oz scenario further imposes several limitations; for example on time and place as participants can not carry out the recording unsupervised through a web browser interface. Therefore we selected a test set of 104 items from the FreeDB music database, consisting of 39 albums, 31 artists and 34 titles. The selected items have in common that we expect them to be exemplary candidates for text normalization. For instance, long lists of artist names are a frequent issue. Besides, album names often include additional information like physical packaging or alternative title names. In order to evaluate text normalization and to assess the different evaluation metrics, we need (1) a high quality reference set and (2) a human assessment of the text normalization system. The required information were collected in two steps. First, we asked 16 people how they would select music by speech. Therefore an audio recording tool was used to provide each participant with 30 to 35 pieces of information extracted from MP3 (MPEG-1 Audio Layer 3) files and music databases like FreeDB and to record the spoken utterances. To make the survey more realistic and to prevent users from simply reading out the displayed information, the music information was made invisible 2 seconds before the recording was started. The collected recordings were then transcribed according to their spelling; for example it makes a difference in the transcription whether one said "zero eighty-four" or "zero eight four". For each category (Album, Artist or Title) we have a minimum of 2 recordings and a maximum of 6 recordings. A first analysis of the recorded data has shown that (1) there is a certain agreement among the participants how to select music by speech, (2) the agreement is on average higher on titles than on artists than on albums and (3) the participants prefer short "queries" [Martin Pfeil, 2007].

In the second step we asked 22 people, 13 of them also participated in the recording session before, to assess both the collected human normalizations from the recording session and the automatically generated normalizations. Using a

Table 2. Transcribed human hypotheses of two items

Original item	Human hypotheses
What Good Did You Get (Out of Breaking My Heart) 1964	1. What Good Did You Get Nineteen Sixty-Four 2. What Good Did You Get 3. What Good 4. What Good Do You Get 5. What Did You Get
A Fistful Of Dollars (Original Soundtrack)	1. Fistful Dollars 2. A Fistful Of Dollars 3. Fistful Of Dollars 4. Soundtrack von Eine Hand-voll Dollars

webform, the participants could rate each normalization ranging from "I would select exactly in this way" (5 points) to "I would not select in this way at all" (1 point). A primary feedback of the participants of the recording session was that they think their normalizations made implicitly when selecting the shown items by speech are highly affected by chance due to the fact that most of the items were unknown to them; thus we have to expect that the collected data does not reflect a consistent impression of "good" references. Using the data of the second evaluation phase we see that more than 70% assigned the maximum given points to their own normalization made in the recording session. Even if this is quite a good result when remembering the feedback of the participants, this is an further indication that not all of the collected hypotheses are of high quality as we can also see from Table 3.

Table 3. Statistics of human evaluation; * of the means per normalization

	Human references	Automatic normalizations
Total number	345	244
Number of ratings	2557	1796
Average per item	7.41	7.36
Average score *	3.05	2.71
Median score *	3.00	2.65
Standard deviation *	0.80	0.96

3   Evaluation Metrics

As already mentioned, the quality of a normalization is a rather subjective impression and there is no quantifiable notion of whether a normalization is "good" or not; especially the second point is a problem for automatic evaluation. With respect to our rather small corpus, we looked into evaluation metrics from different disciplines. Disciplines facing the same problems in evaluation are for example machine translation and speech recognition. From the common available automatic evaluation metrics we selected three, which we think may be suitable to evaluate text normalization. These are a multi reference version of the word error rate (m-WER) [Sonja Nießen, 2002] [McCowan et al., 2004], the Bilingual Evaluation Understudy (BLEU) metric [Papineni et al., 2001] [Callison-Burch et al., 2006] and the Metric for Evaluation of Translation with Explicit ORdering (METEOR) [Banerjee and Lavie, 2005].

The word error rate is the most obvious metric to evaluate text normalization because text normalization is a string editing problem and it was already used before to evaluate text normalization in the context of TTS by Sproat et al. [Sproat et al., 1999]. The m-WER is an error rate and we want a measure for the goodness; therefore we report $1 - Score_{m-WER}$ instead. In order to get a recognition/success rate between 0 and 1, the m-WER score is limited to 1. Further we tested a different normalization of the edit distance by the length of the best match reference, but initial tests were rather disappointing and we will not continue to pursue this approach. Initial tests also indicated that the micro-average of the m-WER might be inappropriate; its macro-averaged version states better results.

The METEOR metric favours recall in that it applies a 9:1 weighting when combining it with precision. Precision penalizes candidate normalizations being too long and recall those normalizations being too short, both in comparison to a reference. The analysis of the survey data gave no evidence that the participants favour candidate normalizations being too short nor being too long in comparison to a reference. Therefore we evaluate a version of the METEOR metric equally weighting precision and recall (1:1), which is referred as METEOR-1 in the following, too.

An analysis of the data collection and human evaluation has shown that human references have an average length (in terms of words) of around 3; therefore we apply the BLEU metric on unigrams, bigrams and trigrams only.

4   Experimental Evaluation/Results

The selected evaluation metrics return a (decimal) score between 0 and 1. To compare these scores with the scores assigned by the human judges, we apply the following linear regression:

$$score_{Metric,scaled} = 1 + 4 \cdot score_{Metric}$$

All evaluated metrics assess a hypothesis in that they try to compute on its closeness to a set of references in some way; therefore the reference set should be selected carefully. Filtering out "worse" references also reduces the number of items that can be evaluated. Fortunately, this has no significant impact on the assessment of the remaining automatic normalizations as we can see from Table 4.

Table 4. Test set size

	References with average score			
	≥ 1	≥ 2	≥ 3	≥ 4
Number references	345	318	187	51
Evaluated items	103	103	100	48
Avg. human assessment	2.71	2.71	2.71	2.78

The final test set contains 48 items, having 114 candidate normalizations and 51 human references, all having an average score greater equal 4. The candidate normalizations have an average human assessment of 2.78.

Table 5. Final reference set of six items

Original item	Reference(s)
What Good Did You Get (Out of Breaking My Heart) 1964	What Good Did You Get
A Fistful Of Dollars (Original Soundtrack)	A Fistful Of Dollars
Celtic Christmas II - A Windham Hill Collection	Celtic Christmas 2
101% Soul - Disc 1 - Souled out	101% Soul
Fats Waller,Fats Waller and His Rhythm	1. Fats Waller 2. Fats Waller and His Rhythm
Vamos Ya (Dame Mas/Give It Up)	Vamos Ya

The m-WER and METEOR metric produce scores per normalization. We compare both at normalization level to human assessment in that we compute the correlation coefficient on the average human assessment and metric score per normalization; we can not do that for BLEU. An important part of the BLEU metric is the brevity penalty, which is computed at corpus level; therefore it is pointless to report the BLEU scores at normalization level because (1) the brevity penalty at normalization level would be too harsh and (2) reporting the score without the brevity penalty is one half of the game only. Therefore we compare the metrics at corpus level to get comparable figures for the BLEU metric.

The results of the evaluation at corpus put the correlation figures at candidate level into perspective: the correlation of the METEOR variants, especially

Table 6. Spearman Correlation at normalization level

	Correlation
m-WER	0.70
METEOR	0.57
METEOR-1	0.66

Table 7. Metric scores at corpus level

	Score
m-WER	1.60
m-WER (macro-average)	2.73
METEOR	4.15
METEOR-1	3.58
BLEU-1	3.12
BLEU-2	2.88
BLEU-3	2.54
Human assessment	2.78

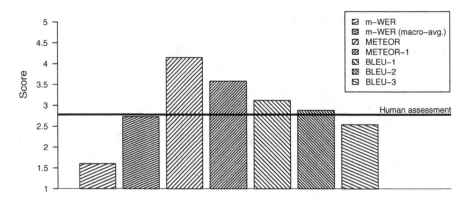

Fig. 2. Metric scores at corpus level

METEOR-1, with human judgement seems to be too high. This is probably related to Spearman's rank correlation coefficient, which computes the correlation on the differences in ranking, and may extenuate the difference in the absolute scores. Of the three BLEU variants, the BLEU metric on bigrams seems to track human judgement best; this result is not really unexpected. The BLEU-1 metric does not take word order into account, but human judges seem to consider word order to some extent in their judgement; on the other hand the higher the n-grams get the less variation BLEU allows in word order.

The low scores of the micro-averaged/original version of the m-WER metric are an indicator that the micro-average is more susceptible to outliers than the macro-average. This effect is extremely high on the word error rate than on BLEU and both METEOR variants which also use the micro-average because the numerator can exceed the denominator in the word error rate. Thus a few "worse" candidates, having a high edit distance, can skew the whole micro-average value.

Using the Mann-Whitney-U test, there is no significant (detectable) difference at a significance level of $\alpha = 0.05$ between human judgement and the m-WER metric at candidate level but for both METEOR variants. The 95%

confidence interval of the difference of human judgement and the m-WER metric is $[-0.19, 0.57]$.

5   Conclusions

We have presented our effort to create an initial corpus for the evaluation of text normalization in the context of speech-based dialogues, in special speech-based music selection. On this rather small test set, the m-WER metric and BLEU metric on bigrams state the closest results to human judgement. The next logical step is to enhance our evaluation corpus in terms of number of items and references and to confirm our findings on a larger scale. However, the experiences made with data collection and human assessment here impose that this will be a time consuming and perhaps expensive task and new approaches have to be applied for example to transcribe the collected data. A possible improvement may be the use of an automatic or semi-automatic transcription of the recorded human references. Another question, which may reduce the effort of collecting references, concerns in how far one can reuse textual music queries, for example from online music shops, as an indicator how humans would like to select music by speech.

A general drawback of the currently applied automatic evaluation methods is its dependency on a reference set. Thus a long-term goal for future work is to develop evaluation methods being independent of such a reference set; statistical models could be a possible solution to this problem.

References

[Akiba et al., 2004] Akiba, Y., Federico, M., Kando, N., Nakaiwa, H., Paul, M., Tsujii, J.: Overview of the IWSLT04 evaluation campaign. In: Proc. of the International Workshop on Spoken Language Translation, Kyoto, Japan, pp. 1–12 (2004)

[Banerjee and Lavie, 2005] Banerjee, S., Lavie, A.: METEOR: An automatic metric for MT evaluation with improved correlation with human judgments (2005)

[Callison-Burch et al., 2006] Callison-Burch, C., Osborne, M., Koehn, P.: Re-evaluating the role of BLEU in Machine Translation Research (2006)

[Martin Pfeil, 2007] Pfeil, M.: Automatic evaluation of text normalization (2007)

[McCowan et al., 2004] McCowan, I., Moore, D., Dines, J., Gatica-Perez, D., Flynn, M., Wellner, P., Bourlard, H.: On the Use of Information Retrieval Measures for Speech Recognition Evaluation. IDIAP-RR 73, IDIAP, Martigny, Switzerland (2004)

[Minker et al., 2005] Minker, W., Buehler, D., Dybkjaer, L. (eds.): Spoken Multimodal Human-Computer Dialogue in Mobile Environments. Text, Speech and Language Technology, vol. 28. Springer, Heidelberg (2005)

[Papineni et al., 2001] Papineni, K., Roukos, S., Ward, T., Zhu, W.: BLEU: a method for automatic evaluation of machine translation (2001)

[Sonja Nießen, 2002] Nießen, S.: Improving Statistical Machine Translation using Morpho-syntactic Information (2002)

[Sproat et al., 1999] Sproat, R., Black, A.W., Chen, S., Kumar, S., Ostendorf, M., Richards, C.: Article Submitted to Computer Speech and Language Normalization of Non-Standard Words (1999)

A Two Phases Statistical Approach for Dialog Management*

David Griol, Lluís F. Hurtado, Encarna Segarra, and Emilio Sanchis

Departament de Sistemes Informàtics i Computació
Universitat Politècnica de València, E-46022 València, Spain
{dgriol,lhurtado,esegarra,esanchis}@dsic.upv.es

Abstract. In this paper, we present a statistical methodology for dialog management. This methodology is based on a classification procedure that considers all of the previous history of the dialog and the result of the queries to the module that controls the application. The classification procedure is divided into two phases to generate the next system turn. We summarize the work that has been carried out to apply this methodology for developing a dialog system for booking sports facilities. A dialog simulation technique has been used to acquire a dialog corpus for this task and to develop a dialog manager following the proposed methodology. The final model has been evaluated using a corpus recorded for the task with real users.

1 Introduction

The use of statistical techniques for the development of the different modules that compose a dialog system has been of growing interest during the last decade [Young, 2002]. These approaches are usually based on statistically modeling the different processes and learning the parameters of the model from a dialog corpus. This type of methodologies has been traditionally applied within the fields of speech recognition and natural language understanding [Minker et al., 1999], [Esteve et al., 2003]. The application of statistical methodologies to model the behavior of the dialog manager is providing interesting results in more recent years [Lemon et al., 2006], [Williams and Young, 2007].

In this field, we have developed an approach to manage the dialog using a statistical model learned from a labeled dialog corpus [Hurtado et al., 2006]. This work was carried out within the framework of a Spanish project called DIHANA [Benedí et al., 2006]. The task defined for this project was the telephone access to a system that provides railway information in Spanish.

In this paper, we describe our work to use this methodology to develop a dialog manager within the framework of a new Spanish project called EDECAN [Lleida et al., 2006]. The main objective of the EDECAN project is to increase the robustness of a spontaneous speech dialog system through the development of technologies for the adaptation and personalization of the system to the different

* This work has been partially funded by Spanish MEC and FEDER under project TIN2005-08660-C04-02, Spain.

E. André et al. (Eds.): PIT 2008, LNAI 5078, pp. 60–71, 2008.

acoustic and application contexts in which it can be used. The task defined for the EDECAN project is the multilingual query to an information system for the booking of sport activities in our University. Users can ask for the availability, the booking or cancellation of facilities and the information about their current bookings.

The success of statistical approaches depends on the quality and quantity of the data used to develop the dialog model. A great effort is necessary to acquire and label a corpus with the data necessary to train a good model. One solution for this problem consists of the development of a module that simulates the user answers. Different techniques have been developed in recent years to learn user models [Schatzmann et al., 2006], [Cuayáhuitl et al., 2006], [Georgila et al., 2006].

We have recently presented an approach to acquire a labeled dialog corpus from the interaction of a user simulator and a dialog manager simulator [Griol et al., 2007]. In this approach, a random selection of the system and user answers is used. The only parameters that are needed for the acquisition are the definition of the semantics of the task (that is, the set of possible user and system answers), and a set of criterions to automatically discard unsuccessful dialogs. We have acquired a corpus for the EDECAN task using this approach. This corpus has been used for learning an initial dialog manager for the EDE-CAN task. In this paper, we present the evaluation of this manager using a set of 150 dialogs that was recorded at the telephone sport service of our University.

2 Dialog Management in the EDECAN Project

In most dialog systems, the dialog manager takes its decisions based only on the information provided by the user in the previous turns and its own model. This is the case of most of slot-filling dialog systems, like the system designed for the DIHANA project [Hurtado et al., 2006]. This process is as follows:

Let A_i be the output of the dialog system (the system answer) at time i, expressed in terms of dialog acts. Let U_i be the semantic representation of the user turn (the result of the understanding process of the user input) at time i, expressed in terms of frames. We represent a dialog as a sequence of pairs (*system-turn, user-turn*):

$$(A_1, U_1), \cdots, (A_i, U_i), \cdots, (A_n, U_n)$$

where A_1 is the greeting turn of the system, and U_n is the last user turn. We refer to a pair (A_i, U_i) as S_i, the state of the dialog sequence at time i.

In this framework, we consider that, at time i, the objective of the dialog manager is to find the best system answer A_i. This selection is a local process for each time i and takes into account the previous history of the dialog, that is to say, the sequence of states of the dialog preceding time i:

$$\hat{A}_i = \operatorname*{argmax}_{A_i \in \mathcal{A}} P(A_i | S_1, \cdots, S_{i-1})$$

where set $\mathcal{A}$ contains all the possible system answers.

As the number of all possible sequences of states is very large, we define
a data structure in order to establish a partition in the space of sequences of
states (i.e., in the history of the dialog preceding time i). This data structure,
that we call Dialog Register (DR), contains the information provided by the
user throughout the previous history of the dialog. All the information captured
by the DR_i at a given time i is a summary of the information provided by the
sequence $S_1, \cdots, S_{i-1}$. Using the DR, we obtain a great reduction in the number
of different histories in the dialogs at the expense of a loss in the chronological
information. We consider this to be a minor loss because the order in which the
information is supplied by the user is not a relevant factor in determining the
next system answer A_i. After applying the above considerations and establishing
the equivalence relation in the histories of dialogs, the selection of the best A_i is
given by:

$$\hat{A}_i = \operatorname*{argmax}_{A_i \in \mathcal{A}} P(A_i | DR_{i-1}, S_{i-1})$$

The last state (S_{i-1}) is considered for the selection of the system answer due
to the fact that a user turn can provide information that is not contained in the
DR, but is important to decide the next system answer. This is the case of the
task-independent information (e.g., *Affirmation*, *Negation* and *Not-Understood*
dialog acts).

In other dialog systems (for instance, the system defined for the EDECAN
project), the dialog manager generates the following system answer taking into
account not only the information provided by the user, but also the information
generated by the module that controls the application (that we call *Application
Manager, AM*).

The *AM* developed for the EDECAN dialog system performs two main functions. On the one hand, this module performs the queries to the database. On
the other hand, it has to verify if the user query follows the regulations defined
for the task (a user can book only one court a day, the facilities can not be
booked if the user is suspended, etc.).

Then, the result of queries to the *AM* has to be considered in order to generate
the following system answer. For instance, in order to book the facilities (e.g., a
tennis court), several situations can happen:

- After the query to the database, it is detected that the user is suspended.
  The system must inform the user that s/he will not be able to book sport
  facilities until the period of sanction has finished.
- After the database query, if it is verified that there is not any facility that
  fulfills the user requirements, the system must inform about it. In this situation, the system can inform the user if the required facility is available if
  one or several of these requirements are changed (e.g., the hour).
- As a result of the query to the database, it is verified that there is only one
  available facility that fulfills the user requirements. The system must confirm
  that everything is correct to complete the booking.

- If there are two or more available facilities that fulfill the user requirements, the system must verify which of them the user want to book.

We have decided that two phases are required for the selection of the next system turn in this type of tasks. In the first phase, the information contained in the DR and the last state S_{i-1} are considered to select the best request to be made to the AM ($\hat{A}_{1_i}$):

$$\hat{A}_{1_i} = \operatorname*{argmax}_{A_{1_i} \in \mathcal{A}_1} P(A_i | DR_{i-1}, S_{i-1})$$

where $\mathcal{A}_1$ is the set of possible requests to the AM.

In the second phase, the final system answer ($\hat{A}_{2_i}$) is generated taking into account $\hat{A}_{1_i}$ and the information provided by the AM (AM_i):

$$\hat{A}_{2_i} = \operatorname*{argmax}_{A_{2_i} \in \mathcal{A}_2} P(A_i | AM_i, A_{1_i})$$

where $\mathcal{A}_2$ is the set of possible system answers.

In our previous work on dialog management, we proposed the use of a multilayer perceptron (MLP) to obtain the system answer [Hurtado et al., 2006]. Figure 1 shows the scheme proposed for the development of the dialog manager for the EDECAN project, detailing the two phases described for the generation of the final system answer. We propose the use of two MLPs, each one to deal with the specific information defined for each phase.

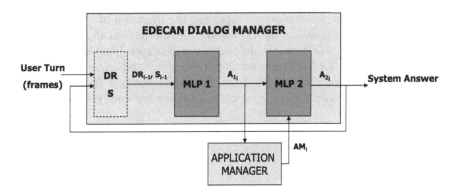

Fig. 1. Scheme of the dialog manager designed for the EDECAN project

3   The Semantics of the EDECAN Task

The definition of the semantics of the EDECAN task has been carried out considering the different functionalities required for the booking system and the information that is required to complete them. A set of dialogs recorded at the telephone sport service of our University with real users has been labeled in terms of dialog acts to make this definition. This corpus contains 150 dialogs (873 user turns). Figure 2 shows an example of a dialog taken from this corpus.

S1: Welcome to the sport service. How can I help you?
U1: I want to book a tennis court for March the 3rd.
S2: What time do you want to play?
U2: At three o'clock in the afternoon.
S3: Tennis courts number 1 and number 3 are available on March the 3rd. Which do you want to book?
U3: Tennis court number 1.
S4: I have just booked you the tennis court number 1 for March the 3rd at 15:00. Anything else?
U4: Yes, I want to cancel a paddle court for tomorrow.
S5: Do you want to cancel the booking of a paddle court for March the 1st at 19:00?
U5: Yes.
S6: I have just cancelled you the required court. Anything else?
U6: No, thank you.
S7: Thank you for using the sport service. Goodbye.

Fig. 2. An example of a dialog for the EDECAN task

3.1   User Dialog Acts

In the case of user turns, the dialog acts correspond to the classical frame representation of the meaning of the utterance. A frame is a structure for representing a concept or situation. Each concept in a domain has usually associated a group of attributes (slots) and values. In the semantic representation defined for the EDECAN task, one or more concepts represent the intention of the utterance, and a sequence of attribute-value pairs contains the information about the values given by the user. In this task, we defined seven concepts (*Availability, Booking, Booked, Cancellation, Affirmation, Negation,* and *Not-Understood*) and six attributes (*Sport, Hour, Date, Court-Type, Court-Number,* and *Order-Number*). An example of the semantic interpretation of an input sentence is shown below:

User Turn
I want to book a squash court for tomorrow afternoon.
Semantic Representation
(*Booking*)
 Sport: squash
 Date: tomorrow
 Hour: afternoon

3.2   System Dialog Acts

The labeling of the system turns is similar to the labeling defined for the user turns. A total of 25 task-dependent concepts has been defined:

- Task-independent concepts (*Affirmation, Negation, Not-Understood, New-Query, Opening*, and *Closing*).
- Concepts used to inform the user about the result of a specific query (*Availability, Booking, Booked*, and *Cancellation*).
- Concepts defined to require the user the attributes that are necessary for a specific query (*Sport, Date, Hour*, and *Court-Type*).
- Concepts used for the confirmation of concepts (*Confirmation-Availability, Confirmation-Booking, Confirmation-Booked, Confirmation-Cancellation*) and attributes (*Confirmation-Sport, Confirmation-Date, Confirmation-Hour, Confirmation-CourtType*).
- Concepts relative to the *AM*: the non-fulfillment of the booking regulations (*Rule-Info*) or the need of selecting some of the available facilities (*Booking-Choice, Cancellation-Choice*).

A total of six attributes has been defined (*Sport, Court-Type, Court-Number, Date, Hour*, and *Availability-Number*). An example of the labeling of a system turn is shown below:

System Turn
Do you want to book the squash court number 1 in the sports hall on March the 5th from 20:00 to 20:30?
Labeling
(*Confirmation-Booking*)
    Sport: squash
    Date: 03-05-2008
    Hour: 20:00-20:30
    Court-Type: sports_hall
    Court-Number:1

3.3   Dialog Register Representation

For the EDECAN task, the *DR* is a record structure of 10 fields, where each concept or attribute has a field associated to it. The sequence of fields for concepts and attributes is shown in Table 3.

For the dialog manager to determine the next answer, we have assumed that the exact values of the attributes are not significant. They are important to access the database and to generate the output sentences of the system. However, the only information necessary to determine the next action by the system is the presence or absence of concepts and attributes, and their confidence scores. Therefore, the information we used from the *DR* is a codification of this data in terms of three values, $\{0, 1, 2\}$, for each field in the *DR* according to the following criteria:

- **0:** The concept is not activated, or the value of the attribute is not given.
- **1:** The concept or attribute is activated with a confidence score that is higher than a given threshold (a value between 0 and 1).

Concepts	Attributes
Availability	*Sport*
Booking	*Court-Type*
Booked	*Court-Number*
Cancellation	*Date*
	Hour
	Order-Number

Fig. 3. Dialog Register (*DR*) defined for the EDECAN task

- **2:** The concept or attribute is activated with a confidence score that is lower than the given threshold.

Therefore, each DR can be represented as a 10-length string from $\{0, 1, 2\}^{10}$.

3.4   Representation Defined for the Information

The representation defined for the input pair (DR_{i-1}, S_{i-1}) is as follows:

- The dialog register (DR): As stated above, the DR defined for the EDECAN task stores a total of ten characteristics (four concepts and six attributes). Each one of these characteristics can take the values $\{0, 1, 2\}$. Therefore, every characteristic has been modeled using a variable with three bits.

$$\boldsymbol{x}_i = (x_{i_1}, x_{i_2}, x_{i_3}) \in \{0, 1\}^3 \; i = 1, ..., 10$$

- The codification of the dialog acts corresponding to the last answer generated by the system (A_{i-1}): This information is modeled by means of a variable, which has as many bits as possible different system answers detailed for our system in terms of frames (25).

$$\boldsymbol{x}_{11} = (x_{11_1}, x_{11_2}, x_{11_3}, \cdots, x_{11_{25}}) \in \{0, 1\}^{25}$$

- Task-independent information, that is not included in the DR (*Affirmation, Negation,* and *Not-Understood* dialog acts): These three dialog acts have been coded with the same codification used for the information in the DR; that is, each one of these three dialog acts can take the values $\{0, 1, 2\}$. Therefore, this information is modeled using three variables with three bits.

$$\boldsymbol{x}_i = (x_{i_1}, x_{i_2}, x_{i_3}) \in \{0, 1\}^3 \; i = 12, ..., 14$$

Therefore, the pair (DR_{i-1}, S_{i-1}) can be modeled with a variable with 14 characteristics:

$$(DR_{i-1}, S_{i-1}) = (\boldsymbol{x}_1, \boldsymbol{x}_2, \boldsymbol{x}_3, \cdots, \boldsymbol{x}_{14})$$

The answer generated by the AM has been coded considering the set of possible answers after carrying out a query to the AM. This set includes the different situations that a query to the *AM* developed for the EDECAN task can generate, and that are reflected in our corpus:

- Case 1: The *AM* has not taken part in the generation of the final system answer, for example, when the dialog manager selects the confirmation of an attribute, the closing of the dialog, etc.
- Cases 2-4: After a query to the database, the *AM* informs that there is not any facility that fulfills the user requirements (case 2), only one facility is available (case 3) or more than one facility is available (case 4).
- Case 5: The *AM* informs that the user query cannot be completed because it does not fulfill the regulations.

Then, the answer generated by *AM* has been modeled with a variable of five bits:

$$AM = (x_1, x_2, x_3, x_4, x_5) \in \{0, 1\}^5$$

Our objective is to incorporate new functionalities to the *AM* by introducing a user profile for adapting the system behavior to the user preferences. Then, it will be also possible to incorporate personalized suggestions that take into account this profile.

4 Our Approach for Automatically Acquiring a Dialog Corpus

As stated in the introduction, our approach for acquiring a dialog corpus is based on the interaction of a user simulator and a dialog manager simulator. Both modules use a random selection of one of the possible answers defined for the semantics of the task (user and system dialog acts). At the beginning of the simulation, the set of system answers is defined as equiprobable. When a successful dialog is simulated, the probabilities of the answers selected by the dialog manager during that dialog are incremented before beginning a new simulation.

The user simulation simulates the user intention level, that is, the simulator provides concepts and attributes that represent the intention of the user utterance. Therefore, the user simulator carries out the functions of the ASR and NLU modules.

The semantics selected for the dialog manager is represented through the 25 possible system answers defined for the task. The selection of the possible user answers is carried out using the semantics defined for the NLU module.

An error simulator module has been designed to perform error generation and the addition of confidence measures in accordance with an analysis of a corpus of 900 dialogs acquired using the DIHANA dialog system with real users. This information modifies the frames generated by the user simulator and also incorporates confidence measures for the different concepts and attributes. Experimentally, we have detected 2.7 errors per dialog. This value can be modified to adapt the error simulator module to the operation of any ASR and NLU modules.

4.1 The Corpus Acquisition

A maximum number of system turns per dialog was defined for acquiring a corpus. The dialog manager considers that the dialog is unsuccessful and decides to abort it when the following conditions take place:

- The dialog exceeds the maximum number of system turns.
- The answer selected by the dialog manager corresponds with a query not required by the user simulator.
- The *AM* provides an error warning because the user simulator has not provided the mandatory information needed to carry out the query.
- The answer generator provides a error warning when the selected answer involves the use of a data not contained in the DR, that is, not provided by the user simulator.

A user request for closing the dialog is selected once the system has provided the information defined in the objective(s) of the dialog. The dialogs that fulfill this condition before the maximum number of turns are considered successful.

Table 1 summarizes the statistics of the acquisition of a corpus for the EDE-CAN task. A total of 100,000 dialogs were simulated. A set of 15 scenarios was defined to specify the objectives of the simulation.

Table 1. Statistics of the corpus acquisition

Simulated dialogs	100, 000
Successful dialogs	2,521
Different dialogs	1,973
Number of user turns per dialog	4.2

4.2 Dialog Example

Table 2 shows an example of a dialog that compose the acquired corpus. The objective defined for the dialog was the booking of a tennis court for March the 14th at eight o'clock. The confidence scores generated by the error simulator are shown between brackets. A sentence in natural language, that is equivalent to the labeled system turn selected by the dialog manager, has been incorporated to clarify the explanation.

The dialog begins with a greeting turn generated by the system (S1). In the first turn, the simulated user provides the *Sport*, the *Date* and the *Hour*. The error simulator introduces in this first turn an error value in the *Date* slot (it changes day 14 for day 15) and assigns confidence scores to the different slots. In this case, a low confidence is assigned to this erroneous value.

In the second system turn, a confirmation for the *Date* is selected. Considering the information defined in the objective of the scenario, the user simulator selects

Table 2. An example of a dialog extracted from the simulated corpus

S1: (*Opening*)
Welcome to the sport service. How can I help you?
U1: (*Booking*) [0.9]
Sport: Tennis [0.9]
Date: 03-15-2008 [0.1]
Hour: 08.00-09.00 [0.9]
S2: (*Confirmation-Date*)
Do you want to play on the 15th March?
U2: (*Negation*) [0.9]
Date: 03-14-2008 [0.9]
S3: (*Confirmation-Booking*) *Sport*: Tennis *Date*: 2008-03-14 *Hour*: 08.00-09.00
{*One court available*} Do you want to book tennis court number 2?
U3: Yes.
S4: (*Booking*) *Sport*: Tennis *Date*: 2008-03-14 *Hour*: 08.00-09.00 (*New-Query*)
Tennis court number 2 has been booked. Anything else?
U4: (*Negation*) [0.9]
S5: (*Closing*)
Thank you for using the sport service. Goodbye.

a *Negation* dialog act and provides the correct value for the *Date* according to the objective (U2). In this turn, the error simulator assigns a high confidence value to the information provided by the user. In the following system turn (S3), the dialog manager selects to make a booking query to the database. There is only one court available. The user simulator confirms the booking in U3. Once the objective of the dialog is achieved, the user simulator selects a request for closing the dialog in the following turn (U4).

5 Evaluation

The corpus described in the previous section has been used to learn a statistical dialog manager for the EDECAN task according to the methodology presented in Section 2. The corpus provided by the telephone sport service of our University was used as a test set to evaluate the behavior of this dialog manager with a real user corpus. Software developed in our research group was used to model and train the MLPs. MLPs were trained using the backpropagation with momentum algorithm. The topology used was two hidden layers with 100 and 10 units each one.

We defined three measures to evaluate the performance of the dialog managers. These measures are calculated by comparing the answer automatically generated by the dialog manager for each input in the test partition with regard to the reference answer annotated in the corpus. This way, the evaluation is carried out turn by turn. The first measure is the percentage of answers that are equal to the reference answer in the corpus (*%exact*). The second measure is the percentage of answers that are coherent with the current state of the dialog (*%correct*). Finally, the third measure is the percentage of answers that are considered erroneous according to the current state of the dialog and would cause the failure of the dialog (*%error*). The last two measures have been obtained after a manual revision of the answers provided by the dialog managers.

Table 3 shows the results of the evaluation of the dialog manager. The results obtained after the experimentation show that the statistical dialog management technique successfully adapts to the requirements of the EDECAN task, providing the dialog manager a 89.8% of answers that are coherent with the current state of the dialog. In addition, the 75.3% of answers are equal to the reference answer in the corpus. The percentage of answers provided by the dialog manager that can cause the failure of the dialog is considerable (3.9%). Also, there is a remaining 6.3% of system answers that do not suppose the dialog failure, but are not coherent with the current state of the dialog (for example, answers that require information that the user has already provided). We want to reduce both percentages by incorporating new dialogs to our initial corpus.

Table 3. Results of the evaluation of the statistical dialog manager developed for the EDECAN project

	%exact	%correct	%error
System answer	75.3%	89.8%	3.9%

6   Conclusions

In this paper, we have described a statistical approach for dialog management based on a classification process that takes into account the information provided by the user and the module that controls the application. The dialog model is learned from a corpus of training samples. The performance of the dialog manager depends on the quality and size of the corpus used to learn its model. We have presented a technique for automatically acquiring a dialog corpus. The simulated dialogs are automatically generated in the labeling format defined for the task. Therefore, the effort necessary to acquire a dialog corpus and learn a dialog manager is considerably reduced. The results of the evaluation of the statistical dialog manager learned using the acquired corpus show that it could be used as an initial dialog manager, generated without many effort and with very high performance.

At the moment, our objective is to carry out the evaluation of the different modules that make up the EDECAN dialog system with real users. This evaluation is going to be made in a supervised way, using the statistical dialog manager presented in this work. The acquired dialogs will be used to evaluate and improve the initial dialog model.

References

[Benedí et al., 2006] Benedí, J., Lleida, E., Varona, A., Castro, M., Galiano, I., Justo, R., López, I., Miguel, A.: Design and acquisition of a telephone spontaneous speech dialogue corpus in Spanish: DIHANA. In: Proc. of the 5th International Conference on Language Resources and Evaluation (LREC 2006), Genoa, Italy, pp. 1636–1639 (2006)

[Cuayáhuitl et al., 2006] Cuayáhuitl, H., Renals, S., Lemon, O., Shimodaira, H.: Reinforcement learning of dialogue strategies with hierarchical abstract machines. In: Proc. of IEEE-ACL Workshop on Spoken Language Technology (SLT 2006), Palm Beach, Aruba, pp. 182–185 (2006)

[Esteve et al., 2003] Esteve, Y., Raymond, C., Bechet, F., Mori, R.D.: Conceptual Decoding for Spoken Dialog systems. In: Proc. of European Conference on Speech Communications and Technology (EuroSpeech 2003), Geneva, Switzerland, pp. 617–620 (2003)

[Georgila et al., 2006] Georgila, K., Henderson, J., Lemon, O.: User Simulation for Spoken Dialogue Systems: Learning and Evaluation. In: Proc. of the 9th International Conference on Spoken Language Processing (Interspeech/ICSLP), Pittsburgh, USA, pp. 1065–1068 (2006)

[Griol et al., 2007] Griol, D., Hurtado, L., Sanchis, E., Segarra, E.: Acquiring and Evaluating a Dialog Corpus through a Dialog Simulation Technique. In: Proc. of the 8th SIGdial Workshop on Discourse and Dialogue, Antwerp, Belgium, pp. 39–42 (2007)

[Hurtado et al., 2006] Hurtado, L., Griol, D., Segarra, E., Sanchis, E.: A Stochastic Approach for Dialog Management based on Neural Networks. In: Proc. of the 9th International Conference on Spoken Language Processing (Interspeech/ICSLP), Pittsburgh, USA, pp. 49–52 (2006)

[Lemon et al., 2006] Lemon, O., Georgila, K., Henderson, J.: Evaluating Effectiveness and Portability of Reinforcement Learned Dialogue Strategies with real users: the TALK TownInfo Evaluation. In: Proc. of IEEE-ACL Workshop on Spoken Language Technology (SLT 2006), Palm Beach (Aruba), pp. 182–186 (2006)

[Lleida et al., 2006] Lleida, E., Segarra, E., Torres, M., Macías-Guarasa, J.: EDECÁN: Sistema de diálogo multidominio con adaptación al contexto acústico y de aplicaci 'on. In: Proc. of IV Jornadas en Tecnologia del Habla, Zaragoza, Spain, pp. 291–296 (2006)

[Minker et al., 1999] Minker, W., Waibel, A., Mariani, J.: Stochastically-based semantic analysis. Kluwer Academic Publishers, Boston (1999)

[Schatzmann et al., 2006] Schatzmann, J., Weilhammer, K., Stuttle, M., Young, S.: A Survey of Statistical User Simulation Techniques for Reinforcement-Learning of Dialogue Management Strategies. Knowledge Engineering Review 21(2), 97–126 (2006)

[Williams and Young, 2007] Williams, J., Young, S.: Partially Observable Markov Decision Processes for Spoken Dialog Systems. Computer Speech and Language 21(2), 393–422 (2007)

[Young, 2002] Young, S.: The Statistical Approach to the Design of Spoken Dialogue Systems. Technical report, Cambridge University Engineering Department (2002)

Detecting Problematic Dialogs with Automated Agents

Alexander Schmitt[1], Carolin Hank[1], and Jackson Liscombe[2]

[1] Institute of Information Technology, University of Ulm, Germany
alexander.schmitt@uni-ulm.de
carolin.hank@uni-ulm.de
[2] SpeechCycle Inc., New York City, USA
jackson@speechcycle.com

Abstract. We present a supervised machine learning approach for detecting problematic human-computer dialogs between callers and an automated agent in a call center. The proposed model can distinguish problematic from non-problematic calls after only five caller turns with an accuracy of over 90%. Based on a corpus of more than 69,000 dialogs we further employ the classifier's decision to given business models and present the cost savings that can be achieved by deploying classification techniques to Interactive Voice Response systems.

1 Introduction

Increasingly, companies are looking to reduce the costs of customer service and support via automation. With respect to telephone applications, we are witnessing a growing utilization of spoken dialog technology in recent call centers. Such Interactive Voice Response (IVR) systems are being used in various domains: in call routing, where the system serves as front-end to the actual human expert; as information retrieval systems (train schedules, package tracking, etc.); as transactional applications (money transfer, stock trading, hotel booking); or even as problem solvers, such as technical support automated agents, the most recent and complex application of IVRs. Most of those systems are based on touch-tone input, spoken language keywords or a combination of both. Less often, they are able to deal with natural language input. The intentions behind these automation trends are various. Call center automation

- reduces costs: automated services offer a high ROI (return on investment)
- unburdens the operators: routine requests such as answering frequently asked questions or finding the right contact person at the company's switchboard are left to the automated system
- lowers the holding time for customers: the caller is handled directly without waiting time
- provides constant quality: the caller receives a consistent service and uniform information

E. André et al. (Eds.): PIT 2008, LNAI 5078, pp. 72–80, 2008.

However, not all calls can be handled successfully by automated systems. Common problems are: the topic the customer talks about is out-of-domain (semantic problem), the speech recognition does not work due to bad transmission quality, dialect or background noise (speech recognition problem) or the customer is not used to handling this emerging technology due to low media competence (usability problem).

However, effusive and cumbersome automation lowers customer satisfaction. Hence, an elegant trade-off between automated agents and human operators ultimately needs to be found. An approach that has been discussed in recent years is to let the caller start with the automated system, automatically detect problematic conversations, and change the dialog strategy of the system or bring in a human operator if and when a problem occurs.

2 Related Work

Some of the first models to predict problematic dialogs in IVR systems have been proposed by Walker et al. ([Walker et al., 2000b], [Walker et al., 2000a], [Walker et al., 2002]). Walker et al. employ RIPPER, a rule-learning algorithm, to implement a Problematic Dialogue Predictor forecasting the call-outcome of calls in the HMIHY (How May I Help You) call routing system from AT&T. The classifier is able to determine whether a call belongs to the class "problematic" or "not problematic" and this information is used to adapt the dialog strategy of the dialog manager and to repair problems. The accuracy of the classifier after two turns between the user and the system is 79.9% using automatic features; an improvement of 24.4% compared to the baseline, a random guess of the majority class (64.0%). [Levin and Pieraccini, 2006] combined a classifier with various business models to arrive at a decision to escalate a caller depending upon expected cost savings in so doing. The target application is that of a technical support automated agent. [Horvitz and Paek, 2007] consider the influence of an agent queue model on the call outcome and include the availability of human operators in their decision process. Similarly, [Kim, 2007] present a problematic/non-problematic classifier that is trained with 5-grams of utterances from callers that reaches an accuracy of 83% after 5 turns. Escalation is performed when the quality falls below a certain threshold.

Our approach accounts for both points of view considered in the aforementioned studies. First, we introduce a classification approach that can either serve as indicator to the dialog manager to change the dialog strategy or to escalate to a human agent. Second, we integrate the classification outcome with different business models to consider the expected cost savings.

3 Domain

The following experiments are based on data collected from an automated troubleshooting agent that is currently deployed for a large High Speed Internet provider. The automated agent troubleshoots problems related to billing, provisioning, outages, integration and equipment. Callers are encouraged to describe their problems in natural spoken English. The application belongs to a new generation of dialog systems that goes beyond classical FAQ IVRs in that it takes similar steps as a human agent would to solve the issue and fix the problem. Figure 1 shows a dialog that we refer to as problematic.

The sample dialog has been captured during a conversation between a customer and an automated agent unable to troubleshoot the caller's Internet problems. As we can see, the customer hung up after several turns because the conversation didn't run smoothly. While the automated agent was attempting to ping the customer's modem, the customer continued talking to the agent. Since the agent did not expect an answer from the customer at this point in time and the utterance did not match the activated standard grammars, the ASR module output nomatch-events. Evidently, the customer was not comfortable and/or experienced in dealing with IVRs. At the very least, the caller appeared to be uncooperative. Our aim is to detect such problematic dialogs and intervened before it is "too late." We highlight two different views on classifying problematic dialogs. The first model enables a constant monitoring and re-rating of the call quality wherein the accuracy increases as the dialog progresses. The second view considers call quality monitoring from the point-of-view of a service provider that applies a defined business model. We link the classifier output to a cost function and show the degree of cost reduction a classifier brings.

4 Slipper

We employed SLIPPER, a fast and effective rule learner for classification purposes. SLIPPER stands for **S**imple **L**earner with **I**terative **P**runing to **P**roduce **E**rror **R**eduction [Cohen and Singer, 1999] and is an instance of a supervised learning algorithm. During training it creates easily understandable and compact if-then-else-rules for classification.

Using SLIPPER provides several advantages: it is fast in classification and is thus ideally suited for integration in a real-time system such as a dialog manager. Furthermore, its learned rules are easy to understand and facilitate comprehensible hypotheses that enable good classification accuracies. SLIPPER is based on AdaBoost, a special form of boosting algorithm that combines a number of weak classifiers to arrive at a precise predictor for classification.

For classifying between two classes, SLIPPER creates a strong hypothesis $H(x)$ comprising combination of weak hypotheses $h_t(x)$ that are weighted (α) in an iterative process depending on their significance to the overall outcome. Given a set of features x the classifier outputs "-1" for class 1 and "+1" for class 2 (*sign*-function).

$$H(x) = sign \left(\sum_{t=1}^{T} \alpha_t h_t(x) \right) \qquad (1)$$

Table 1. Example dialog of a problematic call from an automated agent. Caller utterances are transcribed using the predicted (ASR) transcriptions.

Agent:	(chime) This is our automated Internet troubleshooter. Please hold on while I look up your account.
Agent:	Okay. I found it.
Agent:	Are you calling because you've lost your Internet connection? Please say yes or no.
Caller:	um sure thanks yes
Agent:	All right. Lets get that fixed. I'm going to check your modem from my end; one moment please.
Caller:	all ack [nomatch]
Agent:	Oh! Sorry, I'll just say this again. I just need to check your modem.
Caller:	all ack [nomatch]
Agent:	Thanks for waiting. I do see your modem on our network, but I need to make sure it can communicate correctly.
Caller:	have map [nomatch]
Agent:	Oh! Sorry, I'll just say this again. I just wanted to say that I can see your modem but I understand you cannot connect.
Caller:	have map [nomatch]
Agent:	I'm going to reset it in a moment, but before I do I need to know... Are you calling using Acme Telephone Service, a Regional Phone Service, or an Internet-Based Telephone Service? In other words, is your phone plugged into a piece of computer equipment?
Caller:	yes mam yes
Agent:	Okay, Acme's name for this service is Acme Telephone. Do you use Acme's telephone service?
Caller:	no no
Agent:	And who is your Internet Based Telephone Service provider?
Caller:	oh that is

Caller hangs up

This final hypothesis $H(x)$ contains all weighted weak rules that make up the classification algorithm.

In the call classification domain those weak rules for detecting a bad call can be, for example:

- if the average recognition accuracy from the ASR is below 60%
- if we observe the words "operator" or "agent" at least two times
- if the user did not respond more than three times to a question by from the IVR

SLIPPER determines such rules automatically. The model is trained with a set of features and an according label.

5   Corpus and Features

The employed corpus (see Table 2) comprises 69,296 calls from a commercially-deployed recent call center recorded between December 3, 2007 and Dec 14, 2007. It consists of log data that has been captured during the conversation between the caller and the automated agent.

Table 2. Labeled corpus: non-automated calls are escalated ("E"), completely automated and partially automated are not escalated ("DE")

	E	DE	E+DE
Number of calls	31,398	37,898	69,296
Average turns	4.81	18.4	12.25
Average duration (min)	0:52	3:46	2:27
Average duration of 3 turns (min)	0:34	0:42	0:39

The corpus consists of three call types: *completely automated*, i.e. all caller problems were solved by the system; *partially automated*, i.e. some caller problems were solved by the system but others had to be handled by a human agent; or *not automated*, i.e. the system could not help, the caller hung up prematurely or asked for an agent. We labeled all automated and partially automated calls as "don't escalate" (DE) and all not automated calls as "escalate" (E).

For training the model, features from a subset of 36,362 calls were used. The test set consists of 18,099 disjunct calls. We extracted the following features from each dialog turn:

ASR features. Raw ASR transcription of the caller's utterance (*utterance*). ASR confidence of returned utterance transcription, from 0–100 (*confidence*). Name of the grammar that returned the parse (*triggeredgrammarname*). Whether the caller communicated with speech or keypad (*inputmode*). Whether the speech recognizer returned a valid parse ('Complete') or not ('No Input' or 'No Match') (*recognition status*). Whether or not the caller began speaking before the prompt completed (*bargedin*).

NLU features. The semantic parse of the caller utterance as returned by the activated grammar in the current dialog module (*interpretation*). Number of system tries to retrieve parsable caller input (*loopname*). The first time the system prompts the caller, *loopname* has the value 'Initial.' Subsequent re-prompts can either be 'Timeout' or 'Retry.'

Dialog Manager features . The number of previous tries to elicit a valid response from the caller (*roleindex*). Whether the system requested substantive user input or confirmed previous substantive input (*rolename*). Type of dialog activity (*activitytype*), e.g. 'Question' or 'Announcement.' Duration of the dialog turn, in seconds (*duration*).

6   Classification

In order to determine the call outcome accurately, we decided to create a separate model for each position in the dialog. Model 1 was trained with features from turn 1, model 2 with features from turn 1+2, model 3 from turns 1+2+3, and so on. In so doing, we were sure to use an appropriate model for classification at each point in the dialog, one that had been trained only on the dialog features which had been observed so far. As shown in Table 3, classification accuracy increases as the number of observed turns increases. After five turns we observe a call outcome classification rate of 90% being 64% better than the baseline (54,7%).

The decision of whether to escalate or not would ideally be determined dynamically at the earliest possible point in a dialog. For now, though, we choose a fixed position in the dialog where we decide to escalate or to continue with the automated system. Given that we observe high accuracy (83%) after only three turns, it seems appropriate to set this as our fixed point in order to minimize the time callers spend in calls that eventually get escalated. Furthermore, the choice of a fixed detection point after three turns is justified by the fact that the average number of turns in escalated calls in our corpus is rather short (see Table 2).

7   Revenue Modeling

So far, we have only considered the overall performance accuracy of the classifier, but have not analyzed the impact of its behavior on business costs and revenue. This section describes the impact of call escalation prediction on different IVR revenue models.

For comparison reasons, we employed the same two business models presented in [Levin and Pieraccini, 2006], but instead of a dynamic decision point—where the evaluation of the call quality is performed—a fixed decision point is chosen. By "fixed" we mean that we consult the classifier after three dialog turns to estimate the call outcome. If the classifier predicts that the call will be escalated

Table 3. Accuracy of each classifier at turn n

Turns	Accuracy	Test Error Rate	Standard Deviation
2	77.73%	22.27%	0.75%
3	83.74%	16.26%	0.75%
4	88.04%	11.96%	0.69%
5	90.50%	9.5%	0.63%
6	93.09%	6.91%	0.56%
7	94.39%	5.61%	0.53%
8	95.15%	4.85%	0.51%
9	95.51%	4.49%	0.52%
10	95.96%	4.04%	0.53%
11	96.21%	3.79%	0.55%
12	95.13%	4.87%	0.65%

at a later point in time, escalation is performed directly. When the classifier predicts the call will not be escalated, i.e. a revenue for the automation is probable, we don't escalate and let the call proceed without any further classifier-based escalation.

In these models, each call type has an associated cost per minute rate (cpm) and each call can be awarded a value based on some scaled factor of $m * cpm$. In other words, the cost per minute multiplied by the number of minutes the person was on the phone with the system plus a constant revenue for automating the call.

The two models have the following parameters:

– M1: $cpm = \$0.10$ and revenue$= \$1.00$ for an automated call
– M2: $cpm = \$0.05$ and revenue$= \$0.70$ for an automated call

We evaluated the costs of each call on the corpus of 18,099 randomly chosen calls. Note that there are two different labeling methods employed. Labeling method $L1$ assumes that automated and partially automated calls are "good" and are thus labeled as "don't escalate." Non-automated calls get the label "escalate." Levin and Pieraccini (labeling method $L2$) labeled the calls differently: automated calls get the label "don't escalate," partially automated calls and non-automated calls are labeled with "escalate" (their terms are "automated" and "not automated"). According to the latter method, the corpus has a different distribution (see Table 4).

Which labeling method is employed depends again on the business model. If revenues for partially automated calls are granted, an early automation of those calls is not recommendable. In the other case, i.e. there is no revenue granted for partially automated calls, an early escalation saves costs. The results for both labeling methods $L1$ and $L2$, in combination with the two business models $M1$ and $M2$, are shown in Table 5.

Table 4. Corpus labeled according to Levin and Pieraccini: automated calls are escalated ("E"), partially automated and not automated calls are not escalated ("DE")

	E	DE	E+DE
Number of calls	57,673	11,623	69,296
Average turns	11.19	17.47	12.25
Average duration (min)	2:14	3:33	2:27
Average duration of 3 turns (min)	0:22	0:43	0:39

Table 5. Cost savings using different business models and labeling methods. L1: automated calls and partially automated calls are not escalated, non-automated calls are escalated; L2: automated calls are escalated, partially automated and non-automated calls are not escalated.

Labeling method	Model	costs without classifier	costs with classifier	savings
L1	M1	9.95	9.01	0.94 (9.4%)
L1	M2	1.32	1.01	0.31 (23.4%)
L2	M1	9.95	6.1	3.85 (38.7%)
L2	M2	1.32	3.1	-1.78 (-138.5%)

As we can see, the savings strongly depend on the particular business model and the a priori distribution of the call outcomes. While a classifier in combination with a business model can bring significant cost reductions (9.4%, 23.4%, and 38.7% for L1/M1, L1/M2, and L2/M1, respectively), its employment can also cause much lower revenue (-138.5% for L2/M2). [Levin and Pieraccini, 2006] reach cost savings of 5.4 cents per call for model L2/M1 compared to 3.85 cents with our corpus and classifier. This might be attributed to a different distribution of automated and non-automated calls in the corpus. A direct comparison could only be given with the same corpus.

8 Conclusion

We presented a powerful model able to detect problematic calls in an IVR system. After only three turns (in average, after 39 seconds) the classifier is able to detect escalated calls with an accuracy of over 83%. This information can then be employed to change the dialog manager's behavior, i.e. it can lead to an adaption of the dialog strategy or lead to an escalation of the caller to a human operator. Both measures can bring significant cost reductions as well as higher customer satisfaction and caller experience. First, calls that would usually fail can be recovered by an intelligent, adaptive and problem-aware dialog manager, yielding a higher automation rate. Second, early escalation of customers that the system will probably not be able to help saves time fruitlessly spent with the automated system and, moreover, leads to per-minute savings. Furthermore, the impact of including a classifier in the dialog manager has been justified on the basis of various concrete business models. Although these results are corpus-specific, they can be generalized to IVRs with similar class-distributions, feature sets and classification methods and one could expect similar accuracies and cost savings as shown in this study.

Future work will include the extension of the feature space by the emotional state of the caller based on lexical and acoustic information; a further refinement of the classes, i.e. a direct prediction of "automated," "partially automated" and "not automated" instead of "escalate" and "don't escalate"; and the employment of other supervised learning methods such as neural networks and support vector machines.

References

[Cohen and Singer, 1999] Cohen, W.W., Singer, Y.: A simple, fast, and effective rule learner. In: Proceedings of the Sixteenth National Conference of Artificial Intelligence (1999)

[Horvitz and Paek, 2007] Horvitz, E., Paek, T.: Complementary computing: policies for transferring callers from dialog systems to human receptionists. User Modeling and User-Adapted Interaction 17(1-2), 159–182 (2007)

[Kim, 2007] Kim, W.: Online call quality monitoring for automating agent-based call centers. In: Proceedings Interspeech 2007 ICSLP, Antwerp, Belgium (2007)

[Levin and Pieraccini, 2006] Levin, E., Pieraccini, R.: Value-based optimal decision for dialog systems. In: Workshop on Spoken Language Technologies (SLT 2006), Aruba (2006)

[Walker et al., 2000a] Walker, M., Langkilde, I., Wright, J., Gorin, A., Litman, D.: Learning to predict problematic situations in a spoken dialogue system: Experiments with how i help you. In: Proceedings of the first conference on North American chapter of the Association for Computational Linguistics (2000a)

[Walker et al., 2002] Walker, M., Langkilde-Geary, I., Wright, H., Wright, J., Gorin, A.: Automatically training a problematic dialogue predictor for a spoken dialogue system. Journal of Artificial Intelligence Research 16, 293–319 (2002)

[Walker et al., 2000b] Walker, M., Wright, J., Langkilde, I.: Using natural language processing and discourse features to identify understanding errors in a spoken dialogue system. In: Proc. 17th International Conf. on Machine Learning, pp. 1111–1118. Morgan Kaufmann, San Francisco (2000b)

Call Classification with Hundreds of Classes and Hundred Thousands of Training Utterances ... ... and No Target Domain Data

David Suendermann, Phillip Hunter, and Roberto Pieraccini

SpeechCycle, Inc., New York City, USA
{david,phillip,roberto}@speechcycle.com
http://www.speechcycle.com

Abstract. This paper reports about an effort to build a large-scale call router able to reliably distinguish among 250 call reasons. Because training data from the specific application (Target) domain was not available, the statistical classifier was built using more than 300,000 transcribed and annotated utterances from related, but different, domains. Several tuning cycles including three re-annotation rounds, in-lab data recording, bag-of-words-based consistency cleaning, and recognition parameter optimization improved the classifier accuracy from 32% to a performance clearly above 70%.

1 Introduction

The introduction of natural language processing to automate call routing about ten years ago [Gorin et al., 1997] has led to a strong interest in the development of statistical call classifiers as an enabling technology for interactive voice response (IVR) applications. The goal of a statistical spoken language understanding (SSLU) classifier is that of mapping a natural language utterance—typically a caller's response to an open-ended question—to one of a given set of categories, or classes, of call reasons. Today, SSLU, typically performed by natural language speech recognition followed by a sentence classifier, is often used as a more sophisticated replacement of menu-based systems using dual-tone multi-frequency (DTMF) [itu, 1995] technology (... *push 1 for billing push 2 for sales* ...) or speech-recognition-based directed dialog (... *you can say billing, sales, or* ...). While both DTMF and directed dialog can, in principle, provide very high accuracy routing, these simple solutions are often not practical for several reasons:

- In certain applications, the number of classes can be too large to be handled in a single menu. Even succession of menus hierarchically structured would prove unwieldy with hundreds of classes, not to mention the bad caller experience when five or six menu levels are required to reach the correct routing point.

E. André et al. (Eds.): PIT 2008, LNAI 5078, pp. 81–87, 2008.

Table 1. Domains covered by the call classifier with examples and number of classes

domain	description	examples	classes
TV	cable television support	cable box issues, picture problems, On-Demand and Pay-Per-View orders	79
Internet	broadband internet support	internet and e-mail problems, setup, equipment, security	63
Phone	telephone support	voice mail, caller ID, phone features, dial tone	62
General	everything not covered by the above	billing, orders, appointments	46
Target	everything covered		250

- Even when prompted with a clear menu, callers often describe the reason why they are calling in their own words, and that may not be covered by the rule-based grammar typically used with directed dialog systems.
- For complex domains, callers may not understand or be familiar with the terms used in the menu. For example in response to the prompt: *Do you have a hardware, software, or configuration problem?*, they may respond unexpectedly (*My CD-ROM does not work!*) or choose one of the options at random without really knowing if it applies to their case.

Hence, for very complex scenarios like the one we will discuss in the following, the use of natural language call classification is the only feasible solution. The interactive voice response application described in this paper is designed for the customer service hotline of a large US cable provider and has to process a variety of call reasons belonging to one of the four domains introduced in Table 1.

State-of-the-art call classifiers as those described in [Evanini et al., 2007] are based on a statistical model trained on a large number of sample utterances. In commercial interactive voice response systems, utterance gathering is usually performed in several steps:

1. At first, a few thousand utterances are recorded by a simple collection application which prompts callers to describe the reason they are calling and then, after having recorded the utterance, transfer them to a traditional routing system. Speech recognition and utterance classification are not used during this step. This type of collection is typically limited in time and in volume of calls, since prompting for call reason and then being transferred to a different system which collects the call reason again produces a bad caller experience, and providers are generally averse to impose that to a large number of customers.
2. An initial classifier[1] is built based on the utterances collected in Step 1. The performance of this initial classifier is usually far from satisfactory because of the limited number of samples.

---

[1] In this work, we use a maximum-likelihood classifier with boosting similar to the one described in [Evanini et al., 2007].

3. The initial classifier from Step 2 is incorporated into the system, and call routing is performed based on its output. In order to limit the negative caller experience produced by a poorly performing classifier, special care is taken in confirming and rejecting low confidence output and following up with properly designed backup directed dialogs. Massive utterance collection is performed at this stage.

4. At reasonable intervals, new classifiers are trained based on the complete set of available utterances iterating over Steps 2 and 3 until the performance reaches a satisfactory level.

The particular challenge we faced in the application described here was due to a customer constraint forcing us to skip Step 1 of the above procedure. So, an initial collection of utterances was not available, and the initial classifier was to be build without appropriate training data from the Target domain. In order to move to Step 2 with a reasonable classifier, we decided to rely on a large amount of data collected from other deployed applications. Moreover, the number of classes was significantly larger than with comparable classification scenarios which usually incorporate less than 100 classes [Evanini et al., 2007]. A preliminary analysis of the call reasons of the Target domain revealed that the number of classes required for this application was 250.

In the following, we discuss data resources, design, and test environment of the call classifier including the steps undertaken to face the challenges introduced by this project. The performance of the classifier, measured at each step of the process on a limited set of test utterances obtained during an initial deployment of the application, is reported.

2   Data Recources

As discussed in the introduction, no data specifically collected for the Target domain was available at the beginning of the project, and the customer required automated call routing to be performed in the first deployment. Thus, we decided to rely on a large corpus of transcribed and annotated speech including more than 2 million utterances collected during the deployment of systems designed for the automation of TV, Internet, and Phone sub-domains (for details, see [Acomb et al., 2007]). Only utterances recorded at the initial open prompt in those systems were considered.

In order to preserve the frequency distribution of the categories in each sub-domain, we performed an unbiased selection of the samples by using all the utterances in a given time range of the collection. Table 2 shows the resulting number of utterances in each sub-domain including a transcription of the prompt used for their collection. In contrast, the prompt used in the Target application was:

Briefly tell me what you're calling about today, for example *I'm having trouble getting online*, or you can say *Give me some choices*.

Table 2. Number of utterances and prompt for a given domain used for the development of the call classifier

domain	utterances	prompt
TV	32,149	Please briefly describe the reason for your call.
Internet	94,598	Briefly describe the problem, saying something like *I can't send or receive email.* Or you can say *What are my choices?*
Phone	10,819	I'll connect you with someone who can help. To get you to the right place, tell me briefly what you're calling about.

The utterances spoken by callers are affected by the prompt used. Different prompts produce a different distribution on the variety of language used. The prompt for the Internet domain for instance clearly encourages the caller to either say *I can't send or receive email* or *What are my choices?*, whereas the other prompts are entirely open. Very rarely, callers would ask for their choices in this case. This was confirmed looking at the data, where the word *choices* appeared 2,609 times in the Internet domain, whereas there was only 1 occurrence in the TV and Phone domains. Thus, the utterances collected in the different sub-domains poorly reflect the linguistic distribution of the utterances in the Target domain. Another problem with using the available corpora from the sub-domains is due to the different contexts in which the utterances were recorded. In fact, in all those sub-domains, the caller had consciously selected a particular technical support application (TV, Internet, or Phone) before being prompted to speak the reason of the call. Consequently, very often, references to the actual domain are not explicitly mentioned, since it was implied by the initial selection of the caller. As an example, the utterance:

> *it's not working*

may appear as a sample in each sub-domain meaning:

- that *the cable modem is not working* in the TV domain,
- that *there is no Internet connection* in the Internet domain,
- that *something is broken* in the Phone domain.

Instead, when read in the Target domain the very same utterance means that *the reason for calling is completely unclear.* Consequently, by blindly merging the sub-domain corpora, utterances like the one in the above example would appear in several different classes producing an incorrect approximation of the statistical model for the Target domain. We solved this problem by iteratively re-annotating the available corpus according to the Target domain specification.

After the initial call classifier was deployed, we recorded 2991 utterances[2]. These utterances were transcribed and annotated and used as test corpus.

---

[2] This happened only shortly before the submission deadline of this publication preventing us from collecting more data and further tuning the call classifier.

Table 3. Accuracy of the call classifier from the baseline to the production system

version	utterances	enhancements	accuracy
I	164,523	live data from applications	
		+ sample utterances from designers	32.4%
II	194,077	re-annotation round 1	44.5%
III	302,912	in-house utterance recording	
		+ re-annotation round 2	62.8%
IV	242,283	recognizer tuning	
		+ re-annotation round 3	
		+ annotation consistency check	71.6%

3   From Baseline to Production

This section reports about our efforts to achieve the best classification performance given the constraints and the challenges described in Section 1. The classification accuracy on the test set of 2991 utterances introduced in Section 2 is reported in Table 3 for each step of the process.

3.1   Just Let It Go

In spite of the arguments pointed out in Section 2 (different prompts, different contexts), we wanted to estimate the baseline performance by blindly merging the sub-domain corpora without any adaptation to the Target domain. However, since only utterances from three domains (TV, Internet, and Phone) were available, application designers were asked to provide a number of example utterances for each class of the missing domain (General). In total, 290 example utterances were produced, annotated, and merged with the rest of the corpus for the initial training. The utterance counts were artificially adjusted to balance the small number of General domain utterances with the large numbers of the other three sub-domains.

3.2   Not Quite There—Let's Get Rid of Major Confusion

By examining the confusion matrix obtained from a test of the baseline classifier (cf. Section 3.I) on several thousand utterances of the same type like the baseline training data, we observed that 30% of the utterances were not only assigned a wrong class but a wrong domain. Consequently, as predicted in Section 2, the context indeed seems to play a significant role in our scenario. Thus, as a first step to get rid of such confusions, classes showing excessive misclassification rates in the confusion matrix were isolated and subject to a first re-annotation round.

3.3   Still Not Great—We Really Need Live Examples

Although the overall performance already had significantly improved, there was a clear demand for utterances particularly in the General domain, being the one

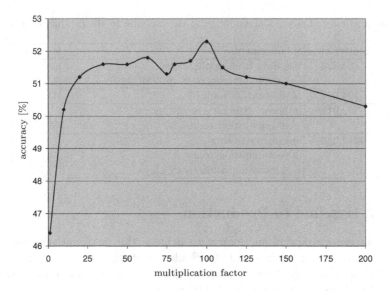

Fig. 1. Influence of the multiplication factor on the call classification accuracy

lacking live training data. The examples provided by the application designers for the initial baseline classifier seemed to be too artificial and different from utterances we would experience in the live system. As a consequence, we set up a platform for recording, transcribing, and annotating calls placed by about 50 subjects recruited internally to the company. A collection system was implemented, and each subject was asked to call it and produce 40 utterances, one for each one of a corresponding number of classes. Utterance categories were randomly distributed among callers with a bias towards those that showed lower performance in the initial experiment. A simple description of each class was provided to the speaker, so as to solicit a reasonably natural response which could also include conversational artifacts such as hesitations, repetitions, linguistic violations, colloquial speech, etc.

A total of 1784 utterances was collected in this step and used in conjunction with the rest of the corpus which included almost 100 times more utterances. To compensate for this count imbalance, the newly collected utterances were split into 67% training and 33% development data. Before merging them with the rest of the corpus, the new utterance counts were inflated by a multiplicative factor learned on the development set. Figure 1 shows the influence of this multiplication factor on the call router accuracy measured on the development set. After including these new utterances, most confused classes were extracted and re-annotated as described in Section 3.II.

3.4 Let's Tease Out the Optimum

As a last step, the training had to be optimized, and the corpus now including more than 300,000 utterances had to be cleaned up as follows:

- speech recognizer tuning (in particular the weighting between acoustic and language model),
- a complete screening of the most frequent utterances among all classes to determine major incorrect annotations still in the data—a third re-annotation round was carried out,
- an annotation consistency cleaning based on bag-of-words matching isolating similar but differently annotated utterances, and
- removal of utterances being over-represented in the data like the one adverted by the Internet prompt in Table 2 (*I can't send or receive email*).

4   Conclusion

Although there was no live training data available for the call classifier's Target domain, we achieved a rather decent accuracy of more than 70% on a task with 250 different classes. This result more than doubled the baseline accuracy and was achieved through a careful re-annotation process involving more than 300,000 utterances and an effort to model the Target behavior by performing in-lab live recordings with 50 people involved.

After the call classifier will be rolled out in a production system, a considerable number of live utterances will be collected and used to further enhance the performance either by enriching the existing classifier or by completely rebuilding it whatsoever achieves higher scores.

References

[itu, 1995] Interactive Services Design Guidelines. Technical Report ITU-T Recommendation F.902, ITU, Geneva, Switzerland (1995)

[Acomb et al., 2007] Acomb, K., Bloom, J., Dayanidhi, K., Hunter, P., Krogh, P., Levin, E., Pieraccini, R.: Technical Support Dialog Systems: Issues, Problems, and Solutions. In: Proc. of the Workshop on Bridging the Gap: Academic and Industrial Research in Dialog Technologies, Rochester, USA (2007)

[Evanini et al., 2007] Evanini, K., Suendermann, D., Pieraccini, R.: Call Classification for Automated Troubleshooting on Large Corpora. In: Proc. of the ASRU, Kyoto, Japan (2007)

[Gorin et al., 1997] Gorin, A., Riccardi, G., Wright, J.: How May I Help You? Speech Communication 23(1/2) (1997)

Hard vs. Fuzzy Clustering for Speech Utterance Categorization

Amparo Albalate[1] and David Suendermann[2]

[1] Institute of Information Technology, University of Ulm
amparo.albalate@uni-ulm.de
[2] SpeechCycle Inc. NY, USA
david@speechcycle.com

Abstract. To detect and describe categories in a given set of utterances without supervision, one may apply clustering to a space therein representing the utterances as vectors. This paper compares hard and fuzzy word clustering approaches applied to 'almost' unsupervised utterance categorization for a technical support dialog system. Here, 'almost' means that only one sample utterance is given per category to allow for objectively evaluating the performance of the clustering techniques. For this purpose, categorization accuracy of the respective techniques are measured against a manually annotated test corpus of more than 3000 utterances.

1 Introduction

A technical support automated agent is a spoken language dialog system devised to perform problem solving tasks over the phone in a similar way as human agents do [Acomb et al., 2007]. These systems are nowadays adopted as an efficient solution to common problems in technical support call centers, such as the long waiting time experienced by the user, the cost of training and maintaining a large base of human agents, and the scalability of the service.

One of the main features of technical support automated agents is the natural modality of interaction with the callers. With an open-ended prompt (e.g. *Please briefly describe the reason for your call*), the system leaves the interaction initiative to the users who are allowed to provide a description of the problem with their own words. Because a symptom can be spoken in multiple ways and styles (natural language), user utterances in response to open prompts may become very complex. A robust semantic analysis of the input utterance is thus necessary in order to identify the underlying problem or symptom from the description provided by the caller. Once the problem has been diagnosed, the automated agent can guide the caller through the relevant troubleshooting steps towards the problem solution.

In technical support applications, the semantic analysis of natural language utterances is commonly based on a technology called statistical spoken language understanding (SSLU). In essence, SSLU performs a mapping of user utterances into one of the predefined problem categories. This is generally achieved through statistical pattern recognition based on supervised classifiers which are trained with manually labelled utterance sets in order to automatically classify new unlabeled utterances.

E. André et al. (Eds.): PIT 2008, LNAI 5078, pp. 88–98, 2008.

However, the manual compilation of large training corpora requires an extensive human labeling effort with high associated time cost: when data for a new application is collected, a number of sample utterances is manually analyzed and initial categories are defined. Then, a large set of utterances is labelled according to these categories. In doing so, the human labeler potentially faces difficulties assigning particular utterances to the predefined set of categories. The labeler will then iteratively extend and alter the category set to cover also utterances he has problems with. On the other end, it is completely unclear if the category set and its definition are reasonable from the statistical classification point of view. If category definitions are too vague, labelers tend to label similar (and sometimes even identical) utterances with different categories. It is also possible that, due to the feature set it relies on, the classifier cannot distinguish between utterances whereas the human labeler can. E.g., the utterances

> *schedule appointment* (the caller wants to set up an appointment) and
> *appointment schedule* (the caller is calling about his appointment which potentially has been setup earlier)

would be labelled with different categories for their meaning being different. A unigram classifier (ignoring the order in which words appear) is unable to distinguish between these utterances, though.

All these issues can potentially be overcome by means of unsupervised categorization methods which aim at producing category definitions by themselves optimizing the separability of the categories. This is done by taking all (non-labelled) utterances of a given training set into account which then are implicitly labelled while optimizing the category definitions.

Unfortunately, it is very hard to analyse the quality of the categories, an unsupervised algorithm comes up with, without a lot of human involvement (basically human labelers going over the algorithm's suggestions and subjectively rating them). Therefore, in this publication, we trigger a basically unsupervised categorization algorithm by means of a single manual example per category providing suggestions on the number and very gross locations of the reference categories. Then, we use a manually labelled test set to estimate the algorithm's performance. As opposed to the above mentioned procedure for evaluating a completely unsupervised technique, this test is repeatable, cheap and allows for frequent tuning cycles.

How can, however, a single example sufficiently represent the entire diversity of utterances in a category? What about the fact that there can be several ways to express the same (or similar) meanings? In the domain this work is carried out (automated troubleshooting for cable television), two example caller utterances for the category *NoPicture* are

– *no picture*,
– *no image*,

and two examples for the category *NoSound* are

– *no sound*,
– *no audio*.

A straight-forward clustering algorithm being given, say, the first of the utterance pairs as the single mentioned training example, would not have the words *image* and *audio* in its vocabulary. It, hence, would assign both *no image* and *no sound* with the same likelihood to the categories *NoPicture* and *NoSound*. If the algorithm knew that *picture* and *image* are synonyms, as *sound* and *audio* are, it would assign the utterances correctly.

Therefore, in this paper, we discuss feature extraction methods which aim at capturing semantic relationships between words such as synonymy and polysemy. In particular, we analyse and compare two approaches to the classification of words based on hard and fuzzy clustering.

The remainder of the paper is organized as follows: In Section 2, we present an overview of the utterance categorization modules. In the next section, we pay special attention to the feature extraction module incorporating either hard or fuzzy clustering. Finally, we describe our evaluation methods and discuss results as well as further directions of the work in Sections 4 and 5, respectively.

2   Utterance Categorization with Three Modules

Automated speech utterance categorization was introduced about ten years ago to allow the caller to use unconstraint natural speech to express the call reason [Gorin et al., 1997]. At the same time, speech utterance categorization was capable of distinguishing many more reasons than directed dialogs, common at that time, could ever handle.

There is a number of approaches to statistical speech utterance categorization (see [Evanini et al., 2007]) which, however, are based on a significant amount of manually labelled training data. Being provided only a single training utterance per category requires special modifications of the categorization procedure as discussed in the following.

Figure 1 provides an overview of the utterance categorization model which consists of three sequential modules: preprocessing, feature extraction, and categorization.

2.1   Preprocessing

The preprocessing module applies morphological analysis, stop word filtering, and bag-of-word representation.

First, a Part of Speech (POS) tagger [Toutanova and Manning, 2000] and a morphological analyser [Minnen et al., 2001] have been applied to reduce the surface word forms in utterances into their corresponding lemmas.

As a next step, stop words are eliminated from the lemmas, as they are judged irrelevant for the categorization. Examples are the lemmas *a, the, be, for*. In this work, we used the SMART stop word list [Buckley, 1985] with small modifications: in particular, we deleted confirmation terms (*yes* and *no*) from the list, whereas words typical for spontaneous speech (*eh, ehm, uh*) were treated as stop words.

The categoriser's vocabulary is then defined as the set of distinct lemmas in the preprocessed training utterances: $W = (w_1, \ldots, w_D)$. In this work, the vocabulary dimension is $D = 1614$ lemmas.

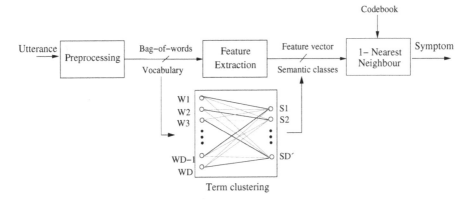

Fig. 1. Utterance categorization components. For feature extraction, hard and fuzzy approaches to term clustering are compared. Hard clustering can be seen as a hard mapping of each input pattern into a single output class (black traces). In contrast, a fuzzy clustering provides a *fuzzy* or *soft* association of each pattern to the output classes through a membership matrix (grey lines). Hard clustering can also be observed as a particular case of fuzzy clustering, where pattern memberships are either '1' or '0'.

Finally, the lemmas for each utterance are combined as a *bag of word*. I.e., each utterance is represented by a D-dimensional vector whose binary elements represent the presence/absence of the respective vocabulary element in the current utterance:

$$BW = (b_1, \ldots, b_D) \tag{1}$$

2.2   Feature Extraction

In order to extract the set of salient features for utterance categorization, we apply clustering to the vocabulary terms. The rational for the use of term[1] clustering is the need for extracting semantic effects, such as synonymy and polysemy, which may not be represented in the original bag of words. Here, we distinguish between hard and fuzzy term clustering.

In hard term clustering, each input pattern is unequivocally allocated to one output cluster. This approach may be adequate for capturing semantically related terms (e.g. synonyms) in output semantic classes. In contrast, a fuzzy clustering algorithm associates the input patterns to all output classes through a matrix with membership degrees. If a considerable number of polysemous terms (with several related meanings) is present in the input data, fuzzy techniques should then be more appropriate.

After the feature extraction phase, each input bag of words (BW) is accordingly transformed into a feature vector F. Details of the feature extraction based on hard and fuzzy clustering and the representation of new feature vectors are discussed in Sections 3.2 and 3.3, respectively.

---

[1] In the following, we also use *term* as a synonym for *lemma*.

2.3   Utterance Categorization

In order to categorise a test utterance represented by its bag of words or feature vector into one of N categories, we use the Nearest Neighbor (NN) algorithm. This algorithm requires a codebook of prototypes composed of one labelled utterance per category. Each input utterance is then assigned to the category of the closest prototype. The proximity of an input utterance to the prototypes is here calculated according to the inner product between their feature vectors, F_a and F_b:

$$s(F_a, F_b) = F_a \cdot F_b. \tag{2}$$

3   Term Clustering

3.1   Term Vector of Lexical Co-occurrences

A frequently reported problem to word clustering is the adequate representation of word lemmas in vector structures so that mathematical (dis)similarity metrics applied to term vectors can reflect the terms' semantic relationships [Montgomery, 1975]. We follow a second-order term co-occurrence criterion [Picard, 1999] for detecting word-semantic proximities:

Two words are similar to the degree that they co-occur with similar words.

Consequently, each vocabulary term w_i is represented in a D-dimensional vector of lexical co-occurrences:

$$W_i = (c_{i1}, \ldots, c_{iD}) \tag{3}$$

wherein the constituents c_{ij} denote the co-occurrence of the terms w_i and w_j, normalized with respect to the total sum of lexical co-occurrences for the term w_i:

$$c_{ij} = \frac{nc_{ij}}{\sum\limits_{k \neq i} nc_{ik}}. \tag{4}$$

Here, nc_{ij} denotes the total number of times that w_i and w_j co-occur. Finally, in order to extract the terms' semantic dissimilarities, we have used the Euclidean distance between term vectors.

3.2   Hard Term Clustering

As mentioned in Section 2.2, a hard clustering algorithm places each input pattern into a single output cluster. Based on the complete-link criterion [Johnson, 1967], the proposed term clustering[2] produces a partition of the vocabulary terms given an input user parameter, the maximum intra-cluster distance d_{th}:

---

[2] The proposed clustering algorithm is a variant of the complete link which uses the cluster merging condition from complete link, while the search criterion is based on a single link approach. Thus, this procedure meets the complete link condition for the maximum intra cluster distance, and simultaneously prevents relatively close patterns to be assigned into different clusters. Note, however, that no hierarchical structure (dendogram) can be drawn for the output partitions. A hierarchical alternative would be a *centroid* or *average link* approach.

1. Construct a dissimilarity matrix U between all pairs of patterns. Initially, each pattern composes its individual cluster $c_k = \{w_k\}$.
2. Find the patterns w_i and w_j with minimum distance in the dissimilarity matrix.
   - If the patterns found belong to different clusters, $c_a \neq c_b$, and $U_{max}(c_a, c_b) \leq d_{th}$, where $U_{max}(c_a, c_b)$ is the distance of the furthest elements in c_a and c_j, merge clusters c_a and c_b.
   - Update U so that $U_{ij} = \infty$.
3. Repeat step 2) while $U_{min} \leq d_{th}$ or until all patterns remain assigned to a single cluster.

As a result of the hard term clustering algorithm, different partitions of the vocabulary terms are obtained, depending on the input parameter d_{th}. Because the elements in each cluster should indicate terms with a certain semantic affinity, we also denote the obtained clusters as *semantic classes*. Table 1 shows examples of clusters produced by this algorithm.

Table 1. Example utterances of semantic classes obtained by hard term clustering for $d_{th1} = d$ on a text corpus comprising 30,000 running words from the cable television troubleshooting domain; the average number of terms per cluster is 4.71; the total number of extracted features is 1458

speak, talk
operator, human, tech, technical, customer, representative, agent, somebody, someone, person, support, service
firewall, antivirus, protection, virus, security, suite, program, software, cd, driver
reschedule, confirm, cancel, schedule
remember, forget
webpage, site, website, page, web, message, error, server
megabyte, meg
technician, appointment
update, load, download
boot, shut, turn
user, name, login, usb
area, room, day

After hard term clustering, the bag of words remains represented in a binary feature vector F_{hard}:

$$F_{hard} = (b_{f_1}, b_{f_2}, \ldots, b_{f_{D'}}) \qquad (5)$$

where the b_{f_i} component denotes the existence of at least one member of the ith extracted class in the original bag of words.

Disambiguation. If applied to bags of words or feature vectors extracted from hard term clusters, the NN classifier rejects a considerable number of ambiguous utterances for which several candidate prototypes are found[3]. A disambiguation module has been

---

[3] Candidate prototypes are such prototypes which share maximum proximity to the input utterance. This happens specially when the similarity metric between the vectors results in integer values, e.g. in the case of using the inner product of binary vectors as the aforeintroduced bags of words and feature vectors extracted after hard word clustering.

therefore developed to resolve the mentioned ambiguities and map an ambiguous utterance to one of the output categories.

First, utterance vectors with more than one candidate prototype are extracted. For each pattern, we have a list of pointers to all candidate prototypes. Then, the terms in each pattern that cause the ambiguity are identified and stored in a competing term list.

As an example, let us consider the utterance *I want to get the virus off my computer* which, after pre-processing and hard term clustering, results in the feature set *computer get off virus*. Its feature vector has maximum similarity to the prototypes *computer freeze* (category *CrashFrozenComputer*) and *install protection virus* (category *Security*). The competing terms that produce the ambiguity are in this case the words *computer* and *virus*. Therefore, the disambiguation among prototypes (or categories) is here equivalent to a disambiguation among competing terms. For that reason, as a further means of disambiguation, we estimate the *informativeness* of a term w_i as shown in Equation 6:

$$I(w_i) = -(log(Pr(w_i)) + \alpha \cdot log(\sum_{\substack{j \\ L_j = N}} c_{ij} Pr(w_j)))$$
(6)

where $Pr(w_i)$ denotes the maximum-likelihood estimation for the probability of the term w_i in the training corpus, and L_j refers to the part-of-speech (POS) tag of w_j, where N refers to nouns). POS tags have been extracted by means of the Standford POS tagger [Toutanova and Manning, 2000].

As it can be inferred from Equation 6, two main factors are taken into account in order to estimate the relevance of a word for the disambiguation:

a) the word probability and
b) the terms' co-occurrence with frequent nouns in the corpus.

The underlying assumption that justifies this second factor is that words representative of problem categories are mostly nouns and appear in the corpus with moderate frequencies. The parameter α is to control the trade-off between the two factors. Reasonable values are in the range of ($\alpha \in [1, 2]$) placing emphasis on the co-occurence term; for our corpus, we use $\alpha = 1.6$ which we found best-performing in the current scenario.

Finally, the term with highest informativeness is selected among the competitors, and the ambiguous utterance vector is matched to the corresponding prototype or category.

3.3 Fuzzy Term Clustering

The objective of the fuzzy word clustering used for feature extraction is a fuzzy mapping of words into semantic classes and leads to the membership matrix M representing this association. We use the Pole-based overlapping clustering (PoBOC) algorithm [Cleuziou et al., 2004] which distinguishes two kinds of patterns: poles and residuals.

Poles are homogeneous clusters which are as far as possible from each other. In contrast, residuals are outlier patterns that fall into regions between two or more poles. The elements in the poles represent monosemous terms, whereas the residual patterns can be seen as terms with multiple related meanings (polysemous). The PoBOC algorithm is performed in two phases: (i) pole construction, and (ii) multiaffectation of outliers.

In the **pole construction** stage, the set of poles $\{P\} = \{P_1, \cdots, P_{D'}\}$ and outliers $\{R\}$ are identified and separated. Poles arise from certain terms, known as the *pole generators*, with a maximal separation inside a dissimilarity graph.

In the **multi-affectation** stage, the outliers' memberships to each pole in $\{P\}$ are computed. Finally, the term w_i is assigned a membership vector to each P_j pole as follows:

$$M_{ij} = \begin{cases} 1, & \text{if } w_i \in P_j \\ 1 - d_{av}(W_i, P_j)/d_{max} & \text{if } w_i \in \{R\} \\ 0, & \text{otherwise} \end{cases} \tag{7}$$

where $d_{av}(w_i, P_j)$ denotes the average distance of the w_i word to all objects in P_j, and d_{max} is the maximum of the term dissimilarity matrix.

Finally, the feature vector obtained with fuzzy term clustering, F_{fuzzy}, is calculated as the normalized matrix product between the original bag of words BW and the membership matrix M:

$$F_{fuzzy} = \frac{BW_{(1xD)} \cdot M_{(DxD')}}{|BW \cdot M|}. \tag{8}$$

4 Experiments

In order to evaluate the proposed hard and fuzzy word clustering methods for utterance classification, we compare the performance of an NN classifier directly applied to the bag of word vectors with that after performing feature extraction. As introduced in Section 1, this is done by comparing the output categories the proposed algorithm assigns to a number of test utterances with manually assigned categories thereof (the reference). If both categories coincide, the automatic categorization is considered correct, otherwise it is counted as error. As overall accuracy, we define

$$\text{accuracy} = \frac{\text{\# correctly classified test utterances}}{\text{\# total utterances in test set}} \tag{9}$$

In the following, we describe the test corpus on which we evaluated the proposed algorithms. Then, we report on the experimental results and finally discuss the outcomes.

4.1 Corpus Description

We used a corpus of 34,848 transcribed and annotated caller utterances gathered from user interactions of a commercial video troubleshooting agent. From this corpus, 31,535 utterances were used for training[4] and 3,285 utterances for test. The remaining 28 utterances (one labelled utterance per category) were manually selected as NN prototypes. Most of the original utterances are composed of 1 to 10 words. After preprocessing, we have an average of 4.45 terms per utterance. The final vocabulary is composed of $D = 1614$ terms; we distinguish $N = 28$ distinct categories in this work.

---

[4] As training corpus we refer to the utterances used in the feature extraction module for lexical analysis and term clustering. None of these methods makes use of the utterances' manual annotations.

4.2 Results

Table 2 shows accuracies on the test set achieved by several configurations of the NN classifier: (i) no feature extraction (bag-of-word matching), (ii) fuzzy term clustering, and (iii) best partition obtained with hard word clustering. Results obtained with the further use of the disambiguation procedure directly applied to bags of words or feature vectors after hard word clustering are also presented. Finally, as a standard of comparison, we also report the accuracy of a 'trivial' classifier which assigns the most frequent category to every utterance.

Table 2. Results of utterance categorization experiments using several feature extraction techniques

Classifier	Clustering	Disambiguation	Accuracy
trivial	–	–	12.5%
NN	–	no	45.0%
NN	–	yes	57.0%
NN	Fuzzy	no	50.0%
NN	Hard	no	50.8%
NN	Hard	yes	62.2%

A second comparison of the utterance classification accuracy rates obtained with hard and fuzzy clustering methods is shown in Figure 2. In the case of hard clustering, results make reference to different cluster partitions obtained with distinct values of the intra cluster threshold distance (d_{th}), normalized with respect to the largest value ($d_{th_{max}}$) used in our experiments[5]. Also, for hard clustering, results are provided before and after disambiguation.

4.3 Discussion

Looking at the plain results without the use of disambiguation, it turns out that both hard and fuzzy word clustering achieve almost the same accuracy (around 50%) out-performing the baseline NN classifier that uses raw bag-of-word vectors by more than 5%.

Although both performances are similar, the nature of the classification errors made by fuzzy and hard word clustering potentially differ. In the fuzzy clustering case, feature vectors are composed of real numbers whereas the hard clustering vectors are binary (cf. Section 3.2). Hence, the distance measures in the former case are real, in the latter case integer. As for the example in Section 3.2, it often happens that one or more competing categories result in the very same distance leading to a considerable number of ambiguous cases.

This fact motivated the use of the disambiguation module. Indeed, the disambiguation led to significant improvements in the utterance categorization performance. The

---

[5] The range of d_{th} values used in hard clustering has been selected through an analysis of the term distances histogram, so that a majority of words are enclosed in this range.

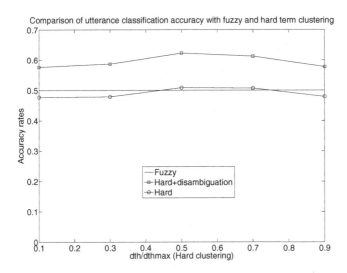

Fig. 2. Comparison of utterance categorization accuracies obtained with feature extraction based on fuzzy and hard clustering, before and after the disambiguation procedure (hard clustering case) is applied

accuracy maximum (62.2%) is reached by the combination of hard term clustering and disambiguation. This classifier configuration outperforms the NN classifier with disambiguation by 5.2% and the baseline by a considerable 17.2%.

5   Conclusion

Given only one sample utterance per category, the proposed categorization scheme produces up to 62.2% correct classification results in our test scenario using hard term clustering as feature extraction in conjunction with a disambiguation procedure. Without disambiguation, utterance categorization accuracies by up to 50% are reached by both fuzzy and hard term clustering. The classification errors observed with hard word clustering are partially due to ambiguities produced during feature vector matching. In this latter case, the categorization can potentially benefit from the further use of a disambiguation scheme as demonstrated in our experiments. We can thus conclude that the most appropriate utterance categorization scheme among the analyzed techniques is based on hard term clustering.

In the future we aim at studying bootstrapping techniques which help enlarge very small training sets automatically. Also subject of analysis are new utterance (dis)similarity metrics which make direct use of terms' semantic (dis)similarities, in order to avoid the limited performance of an intermediate term clustering approach. This is to increase the ratio between correct and incorrect categorizations being one of the most important criteria in commercially deployed applications.

References

[Acomb et al., 2007] Acomb, K., Bloom, J., Dayanidhi, K., Hunter, P., Krogh, P., Levin, E., Pieraccini, R.: Technical Support Dialog Systems: Issues, Problems, and Solutions. In: Proc. of the Workshop on Bridging the Gap: Academic and Industrial Research in Dialog Technologies, Rochester, USA (2007)

[Buckley, 1985] Buckley, C.: Implementation of the SMART information retrieval system. Technical report, Cornell University, Ithaca, USA (1985)

[Cleuziou et al., 2004] Cleuziou, G., Martin, L., Vrain, C.: PoBOC: An Overlapping Clustering Algorithm. Application to Rule-Based Classication and Textual Data. In: Proc. of the ECAI, Valencia, Spain (2004)

[Evanini et al., 2007] Evanini, K., Suendermann, D., Pieraccini, R.: Call Classification for Automated Troubleshooting on Large Corpora. In: Proc. of the ASRU, Kyoto, Japan (2007)

[Gorin et al., 1997] Gorin, A., Riccardi, G., Wright, J.: How I Help You? Speech Communication 23(1/2) (1997)

[Johnson, 1967] Johnson, S.: Hierarchical Clustering Schemes. Psychometrika 32 (1967)

[Minnen et al., 2001] Minnen, G., Carrol, J., Pearce, D.: Applied Morphological Processing of English. Natural Language Engineering 7(3) (2001)

[Montgomery, 1975] Montgomery, C.A.: A Vector Space Model for Automatic Indexing. Communication of the ACM 18(11) (1975)

[Picard, 1999] Picard, J.: Finding Content-Bearing Terms using Term Similarities. In: Proc. of the EACL 1999, Bergen, Norway (1999)

[Toutanova and Manning, 2000] Toutanova, K., Manning, C.: Enriching the Knowledge Sources Used in a Maximum Entropy Part-of-Speech Tagger. In: Proc. of the EMNLP/VLC, Hong Kong, China (2000)

Static and Dynamic Modelling for the Recognition of Non-verbal Vocalisations in Conversational Speech

Björn Schuller, Florian Eyben, and Gerhard Rigoll

Institute for Human-Machine Communication, Technische Universität München,
Theresienstrasse 90, 80333 München, Germany
{sch, eyb, ri}@mmk.ei.tum.de
http://www.mmk.ei.tum.de

Abstract. Non-verbal vocalisations such as laughter, breathing, hesitation, and consent play an important role in the recognition and understanding of human conversational speech and spontaneous affect. In this contribution we discuss two different strategies for robust discrimination of such events: dynamic modelling by a broad selection of diverse acoustic Low-Level-Descriptors vs. static modelling by projection of these via statistical functionals onto a 0.6k feature space with subsequent de-correlation. As classifiers we employ Hidden Markov Models, Conditional Random Fields, and Support Vector Machines, respectively. For discussion of extensive parameter optimisation test-runs with respect to features and model topology, 2.9k non-verbals are extracted from the spontaneous Audio-Visual Interest Corpus. 80.7% accuracy can be reported with, and 92.6% without a garbage model for the discrimination of the named classes.

1   Introduction

Speech is an essential part of human to human communication. It is perhaps the most natural way for people to exchange information with each other. Therefore, if we want machines that are able to communicate with us via natural speech communication, we need robust and intelligent methods for speech recognition, speech understanding and speech synthesis.

Speech recognition research in the past has mainly focused on well defined recognition tasks. These tasks had a restricted vocabulary and task specific stochastic or rule-based grammar. The utterances used for evaluation were mostly read by native speakers under perfect acoustic conditions. Main focus was laid on phoneme based word recognition. Near perfect recognition results have been reported for such tasks (under laboratory conditions) already more than a decade ago [Young, 1996].

Such a system will, however, not work well for spontaneous, conversational speech in applications like dialog systems, call centre loops or automatic transcription systems for meetings. This is due to various non-verbal sounds and irregularities encountered in spontaneous speech. These include disfluencies (filled

E. André et al. (Eds.): PIT 2008, LNAI 5078, pp. 99–110, 2008.

and unfilled pauses, corrections and incomplete words), interjections (e.g. laughing, crying, agreement/disagreement: "aha/ah ah"), human noises (e.g. yawning, throat clearing, breathing, smacking, coughing, sneezing) and other sounds like background conversation or noise [Ward, 1991].

Read speech conveys only the information contained in the spoken words and sentences. In contrast, spontaneous speech contains more extralinguistic information "between the lines", including irony, speaker emotion, speaker confidence and interest in conversation [Schuller et al., 2007]. Next to prosodic features [Kompe, 1997], disfluencies and non-verbal clues such as filled pauses, laughter or breathing reveal much about this extralinguistic information [Schuller et al., 2007]. An automatic spontaneous speech recognition system will only be able to detect information carried on the verbal level. For understanding the extralinguistic information carried by spontaneous speech, non-verbal information is vital [Campbell, 2007], [Decaire, 2000], [Lickley et al., 1991].

A speech recogniser that is able to understand the meaning of spoken language to some extent, must be capable of spotting non-verbal sounds and identifying their type. In contrast to some previous work, which aimes at detection of non-verbal sounds in order to improve robustness of speech recognition [Schultz and Rogina, 1995], this paper deals with the explicit identification of the type of non-verbal vocalisation. [Schultz and Rogina, 1995] only reports on increase in Word Accuracy, and not on correct identification of non-verbal sounds.

The article is structured as follows: in section 2 existing work is discussed, in section 3 details on the database are provided, in section 4 the proposed methods are introduced before results and conclusions in section 5 and section 6, respectively.

2   Existing Work

Various work exists on automatic recognition of few types of Non-Verbals. Covered are especially filled pauses and laughter [Kennedy and Ellis, 2004], [Truong and van Leeuwen, 2005].

Filled pauses. A filled pause detection system was introduced by M. Goto et al. in [Goto et al., 1999]. A quick summary of the technique is given in the following: the system is able to spot two hesitation phenomena, namely filled pauses and word lengthening, in a continuous stream of spontaneous speech. The basic assumption is that hesitations are uttered when the "speaking process is waiting for the next speech content from the thinking process" and thus the speaker cannot change articulatory parameters in that instant. A voiced sound with nearly constant fundamental frequency (F_0) and minimal spectral envelope deformation over time will be produced. The system detects such voiced sounds with minimal variation in the articulatory parameters, which it assumes to be hesitations. A recall rate of 84.9% percent and a precision rate of 91.5% is reported for the spotting of hesitations.

Laughter. For laughter detection and especially synthesis of laughter various papers have been published by N. Campbell et al. [Campbell et al., 2005]. The basic approach they take is the following: an excessive study about various types of laughter has been conducted. It has been found that laughter consists of four distinguishable basic segments, namely voiced laugh, chuckle, ingressive breathy laugh, and nasal grunt. Hidden-Markov Models (HMM) are trained on these laughter segments. A language model, defining in what sequence laughter segments occur, is further given. A success rate of 81% compared to hand labelled data is obtained in detecting the correct laughter segments. 75% success rate is reported when using the grammar to detect laughter type based on the detected laughter segments. This approach is very suitable for detecting laughter types, once a speech/ laughter discrimination has been performed. The latter, however, is not described in that paper.

Another, quite recent, approach [Knox and Mirghafori, 2007] is presented by M. Knox. Experiments are carried out on a large English Meeting room database (ICSI Meetings database). Features from 25ms frames with a forward shift of 10ms are extracted. 75 consecutive frames are fed as input to a neural network, which assigns a target (speech/laughter) to the centre frame. The output of several such neural networks, operating on different feature sets is again fed into a combiner neural network to produce the final output. In this way a target is assigned to every frame. An Equal-Error Rate of 7.9% is achieved. The paper investigates several feature sets whereby Mel-Frequency Cepstral Coefficient (MFCC) based ones give the best results.

The detection of other sounds, such as breathing, yawning or throat clicking is yet quite unexplored. Further, no work is known to us that approaches the problem in a strictly data-driven manner, independent of the type of non-verbal vocalisation to be detected.

In this paper we will therefore focus on the data-driven detection of non-verbal sounds in general. Various dynamic and static classification methods for discriminating between different classes of isolated Non-Verbals are discussed and evaluated.

3   Database

In our experiments we use a database containing 2.9k isolated Non-Verbals extracted from the Audio-Visual Interest Corpus (AVIC) [Schuller et al., 2007]. The AVIC database contains human conversational speech of 21 subjects (10 of them female, 3 of them Asian, others European with balanced age classes) discussing in English with a product presenter who leads them through a commercial presentation. Voice data is recorded by a headset, and a condenser far-field mic (approx. 50cm distance) at an audio sampling rate of 44.1kHz with 16Bit quantisation. All presenter comments are not included in the extracted segments because this would perturb the balanced distribution of number of utterances among speakers. Thus, the total recording time for males resembles 5:14:30h with 1,907 turns, for females 5:08:00h with 1,994 turns, respectively. The lengths of the utterances range from 0.1s to 10.9s with 2.1s on average. Apart from five levels of interest, the spoken content including non-verbal interjections on a word level is transcribed. These interjections are *breathing, consent, coughing, hesitation, laughter, long pause, short pause,* and *other human noise.* Tab. 1 shows the distribution among classes of the Non-Verbals used in the ongoing, whereby coughing was excluded due to sparse instances. Other human noise was mapped onto the new class *garbage* for the following experiments. Further, of the 4.503 extracted Non-Verbals by Forced Alignment, only such having a minimum of 100 ms are kept. Non-Verbals shorter that 100ms have in most cases been incorrectly aligned. Moreover, feature extraction and model evaluation on such short segments is very error prone. The maximum length of occurring Non-Verbals is 2s. Each turn contains between 0 and 31 words with 4.71 words on average (silence and Non-Verbals are hereby not counted). Of the 3,901 turns in total, 2,710 contain between 1 and 7 Non-Verbals. Likewise, there is a total of 18,581 spoken words, and 23,084 word-like units including Non-Verbals (19.5%).

Table 1. Distribution of the Non-Verbals in *AVIC* across the 5 classes

Breathing	Consent	Garbage	Hesitation	Laughter	TOTAL
452	325	716	1,147	261	**2,901**

4 Proposed Method

In this section we investigate three different methods for the discrimination between 5 classes of Non-Verbals, namely Breathing, Consent, Garbage, Hesitation, and Laughter: Hidden Markov Models (HMM), Hidden Conditional Random Fields (HCRF), and Support Vector Machines (SVM).

Extensive tests are conducted for HMM in order to find an optimal configuration (features and model topology) for the task at hand. These are described in more detail in Sect. 4.1. The HCRF are initialised with the parameters of corresponding trained HMM, and thus are fully comparable to the HMM [Gunawardana et al., 2005]. Six feature sets, based on MFCC and PLP are evaluated in conjunction with the two dynamic classifiers, HMM and HCRF. For static classification with SVM a large feature set based on acoustic low-level descriptors (LLD) is used, which has successfully been used in the field of paralinguistics [Schuller et al., 2008]. The following sections describe each of the three methods in more detail.

4.1 Non-verbals Recognition Using HMM

No previous evaluations for the task of Non-Verbals discrimination regarding HMM topology optimisation have been conducted. Therefore, we must find an optimal topology for the task. In phoneme based speech recognisers HMM with

Table 2. Description of the six feature sets for dynamic classifiers (HMM and HCRF)

Set	Features	Dimension
$MFCC_E$	12 MFCC (1-12) + E + δ + $\delta\delta$	39
$MFCC_0$	13 MFCC (0-12) + δ + $\delta\delta$	39
$MFCC_0^{cms}$	13 MFCC (0-12) + δ + $\delta\delta$ (after Cepstral Mean Subtraction)	39
$PLPCC_E$	12 PLPCC (1-12) + E + δ + $\delta\delta$	39
$PLPCC_0$	13 PLPCC (0-12) + δ + $\delta\delta$	39
$PLPCC_0^{cms}$	13 PLPCC (0-12) + δ + $\delta\delta$ (after Cepstral Mean Subtraction)	39

3 states are used to model phonemes. Non-Verbals can be longer than phonemes (see Sect. 3) and have more acoustic variation. It can thus be assumed that more than 3 states are required for Non-Verbals HMM.

One can approach the task of HMM topology optimisation in many ways. An optimal solution will however only be found if all possible combinations of topology parameters for all classes are evaluated. The topology parameters of interest are: number of emitting states (N), number of Gaussian mixture components (M) for each state's output distribution, and the state transition configuration ($\mathbf{A}$), i.e. which transitions between which states are allowed. Due to the exponentially large amount of evaluations required for finding an optimal topology, such exhaustive search is not computable. In order to get an idea of how the HMM topology and choice of features affects the results, a small set of parameters will therefore be tested. The results can be used in future work to further optimise the model topology. The detailed evaluation procedure, including feature and parameter sets, is described in the following three subsections. Results are given in Sect. 5.

Feature sets. Six feature sets based on Mel-Frequency Cepstral Coefficients (MFCC), and Perceptual Linear Predictive Cepstral Coefficients (PLPCC) [Hermansky, 1990] are evaluated. An overview is given in Tab. 2. All features are extracted from frames of 25ms length sampled at a rate of 10ms. A Hamming window is applied to the frames before transformation to the spectral domain. Using a Mel filter bank of 26 channels, 13 MFCC, and 13 PLPCC including the 0th coefficient are computed. Also, the log-energy E is computed for every frame. First and second order regression coefficients are appended to all six feature sets. Cepstral Mean Subtraction (CMS) is applied to one MFCC and one PLP based feature set. This means, for each cepstral coefficient the mean is computed over all corresponding coefficients in the input and then subtracted.

HMM topology parameters. Three different types of HMM structure are investigated: the first being a linear HMM, i. e. a left-right HMM with no skip-state transitions (only transitions from state n to states n and $n+1$ are allowed). The second being a Bakis topology HMM (left-right) with one skip-state transition ($N_{skip} = 1$), i. e. with allowed transitions from a state n to states n, $n + 1$

and $n+2$. The number N of emitting states is varied from 1 to 10. Each number of states is tested with $M = 1$ and $M = 8$ Gaussian mixture components. This results in a total of 40 different sets of model parameters to be evaluated.

Evaluation procedure. The 40 parameter sets introduced in the previous section are evaluated for all six feature sets independently. Thus, a total of 240 evaluations is conducted. Each single evaluation is performed in a speaker independent 3-fold stratified cross-validation (SCV). For the SCV, the AVIC data set is split into three speaker disjunctive parts, each containing data from one third of the speakers. Parts 1 through 3 are used for testing in folds 1 through 3, respectively. The remaining two parts are used for training. Splitting by speakers, however, introduces some problems that one must be aware of: the types of Non-Verbals and the number of Non-Verbals are not equally distributed among speakers (see Sect. 3 for more details). For example, some speakers are more fluent or confident and thus produce fewer hesitations. Therefore, among the folds and the classes in each fold there will be notable differences in the amount of test data vs. training data. Tab. 3 shows the number of training and test instances for each fold. HMM with $M = 1$ are trained in 4 iterations of

Table 3. Number of occurrences of each class in test and training data for each fold

| Fold | [#] test | | | | | |
	Breathing	Consent	Garbage	Hesitation	Laughter	**Total**
1	129	95	126	340	68	**758**
2	83	88	264	281	100	**816**
3	240	142	326	526	93	**1327**
Fold	[#] train					
	Breathing	Consent	Garbage	Hesitation	Laughter	**Total**
1	323	230	590	807	193	**2143**
2	369	237	452	866	161	**2085**
3	212	183	390	621	168	**1574**

Baum-Welch re-estimation [Young et al., 2006]. Models with $M = 8$ are created from the trained models with $M = 1$ by successive mixture splitting, i. e. the number of mixture components M is doubled three times. After each doubling of M, 4 re-estimation iterations are performed. One model is trained for each Non-Verbal. The most likely model is found by Viterbi evaluation. Priors are integrated by the number of occurrences (in the training set) of the corresponding class.

A discussion of the results and best topology and feature set combination is given in Sect. 5.

4.2 Isolated Recognition of Non-verbals Using HCRF

Hidden Conditional Random Fields (HCRF) have become popular in the last couple of years. They have been successfully applied to tasks such as phone classification [Gunawardana et al., 2005] and meeting segmentation [Reiter et al., 2007]. They are an extension of the Conditional Random Fields first introduced by Lafferty et al. [Lafferty et al., 2001].

In this work we use HCRF that are initialised with the parameters of trained HMM. The HCRF are not trained any further in order to have a direct comparison of the two model types. Configurations with $N = 1..10$ hidden states and 1 and 8 Gaussian mixture components are examined. Only the feature set $PLPCC_E$ is investigated thoroughly because the best HMM recognition results are reported with this feature set. The same speaker independent 3-fold stratified cross-validation procedure as for HMM is used. The results for classification of Non-Verbals with HCRF are also given in Sect. 5.

4.3 Isolated Recognition of Non-verbals Using SVM

In this section a completely different approach for discrimination of different types of Non-Verbals is presented. The previous approach is based on dynamic models (HMM and HCRF) used in speech recognition applications because such models can be easily integrated into existing speech recognisers. Yet, alone for the task of distinguishing the type reliably in a second pass, after segmenting data into speech and Non-Verbal segments, for example, a static classification approach can be used.

Features extracted for the dynamic classifiers are sequences of feature vectors $\mathbf{x}_t$ with a sequence length proportional to the length of the input data. For static classification only one feature vector $\mathbf{x}$ with 622 features is extracted for each Non-Verbal utterance. The number of features is reduced to $D' = 108$ by a sequential forward floating search correlation-based (CFS) feature selection step. For computation of the 622 dimensional feature vector the low-level descriptors (LLD) given in Tab. 4 form the basis. Functionals are applied to the evolution of these LLD over time to obtain time and length independent static features. Statistical characteristics of LLD such as mean, median, minimum and

Table 4. Acoustic LLD used in computation of static feature vector

Type	LLD
Time Signal	Elongation, Centroid, Zero-Crossing Rate
Energy	Log-Frame-Energy
Spectral	0-250 Hz, 0-650 Hz, Flux Roll-Off + δ, Centroid + δ
Pitch	F_0 (fundamental frequency)
Formants	F1-F7 Frequency + δ, BW. + δ
Cepstral	MFCC 1-15 + δ + $\delta\delta$
Voice Quality	Harmonics to Noise Ratio (HNR)

maximum position and value, and standard deviation are used as functionals. These are also computed from first (δ) and second order ($\delta\delta$) regression coefficients of LLD, to better model LLD change over time. For more information see [Schuller et al., 2008].

The exact same speaker independent 3 fold partitioning for test and training as is used for dynamic classifiers in Sect. 4.1 is applied. Basing on previous experience in [Schuller et al., 2007], Support-Vector-Machines (SVM) trained with a Sequential Minimal Optimisation (SMO) algorithm are used as the classifier of choice.

5   Results

Table 5 compares the best results of each feature set. Overall best results are achieved with the feature set $PLPCC_E$. 80.7% of all instances are classified correctly when using linear topology HMM with $N = 9$ emitting states, and $M = 8$ Gaussian mixture components. 4 iterations are used for training models with $M = 1$. 12 additional iterations are required for models with $M = 8$.

Table 5. Discrimination between 5 Non-Verbals classes. HMM as classifier. 3-fold SCV, speaker independent. Best results (accuracies) and model parameters associated with best result for each feature set. Optimal topology is linear, each, meaning zero skip-states.

Parameters	$MFCC_0$	$MFCC_0^{cmn}$	$MFCC_E$	$PLPCC_0$	$PLPCC_0^{cmn}$	$PLPCC_E$
Best acc. [%]	79.5	74.2	77.7	79.3	73.4	79.7 (**80.7**[1])
N	8	7	5	10	9	**9**
M	8	8	8	8	8	**8**

PLP based features seem to require more states in the models for good results, MFCC based features give good results with 8 states. Overall, both feature kinds lead to similar classification results, so that they may be interchanged, in whatever way it is required by their application.

Cepstral Mean Normalisation (CMN) has not proven well throughout all experiments for isolated recognition of Non-Verbals. One explanation for this phenomenon might be as follows: isolated Non-Verbals are very short (< 2 s). Computing the mean over the cepstral feature vectors of short segments, which only contain one uttered sound (such as breathing), more likely leads to a biased mean, i. e. not the long term mean related to noise or recording location properties. Subtracting this biased mean leads to loss of information and thus to lower recognition accuracies.

---

[1] This result was obtained by increasing M in steps of 1 instead of doubling M in each round of mixture increase.

Overall best results are obtained with the feature set $PLPCC_E$ using models with 8 Gaussian mixture components and linear topology. The Bakis topology has not proven well. Tab. 6 gives details on the results. Up to now, only 1 and 8 Gaussian mixture components were evaluated. The models with 8 mixture components are created from the trained models with 1 mixture component by doubling the number mixture components and applying 4 rounds of re-estimation after each increase of the number of mixture components. Likewise, only mixture component numbers M that are a power of 2 can be investigated. To evaluate the effect of M in more detail, configurations with $M = 1 - 16$ are analysed on the winning feature set $PLPCC_E$ using the winning linear HMM topology with $N = 9$. The number of mixture components is now increased in steps of 1. After each step 4 rounds of re-estimation are applied. Fig. 1 visualises the results. The

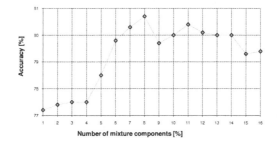

Fig. 1. Discrimination between 5 Non-Verbals classes. HMM as classifier. 3-fold SCV, speaker independent. Feature set $PLPCC_E$. $N = 9$, linear topology. Accuracies obtained with $M = 1 - 16$.

best result is obtained with $M = 8$ is **80.7%** accuracy. With HMM with the same configuration only 79.7% are obtained when creating models with $M = 8$ in fewer steps (i. e. by doubling the number of mixture components instead of increasing it by 1). This shows that more re-estimation iterations during mixture increasing are beneficial and lead to more accurate models.

Table 6. Discrimination between 5 Non-Verbals classes. HMM as classifier. 3-fold SCV, speaker independent. Feature set $PLPCC_E$. Selected numbers of states N vs. number of mixtures M and topology type (linear/Bakis).

[%] correct	$M = 1$		$M = 8$	
	linear	Bakis	linear	Bakis
$N = 1$	68.4	68.4	73.7	73.7
$N = 3$	73.5	72.3	75.5	74.8
$N = 5$	76.3	74.4	77.2	75.2
$N = 7$	77.0	74.8	77.6	76.1
$N = 9$	77.2	73.9	**79.7**	77.8

In order to better understand the sources of classification errors, we now take a look at the confusion matrix. A larger number of confusion matrices has been produced during the evaluations, however, all show one clear tendency, which can be seen in the exemplary confusion matrix shown in table 7: most confusions are related to the garbage model. This is most likely caused by the unspecific nature of the data in the garbage class and poor labeling. The class includes background noises (which, for example, have similar spectral characteristics than breathing), background speech, or speech segments which did not correspond to any word or Non-Verbal. The latter could be most likely confused with hesitation, which in practice would not be too wrong. To better model the individual classes of noise, more than one garbage model and more training data for each of these classes is required. To assess what the performance could be, if a better garbage modelling were available (i. e. more specific annotations and/or separate classes for the individual types of sounds in the garbage class), a test run without the garbage class has been conducted on the winning feature set $PLPCC_E$. As expected, results improve by 5% to 10% in this test run. Using models with 1 mixture component, 89.5% of the Non-Verbals are classified correctly. With 8 mixture components, **92.6%** are classified correctly.

Table 7. Confusion matrix: dynamic discrimination between 5 Non-Verbals classes. 3-fold SCV, speaker independent. Sum over all 3 folds. Optimal configuration: feature set $PLPCC_E$. $N = 9$, $M = 8$, linear topology. Mixture increase in steps of 1.

[#] classif. as →	garbage	hesitation	consent	laughter	breathing
garbage	**515**	93	22	41	41
hesitation	190	**929**	14	13	1
consent	28	37	**255**	3	3
laughter	17	1	2	**229**	12
breathing	18	2	1	19	**412**

Unlike the results obtained in [Reiter et al., 2007], the HCRF did not prove better than HMM for classification of Non-Verbals. The best result for HCRF - **77.8%** - is obtained with the configuration that gives best results for HMM: 9 states, 8 mixture components and linear topology.

With SVM **78.3%** of the instances are classified correctly in a 3-fold SCV. However, this again is below the best result, which is achieved with HMM. Consistent with the results for HMM, the confusion matrix for SVM reveals the garbage class as cause for most confusions. If these instances are ignored, the remaining 4 classes can be discriminated with an accuracy of **91.3%**.

6   Conclusion

We presented the robust recognition of 5 types of Non-Verbals, herein. Diverse models and feature-types were outlined and extensively evaluated on the AVIC database of spontaneous conversational speech. For discrimination between 4 classes of isolated Non-Verbals accuracies of 92.3% are reported using HMM as classifier. When an additional garbage class is added the accuracies drop to 80.7%, which is mainly assumed to be due to the unspecific nature of the garbage class annotations in the AVIC corpus. With SVM and HCRF similar, but slightly (approx. 2%) lower results as with HMM are observed. An additional advantage of HMM is their easy integration within a typical Automic Speech Recognition framework. MFCC and PLP based features were investigated, and lead to similar results. Addition of the extra low-level features in the HMM framework as used for static modelling did not result in any further gain.

In future works we will provide results on integrated decoding of Non-Verbals. Further, approaches for speech/Non-Verbal discrimination based on evolution of low and mid-level descriptors over time need to be investigated. I. e., tracking of voice pitch variations, loudness envelopes and rhythm of speech. Also, parameter optimisation for HMM has to be applied for each class of Non-Verbals, individually. For example, laughter is more complex than breathing, thus it requires more model parameters. Also, other modelling techniques need to be investigated such as HMM/SVM hybrids, and Long-Short-Term-Memory (LSTM) neural networks. Methods for detecting non-verbal vocalisations combined with speech must be researched. Especially laughter often occurs while a person is uttering words. It is a great challenge to detect that the person is laughing, and then detect the spoken content. Speech while laughing is quite different from regular speech regarding its acoustic properties. Also explicit methods for detection of disfluencies such as incomplete words, corrections, stuttering or repetitions must be found as it is not possible to include all combinations of incomplete words in the dictionary and the language model.

Acknowledgment

The research leading to these results has received funding from the European Community's Seventh Framework Programme (FP7/2007-2013) under grant agreement No. 211486 (SEMAINE).

References

[Campbell, 2007] Campbell, N.: On the use of nonverbal speech sounds in human communication. In: COST 2102 Workshop, pp. 117–128 (2007)

[Campbell et al., 2005] Campbell, N., Kashioka, H., Ohara, R.: No laughing matter. In: Proceedings of INTERSPEECH 2005, pp. 465–468 (2005)

[Decaire, 2000] Decaire, M.W.: The detection of deception via non-verbal deception cues. Law Library 1999 - 2001 (2000)

[Goto et al., 1999] Goto, M., Itou, K., Hayamizu, S.: A real-time filled pause detection system for spontaneous speech recognition. In: Eurospeech 1999, pp. 227–230 (1999)

[Gunawardana et al., 2005] Gunawardana, A., Mahajan, M., Acero, A., Platt, J.C.: Hidden conditional random fields for phone classification. In: Proceedings of the International Conference on Speech Communication and Technology (INTER-SPEECH), Lisbon, Portugal (2005)

[Hermansky, 1990] Hermansky, H.: Perceptual linear predictive (plp) analysis of speech. Journal of the Acoustical Society of America 87(4), 1738–1752 (1990)

[Kennedy and Ellis, 2004] Kennedy, L.S., Ellis, D.P.W.: Laughter detection in meetings. In: NIST ICASSP 2004 Meeting Recognition Workshop, Montreal (2004)

[Knox and Mirghafori, 2007] Knox, M., Mirghafori, M.: Automatic laughter detection using neural networks. In: Proceedings of INTERSPEECH 2007 (2007)

[Kompe, 1997] Kompe, R.: Prosody in Speech Understanding Systems. Springer, Heidelberg (1997)

[Lafferty et al., 2001] Lafferty, J., McCallum, A., Pereira, F.: Conditional random fields: Probabilistic models for segmenting and labeling sequence data. In: Proceedings of International Conference on Machine Learning (ICML) (2001)

[Lickley et al., 1991] Lickley, R., Shillcock, R., Bard, E.: Processing disfluent speech: How and when are disfluencies found? In: Proceedings of European Conference on Speech Technology, vol. 3, pp. 1499–1502 (1991)

[Reiter et al., 2007] Reiter, S., Schuller, B., Rigoll, G.: Hidden conditional random fields for meeting segmentation. In: Proc. ICME 2007, Beijing, China, pp. 639–642 (2007)

[Schuller et al., 2007] Schuller, B., Batliner, A., Seppi, D., Steidl, S., Vogt, T., Wagner, J., Devillers, L., Vidrascu, L., Amir, N., Kessous, L., Aharonson, V.: The Relevance of Feature Type for the Automatic Classification of Emotional User States: Low Level Descriptors and Functionals. In: Proc. INTERSPEECH 2007, Antwerp, Belgium, pp. 2253–2256 (2007)

[Schuller et al., 2007] Schuller, B., Müller, R., Hörnler, B., Hoethker, A., Konosu, H., Rigoll, G.: Audiovisual recognition of spontaneous interest within conversations. In: Proc. of Intern. Conf. on Multimodal Interfaces, ACM SIGHI, Nagoya, Japan, pp. 30–37 (2007)

[Schuller et al., 2008] Schuller, B., Wimmer, M., Mösenlechner, L., Kern, C., Arsic, D., Rigoll, G.: Brute-forcing hierarchical functionals for paralinguistics: A waste of feature space? In: Proceedings of ICASSP 2008, Las Vegas, Nevada, USA (2008)

[Schultz and Rogina, 1995] Schultz, T., Rogina, I.: Acoustic and Language Modeling of Human and Nonhuman Noises for Human-to-Human Spontaneous Speech Recognition. In: Proc. ICASSP-1995, Detroit, Michigan, vol. 1, pp. 293–296 (1995)

[Truong and van Leeuwen, 2005] Truong, K.P., van Leeuwen, D.A.: Automatic detection of laughter. In: Proceedings of Interspeech, Lisbon, Portugal, pp. 485–488 (2005)

[Ward, 1991] Ward, W.: Understanding spontaneous speech: the phoenix system. In: Proceedings of ICASSP, Toronto, pp. 365–367 (1991)

[Young, 1996] Young, S.: Large vocabulary continuous recognition: review. IEEE Signal Processing Magazine 13(5), 45–57 (1996)

[Young et al., 2006] Young, S., Evermann, G., Gales, M., Hain, T., Kershaw, D., Liu, X., Moore, G., Odell, J., Ollason, D., Povey, D., Valtchev, V., Woodland, P.: The HTK book (v3.4). Cambridge University Press, Cambridge (2006)

Writing with Your Eye: A Dwell Time Free Writing System Adapted to the Nature of Human Eye Gaze

Nikolaus Bee and Elisabeth André

Institute of Computer Science, University of Augsburg,
86135 Augsburg, Germany
{bee,andre}@informatik.uni-augsburg.de

Abstract. We investigate the usability of an eye controlled writing interface that matches the nature of human eye gaze, which always moves and is not immediately able to trigger the selection of a button. Such an interface allows the eye continuously to move and it is not necessary to dwell upon a specific position to trigger a command. We classify writing into three categories (typing, gesturing, and continuous writing) and explain why continuous writing comes closest to the nature of human eye gaze. We propose Quikwriting, which was originally designed for handhelds, as a method for text input that meets the requirements of eye gaze controlled input best. We adapt its design for the usage with eye gaze. Based on the results of a first study, we formulate some guidelines for the design of future Quikwriting-based eye gaze controlled applications.

1   Introduction

As new video-based methods improve contact-free eye tracking and first systems are emerging that can be used with common webcams, the interest in gaze-based interaction increases. Eye tracking systems based on webcams, such as Opengazer[1], have become affordable and thus can be used by the masses in everyday human-computer interaction.

One domain for gaze-based interaction, mainly of interest to physically handicapped people, is gaze-based writing. We will introduce a gaze-controlled input system that enables users to write with their eyes. A human's eye continuously gazes, wanders and normally stops only for a fraction of a second. Common gaze-based writing systems force the users to dwell upon a specific position for a certain time to trigger a command. In contrast to this, we will present a dwell-time free gaze-controlled writing system which matches the nature of human eye gaze in a better manner.

Unfortunately, eye gaze as an input method is more problematic than hands and fingers. The eye is normally used to gain information only and not to trigger any commands or control devices. [Ashmore et al., 2005] summarizes four

---

[1] More information about this open source eye tracker and a video can be found under:
http://www.inference.phy.cam.ac.uk/opengazer/

E. André et al. (Eds.): PIT 2008, LNAI 5078, pp. 111–122, 2008.

problems which interface developers should consider when using eye gaze for human-computer interaction. (1) The accuracy of eye tracking devices is limited to about 0.5-1°visual angle. 1°corresponds approximately to the size of a thumbnail at arm length [Duchowski, 2007]. This restricts the interaction elements in an interface to a certain size. (2) Eye gaze is recognized with a delay dependent on the frame rate. A 50 Hz system, for instance, incurs delays of 20 ms. When using webcams with 25 Hz, the delay would be 40 ms. (3) Eye gaze is never perfectly still even if one concentrates on a point. It slightly jitters with flicks less than 1°, small drifts of about 0.1°/s and tremors (tiny, high frequency eye vibrations). (4) The Midas touch problem [Jacob, 1991] leads to ambiguities in gaze-controlled interaction. Eyes are used for seeing and gathering information. Naturally, they follow any salient or moving point of interest. Interfaces that use eye gaze should thus be carefully designed and not use too many or intrusive elements that could attract the attention of the user's eye gaze.

We will first give an overview of existing writing systems that are based on eye gaze control. Three kinds of writing approach can be distinguished: typing, gesturing and continuous writing. We will describe our interface that considers the specific characteristics of human eye gaze, i.e. always moving and not able to press something. An experiment to measure the performance and usability of our new input method and its results follow.

2   Related Work

Three types of writing can be distinguished: typing, gesturing and continuous writing.

1. *Typing* – can be performed by pressing keys on a physical keyboard or by selecting letters on an onscreen keyboard using, for example, a game controller.
2. *Gesturing* – is comparable to block lettering. Gesture-based input methods may be found in handhelds with pen-based input devices, such as the Graffiti system from Palm. Each input of a letter is separated by a short interruption (lifting of the pen).
3. *Continuous writing* – reduces the interruptions between letters to a minimum. Cursive handwriting comes close to it.

Taking the humans' eye gaze behavior into consideration, *continuous writing* matches best the requirements of interfaces that utilize eye gaze for input control. Human eye gaze is always moving and always 'on', which can be seen as a pen that always draws. We cannot simply switch off our eye gaze. For handwriting it is necessary to lift the pen to separate single words. As we cannot switch off eye gaze, it would be fascinating to design a gaze-driven interface, where switching is not necessary at all. Before presenting our own system, we will discuss applications that were developed for gaze-controlled writing that fall into the categories introduced above.

2.1   Gaze-Controlled Typing

There are two kinds of common keyboard writing. In the case of direct writing, a keyboard with the keys arranged in alphabetical order or using a typical keyboard layout is displayed. Unlike this, multi-tap writing is based on a hierarchical arrangement of letters. Here the letters are grouped on keys together and users have to repeatedly press buttons to get a single letter. This method is frequently used in mobile phones. To adapt common keyboard writing for eye gaze writing, users have to directly select the keys with their gaze, in a similar way as they would type on a keyboard. They simply type with their eye. Both gaze-controlled direct writing and gaze-controlled multi-tap use dwell time, i.e. users have to fixate a specific point for a specific time, to trigger a key.

[Majaranta et al., 2006] used gaze-controlled interfaces for writing. To write letters, users simply must look at the on-screen button for a certain amount of time. As users write with their eyes in a contact-free manner, there is at first no haptic or acoustic feedback which they might be familiar with from typewriters or keyboards. [Majaranta et al., 2006] investigated several kinds of typing feedback for users: visual, speech and click noise. The visual feedback was implemented with a small highlighted border around the key which is displayed when the user looks at the key. Furthermore, the size of the character on the key shrinks linear to the dwell time. On selection, the background of the key changes its color and the key goes down. When speech is used, the letter is simply spoken out as feedback after its selection. The click noise as feedback is self-explanatory. The authors found in their comparison of speech only, click + visual, speech + visual, and visual only, that click + visual enabled the users to write fastest with their eyes. The maximum writing speed they achieved was about 7.5 wpm (words per minute).

[Hansen et al., 2001] developed a writing system with a hierarchical structure called GazeTalk. They reduced the approximately 30 on-screen keys, common for gaze-controlled keyboard-based systems, to ten in their gaze-based multi-tap system. They applied two different methods. The version for novice users arranges the letters alphabetically. First, letters and special characters are grouped on four buttons. After selecting a button the single characters are shown on single buttons and can be selected for writing. Whereas a gaze-controlled system can select a letter with a single step, this system needs two. The version for advanced users automatically predicts the next letter while the user is writing. In prediction mode only the six most likely letters are shown. If the desired letter is not among them, the user must trigger another button to get back to the alphabetical display.

Among systems without any probabilistic letter prediction or word completion, gaze-controlled keyboard-based systems are the fastest as it takes only one step to enter a letter. But such systems must display all letters at once on the screen. The alphabet has 26 letters adding some command buttons (i.e. space, delete etc.), space for at least 30 buttons is required. Depending on the accuracy of the eye tracker, the buttons need a certain size. And in the end, the writing interface will need a lot of space. With multi-tap systems, the buttons can be larger and are therefore less vulnerable to inaccuracies of the eye tracking system.

Both the direct writing and the multi-tap approach use dwell time to trigger keys. Dwell time strongly depends on the experience of users and thus has an impact on typing speed and error rate. If the chosen dwell time is too short, users will make more mistakes and if the dwell time is too long, users will strain their eyes. Thus, a reasonable trade-off between typing speed and error rate needs to be found. [Špakov and Miniotas, 2004] developed an algorithm to adjust dwell time in real-time. They found that a dwell time of 700 ms enables the user to type nearly without any wrongly selected keys. [Hansen et al., 2001] used a dwell time of 750 ms for novice users which they decreased after several hours of usage to 500 ms.

2.2   Gaze-Controlled Gesturing

[Isokoski, 2000] developed a system called MDITIM (Minimal Device Independent Text Input Method) for device-independent text input. Originally it was only tested with a touchpad, a trackball, a computer mouse, a game controller and a keyboard. To adopt it for eye gaze control, practically no changes were necessary. Only a modifier key, which was previously controlled by pressing a button, was replaced by an area-of-interest, where users had to look at to trigger it. MDITIM encodes letters in commands of directions, i.e. a = NSW, b = SEW, c = ESW, d = SWE, and so forth. The codes consist of three or four directions. If a user, for instance, wishes to write 'c', her eyes have to go to the right, then down and finally to the left. Writing 'cab' results in ESWNSWSEW, which comes close to a continuous writing system. Nevertheless, MDITIM is not a real continuous writing system. For example, combinations, such as 'dc', are encoded by SWEESW, which includes two equal codes in a row. If the system shall be able to recognize such a combination, there must be an interruption in between.

EyeWrite developed by [Wobbrock et al., 2008] is a pure gesture-based eye writing system similar to Graffiti for Palm handhelds. It is the first system that uses letter-like gestures for eye input, in contrast to MDITIM which encodes the alphabet. The interface – the authors chose a window size of 400 × 400 – is aware of five areas: the four corners and the middle. To provide some guidance for the eye gaze to write gestures, there are points placed in the corners and in the middle. To write a 't' for example, the gaze must move from the upper left corner to the upper right corner, then to the lower right corner and finally to the middle to indicate that the gesture is terminated. Glancing at the corners suffices to draw the gesture. The system works not completely dwell time free as the eye gaze must stay for a specified time in the middle for segmentation. The authors specified a dwell time of about 250 ms, which corresponds to half of the typical dwell time that systems use or to twice as much as the average fixation time. The usage of this system is rather similar to MDITIM, but with letter-like gestures, it is easier for users to remember the gestures.

A disadvantage of gesture-based typing systems is that users have to learn the gestures by heart or look it up. That makes the systems difficult to use for occasional users. EyeWrite could be easier to use than MDITIM as EyeWrite uses letter-like gestures, which makes the gestures easier to memorize. The authors of MDITIM do not provide a user study with performance measurements. [Wobbrock et al., 2008] conducted a longitudinal study about the performance of their system. Novice users wrote from about 2.5 wpm (words per minute) up to about 5 wpm after 14 sessions.

2.3   Gaze-Controlled Continuous Writing

[Urbina and Huckauf, 2007] introduce three dwell-time free eye writing applications. In Iwrite, keys are arranged alphabetically in a rectangular horseshoe shape. To select a letter users must look at the letter and then look outside the shape. The inner area of the horseshoe displays the currently written text. A similar system called StarWrite arranges the letters on a half-circle in the upper part and a display for the written text in the lower part. Looking at a letter enlarges it and its two neighbors. To select a letter one must then 'drag' it to the lower text field. Again all letters must be displayed at once. Thus, this method is space consuming or vulnerable to inaccuracy of eye tracking.

pEYEwrite [Huckauf and Urbina, 2007] is their third concept of dwell-time free writing. Here letters are arranged hierarchically using pie menus with six sections, where each section groups five letters or special characters. Letters are again arranged alphabetically. The pie is further divided into an inner and an outer part. The letters are displayed in the inner part of the pie and to trigger a selection of a letter, users must gaze at the corresponding section on the outer frame. To write a letter, a user first selects the section that contains the intended letter. After that, a new pie menu pops up that contains one letter in the single sections. After the selection, the pie disappears and the user can continue. This system needs two activations to write a letter.

Maybe the most prominent gaze-controlled text entry system for continuous writing is Dasher [Ward and MacKay, 2002]. It does not use any static elements in its design. Letters move from the right to the left and as soon as a letter crosses a border it is selected. The letters move continuously as long as the users look at the letters. At start the letters are arranged vertically on the very right border of the application. As soon as the user looks at a letter the letter starts to enlarge and moves to the left. Dasher uses probabilistic prediction of letters and word completion. Both concepts are seamlessly integrated in the interface. The probability of a letter is directly depicted by its size which facilitates its selection.

[Isokoski, 2000] describes an adaption of Quikwriting for usage with eye gaze. Quikwriting was developed by [Perlin, 1998] as a new text input interface for stylus-based systems, i.e. handhelds or smartphones. The system is based on two input concepts. First, with Quikwriting users must never lift their stylus from the surface. This approach perfectly matches the nature of human eye gaze. The eye is always gazing at something, e.g. the screen, and we cannot 'lift' our eye gaze from the screen unless we close our eyes. But then we can no longer see anything. Lifting, we better say triggering or switching, is not a natural human eye gaze behavior. Second, the user never has to stop moving the stylus. Of course eyes stop often to fixate something in a scene, but these fixations normally just last around 150-300 ms. This is much shorter than the trigger time in a dwell-time system. As soon as the dwell time is equal to fixation time, everything users look at is selected.

The interface of Quikwriting is divided into eight equally sized sections around a central resting area. To write a letter, the user moves from the center to one of the outer sections, optionally to another adjacent section, and back to the center, which triggers the selection of the letter. Every section is linked to a group of letters. In general, the letters are arranged in such a way that frequent characters can be written faster. Thus training speeds up writing since users familiar with the arrangement would be able to find an intended letter faster than novice users. For instance, one section contains 'h', 'e', and 'c' in this order. To write an 'e', users simply move their stylus to this section and back to the resting area. If they want to write the 'h', they move to this section, after that to the adjacent left section and finally directly back to the central area. [Isokoski, 2000] never seemed to have implemented this system and thus results about its usability are not available.

3   Implementation of Eye Writing Applications

Our objective is to develop a new gaze-controlled dwell-time free system for continuous writing. We hope that such a system would come close to the nature of human eye gaze behavior. Based on earlier research, we will concentrate on an interface design which does not require learning any gestures by heart. Taking the Midas touch problem [Jacob, 1991] into account, our interface shall be comfortable for the eye. Therefore, distracting visual feedback should be handled with care. Taking these requirements into account, we decided to explore the potential of Quikwriting, which was designed for the usage with handhelds in the first place, for a gaze-controlled interface (see Figure 1). In addition, we will provide a comparison with a gaze-controlled keyboard-based system.

3.1   Gaze-Controlled Quikwriting

Two problems occur with the original design of Quikwriting when simply substituting the stylus by eye gaze. When interacting with a stylus, users first search for the section that contains the letter to write and then they move the stylus there to select it. To avoid that the selection of a letter is unintentionally triggered by a visual search process, we decided not to display the letters within the original sections. Instead, we displayed them in the inner resting area, each group of letters close to its linked section. Further, we had to help users memorize which adjacent section is linked to which single letter since users might already forget during the interaction which section they have to gaze at. This would be fatal for our system. Imagine that the user has selected a group of letters by moving his eye gaze out of the center to an outer section and now has to gaze at an adjacent section to trigger the selection of a letter. Let us assume that the user forgot whether the first or the second adjacent section is the correct one. Thus his gaze would move back again to the resting area. But this process already triggers the selection of a letter. To avoid this problem, we display each single letter within the section the user has to gaze at in order write a letter after having selected a group of letters by moving his eye gaze out of the center (see Figure 1). Then he can look at the section for the letter to write and gaze back to the center.

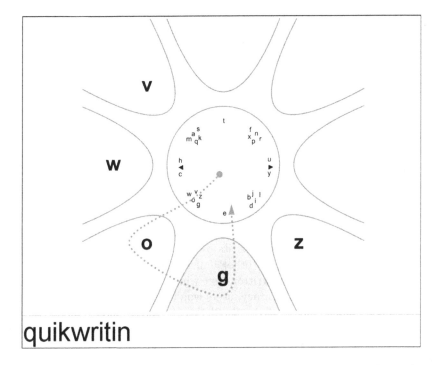

Fig. 1. Adapted interface of Quikwriting for use with eye gaze. The dotted line indicates the gaze path to write the letter 'g'. The user currently looks at 'g'. The light shaded background follows the gaze and indicates which section the user is looking at.

Another problem occurs when a user wants to check what she or he already wrote. For instance, if we place the text area below the writing interface, users may gaze from the center at the text area and pass writing sensitive sections. Looking back to the center would result into the selection of a letter. To avoid this kind of unintended writing actions, we check whether the user is looking at the text field and disable any writing function until the gaze is back in the central area.

3.2   Gaze-Controlled Keyboard-Based System as a Baseline

The performance of writing systems distinguishes a lot in the literature. Some authors measure in characters per minute and others measure in words per minute. Sometimes, the authors do not even describe how many characters make up their words. Most literature considers for European languages a sequence of five characters including spaces and punctuation marks for one word. [MacKenzie, 2003] describe in detail how to measure writing speed in theory and practise for various kinds of interaction device. Not only the measurement methods differ frequently, also the writing speed of gaze-controlled keyboard-based systems, for instance, ranges from about 5 wpm [Wobbrock et al., 2008] to about 11 wpm [Urbina and Huckauf, 2007] for novice users. [Majaranta et al., 2004] report that even among subjects the speed for gaze-controlled writing varies from 7 wpm to over 14 wpm. The huge variance could come from the different eye tracking systems and their accuracy, tracking capabilities and delay. Further, it is important to know if only correctly written letters or all written letters are taken into account. Including wrongly written letters in our analysis, would falsify our results, as they might have been written randomly and unwillingly.

This all makes it difficult for us to compare the performance of our newly developed application with results in the literature. As among systems without word completion, keyboard-based systems are the fastest way to write with eye gaze control, we decided to implement such a system. This gives us a trustier way to compare writing speeds. Our implementation of a keyboard-based system used a dwell time of 750 ms as our study only included novice users that never used an eye tracking system before. The system's response during the writing process was limited to visual feedback. Users were allowed to interrupt looking at a key to trigger it. Every key has its own dwell time buffer. As soon as a dwell time of one key exceeds, all other buffers are reset. This gives users the freedom to look at the already written text while writing a letter. Also for eye tracking systems with lower accuracy, users won't get easily annoyed if the gaze leaves the key for a glance and the dwell time is reset. While looking at one key, the background color changes and slowly fills the button from inside. The letters were arranged in alphabetical order. Additionally we had three command buttons for space, delete and enter.

4   Experiment

To investigate whether the new interface is usable and whether the writing speed can compete with a gaze-controlled keyboard-based interface, we conducted a study with 3 subjects.

We used the iView X RED eye tracking system from SensoMotoric Instruments (SMI), which is contact-free. The eye tracker operates with a sampling rate of 50 Hz and is used in combination with a 19-inch screen with a resolution of 1280 × 1024. When a subject is placed in front of the eye tracking system, the system automatically recognises the position of the head and gives hints about its best position. While the subjects' eye gaze is tracked, they are allowed to move their head freely to a certain extent.

After the subjects were placed in front of the eye tracker, we gave them a short introduction about the eye tracking system. We explained them how they would use their eye gaze to write. Before we started the study, we gave them about 5 minutes to get used to the applications, as our subjects never used an eye tracker before. This was to ensure that the subjects were able to work with our eye tracking system and the tracking accuracy was high enough. We prepared 30 short sentences on small index cards, which were shown and read to them before they started to write a sentence. Every subject had to use the adapted Quikwriting system and the keyboard-based system. Per application they had to write 10 sentences. The sentences were selected randomly per subject. We showed the cards to the subjects to avoid misspelling which would have a side effect on the analyzed error rate. The applications logged the users' writing interactions with a time stamp into a file.

5   Results and Discussion

We analysed the log files and removed all unwillingly and wrongly written letters. This was necessary as sometimes the users wrote letters although they did not intend to do so. And as we were only interested in the writing speed of correctly written letters, the wrong ones were removed. Removing the wrongly written letters normally worsens the writing speed. Writing unwillingly letters often occurs randomly and unexpectedly and therefore the selection of such letters takes a shorter time. We observed (see Table 1) that users were able to write with our adapted Quikwriting 5 wpm. The same subjects achieved a writing speed of about 8 wpm with the keyboard-based interface.

Table 1. Comparison of writing speeds in wpm (words per minute)

	eyeKeyboard	Quikwriting
avg	7.8	5.0
var	0.02	0.3

For all users the keyboard-based system was easier to use, but more exhausting. This was surprising to us since the users were familiar with keyboards, while the adapted Quikwriting was new to them and their usage had to be learned. The reason for the keyboard-based system to be exhausting is the Midas Touch problem. The users always feared that something happened, when they looked somewhere. Some asked if there is a place where nothing happens and they can rest their eyes. In the adapted Quikwriting we have automatically a resting area in the middle of the interface. On the other side the keyboard-based system could be speed up by reducing our current dwell time of 750 ms. For instance,

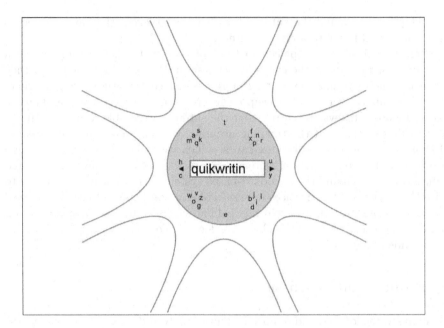

Fig. 2. In a new design of the adapted Quikwriting, we will place the text field in the resting area. This will enable users to check what they have written without moving their eyes to any place outside the control interface.

with a dwell time of 500 ms the writing speed would increase to about 9 wpm. A significant improvement by training is possible since letters are arranged dependent on their probability. We expect that an experienced (i.e. training of 5 days with 15 minutes each day) user could achieve an increased writing speed with Quikwriting up to 9.5 wpm, which comes close to that of a keyboard-based layout.

The error rate of the Quikwriting based system was much higher than the error rate of the keyboard based system. After analysing the log data we found that errors mainly occurred when the user checked what he or she already had already written. We further found that the blocking of any interaction after the users looked at the text field with the already written text did not work in a satisfying manner. Obviously, users did not focus on the written text, as a half glance already sufficed for a human eye to recognise what was written. Therefore, we intend to change the layout of the interface. In particular, we plan to place the text field in a next step to the middle (see Figure 2). This will match the layout of Quikwriting as the eye gaze starts and stops in the middle resting area. Another point is the arrangement of the letters. We kept the layout of Quikwriting as it was originally designed by [Perlin, 1998]. This includes the probability distribution of the characters in the English language. The first six most probable letters in English are E, T, A, O, I, and N, whereas in German they are E, N, I, S, R, and A.

The keyboard-based system could be improved by providing audio feedback to the users after a letter was written. Indeed, subjects already looked at the next letter although the current one was not yet written. Also the dwell time should be adjusted to the users, as for some of them staring for 750 ms was too long.

Comparison With Other Input Methods. The speed of handwriting is about 30 wpm. An average typist writes with 50 to 70 wpm on a computer keyboard. Of course eye gaze controlled writing systems cannot compete with these input methods, but users would need their hands. An input method that needs hands as well uses game controllers. Normally the controller is used to select the letters on a keyboard-based interface displayed on the screen, similar to the one we described in section 2.1. [Költringer et al., 2007] conducted a study with common game controllers. They found that the writing speed of novice users is about 8 wpm using such devices. Experienced users after 15 sessions were able to write 12 wpm. The speed of this input method is comparable to that of eye gaze controlled systems. Since text input becomes more and more important for gaming consoles, eye gaze based input methods will become interesting as soon as webcam-based eye tracking systems become more accurate and reliable.

6   Conclusion

Eye gaze interaction has the potential of becoming a new form of interaction in human-computer interfaces. Currently the interest in such interaction systems mainly comes from physically handicapped people that, for instance, cannot keep their hands calm or move them at all.

We developed a new writing system for eye gaze controlled interaction. Our very first prototype can easily compete with gaze-controlled keyboard-based systems. As we were testing the system for the German language, we expect an improvement after we place the letters according to the occurrence probability of German letters. And with moving the text field from the bottom to the center, a more continuous flow of writing should become possible and increase writing speed.

Based on the results of a first user study, we formulated some guidelines for the design of future Quikwriting-based eye gaze control. Quikwriting was originally designed for the usage with stylus-based input devices. The underlining principles of Quikwriting, (1) always move and (2) never lift the stylus, perfectly match the nature of human's eye gaze and should be considered in future designs for eye gaze interaction. We were able to show that such a system can compete with common writing systems without word completion for eye gaze, such as GazeTalk or pEYEwrite.

References

[Ashmore et al., 2005] Ashmore, M., Duchowski, A.T., Shoemaker, G.: Efficient eye pointing with a fisheye lens. In: GI 2005: Proceedings of Graphics Interface 2005, pp. 203–210. CHCCS (2005)

[Duchowski, 2007] Duchowski, A.T.: Eye Tracking Methodology: Theory and Practice. Springer, Heidelberg (2007)

[Hansen et al., 2001] Hansen, J.P., Hansen, D.W., Johansen, A.S.: Bringing Gaze-based Interaction Back to Basics. Systems, Social and Internationalization Design Aspects of Human-computer Interaction (2001)

[Huckauf and Urbina, 2007] Huckauf, A., Urbina, M.: Gazing with pEYE: new concepts in eye typing. In: APGV 2007: Proceedings of the 4th symposium on Applied perception in graphics and visualization, pp. 141–141. ACM, New York (2007)

[Isokoski, 2000] Isokoski, P.: Text input methods for eye trackers using off-screen targets. In: ETRA 2000: Proceedings of the 2000 symposium on Eye tracking research & applications, pp. 15–21. ACM, New York (2000)

[Jacob, 1991] Jacob, R.J.K.: The use of eye movements in human-computer interaction techniques: what you look at is what you get. ACM Transactions on Information Systems 9(2), 152–169 (1991)

[Költringer et al., 2007] Költringer, T., Van, M.N., Grechenig, T.: Game controller text entry with alphabetic and multi-tap selection keyboards. In: CHI 2007: CHI 2007 extended abstracts on Human factors in computing systems, pp. 2513–2518. ACM, New York (2007)

[MacKenzie, 2003] MacKenzie, S.I.: Motor behaviour models for human-computer interaction. In: Carroll, J.M. (ed.) HCI Models, Theories, and Frameworks: Toward a Multidisciplinary Science (2003)

[Majaranta et al., 2004] Majaranta, P., Aula, A., Räihä, K.-J.: Effects of feedback on eye typing with a short dwell time. In: ETRA 2004: Proceedings of the 2004 symposium on Eye tracking research & applications, pp. 139–146. ACM, New York (2004)

[Majaranta et al., 2006] Majaranta, P., Mackenzie, I., Aula, A., Räihä, K.-J.: Effects of feedback and dwell time on eye typing speed and accuracy. Universal Access in the Information Society 5(2), 199–208 (2006)

[Perlin, 1998] Perlin, K.: Quikwriting: continuous stylus-based text entry. In: UIST 1998: Proceedings of the 11th annual ACM symposium on User interface software and technology, pp. 215–216. ACM Press, New York (1998)

[Urbina and Huckauf, 2007] Urbina, M.H., Huckauf, A.: Dwell time free eye typing approaches. In: COGAIN 2007: Gaze-based Creativity and Interacting with Games and On-line Communities (2007)

[Špakov and Miniotas, 2004] Špakov, O., Miniotas, D.: On-line adjustment of dwell time for target selection by gaze. In: NordiCHI 2004: Proceedings of the third Nordic conference on Human-computer interaction, pp. 203–206. ACM, New York (2004)

[Ward and MacKay, 2002] Ward, D.J., MacKay, D.J.C.: Fast hands-free writing by gaze direction (2002)

[Wobbrock et al., 2008] Wobbrock, J.O., Rubinstein, J., Sawyer, M.W., Duchowski, A.T.: Longitudinal evaluation of discrete consecutive gaze gestures for text entry. In: ETRA 2008: Proceedings of the 2006 symposium on Eye tracking research & applications (2008)

Unsupervised Learning of Head Pose through Spike-Timing Dependent Plasticity

Ulrich Weidenbacher and Heiko Neumann

University of Ulm, Institute of Neural Information Processing, 89069 Ulm
{ulrich.weidenbacher,heiko.neumann}@uni-ulm.de

Abstract. We present a biologically inspired model for learning prototypical representations of head poses. The model employs populations of
integrate-and-fire neurons and operates in the temporal domain. Times-
to-first spike (latencies) are used to develop a rank-order code, which is
invariant to global contrast and brightness changes. Our model consists
of 3 layers. In the first layer, populations of Gabor filters are used to extract feature maps from the input image. Filter activities are converted
into spike latencies to determine their temporal spike order. In layer 2,
intermediate level neurons respond selectively to feature combinations
that are statistically significant in the presented image dataset. Synaptic connectivity between layer 1 and 2 is adapted by a mechanism of
spike-timing dependent plasticity (STDP). This mechanism realises an
unsupervised Hebbian learning scheme that modifies synaptic weights according to their timing between pre- and postsynaptic spike. The third
layer employs a radial basis function (RBF) classifier to evaluate neural
responses from layer 2. Our results show quantitatively that the network
performs well in discriminating between 9 different input poses gathered
from 200 subjects.

1 Introduction

1.1 Motivation

Over the last decades, several researchers put their effort on the investigation
of methods to reliably estimate gaze directions of persons attending to certain
objects or persons. This field of research is closely linked to other face related
topics such as face detection, face recognition or facial expression analysis since
most of them have to account for pose variations (see [Zhao et al., 2000] for a
literature survey).

Here, we focus on the reliable estimation of head pose from monocular greyscale
images since this question seems to be very crucial for all fields of research that
are involved in human-machine-interaction (HMI) [Weidenbacher et al., 2006] or
human-robot-interaction (HRI) [Nagai, 2005]. Furthermore, in a car driver scenario, it would be very informative to know which direction the driver is attending
to in order generate warnings in case of an unattended threat [Beardsley, 1998].
Interestingly, humans have remarkable skills in making reliable pose discriminations [Poppe et al., 2007], as it can be observed in, e.g., conversations to estimate

E. André et al. (Eds.): PIT 2008, LNAI 5078, pp. 123–131, 2008.

in which direction a dialog partner is attending to [Strauss, 2006]. There are quite a number of existing methods for pose estimation which can be divided into two different categories: Model-based approaches try to find landmarks points in the face to build a pose specific graph [Krüger et al., 1997, Vatahska et al., 2007] . While appearance-based approaches use the whole image of the face to estimate head pose using PCA [Pentland et al., 1994, Cootes et al. 1998] or neural networks [Voit et al., 2007]. The advantage of appearance-based models is that no facial landmarks have to be detected which is often a problem due to occlusion when the face is in profile view or an eye is covered by hairs. On the other hand, appearance-based approaches need more training data to achieve sufficient performance.

1.2   Biological Plausibility

In the last ten years, it became more an more clear that the development of new machine learning algorithms alone might not be the best way to solve recognition problems, and that the feature set used has a strong impact on the performance of these appearance based algorithms [Meyers and Wolf, 2008]. Since the human visual system can perform pose discrimination tasks at a level of high accuracy [Poppe et al., 2007], it seems natural to try to understand and emulate how it represents visual data in order to derive features that will be useful in computer vision systems. Recently, [Masquelier and Thorpe, 2007] have proposed a biologically motivated model for learning visual features that was also inspired by the well-known Riesenhuber & Poggio model [Riesenhuber and Poggio, 1999] in which high level features such as object categories are composed in a hierarchical fashion from low-level features such as simple contrast detectors. While most of the neurally inspired models interpret activities (e.g. filter responses) as spike rates, Thorpe and colleagues use the temporal order of incoming spikes (rank-order) as an efficient code. This offers the advantage to use spike-time-based learning techniques such as STDP, a Hebbian learning rule that changes synaptic weights based on the timing between pre- and postsynaptic spike time [Bi and Poo, 2001]. This kind of coding strategy has been already tested successfully for face identification [Delorme and Thorpe, 2001].

1.3   Brief Overview

In this contribution, we present an extended version of the model proposed by [Masquelier and Thorpe, 2007] to learn pose specific neural representations. They incorporate STDP which is known to have the effect of concentrating high synaptic weights on afferents that systematically fire early [Guyonneau et al., 2005]. Moreover, the authors trained their model with images of different categorical objects in front of changing backgrounds. The model finds statistical regularities in the feature domain which are used in combination with a radial basis function classifier (RBF) to discriminate between different object classes (faces, motorbikes, and background). We provided the model with additional feature dimensions (scale and phase) to learn pose specific representations of faces. This is a more challenging task as in-class discriminations in general are harder than between-class discriminations. More clearly, a face in frontal pose has more similarity with a slightly rotated face than a face with a motorbike.

2   Methods

2.1   Model Outline

A greyscale intensity image is filtered with Gabor filters of different orientation, scale and phase polarity, followed by a local normalisation (shunting inhibition). This leads to 48 feature maps providing feature specific neural activity. These activities are further converted into spike ranks by sorting all activities over all feature maps in descending order. In the following layers, only spike ranks, i.e., the temporal order of spiking neurons is used. Spikes are propagated consecutively from layer 1 through STDP synapses to layer 2, where integrate-and-fire neurons compete to elicit their first spike. The prototype who fires first is the winner, whose weights are updated according to the STDP rule (winner-take-all). Final pose classification is done in layer 3 by evaluating a trained RBF classifier using binary pose labels and layer 2 responses as input. The major steps of the model are depicted in Fig. 1.

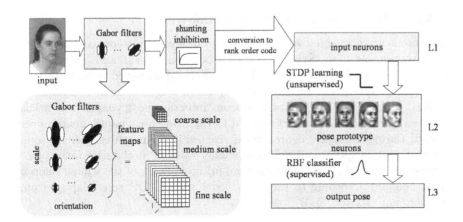

Fig. 1. Overview of the model. Our model consists of three major processing steps. Beginning with a preprocessing stage low level features are extracted and further converted into a rank-order code. Following, pose prototypes are learned from these temporal codes by applying an unsupervised STDP specific leaning rule. After learning has converged, an RBF classifier is used to evaluate the responses from prototypical pose neurons.

2.2   Feature Extraction

The initial stage of processing face images is represented by Gabor wavelets functions [Daugman, 1988] which resembles simple cells in the primary visual cortex. A Gabor filter bank applied to an input image results in different feature maps which selectively respond according to their feature type. Here we used 8 orientations, 3 scales and 2 phases (ON/OFF centre receptive field, responding to positive and negative local contrast) resulting in 48 feature maps (Fig. 1). Furthermore we apply shunting inhibition [Sperling, 1970] to each feature map which has the effect of normalizing filter activity in a spatial neighbourhood within individual feature maps.

2.3   Rank-Order Code

Filter responses from each feature map can be interpreted as neural activity. The more strongly a cell is activated the earlier it fires. This conversion from activity to latency is in accordance with physiological data that response latency decreases with increases in stimulus contrast [Albrecht et al., 2002]. [Thorpe, 1990] has proposed to use the temporal *order* of spike latencies rather than the latencies themselves. This has several advantages: first keeping only the temporal oder saves memory (and computational time) and second the code becomes invariant against global brightness and contrast changes. Such a rank-order code is invariant against global contrast changes since it only represents the *order* but not the precise times to first spike.

2.4   Model Dynamics and STDP Learning

Input neurons are connected with each neuron in layer 2 via connections which define a retinotopic map. Synaptic weights between layer 1 and layer 2 neurons are initially set to 0.5 augmented by Gaussian distributed noise (σ=0.01). Layer 1 (presynaptic) neurons subsequently fire a single spike in temporal order according to their rank. Layer 2 neurons integrate postsynaptic potentials determined by weights that are connected to the firing presynaptic neuron over time until the postsynaptic neuron itself reaches its firing threshold. As soon as the first postsynaptic neuron fires, a winner-take-all mechanism takes place and prevents all other layer 2 neurons from firing. Weights of the winner neuron are now updated according to the simplified binary STDP rule adapted from [Masquelier and Thorpe, 2007]

$$\Delta w = a^+ \cdot w \cdot (1 - w), \text{ if } \quad t_i - t_j \leq 0$$
$$\Delta w = a^- \cdot w \cdot (1 - w), \text{ if } \quad t_i - t_j > 0 \qquad (1)$$

where i and j refer to the pre- and postsynaptic neurons, respectively, t_i and t_j are the corresponding spike ranks. Δw is the synaptic weight modification and a^+ and a^- are the two parameters specifying the amount of change for potentiation and depression of connection weight, respectively. Note, that the learning rule assures that weights remain in range [0,1], therefore no uncontrolled growth of weights can occur.

2.5 RBF Classifier

To evaluate the responses of self-organised prototype neurons, we used a radial basis function classifier. The RBF network was trained with vectors of postsynaptic spike latencies (i.e. the number of presynaptic spikes that were necessary to trigger the spike of a layer 2 neuron). As teacher signal, we used binary class labels from the FERET pose dataset [Phillips et al., 2000]. Training of the RBF classifier did not start until learning of STDP synapses of layer 1-to-layer2 connectivities had finished.

3 Model Simulations

As input of the model we used images of 200 subjects in 9 different poses taken from the FERET database [Phillips et al., 2000]. The size of the input images was 72x64 pixels. In our simulations we used 9 pose neurons initialised with 0.5 in combination with an additive Gaussian noise term($\sigma = 0.01$, $\mu = 0$). Receptive field sizes (RF) of layer 2 pose neurons were set to 65x55 pixels. RFs were duplicated in overlapping retinotopic maps (2 pixels steps), in order to preserve translation invariance. The threshold for the pose neurons to emit a spike was set to 10 % , i.e., when the sum of integrated STDP weights exceeded 10% of the total number of weights within the receptive field[1]. The learning rates a^+ and a^- in Eq. 1 were set to 2^{-5} and $-0.7 \cdot 2^{-5}$. After subsequent presentations of faces in arbitrary poses, neurons in layer 2 began to show a preference for specific head poses (Fig. 2). After 4000 learning steps, weights had converged to a stable state (Fig. 3).

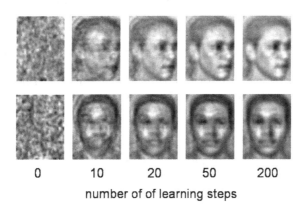

0   10   20   50   200

number of of learning steps

Fig. 2. The figure shows snapshots over time of reconstructed receptive fields for two example pose neurons. Both neurons become selective for distinct head poses. After 200 postsynaptic spikes (weight changes) the weights remain stable.

---

[1] Exact parameter setting was not critical for the system.

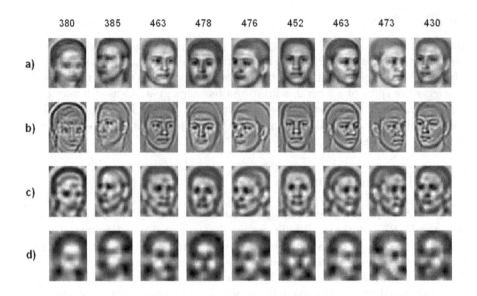

Fig. 3. Receptive fields of all layer 2 neurons after 4000 learning steps. Images in a) show additive reconstructions of learned weights from all feature channels (scale, orientation and phase polarity). b) - d) show weight distribution separate for each Gabor scale from fine to coarse. It is clearly visible that layer 2 neurons show a preference for particular head poses. The numbers over each column denote the quantity of learning steps for each neuron.

To evaluate the resulting pose prototypes, we turned off learning and again processed all images of the database until the stage of layer 2 where each pose neuron reached a certain potential depending on its pose preference. Note that up to this point, solely unsupervised learning was performed, meaning that no external teacher signal was given to the model. Consequently, the model had no knowledge about which prototype neuron is related to which pose. Poses were only learned due to hidden statistical regularities in the dataset. This vector of postsynaptic potentials was then used as input code to train an RBF classifier. As a teacher signal, we provided the RBF classifier with pose class memberships of each input image. After successful training of the RBF classifier, the output neuron of the RBF that responded maximally determines the pose class of the input image. We performed a 200-fold cross-validation on the dataset to evaluate the performance of the multi-class RBF classifier. More clearly, we tested each of the 9 poses from one subject which the system had never seen before while the system was trained with the remaining 199 subjects (including all poses). Then we compared the pose responses from the RBF network with the correct pose. Fig. 4 illustrates the confusion matrix which demonstrates that the vast majority of the data had been classified correctly. In quantitative terms 94.7 % of all poses were classified within +/- one pose class around the correct one.

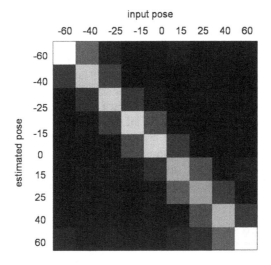

Fig. 4. Confusion matrix of RBF classifier output using a 200-fold cross-validation. The figure shows that nearly all pose classification results lie within the range of +/- one pose class around the correct pose (corresponding to 94.7 % classifications).

4   Discussion and Conclusion

We have presented a model that learns pose selective representations from feature ensembles of oriented faces. Moreover we have shown, that this intermediate complexity level representation can be used as input for a final RBF classifier in order to produce consistent pose estimates. This type of hybrid model has several advantages compared to other leaning approaches such as e.g. back propagation networks. First, selectivity in the STDP layer for significant input patterns is achieved after only few learning steps (cp. Fig. 2). Second, there is no problem to deal with local minima and finally, the intermediate level representation of a pose does not depend on an external teacher signal. This means that in principle all significant variations of the dataset are captured by an unsupervised learning process. This is closely linked to principal component analysis (PCA) [Pentland et al., 1994] an alternitive unsupervised learning approach where a system of orthogonal eigenvectors represents significant second-order variations in the data represented by prototypes that are termed *eigenfaces*. However, the eigenfaces approach is based on the rate code assumption and therefore does not take temporal correlations into account. Moreover, eigenfaces are restricted to be orthogonal to each other.

A problem that many models are confronted with is to find an optimal parameter setting to achieve accurate behaviour. That is in our model, for instance, to choose the number of postsynaptic neurons in layer 2 of the model. It is unclear how many neurons are needed to optimally capture a certain property from the data such as pose. Furthermore, the threshold for a postsynaptic neuron to emit a spike has also strong influence on the learning behaviour, since too small thresholds would only focus on the very strongest contrasts (earliest spikes) while high thresholds would cause STDP to loose focus on the most important features and selectivity will get worse.

We plan to further improve the model by developing a scheme for dynamic prototype allocation. This would have the benefit that the user would not have to select a static number of STDP neurons prior to the learning. Moreover, we will investigate the extension of the model to learn combinations of patterns (such as eyes, nose and mouth) and their spatial relationships as it is proposed, e.g., in [Krüger et al., 1997]. Furthermore, we are currently experimenting with video sequences of continuous pose variations which constitute a more natural input pattern than randomly shuffled images. Finally, with these continuous frame sequences optical flow estimates could also be taken into account.

Acknowledgments

This work was supported by a grant from the Ministry of Science and Arts of Baden-Württemberg, Germany.(Az.: 32-7532.24-14-19/3) to Heiko Neumann.

References

[Albrecht et al., 2002] Albrecht, D., Geisler, W., Frazor, R., Crane, A.: Visual cortex neurons of monkey and cats: Temporal dynamics of the contrast response fucntion. Neurophysiology 88, 888–913 (2002)

[Beardsley, 1998] Beardsley, P.A.: A qualitative approach to classifying head and eye pose. In: IEEE Workshop on Applications of Computer Vision, p. 208. IEEE Computer Society Press, Los Alamitos (1998)

[Bi and Poo, 2001] Bi, G., Poo, M.: Synaptic modification by correlated activity: Hebb's postulate revisited. Annu. Revi. Neurosci. 24, 139–166 (2001)

[Cootes et al., 1998] Cootes, T.F., Edwards, G.J., Taylor, C.J.: Active appearance models. In: Proc. of the European Conference on Computer Vision, vol. 2, pp. 484–498 (1998)

[Daugman, 1988] Daugman, J.: Complete discrete 2d gabor transforms by neural networks for image analysis and compression. Transactions on Acoustics, Speech, and Signal Processing 36(7), 1169–1179 (1988)

[Delorme and Thorpe, 2001] Delorme, A., Thorpe, S.: Face identification using one spike per neuron. Neural Networks 14, 795–803 (2001)

[Guyonneau et al., 2005] Guyonneau, R., van Rullen, R., Thorpe, S.: Neurons tuned to the earliest spikes through stdp. Neural Computation 17(4), 859–879 (2005)

[Krüger et al., 1997] Krüger, N., Pötzsch, M., von der Malsburg, C.: Determination of face position and pose with a learned representation based on labelled graphs. Image Vision Comput. 15(8), 665–673 (1997)

[Masquelier and Thorpe, 2007] Masquelier, T., Thorpe, S.: Unsupervised learning of visual features through spike timing dependent plasticity. PLoS Comput. Biol. 3(2), 31 (2007)

[Meyers and Wolf, 2008] Meyers, E., Wolf, L.: Using biologically inspiered features for face processing. International Journal of Computer Vision 76, 93–104 (2008)

[Nagai, 2005] Nagai, Y.: The role of motion information in learning human-robot joint attention. In: Proceedings of the 2005 IEEE International Conference on Robotics and Automation, pp. 2069–2074 (2005)

[Pentland et al., 1994] Pentland, A., Moghaddam, B., Starner, T.: View-based and modular eigenspaces for face recognition. In: IEEE Conference on Computer Vision and Pattern Recognition (1994)

[Phillips et al., 2000] Phillips, P., Moon, H., Rauss, P., Rizvi, S.: The feret evaluation methodology for face recognition algorithms. IEEE Transactions on Pattern Analysis and Machine Intelligence 22(10), 1090–1104 (2000)

[Poppe et al., 2007] Poppe, R., Rienks, R., Heylen, D.: Accuracy of head orientation perception in triadic situations: Experiment in a virtual environment. Perception 36(7), 971–979 (2007)

[Riesenhuber and Poggio, 1999] Riesenhuber, M., Poggio, T.: Hierarchical models of object recognition in cortex. Nature Neuroscience 2, 1019–1025 (1999)

[Sperling, 1970] Sperling, G.: Model of visual adaptation and contrast detection. Perception and Psychophysic 8, 143–157 (1970)

[Strauss, 2006] Strauss, P.-M.: A slds for perception and interaction in multi-user environments. In: 2nd Int'l Conf. on Intelligent Environments, pp. 171–174 (2006)

[Thorpe, 1990] Thorpe, S.: Parallel processing in neural systems and computers. In: Spike arrival times: A highly efficient coding scheme for neural networks, pp. 91–94. Elsevier, Amsterdam (1990)

[Vatahska et al., 2007] Vatahska, T., Bennewitz, M., Behnke, S.: Feature based head pose estimation from images. In: IEEE Conf. on Humanoid Robots (2007)

[Voit et al., 2007] Voit, M., Nickel, K., Stiefelhagen, R.: Neural Network-Based Head Pose Estimation and Multi-view Fusion. In: Stiefelhagen, R., Garofolo, J.S. (eds.) CLEAR 2006. LNCS, vol. 4122, pp. 291–298. Springer, Heidelberg (2007)

[Weidenbacher et al., 2006] Weidenbacher, U., Layher, G., Bayerl, P., Neumann, H.: Detection of Head Pose and Gaze Direction for Human-Computer Interaction. In: André, E., Dybkjær, L., Minker, W., Neumann, H., Weber, M. (eds.) PIT 2006. LNCS (LNAI), vol. 4021, pp. 9–19. Springer, Heidelberg (2006)

[Zhao et al., 2000] Zhao, W., Chellappa, R., Rosenfeld, A., Phillips, P.: Face recognition: A literature survey. ACM Computing Surveys 35(4), 399–458 (2000)

Spoken Word Recognition from Side of Face Using Infrared Lip Movement Sensor

Takahiro Yoshida, Erika Yamazaki, and Seiichiro Hangai

Department of Electrical Engineering, Tokyo University of Science
1-14-6 Kudan-kita, Chiyoda-ku, Tokyo, 102-0073, Japan
yoshida@ee.kagu.tus.ac.jp,
yamazaki@hanlab.ee.kagu.tus.ac.jp,
hangai@ee.kagu.tus.ac.jp

Abstract. In order to realize multimodal speech recognition on a mobile phone, it is necessary to develop a small sensor which enables to measure lip movement with small calculation cost. In the previous study, we have developed a simple infrared lip movement sensor located on the front of mouth and cleared that the possibility of HMM based word recognition with 87.1% recognition rate. However, in practical use, it is difficult to set the sensor in front of mouth. In this paper, we developed a new lip movement sensor which can extract the lip movement from either side of a speaker's face and examine the performance. From experimental results, we have achieved 85.3% speaker independent word recognition rate only with the lip movement from the side sensor.

1 Introduction

The information of lip movement is very effective especially for speech recognition, because we cannot utter words and sentences without moving lip and mouth. In the research area of multi-modal automatic speech recognition (ASR), the addition of speaker's lip movement to the speech signal is an effective approach for robust recognition against acoustic noise [Meier et al., 1996; Thambiratnam et al., 1997; Luettin et al., 2001; Yoshida et al., 2001; Zhi et al., 2001; Potamianos et al., 2003]. The information of lip movement is available for not only in multi-modal ASR but also in password authentication without audio speech, and multi-modal speaker identification [Wark et al., 2000]. In such a case, however, video camera, large amount of memory, video interface and high speed processor to get the information of lip movement are necessary. In addition, such a system tends to be expensive and large. This is one of reasons to prevent the use of multi-modal speech signal processing. Especially in the mobile use of multi-modal speech signal processing, it is well expected that the performance of mobile equipments is too poor to extract features for word recognition from lip movement in real time.

In order to improve this problem, we have developed a simple infrared lip movement sensor mounted on a head set and made it possible to acquire lip movement [Yoshida et al., 2007]. The sensor consists of an infrared light emitting diode (IR-LED) and an IR photo transistor, and measures the speaker's lip movement by the reflected light from the mouth region. The sensor has also an advantage in small

E. André et al. (Eds.): PIT 2008, LNAI 5078, pp. 132–140, 2008.
© Springer-Verlag Berlin Heidelberg 2008

calculation cost for extracting the lip movement features. By using the sensor, we have achieved the 66% word recognition rate only by the lip movement features [Yoshida et al., 2007]. We also have reported the results that the developed sensor can track a speaker's lip movement and extract a lip movement feature successfully as well as the lip height feature which is extracted using video camera and a post image processing. The headset with this sensor enabled personal digital assistance (PDA) and mobile phone to acquire and handle lip movement information.

However, the sensor must have the capability to acquire the lip movement from either side of a speaker's face when a person holds only a mobile phone to call without a head set. Therefore, we have developed a new lip movement sensor which can extract the lip movement from the side of a speaker's face for a mobile phone.

In this paper, the performance of the new sensor for side face is evaluated by the spoken word recognition using 50 words only with lip movement features. Also, the details of the side sensor and the experimental results of spoken word recognition are shown in comparison with our previous lip movement sensor for front face.

2 Related Works

There are many excellent works realized the real-time lip extraction methods of the lip movement on their personal computer or workstation [Chan et al., 1998; Kaucic et al., 1998; Zhang et al., 2001; Delmas et al., 2002; Beaumesnil et al., 2006]. Their frame rate is range from 10 frame per second (fps) to 30 fps. The 30 fps is not enough to use the lip movement information for speech application such as ASR or password authentication. All methods extract the lip movement from the moving pictures of speaker's face by image processing. For this purpose, temporary and spatial image processing and huge memory size are required. However, the processing costs and available memory are limited in mobile phone.

In contrast, our infrared lip movement sensor does not require such big resources. Our sensor outputs only 1 channel analog signal related to lip movement. Mobile equipments can get the lip movement information directly with extremely low speed analog to digital converter (ADC) without software image processing. Only 200Hz sampling frequency enables to acquire 100 fps lip movement data.

There are a few related works of using IR sensor to get lip movement information. One of works was reported by J. Huang, et al. [Huang et al., 2003]. Their headset had an IR charge coupled device (CCD) camera to get moving pictures of speaker's mouth region. Their method needed the large calculation costs and memory to get the information of lip movement as previous method using video camera, because their headset captures moving pictures. In the excellent previous work by Z. Zhang, et al. [Zhang et al., 2004], they developed the multi-sensory headsets. One of their prototype headsets had an infrared sensor. The main specialty of their prototype headset was the born conductive microphone. Their infrared sensor is similar to our sensor in the point of lip movement sensing. However, the lip movement information from the infrared sensor was used only for voice activity detection. In addition, they did not report the details of infrared sensor and its lip movement features. We could not find any other work in which the lip movement features from an infrared sensor were used for ASR or multi-modal ASR.

3 Lip Movement Sensor for Capturing from Either Side of Face

3.1 Detail of the Side Sensor

A closed view of the developed side sensor is shown in Fig. 1(a). A whole view of the side sensor mounted on a headset is shown in Fig. 1(b). The sensor consists of an IR-LED for radiating infrared light and an IR photo transistor for measuring the power of reflected infrared light. In this new prototype, we use Toshiba TLN103A IR-LED which has 80 degree half-value angle and 940 nm peak wavelength as infrared light. We also use Toshiba TPS611F IR photo transistor which has a visible light cut filter to suppress external visible light, 8 degree half-value angle, and 900 nm center wavelength.

The infrared light is radiated to the mouth region of speaker continuously, and the reflected light is measured. When a speaker opens mouth widely, the power of the reflected light decreases, because the infrared light passes through the gap between the lips as shown in Fig. 2(a). When the speaker closes mouth, the reflected light becomes stronger as shown in Fig. 2(b). This means that the intensity of the sensor output shows the size of mouth opening, which corresponds to the height of the mouth. To improve the dynamic range and signal-to-noise ratio (S/N) of the sensor, we choose the infrared photo transistor with small half-value angle to sharpen the directivity of the infrared sensor.

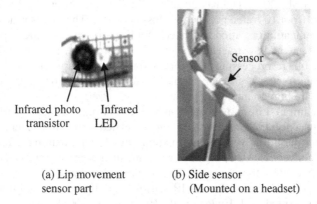

Infrared photo   Infrared
transistor   LED

(a) Lip movement   (b) Side sensor
sensor part   (Mounted on a headset)

Fig. 1. A closed view of the developed side sensor

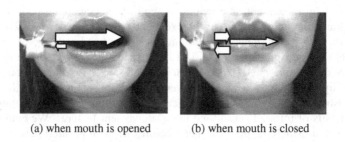

(a) when mouth is opened   (b) when mouth is closed

Fig. 2. The mechanism of changing of reflected light with lip movement

We also measured the dynamic range of the output signal from the previously developed front sensor and the new side sensor to compare the sensing performance. In this measurement, the side sensor is set to the position with 3.0 cm right and 1.5 cm below from the center of mouth and 1.0 cm far from the surface of cheek. The front sensor is set to the position with 1.5 cm below from the center of mouth and 1.0 cm far from the surface of cheek.

The measured results of the dynamic range are shown in Table 1. The dynamic range of the side sensor increases 2.7 dB higher than that of front sensor. This result indicates the new side sensor can track the lip movement more clearly.

Table 1. The measured results of the dynamic range

	Condition of the mouth	Output voltage	Dynamic range
Front sensor	11mm opened	0.90 V	4.4 dB
	Closed	1.50 V	
Side sensor	11mm opened	0.55 V	7.1 dB
	Closed	1.25 V	

3.2 Details of the Interface Part and Extraction Process

In order to feed lip movement information through computer, we use a conventional analog to digital converter (ADC). In that case, only 200Hz sampling rate is required for capturing lip movement, because the effective framerate of lip movement for spoken word recognition does not exceed 100 times/sec.

On the other hand, in developing the prototypical sensor, we designed a special interface (I/F), which enables to connect the sensor to existent PDA or personal computer (PC) via audio input port of sound card. If the sensor has this I/F, no special interface on PC or PDA is required. In this study, we used this interface for capturing the sensor signal into PC to make experiments of spoken word recognition. An amplitude modulation of the sensor output enables to input via audio input port. For the application of multi-modal ASR, this sensor and a microphone mounted on a headset will become an excellent tool, because PC or PDA gets the sensor signal and audio speech signal via basic 2 channel audio input port simultaneously.

The block diagram of I/F hardware and extraction process in PC is shown in Fig. 3. The sensor signal from the photo transistor is amplified, and the amplitude modulated sensor signal is made by multiplying 1 kHz sine wave and the sensor signal together. This modulated frequency determines the maximum transfer rate of lip movement. In this case, the maximum transfer rate is 1000fps because the modulated frequency is 1 kHz. After the PC captured the modulated sensor signal via PC audio input, peak-picking process on PC extracts the lip movement feature. The down sampling process for frame rate conversion can be done by a little bit of additional calculation, if an adaptation of the frame rate for ASR engine or multi-modal ASR engine is necessary.

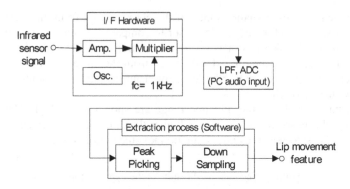

Fig. 3. The block diagram of extraction process

3.3 Example of the Sensor Signal

Fig. 4 shows examples of sensor signals from the side sensor and the front sensor, when the speaker utters the Japanese word "Genzaichi". The waveforms in upper part show audio signals. From Fig. 4 (a) and (b), it is found that the shapes of both sensor signals are similar. When the speaker utters the phoneme, mouth opens and the amplitude of the sensor signal becomes smaller. In contrast, when the speaker closes mouth, the amplitude becomes bigger. This means that the signal of the sensor output highly correlates with the amplitude of speech signal. At the beginning of the sequence, the sensor output is low. The reason is that the speaker opens the mouth before utterance unconsciously. In contrast, at the end of the sequence, the sensor output is high because the speaker closes the mouth after utterance.

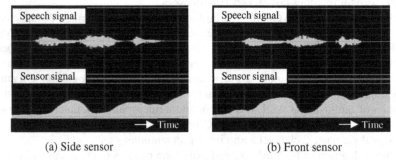

(a) Side sensor   (b) Front sensor

Fig. 4. Measured signals from microphone and the side sensor are shown in (a) and those from the front sensor are shown in (b). (Utterance is a Japanese word "Genzaichi").

4   Spoken Word Recognition Only with the Lip Movement Signal Extracted by the Developed Side Sensor

4.1 Experimental Condition

To evaluate the effectiveness and performance of the lip movement information from the side sensor, we examined isolated word recognition of 50 words only with the lip movement signal from the sensor. We developed the ASR engine for lip movement signal by hidden markov model (HMM). The experimental condition is shown in Table 2. For multi-modal test in future, we record the sensor output signal as right-channel audio signal and speech signal as left-channel audio signal simultaneously. This multi-modal database consists of 7 speakers and 50 Japanese words for car navigation system. Each speaker utters 50 words by 10 times. We used the first 8 times, i.e. 2800 utterances, for training of HMMs. The latter 2 times, i.e. 700 utterances, was used for recognition.

Table 2. Experimental condition of the isolated word recognition of 50 words

Multi-modal database	Vocabulary: 50 words for car-navigation Utterances: 7 persons (3 Males, 4 Females), Each 10 times (Total: 3500 utterances) Used sensor: Side sensor and Front sensor

Sensor position	Side sensor:
	  3.0 cm right and 1.5 cm below from center of mouth
	  1.0 cm far from cheek
	Front sensor:
	  1.5 cm below from center of mouth
	  1.0 cm far from cheek

HMM	4 states Left-to-Right, 33 phoneme models, HTK (HMM Tool Kit) Each 8 times of utterances for training HMMs (Total: 2800 utterances) Each 2 times of utterances for recognition experiment (Total: 700 utterances)
Lip movement feature vectors	28 dimensional QMF filter output signal, 90 frame/sec

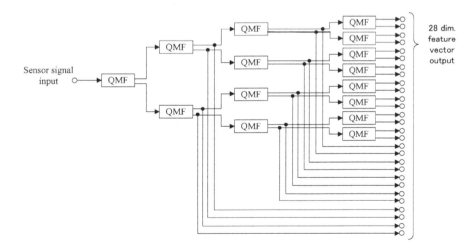

Fig. 5. The 28 dimensional lip movement feature vector from QMF bank

In the experiment of speaker independent word recognition, the training of 50 word HMMs was done by the first 8 times utterances of all 7 speakers. The word recognition tests were done by the latter 2 times utterances of all 7 speakers.

In the experiment of speaker dependent word recognition, we prepare 350 HMMs for 50 words and 7 speakers. Each HMM was trained by the first 8 times utterances of the speaker. The word recognition tests were done by the latter 2 times utterances of the each 7 speakers separately.

Four-state Left-to-Right HMMs are adopted for each of the 33 Japanese phonemes. Each HMM model has 12 Gaussian mixtures for the side sensor and 9 mixtures for the front sensor.

For the lip movement feature, we use the 28 dimensional feature vector. This is obtained from the quadrature mirror filter (QMF) bank as shown in Fig. 5.

4.2 Experimental Results

The experimental results of speaker independent word recognition rate using only lip movement features from the side sensor or the front sensor are shown in Fig. 6. We achieved 85.3% word recognition rate by using the side sensor without audio speech information. It is extremely high recognition performance only with the lip movement. This recognition performance is equivalent to that of the front sensor.

The results of speaker dependent word recognition rate and its average are shown in Fig. 7. In the figure, the numbers show speaker ID and F/M shows gender. We achieved 87.6% word recognition rate in average by the side sensor. This recognition performance is also equivalent to that of the front sensor. The recognition rates of speaker ID 02, 04 and 07 between sensors are different. This is because that we did not record the sensor signals simultaneously. It is necessary to investigate further influence of sensor position to the recognition rate in future.

The recognition rate of the side sensor ranges from 82% to 96%. On the contrary, the recognition rate of the front sensor ranges from 79% to 90%. These variances of the word recognition rates are caused because the lip movement is different even if the speakers utter the same word.

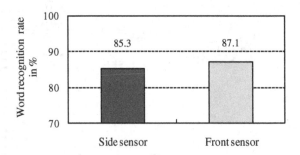

Fig. 6. Comparison of the speaker independent word recognition rate between the lip movement features from the side sensor and the front sensor

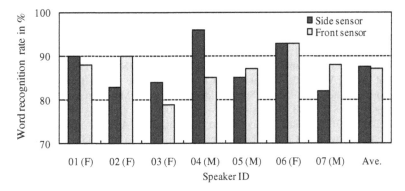

Fig. 7. Comparison of the speaker dependent word recognition rate between the lip movement features from the side sensor and the front sensor

5 Conclusion

In this study, we have developed a new infrared lip movement sensor for capturing from either side of a face. This sensor has advantages for sensing the lip movement from a side of face in low hardware cost, simple structure, small calculation, and connectivity. From these experimental results, it is found that we can achieve 85.3% speaker independent word recognition rate only with the lip movement signal from the side sensor. Also, the side sensor and the front sensor show similar word recognition rate. This experimental result promises the installation of the sensor into a mobile phone to realize multimodal word recognition.

References

[Beaumesnil et al., 2006] Beaumesnil, B., Luthon, F.: Real Time Tracking for 3D Realistic Lip Animation. In: Proceedings of 18th International Conference on Pattern Recognition 2006, vol. 1, pp. 219–222 (2006)

[Chan et al., 1998] Chan, M.T., Zhang, Y., Huang, T.S.: Real-time lip tracking and bimodal continuous speech recognition. In: Proceedings of IEEE Second Workshop on Multimedia Signal Processin 1998, pp. 65–70 (1998)

[Delmas et al., 2002] Delmas, P., Eveno, N., Lievin, M.: Towards robust lip tracking. In: Proceedings of 16th International Conference on Pattern Recognition, vol. 2, pp. 528–531 (2002)

[Huang et al., 2003] Huang, J., Potamianos, G., Neti, C.: Improving Audio-Visual Speech Recognition with an Infrared Headset. In: Proceedings of AVS 2003, pp. 175–178 (2003)

[Kaucic et al., 1998] Kaucic, R., Blake, A.: Accurate, real-time, unadorned lip tracking. In: Proceedings of Sixth International Conference on Computer Vision, pp. 370–375 (1998)

[Luettin et al., 2001] Luettin, J., Potamianos, G., Neti, C.: Asynchronous Stream Modeling For Large Vocabulary Audio-Visual Speech Recognition. In: Proceedings of IEEE ICASS 2001 (2001)

[Meier et al., 1996] Meier, U., Hurst, W., Duchnowski, P.: Adaptive Bimodal Sensor Fusion for Automatic Speechreading. In: Proceedings of ICASS 1996, pp. 833–836 (1996)

[Potamianos et al., 2003] Potamianos, G., Neti, C., Gravier, G., Garg, A., Senior, A.W.: Recent Advances in the Automatic Recognition of Audio-Visual Speech. Proceedings of the IEEE, 91,9 (2003)

[Thambiratnam et al., 1997] Thambiratnam, D., et al.: Speech Recognition in Adverse Environments using Lip Information. In: Proceedings of IEEE TENCON (1997)

[Wark et al., 2000] Wark, T., Sridharan, S., Chandran, V.: The Use of Temporal Speech and Lip Information for Multi-Modal Speaker Identification via Multi-Stream HMM'S. In: Proceedings of ICASSP 2000, vol. 6, pp. 2389–2392 (2000)

[Yoshida et al., 2001] Yoshida, T., Hamamoto, T., Hangai, S.: A Study on Multi-modal Word Recognition System for Car Navigation. In: Proceedings of URSI ISSS 2001, pp. 452–455 (2001)

[Yoshida et al., 2007] Yoshida, T., Hangai, S.: Development of Infrared Lip Move-ment Sensor for Spoken Word Recognition. In: Proceedings of WMSCI 2007, vol. 2, pp. 239–242 (2007)

[Zhang et al., 2001] Zhang, J., Kaynak, M.N., Cheok, A.D., Ko, C.C.: Real-time lip tracking for virtual lip implementation in virtual environments and computer games. In: Proceedings of 10th IEEE International Conference on Fuzzy Systems, vol. 3, pp. 1359–1362 (2001)

[Zhang et al., 2004] Zhang, Z., Liu, Z., Sinclair, M., Acero, A., Deng, L., Droppo, J., Huang, X., Zheng, Y.: Multi-Sensory Microphones for Robust Speech Detection, Enhancement and Recognition. In: Proceedings of IEEE ICASSP (2004)

[Zhi et al., 2001] Zhi, Q., et al.: HMM Modeling for Audio-Visual Speech Recognition. In: Proceedings of IEEE ICME 2001 (2001)

Neurobiologically Inspired, Multimodal Intention Recognition for Technical Communication Systems (NIMITEK)

Andreas Wendemuth[1], Jochen Braun[1], Bernd Michaelis[1], Frank Ohl[2],
Dietmar Rösner[1], Henning Scheich[2], and Ralf Warnemünde[3]

[1] Otto-von-Guericke University, 39106 Magdeburg, Germany
first.last@ovgu.de
[2] Leibniz Institute for Neurobiology, 39118 Magdeburg, Germany
firstname.lastname@ifn-magdeburg.de
[3] Fraunhofer IFF, 39106 Magdeburg, Germany
first.last@iff.fraunhofer.de

Abstract. NIMITEK investigates basic principles of the processing of input (speech, mimics, direct modes), knowledge representation and decision making in dialogue situations between biological / human and technical cognitive systems. This is prototypical for the basic problem of modeling intelligent behavior in interaction with a non-transparent and rapidly changing environment. NIMITEK provides a technical demonstrator to study these principles in a dedicated prototypical task, namely solving the game "Towers of Hanoi". In this paper, we will describe the general approach NIMITEK takes to emotional man-machine interactions, and we will present the principles of the demonstrator.

1 NIMITEK – A Bio-Inspired Approach

In NIMITEK, the results of both experimental and computational biological investigations are taken to model and construct man-machine interfaces. Consequently, the project **integrates** relevant fields which contribute to that approach:

- Knowledge representation, dialogue management and prosody in dialogues,
- Situation dependent reinforcement learning,
- Neurophysiological mechanisms of stimuli classification,
- fMRI imaging of brain areas in prosodic information processing,
- Detection and recognition of emotion in mimics,
- Automatic recognition of speech, prosody and emotion,
- Systems integration, prototyping.

In terms of **methodology**, experiments with animals (gerbils) and interaction with humans (fMRI, situation-dependent learning, Wizard-of-Oz experiments) motivate neurocomputational models [Hamid and Braun, 2007] which explain the basic principles of behavior in dialogue situations with prosodic speech and mimics. This gives ideas for Human Machine Interfaces (HMI). A technical system (demonstrator) enables multimodal processing of input. By recognizing the emotional state of the user

E. André et al. (Eds.): PIT 2008, LNAI 5078, pp. 141–144, 2008.

from speech and mimics, and by identifying the focus of attention in the dialogue, the system dynamically adapts its dialogue strategy for supporting the user in order to be more efficient and more helpful, and to avoid frustration and termination of use. The interaction between the biological and the technical research within NIMITEK works both ways: basic principles of behavior from the biological research are cast into theoretical models which govern the dialogue management in the technical system. In the other direction, experiments with subjects using the demonstrator under fMRI surveillance reveal neural activity within certain emotional states. Technical methodology is used to frame methods to explain the findings from human and animal experiments.

NIMITEK aims at a number of long-range interdisciplinary **goals**:

- Multimodal classification of acoustic and visual emotional data.
- Emotion based control will not only be switched between scenarios, but will be able to learn scenarios and adapt to them.
- Intentions and expectations will be classified from semantics and emotionality of the utterances. This will be used to control e.g. dialogue speed or restart.
- System output (speech, other modes) will be emotional, i.e. uttering prosodic speech or displaying emotional pictures.
- Dialogue control will anticipate intentions and expectations. Control will be constructed by motivation through biological / behavioral models. It will consult the dialogue history and accumulate meaningful past experiences.
- The biological / behavioral models will emerge from experiments designed to explore the limits of biological learning.

These goals are not formulated in abstract scientific space, but the degree of their completion is continuously tested in biological and human experiments, and in particular within the NIMITEK demonstrator, which will be shown at the workshop.

2 Human Machine Interface

In the NIMITEK **modular technology** (fig. 2), the left side shows the acquisition and recognition of the user's facial expression which is done by a stereo camera. The right hand side shows the speech acquisition via microphone. From speech, obviously commands are recognized. But also, speech (in particular the prosody within speech) and mimics together serve as a multimodal emotion source. Emotions are then classified [Vlasenko et al., 2007] into one of the 7 basic emotion classes. Taking also into account the history of the previous system-user interaction, intentions are classified such as "co-operative", "explorative" or "destructive". The latter applies to users who wish to drive the system into dead ends, e.g. by deliberately mispronouncing words or giving contradictory commands. With the recognized commands and the emotional and intentional state, the task controller is driven which is displayed at the center of fig. 2. The effect of the commands are displayed as a new state of the demonstrator.

We will here describe how the recognition and classification of **emotion** is realized on the basis of mimics [Niese et al., 2007]. The facial muscles and certain focal points

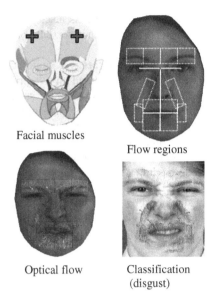

Facial muscles

Flow regions

Optical flow

Classification
(disgust)

Fig. 1. Emotion recognition from facial expression

within the face (crosses in fig. 1) are the basis for human generation of mimics. Most effectively the classification of mimics from muscle activity is done through computation of the optical flow. From the flow regions, the emotion can be classified correctly into one if the seven basis emotions. As an example, in fig. 1 the classification of disgust is shown. As an outlook, research is under way to identify particular brain areas by decoupling the sources of several emotions which are detected in the described fashion. This decoupling can be affected through standard methods like Independent Component Analysis and will reveal first biological insight into the combined generation of emotion from various areas of the brain.

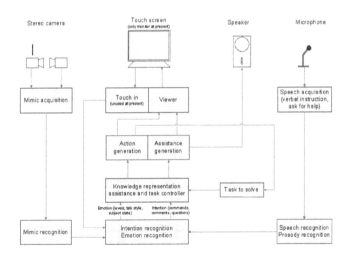

Fig. 2. Systematic overview of the technical modules involved in the demonstrator

The NIMITEK **demonstrator** implements, as a dedicated prototypical task, support for users when interacting with a graphics systems, i.e. playing the game "Towers of Hanoi" and solving the challenge of this task. All interactions are by speech only, which adds additional emotionality to the game. In particular, the task in "Towers of Hanoi" (for those who do not know it) requires to "cross a threshold" in understanding, where after doing so the recursive nature of the game is understood. Naturally, this poses a barrier to the subject which elicits emotional man-machine interactions. As a scientifically novel feature it is further possible to **provoke** emotional states of the user, either to motivate him, or to have a pedagogical effect.

The NIMITEK demonstrator dynamically adapts the **dialogue strategy** [Gnjatović and Rösner, 2008a] according to the current state of the interaction, based on five priors: the emotional state of the user, obtained from the emotion classification; the state of the task and the focus of attention, obtained from the task manager; the user's command, obtained from the natural language understanding module; and the history of interactions, which has been stored. A dialogue strategy includes three decision making processes: *When to provide support? What kind of support? How to provide support?* Further, the natural language understanding module is able to process users' commands that have different syntactical structure: elliptical, complex and context dependent commands. This research is essentially supported by the corpus of affected users behavior in human-machine interaction collected in a Wizard-of-Oz experiment [Gnjatović and Rösner, 2008b].

3 Conclusion

We have shown that basic principles of the processing of input (speech, mimics, direct modes), knowledge representation and decision making can be affected in dialogue situations between biological / human and technical cognitive systems through a technical demonstrator. Emotions play a central role in that approach and have been discussed separately. The research stimulation in this project works from technology to biology and vice versa.

Acknowledgements. We acknowledge grants of the Federal State of Sachsen-Anhalt (2005-2010), FKZ XN3621H/1005. This project is associated to and supported by the Magdeburg Center for Behavioral Brain Sciences (Neuroscience Excellence Cluster).

References

[Gnjatović and Rösner, 2008a] Gnjatović, M., Rösner, D.: Emotion Adaptive Dialogue Management in Human-Machine Interaction. In: Proceedings of the 19th European Meetings on Cybernetics and Systems Research (EMCSR 2008), Vienna, Austria, pp. 567–572 (2008)

[Gnjatović and Rösner, 2008b] Gnjatović, M., Rösner, D.: On the Role of the NIMITEK Corpus in Developing an Emotion Adaptive Spoken Dialogue System. In: Proceedings of the Language Resources and Evaluation Conference (LREC 2008), Marrakech, Morocco (2008)

[Hamid and Braun, 2007]Hamid, O., Braun, J.: Task-irrelevant temporal order and learning of arbitrary visuo-motor associations. In: Proceedings of the European Conference on Visual Perception (ECVP 2007), Arezzo, Italy (2007)

[Niese et al., 2007] Niese, R., Al-Hamadi, A., Michaelis, B.: A Novel Method for 3D Face Detection and Normalization. Jour. of Multimedia 2(5), 1–12 (2007)

[Vlasenko et al., 2007]Vlasenko, B., Schuller, B., Wendemuth, A., Rigoll, G.: Frame vs. Turn-Level: Emotion Recognition from Speech Considering Static and Dynamic Processing. In: Paiva, A., Prada, R., Picard, R.W. (eds.) ACII 2007. LNCS, vol. 4738, pp. 139–147. Springer, Heidelberg (2007)

Deploying DSR Technology on Today's Mobile Phones: A Feasibility Study

Dmitry Zaykovskiy and Alexander Schmitt

Institute of Information Technology, University of Ulm, Germany
{dmitry.zaykovskiy,alexander.schmitt}@uni-ulm.de

Abstract. In this paper we study the feasibility for the deployment of Distributed Speech Recognition (DSR) technology on today's mobile phones using publicly available tools and architectures. The existing standards for DSR front-ends are presented and discussed; arguments for the choice of an appropriate standard for a deployment on the particular platform are given. We point out hindrances and pitfalls during development and deployment. Standard conform solutions for the two most prominent development environments, Symbian C++ and Java Micro Edition, are presented and evaluated on real end-user devices.

1 Introduction

The days are numbered where we used our mobile phones exclusively for telephone conversation. Today we have access to thousands of different applications and services for our mobile companions and their number is rapidly growing. Although the devices have stopped getting smaller and smaller, we see ourselves confronted with a limited user interface consisting of tiny keys and a miniature display, which suffices for making phone calls, but which is unsuited to control applications. The most promising answer to this challenge is the use of speech recognition.

If we take a glance at modern mobile phones, we indeed discover basic speech recognition functionality: most mobile devices on the market support voice control such as voice dialling or hands-free commands for Bluetooth headsets. Instead of searching names in the telephone book, the user can dictate the name of a person he wants to call or, on some devices, use a voice command to launch a certain phone function.

Although this technology points out new ways to improved user interfaces on mobile phones, it still has several limitations:

- the number of recognizable words is very limited,
- the words have to be recorded by the user beforehand,
- the recognition system is speaker dependent.

Some recent devices spare the user the necessity to pre-record the commands and feature speaker-independent, embedded speech recognition. This functionality, however, is also restricted to a very limited quantity of words. With a growing

E. André et al. (Eds.): PIT 2008, LNAI 5078, pp. 145–155, 2008.

number of entries in the phone book, the recognition rate suffers severely due to built-in low-cost processors, limited storage and RAM. With this embedded strategy applications such as SMS dictation or the use of natural language are far out of reach in the next years. The most vividly discussed proposal to overcome this challenge is the principle of Distributed Speech Recognition. In this approach, the speech recognition process is separated into two parts: a *front-end* on the client-side and a *back-end* on the server-side.

The front-end extracts characteristic features out of the speech signal, whereas the back-end, making use of the language and acoustic models performs the computationally costly recognition.

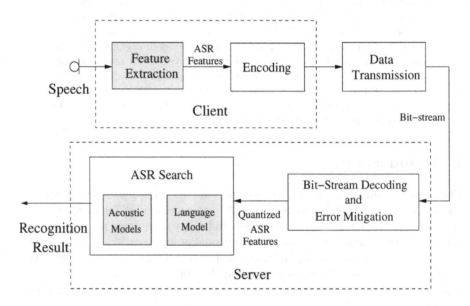

Fig. 1. Architecture of a client-server DSR system

Figure 1 shows a system architecture for DSR. The client captures the speech signal using a microphone and extracts features out of the signal. The features are compressed in order to obtain low data rates and transmitted to the server. At the server back-end, the features are decompressed and subject to the actual recognition process.

2   Related Work

While there have been a number of studies on theory of DSR, little research has been done on deploying of this technology to real mobile devices. Such in [Burileanu and Popescu, 2004] authors proposed a modified version of the widely-spread ETSI FE-standard for DSR, implemented as a hardware-based front-end solution for a Motorola Digital Signal Processor (DSP). A software-based implementation of the ETSI AFE-standard for PDAs using Sphinx-4 as speech recognizer in the back-end is presented in [Xu et al., 2005]. In this approach, the client has been deployed in ANSI C requiring Windows CE as operating system.

In contrast to these works, we are focusing on software-based solutions for the less powerful devices, the mobile phones. In former work, we proposed a DSR front-end for Java-enabled mobile phones [Zaykovskiy and Schmitt, 2007] and came up with a fully Java-based architecture for speech-enabled information services for mobile phones, using the example of a public transport information system [Zaykovskiy et al., 2007].

3   ETSI Standards for DSR Front-Ends

As mentioned previously, the speech recognition process in DSR is distributed between the client and the server. In order to enable a unified communication between DSR clients and DSR servers certain standards are needed. Namely, both parties have to assume the same procedure for feature extraction, the same feature compression algorithm and the same format for the bit-stream.

Four standards specifying the above issues were developed under the auspices of the European Telecommunications Standards Institute (ETSI), see Table 1.

Table 1. Overview of ETSI standards for DSR front-ends

		Noise robustness	
		basic	advanced
Speech recon-struction possible	no	**FE** [ets, 2000] ES 201 108	**AFE** [ets, 2002] ES 202 050
	yes	**xFE** [ets, 2003b] ES 202 211	**xAFE** [ets, 2003a] ES 202 212

The first standard for DSR, the front-end ES 201 108 [ets, 2000], has been published by ETSI in year 2000. This is a basic version of a front-end, let us refer to it as **FE**. The standard specifies a feature extraction scheme based on the widely used mel frequency cepstral coefficients (MFCC). It consists of the following components (see Figure 2):

- an algorithm for creating mel-cepstrum coefficients,
- an algorithm for feature compression,
- a mechanism for error protection and bit-stream generation and
- an algorithm for decoding the bit-stream on the server-side.

In the cepstrum calculation module the speech signal in 8kHz 16 bit/sample PCM format is sent frame by frame through the different processing steps. These include the compensation of the constant level offset, the pre-emphasis of high frequency components, the calculation of the spectrum magnitude, the bank of mel-scale filters, the logarithmic transform and finally the calculation of the discrete cosine transform. Altogether for a single frame this results in a 14-dimensional feature vector consisting of 13 cepstral coefficients and an energy value of the frame.

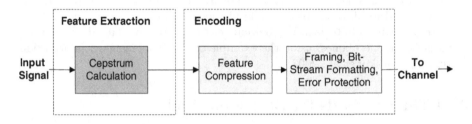

Fig. 2. Block scheme of the basic front-end (FE), ES 201 108

The front-end operates at a bit rate of 4800 bit/s. In order to obtain this bit-rate the feature vectors are compressed. For the feature compression all ETSI DSR standards use the split vector quantization (VQ) approach, which works as follows. First, all the components of the 14-dimensional feature vector are grouped in pairs. For each pair the closest entry from the predefined lookup table (code-book) is determined by using weighted Euclidean distance. By this all the pairs are replaced by the corresponding code-book indices. Later the indices of 24 frames are combined together as 144 bytes multi-frame packages, in order to reduce transmission overhead.

The FE front-end is known to perform inadequately under more demanding background noise conditions such as subway or car environments. Thus, a noise robust version of the front-end has been conformed in 2002. This version is called Advanced Front-End (**AFE**) and was published as ETSI standard document ES 202 050 [ets, 2002]. On the connected digits recognition task the AFE front-end provides a 53% reduction in error rates compared to the FE standard [Macho et al., 2002].

Figure 3 shows a block diagram of the AFE front-end. As we can see, some additional modules have been introduced in order to improve the recognition rates. These are: Wiener filter based noise reduction, waveform processing improving the overall SNR, and blind equalization for compensating the convolutional distortion. Additionally a voice activity detection block (VAD) has been introduced. The core feature extraction module, the calculation of the cepstral coefficients, remains the same as it was in the FE standard. The only difference in both implementations, which we observed in practice, is that the Fourier transform of the AFE cepstrum calculation also incorporates a certain high-pass filtering [Zaykovskiy and Schmitt, 2007].

In 2003 both standards have been enriched to the extended versions ES 202 211 (**xFE**) [ets, 2003b] and ES 202 212 (**xAFE**)[ets, 2003a] allowing for the cost of

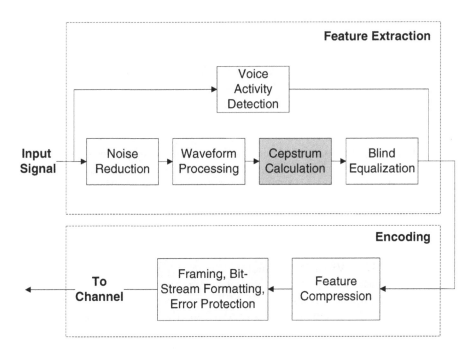

Fig. 3. Block scheme of the advanced front-end (AFE), ES 202 050

additional 800 bit/s a reconstruction of the intelligible speech signal out of the feature stream.

ETSI provides publicly available ANSI C implementations for all four standards. Moreover, for the xAFE front-end there is also a standardized C realization TS 126 243 [ets, 2004] using only fixed-point arithmetic (**xAFE-FP**).

4   Implementation Issues

Conforming to the ETSI standards, we present front-end implementations for the by far most widest spread platforms for mobile phones: Java ME and Symbian. We point out problems that occurred during development and show how to take hurdles appearing in the deployment process.

4.1   Java Mobile Edition

Our first approach towards a speech recognition front-end for mobile phones is based on ETSI's ANSI C reference implementation of FE, and is implemented in Java ME, formerly known as J2ME. Although Java, especially its Micro Edition realization, is meant to be a slow language, we proved that Java-based feature extraction on today's mobile phones is possible within real-time [Zaykovskiy and Schmitt, 2007]. Now what reasons argue for Java when it is considered as 'slow'? Most mobile phones are shipped with proprietary operating systems, enabling developers to provide only Java applications for such devices. Consequently Java is the widest spread technology on today's mobile phone market and experiences a tremendous extension. Sun stated already in June 2005, that more than 708 million Java-enabled handsets have been shipped, and thus outnumbering Java installations on PCs. For deploying applications on *consumer* mobile phones there is no other choice than Java. We had to go over several hindrances on our way to a Java front-end:

Missing functions. Since small devices are very limited in processor speed and memory, the Java ME platform abandons several mechanisms and classes being part of the Java Standard Edition for desktop PCs. Neither generics are supported, nor the sophisticated Collections framework or basic mathematical functions like *java.math.log()* or *java.math.pow()*. The missing log- and pow-function have to be programmed from scratch.

Mobile Media API. Virtually all mobile phones on the market support Java multimedia functions, being implemented within the *Java Mobile Media API* (MMAPI). The implementation of this API, however, differs from manufacturer to manufacturer. Although the Java standard for the MMAPI demands a support for capturing uncompressed PCM-files from the devices microphone, not all manufacturers ship their devices with this capability; e.g. SonyEricsson provides only capturing of compressed AMR-audio within Java, which is worthless for reliable feature extraction. The MMAPI implementations of Nokia Series 60 devices turned out to be reliable.

Multithreading. For achieving low memory consumption on the heap, we propose a front-end design being capable of running in single threading as well as in multithreading mode, i.e. that the feature extraction and the vector quantization modules can either be launched sequentially or in parallel. The first alternative requires more memory, since the extracted features have to be buffered before the VQ is launched, which can be crucial regarding larger utterances. The multithreading version should be set-up as producer-consumer pattern. The feature extraction thread creates features that the quantizer thread consumes by compressing it. This results in slightly slower processing times compared to single threading mode. Details will follow in Section 5. The advantage, however, is that the length of the utterance can be disregarded, since the calculation is processed on-the-fly and thus only a very small buffer has to be allocated.

Security. Capturing the user's voice on a mobile phone is a security critical operation. Thus, launching the capture process within Java causes the mobile phone to prompt for authorization. The same is true for network access. By signing the front-end before deployment with a certificate and by that, making the program a "trusted" one, this behavior can be prevented. Signing allows tracing back the author of potential malicious code. Such code signing certificates can be obtained from Certificate Authorities such as Thawte, VeriSign etc.

Fixed-point Arithmetic. Newer versions of Java ME (since CLDC 1.1) allow the use of floating point numbers by offering the data type *float*. Floating-point operations on phones lacking a *Floating Point Unit* (FPU), however, are computationally extremely costly, since they are software-emulated thwarting out each front-end implementation. Since most mobile phones are lacking an FPU, we highly recommend deploying a front-end being based on fixed-point instead of floating-point arithmetic. There, real numbers are simulated with other data types like *integer* or *char*. The radix point is imaginary and separates the available bits of the data type into an integer and a fractional part.

Regarding the DSR front-ends, the entire algorithm has to be redesigned in order to switch from the floating point arithmetic to the fixed-point one. The ETSI AFE-standard comes with a fixed-point implementation that can be converted with limited effort into a fixed-point based FE-standard.

4.2 Symbian C++

Being designed for the mass market, the mobile phone manufacturers equip their consumer phones with proprietary operating systems. By contrast, the more elaborated smartphones targeting on business clientele are mostly shipped with Symbian OS, a more powerful and flexible operating system.

On this platform, we are enabled to develop not only in Java, but also in C++, Python and Flash Lite. Since C++ programs can be considered as fastest ones in this environment, we ported the noise-robust floating point AFE-standard to Symbian C++. The existing ANSI C implementations from ETSI make a rapid, straight-forward porting possible, so there are less hurdles to clear:

Different functions. Generally the ANSI C commands are the same under Symbian C++. However, there are a few differences: e.g. memory operations are not performed with alloc(), calloc() and free(), but with User::Alloc(), User::AllocZ() and User::Free() respectively.

Security. Within Symbian, security issues are similarly treated as in Java. Whereas Java asks the user to confirm a security critical operation when the application is unsigned, Symbian C++ applications generally crash without warning. Consequently, signing the application with a code signing certificate before deploying is a prerequisite for a successful execution of the front-end.

Multithreading. Although Symban C++ supports multithreading, its use is not mandatory in the front-end task. Data generated by the feature-extraction part can be stored temporarily on the device's permanent storage before vector quantization carries over with the compression. In contrast to Java, where the possibility to access the storage medium depends on the manufacturer, every Symbian phone provides direct disk access. In our implementation we do without multithreading and use the storage between both processes, which turned out to be sufficiently fast.

5 Practical Evaluation

Due to the integration on the lower system level, Symbian C++ offers a certain gain in execution speed compared to Java ME. Hence it can cope with computationally more demanding tasks like noise reduction. That is why we can afford the deployment of the AFE standard to Symbian platform. Contrary, the Java ME applications are run within a virtual machine on a higher system level. Consequently the only realistic standard for this platform is the basic FE front-end.

In the following we present the results of the experiments with real mobile phones regarding the recognition accuracy and time efficiency.

In order to guarantee the correctness of the front-end implementations we have conducted a number of tests recognizing English connected digits. With "clean-condition" settings [Hirsch and Pearce, 2000] we have trained the Sphinx-4 recognizer using the features computed by the original ETSI FE and AFE front-ends. These two acoustic models have been used with the different front-ends to recognize data with subway noise from test set A. The recognition accuracy is shown in Figure 4.

Here, from the first two bars we can conclude that the Java ME floating point implementation and the original ANSI C version of the FE front-end show as good as identical accuracy over all the noise levels. The same holds true for the Symbian C++ and ANSI C implementations of the AFE standard, cf. last two bars. It means that rounding errors, which are especially significant in the case of AFE, do not lead to a variation in performance. Also it is observable that AFE is much more robust against background noise than the FE front-end.

The performance of our Java ME FE-FP front-end (third bar in Figure 4) deserves some explanations. Since there is no standardized fixed-point implementation of the basic FE front-end, we had to use the cepstrum calculation module of the advanced xAFE-FP standard to realize FE-FP. As it was mentioned, the Fourier transform of the AFE front-end incorporates a high-pass filtering. This finally results in varied MFCCs in FE and our FE-FP implementations. The above difference in cepstral coefficients can be compensated by the simple scaling of the cepstrum (similarly as it is done in the blind equalization module [Mauuary, 1998]). The scaling factors were found by minimizing the least mean square error computed as a difference between the original FE and FE-FP cepstra, see [Zaykovskiy and Schmitt, 2007] for details. The high-pass filtering together with the cepstral compensation constitute the computationally inexpensive, yet efficient solution to the noise robustness problem.

The real-time efficiency (time needed for the processing of one second of speech) for the Java ME platform is given in Table 2. It is noted that the use of fixed-point arithmetic can provide a two to four times acceleration making real-time feature extraction possible. It is also noted that the operation in multi-threaded mode on average requires just 13% of additional time.

Table 3 shows the efficiency of the AFE front-end with and without quantization. As we can see none of the tested devices was able to perform the advanced feature extraction within real-time.

Table 2. Real-time efficiency of feature extraction (FE only) and compression (FE+Q) in Java ME. ST and MT stand for the single- and multi-threaded feature compression.

Name of device	Alg.	FE only	FE+Q	
			ST	MT
PDA Dell	Float	1.0	1.4	1.5
Axim X51v	Fixed	0.4	0.5	0.6
Nokia	Float	1.3	1.8	2.0
E70, 6630	Fixed	0.7	0.9	1.4
Nokia	Float	1.2	1.6	1.7
7370	Fixed	2.7	3.7	3.8
Siemens	Float	3.1	4.4	5.0
CX65, CX75	Fixed	2.1	2.7	3.8
Nokia	Float	1.3	1.8	2.1
7390	Fixed	1.6	2.2	2.3
Nokia	Float	1.1	1.5	1.5
6136, 6280, 6234	Fixed	2.2	3.0	3.1
Sony-Ericsson	Float	7.9	12.5	13.4
W810i	Fixed	2.0	2.9	3.1

Table 3. Real-time efficiency for Symbian C++ implementation of the AFE front-end

	Nokia N93	Nokia N71	Nokia E70
AFE	1.35	2.01	2.08
AFE+Q	1.48	2.22	2.28

Table 4. Detailed real-time efficiency of Symbian C++ AFE compared with Windows CE implementation on H5550 HP iPAQ PDA [Xu et al., 2005]

Device	NS	WP	CC	BE	VAD	Total
Nokia E70	1.46	0.12	0.52	<0.01	<0.01	2.08
PDA [Xu et al., 2005]	2.9	0.14	0.95	<0.01	<0.01	3.98

The time required by the major components of AFE (noise suppression, waveform processing, cepstral calculation, blind equalization and VAD) is given in Table 4. It is evident that the noise reduction accounts for nearly 75% of the overall processing time. Comparing the time needed for cepstral processing alone (0.52) and FE feature extraction (1.3) in Java ME on a Nokia E70 we observe that the migration from Java ME to Symbian C++ brings a 2.5-fold acceleration. Similarly, a two-fold gain is observed comparing the Symbian C++ and Windows CE implementations, cf. Table 4.

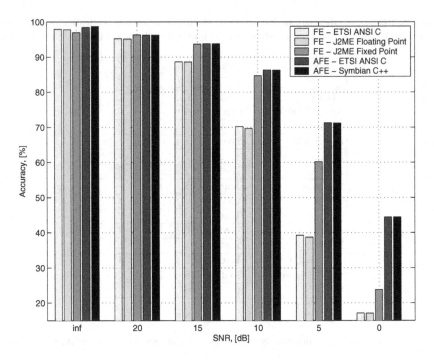

Fig. 4. Recognition accuracy with different implementations of the FE and AFE front-ends

6   Conclusions

In this paper we presented guidelines for the successful deployment of DSR front-ends on mobile phones using open platforms. We addressed both, consumer mobile phones and smartphones by presenting the appropriate front-end implementations based on the two most widely spread technologies: Java ME and Symbian C++.

The results of the experiments carried out with real handhelds provide the basis for the comparative analysis of a performance over different operating systems, standards and devices.

As future work we consider the implementation and evaluation of the fixed-point version of the AFE standard in Symbian C++.

Acknowledgement

We would like to thank the following students for the contribution in the presented research project: Wenbin Li, Ming Sun, Ali Khairat, and Helmut Lang.

References

[ets, 2000] Speech Processing, Transmission and Quality Aspects (STQ); Distributed Speech Recognition; Front-end Feature Extraction Algorithm; Compression Algorithm. ETSI Standard ES 201 108 (2000)

[ets, 2002] Speech Processing, Transmission and Quality Aspects (STQ); Distributed Speech Recognition; Advanced Front-end Feature Extraction Algorithm; Compression Algorithm. ETSI Standard ES 202 050 (2002)

[ets, 2003a] Distributed Speech Recognition; Extended Advanced Front-end Feature Extraction Algorithm; Compression Algorithm, Back-end Speech Reconstruction Algorithm. ETSI Standard ES 202 212 (2003a)

[ets, 2003b] Distributed Speech Recognition; Extended Front-end Feature Extraction Algorithm; Compression Algorithm, Back-end Speech Reconstruction Algorithm. ETSI Standard ES 202 211 (2003b)

[ets, 2004] Digital cellular telecommunications system (Phase 2+); Universal Mobile Telecommunications System (UMTS); ANSI C code for the fixed-point distributed speech recognition extended advanced front-end. ETSI Technical Specification TS 126 243 (2004)

[Burileanu and Popescu, 2004] Burileanu, C., Popescu, V.: An efficient distributed speech recognition frontend implementation using a Motorola Star Core 140 based platform. In: Volume du Symposion International d'Electronique et Télécommunications, ETC 2004, University of Timisoara, Romania (2004)

[Hirsch and Pearce, 2000] Hirsch, H.-G., Pearce, D.: The AURORA experimental framework for the performance evaluation of speech recognition systems under noisy conditions. In: Proc. ISCA ITRW ASR2000, Paris, France, pp. 181–188 (2000)

[Macho et al., 2002] Macho, D., Mauuary, L., Noe, B., Cheng, Y., Eahey, D., Jouvet, D., Kelleher, H., Pearce, D., Saadoun, F.: Evaluation of a noise-robust DSR front-end on AURORA databases. In: Proc. ICSLP, pp. 17–20 (2002)

[Mauuary, 1998] Mauuary, L.: Blind equalization in the cepstral domain for robust telephone based speech recognition. In: Proc. EUSPICO 1998, pp. 359–363 (1998)

[Xu et al., 2005] Xu, H., Tan, Z.-H., Dalsgaard, P., Mattethat, R., Lindberg, B.: A configurable distributed speech recognition system. In: Proc. of the 9th European Conference on Speech Communication and Technology (2005)

[Zaykovskiy and Schmitt, 2007] Zaykovskiy, D., Schmitt, A.: Java (J2ME) front-end for distributed speech recognition. In: AINAW 2007: Proceedings of the 21st International Conference on Advanced Information Networking and Applications Workshops, pp. 353–357. IEEE Computer Society Press, Los Alamitos (2007)

[Zaykovskiy et al., 2007] Zaykovskiy, D., Schmitt, A., Lutz, M.: New Use of Mobile Phones: Towards Multimodal Information Access Systems. In: 3rd IET International Conference on Intelligent Environments, Ulm, Germany (2007)

Real-Time Recognition of Isolated Vowels

Mara Carvalho[1,2] and Aníbal Ferreira[1,2]

[1] Faculdade de Engenharia da Universidade do Porto, Rua Dr. Roberto Frias,
s/n 4200-465 Porto, Portugal
[2] Seegnal Research, TecMaia - MaiaDigital, sala 3, Rua Frederico Ulrich,
nº 2650, 4470-605 Moreira da Maia, Portugal
mara.carvalho@seegnal.pt, anibal.ferreira@seegnal.pt

Abstract. In this paper we present a new approach to the problem of isolated vowel recognition in real-time. Language learning and speech therapy are examples of application areas that require real-time biofeedback of acoustic features. As the performance of known approaches usually drops for child speakers, we evaluated different alternatives of feature extraction and pattern recognition techniques, including PCA, LDA, ANN and Bayesian classification. In addition, we studied the explicit inclusion of pitch as a main parameter in both simulation and the real-time feature extraction process. Best results were obtained with our dataset when MFCCs are mapped, using LDA, to a 4-dimensional subspace that is followed by Bayesian classification. An interactive game was designed that implements the selected real-time vowel recognition technique.

1 Introduction

Over the last years, major advances were made in the speech recognition area. Although one may think that the isolated vowel recognition is a simple problem in this context, that assumption is far from true. The lack of contextual information makes this a complex and still unsolved problem: only by correctly identifying the unique characteristics of each sound it is possible to effectively identify a vowel. Areas such as speech recognition and language learning urge for solutions to this problem. The use of an automatic system, capable of correctly identifying which vowel is uttered is a major advance in these fields, since that allows to reinforce the natural feedback provided by the auditory system with an objective visual feedback on a computer screen.

Children represent the target audience in this context. Some lack of motivation arising from traditional training methods also contributes to make them the most eager audience to solutions that rely on new technologies. Interactive computer games have shown a significant success in this area. In fact, the attractive visual feedback motivates children to train more often, and the immediate observation of the effects of a correct production helps them to be aware of their real improvement.

However, the real-time requirement brings extra difficulties to this task since the allowed latency between input and output is very small (about 30 ms as

E. André et al. (Eds.): PIT 2008, LNAI 5078, pp. 156–167, 2008.
© Springer-Verlag Berlin Heidelberg 2008

this is usually considered as the maximum acceptable delay in the lip sync problem [Escobar and Partridge, 1994]) and must be commensurate with human perception.

There are some applications that pursue this goal, examples are *VATA (Vowel Articulation Training Aid)* [Zimmer, 2002], *OLTK (Optical Logo-Therapy Kit)* [Hatzis, 1999], *Jogos Fonoarticulatórios* [de Lima Araújo, 2000]. They all have limitations, and do not provide the desired robust method for real-time identification of vowels.

The most traditional way of building a vowel recognizer relies on the estimation of the first three formants using the short-time Fourier spectrum from the speech signal. However, this technique provides solutions "very reliable and robust for male speakers, but not for female or child speakers" ([Ferreira, 2005]).

VATA is one of the most remarkable efforts in developing an interactive application controlled by the articulation of vowels. It presents not only 2D vowel displays but also interactive games controlled by vowel sounds. Over the years, several improvements have been made to this application (the last version is dated of 2006). VATA uses DCTCs (Discrete Cosine Transform Coefficients) which are mapped to 2D vowel areas using Artificial Neural Networks (ANNs). These are based on a feedforward MLP (Multi-Layer Perceptron) with one hidden layer, and are trained using a backpropagation algorithm. Neural Networks are mainly affected by the size of the training set and the number of nodes in the hidden layer. In [Zimmer, 2002] results are presented regarding several experiments using a 400-speakers database. This database is approximately equally divided between adult men, adult women and children. In the first test stage, datasets with only male speakers, only female speakers, and both male and female speakers were used. The best classification rates obtained were slightly above 90% for male speakers only, and slightly above 80% for both female speakers and the mixed dataset. No similar test results (for training or testing sets alone) regarding the child database alone are shown. However, the authors also tested their methodology using all available samples for training the MLP. The results obtained were 89.99% of recognition rate for male speakers, 87.33% for female speakers, 83.33% for child speakers and 84.96% when combining all the samples.

OLTK is an interactive tool designed to build a 2D visual display of vowels, and thus allowing the visualization of the distance between the current utterance and the intended one. In this approach 9 cepstral coefficients are obtained from the input sounds, and then mapped to a 2D space by means of an ANN.

In our work, the purpose is to build a robust real-time vowel classifier for 5 of the 8 oral vowels in the European Portuguese: /a/, /e/, /i/, /o/, /u/. The use of such a reduced set of vowels is related to the target audience of such an application: the training of vowel production by young children(i.e., up to about 7 years old) must be simplified, in order to avoid an excessive complexity and in order to avoid the child giving up the training. The classifier will later be integrated in an interactive computer game, providing a training environment for children.

The remainder of this paper is structured as follows. Section 2 presents the methodology used in the development of the classifier. A general pattern recognition scheme was followed, and each one of its steps is detailed in this section. In section 3, we present both the simulation and the real-time test results. Section 4 describes the real-time game that has been implemented, and in Section 5 we present the main conclusions.

2   Methodology

The isolated vowel recognition problem can be seen as a specific pattern recognition problem: our aim is to identify a sound as one of the 5 selected vowels. The basic process flow in pattern recognition is divided in two main steps: Feature Analysis and Pattern Classification. The first step can be further divided in two steps: Parameter Extraction and Feature Extraction.

2.1   Parameter Extraction

The purpose of the Parameter Extraction step is to obtain information from the input data that is relevant to the classification process. In our context, the input data consists of frames of PCM audio samples taken from a continuous sound source. The representation of a sound signal can be made in many different ways. For the particular problem of isolated vowel recognition, linear prediction (LP) techniques are commonly used. However, these techniques perform satisfactory when the fundamental frequency (F0) is significantly lower than the frequency of the first formant. When that is not the case (namely in the case of women or child speech), LP techniques fail [Blandon, 1982]; [Zahorian and Jagharghi, 1993]. As child speech is the main target in our research and application scenario (interactive computer game), the use of such a traditional approach seems of little use.

Mel-Frequency Cepstral Coefficients (MFCC) are widely used in the speech recognition area. These coefficients represent an audio signal using the mel scale, which approximates the response of the human auditory system regarding frequency organization and intelligibility. Additionally, these are noise-robust features. Those reasons led us to chose to use these coefficients in our work. However, MFCC are known to discard some signal characteristics that are important in the context of vowel recognition, namely, the pitch. Vowels have different intrinsic pitches [Whalen and Levitt, 1995], so this is also a discriminatory characteristic that was added to our parameter vector.

2.2   Feature Extraction and Dimensionality Reduction

The second step in the Feature Analysis procedure is the Feature Extraction. The Feature Extraction has the purpose of seeking, among the different parameters obtained from the input signal, distinctive features that allow a reliable classification of each input sound. Ideally, it discards the input parameters that bring no additional distinctive information to the problem. This step also reduces the dimensionality of the input set of parameters, by making combinations of several parameters. For practical reasons, it is impossible to find an ideal feature extractor, and some kind of compromise has to be reached: we will definitively lose some information, but the new features should be capable of identifying each isolated sound as belonging to a certain class. The feature extraction step has also the advantage of allowing a significant dimensionality reduction, as it does the mapping of the data to a lower dimensional space, in which each one of the dimensions is perceptually relevant and thus actively responsible for improving the separation between the different classes. This should be seen as an advantage, as it reduces the size of the vector that the classifier will have to process to obtain a result (which is good for real-time operation). There are many dimensionality reduction techniques: the most traditional are the linear ones - Principal Component Analysis (PCA) and Linear Discriminant Analysis (LDA). There are also many non-linear techniques that can be more effective than the former, namely for highly non-linear data [van der Maaten, 2007]. Additionally, linear techniques are very interesting as they allow simple calculations, which facilitates real-time operation.

PCA (or Karhunen-Loève Transform). With this technique the lower dimensional representation of the data is obtained by maximizing the resulting variance of the data.

Given n samples of a multidimensional data vector $\mathbf{X} = [\mathbf{x}_1, \ldots, \mathbf{x}_n]$, one can define the scatter matrix S (see Equation 1).

$$S = \sum_{k=1}^{n} (\mathbf{x}_k - \mathbf{m})(\mathbf{x}_k - \mathbf{m})^t \qquad (1)$$

In Equation 1, $\mathbf{x}_k$ represents each of the samples, and $\mathbf{m}$ the mean of all the samples.

It can be proven [Duda et al., 2001] that the direction where the dispersion is higher (and hence the squared-error is minimized) is the one given by the eigenvector corresponding to the higher eigenvalue of the scatter matrix. Generalizing this result, a mapping in a subspace with k dimensions is achieved by making a linear transformation using the k eigenvectors matching the k higher eigenvalues of the scatter matrix, which are hence called principal components.

LDA (or Fisher Mapping). The former mapping (PCA) gives rise to components that are useful for data representation, but has no concerns in whether these components are suitable for discriminating the different classes.

The LDA approach tries to project the data in directions such that the different classes are well-separated. To achieve this goal, one can maximize the Fisher's criterion ($\mathbf{J}_w$, see Equation 4), that basically states that the between-class scatter ($\mathbf{S}_B$, see Equation 3) should be maximized as the within-class scatter ($\mathbf{S}_w$, see Equation 2) is minimized [Duda et al., 2001].

$$\mathbf{S}_w = \sum_{i=1}^{c} \sum_{\mathbf{x} \in \mathbf{W}_i} (\mathbf{x} - \mathbf{m}_i)(\mathbf{x} - \mathbf{m}_i)^t \qquad (2)$$

$$\mathbf{S}_B = \sum_{i=1}^{c} n_i (\mathbf{m}_i - \mathbf{m})(\mathbf{m}_i - \mathbf{m})^t \qquad (3)$$

$$\mathbf{J}_w = \frac{\mathbf{T}^t \mathbf{S}_B \mathbf{T}}{\mathbf{T}^t \mathbf{S}_w \mathbf{T}} \qquad (4)$$

In these equations, c represents the number of classes, $\mathbf{w}_i$ represents class i, $\mathbf{x}$ represents each sample, $\mathbf{m}_i$ is the mean of the samples belonging to class i, n_i is the number of samples belonging to class i, $\mathbf{m}$ is the total mean vector and $\mathbf{T}$ is the transformation matrix.

The second approach (LDA) has the advantage of using the training data labels to improve the quality of the mapping (i.e., it is a supervised technique). This is definitely an improvement over the first technique (PCA), but also requires the training set to be a good representation of the total data.

Among all the common non-linear techniques, the most used is the artificial neural network (ANN). This is a very powerful technique that is commonly used in the area of sound identification. One of the reasons of this popularity is the fact that a 3-layer (input layer, hidden layer and output layer) neural network can theoretically approximate any function [Duda et al., 2001]. In an ANN, every node generates an output by making combinations of its inputs. To each input, a different scaling factor and a different bias are applied. These weights and mappings are obtained from the training process of the network. However, this is in fact a non-linear technique, where much of the behavior escapes from human control and understanding - it works like a black box. Additionally, the linear techniques are much easier to apply to a real-time framework, as they simply require matrix multiplication operations. Nevertheless, solutions using ANNs were evaluated during our research. Table 1 shows the error rates obtained by applying bayesian classifiers to the data resulting of the 2-dimensional mapping of 12 MFCCs. First, four mapping techniques were used to achieve the 2-dimensional mapping, namely ANNs, PCA and LDA. Secondly, two bayesian classifiers were trained to perform the classification task: LDC (linear discriminant classifier) and QDC (quadratic discriminant classifier). The results show that no significant differences exist between the error rates obtained by mappings using ANNs and linear techniques. On the other hand, the use of ANNs results in a significant increase in the complexity of the real-time implementation. Therefore, the approach using ANNs was not pursued. Furthermore, previous works in this area [Wang and Paliwal, 2003] show no relevant improvements in the vowel recognition task when using more complex (and hence less capable of being used in real-time operation) mappings, including SVM (Support Vector Machines).

Table 1. Comparison of the error rates for several extraction techniques (ANN, PCA and LDA) and several pattern recognition techniques (LDC and QDC)

	ANN	PCA	LDA
LDC	9.83%	9.21%	10.44%
QDC	9.47%	10.50%	10.33%

2.3   Pattern Classification

Once the feature extraction step is completed, the classification of the resulting patterns is the final step in our classifier design.

Bayesian Classifiers are one of the most simple kind of classifiers. The Bayesian Decision Theory is a statistical approach to the pattern recognition problem [Duda et al., 2001]. These classifiers are based on the computation of the posterior probabilities, for each class. According to the Bayes formula (Equation 5), the posterior probabilities can be calculated from the prior probabilities and the class conditional probabilities [Duda et al., 2001].

$$P(w_j|\mathbf{x}) = \frac{p(\mathbf{x}|w_j)P(w_j)}{p(\mathbf{x})} \tag{5}$$

In this equation, w_j represents class j and $\mathbf{x}$ represents the current sample. $P(w_j|\mathbf{x})$ represents the conditional probability that the class is w_j given that the object is $\mathbf{x}$, $P(w_j)$ is the probability of the occurrence of class w_j and $p(\mathbf{x})$ the probability of occurrence of sample $\mathbf{x}$. In order to achieve a decision, one has to decide to which class a certain sample belongs. Defining discriminant functions $(g_i(\mathbf{x}))$ as the posterior probabilities $P(w_i|\mathbf{x})$, it is straightforward that for minimizing the average probability of error we should choose the class based on the following rule (w_i denotes class i):

$$\mathbf{x} \in w_i \Rightarrow g_i(\mathbf{x}) > g_j(\mathbf{x}) \qquad \forall j \neq i. \tag{6}$$

Developing a classifier basically consists in defining the set of discriminant functions. According to the assumptions made, different discriminant functions may be devised. In this work, two functions were considered. Thus, two different bayesian classifiers were used.

Linear discriminant classifier: Assumes that the covariance of each class is equal.

$$g_i(\mathbf{x}) = -\frac{1}{2\sigma^2}[\mathbf{x}^t\mathbf{x} - 2\mathbf{m}_i^t\mathbf{x} + \mathbf{m}_i^t\mathbf{m}_i] + \ln P(w_i) \tag{7}$$

where σ is the standard deviation and $\mathbf{m}_i$ is the mean of class i.

Quadratic discriminant classifier: Assumes that the covariance matrixes are different for each category. The surfaces delimiting each class space are hyperquadrics [Duda et al., 2001].

$$g_i(\mathbf{x}) = \mathbf{x}^t\mathbf{W}_i\mathbf{x} + \mathbf{w}_i^t\mathbf{x} + w_{i0} \tag{8}$$

where

$$\mathbf{W}_i = -\frac{1}{2}\Sigma_i^{-1} \tag{9}$$

$$\mathbf{w}_i = \Sigma_i^{-1}\mathbf{m}_i \tag{10}$$

$$w_{i0} = -\frac{1}{2}\mathbf{m}_i^t\Sigma_i^{-1}\mathbf{m}_i - \frac{1}{2}\ln|\Sigma_i| + \ln P(w_i) \tag{11}$$

$$\Sigma = \mathbf{E}[(\mathbf{x} - \mathbf{m})(\mathbf{x} - \mathbf{m})^t] \tag{12}$$

In these equations, Σ_i represents the covariance of class i, defined in Equation 12, $\mathbf{E}[]$ denotes the expected value, and $\mathbf{m}_i$ is the mean of class i.

In our particular problem, we can assume that the prior probabilities are equal for the 5 classes (i.e., there is equal probability in uttering each one of the vowels). As for the class conditional probabilities, we have to use the estimation obtained from the training set. It is thus extremely important that the training set correctly characterizes the global data. Once the computation of the parameters (based on the training dataset) is completed, the classification is done simply by calculating the value of the discriminating functions and selecting the class corresponding to the higher value.

3   Results

Several approaches were tested using the basic methodology described. As mentioned above, for simplicity reasons and real-time constraints, we focused on the use of bayesian classifiers, and linear mappings.

First, the training and test sets were defined. The database used in this work consists of 220 files, each one having a duration of 400ms, sampled at a frequency of 32000 Hz. Each file corresponds to a vowel utterance by a specific speaker. A total of 44 speakers (27 children, 11 female and 6 male) contributed to this database [Ferreira, 2007]. The utterances were obtained in a quiet environment, using a simple laptop with an electret microphone with good frequency response between 50 and 8000 Hz. The sampling frequency was set to 32000 Hz. For our dataset, we used each one of the frames obtained in each file as a different sample (hence using a total of 5060 samples). When dividing the training and test datasets, however, we were careful in order to avoid that samples belonging to the same speaker were present in the two datasets. The training dataset has a total of 70% of the total samples, consisting of the parameters obtained for each one of the frames of 19 child speakers, 8 female speakers and 4 male speakers. The remaining samples were used in the test dataset.

For each sample, the chosen parameters (MFCC and pitch) were calculated. Also, other sets of parameters extracted from the input data were tested, namely combinations using Linear Prediction Coefficients. However, the results achieved using these parameters were much worse than the ones obtained using MFCCs and pitch, and therefore are not presented in the current paper.

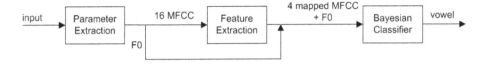

Fig. 1. Classifier developed

Our general classifier is represented in Fig. 1. This classifier was selected after testing different alternatives. We tested four different combinations of mappings/features, as described next.

The choice of using 4 mapped features was not random: for LDA, this is in fact the maximum number of dimensions allowed (corresponding to $c - 1$, where c is the number of classes - 5). Experiments further reducing the number of dimensions tend to yield worse results. As for PCA, experiments using different numbers of mapping dimensions have shown that there are no effective benefits in keeping more than 4 dimensions. In fact, although keeping more than 4 dimensions might result in a slightly smaller error rate, the corresponding increase in complexity of the problem is not justifiable.

Scenario 1: From the 16 MFCC coefficients existing in the parameter vector, we used LDA to achieve a mapping to a 4-dimensional subspace. To these 4 features we added the pitch. These 5 features were used by the bayesian classifiers to identify the current vowel.

Scenario 2: From the 16 MFCC coefficients existing in the parameter vector, we used LDA to achieve a mapping to a 4-dimensional subspace. These 4 features were used by the bayesian classifiers to identify the current vowel.

Scenario 3: From the 16 MFCC coefficients existing in the parameter vector, we used PCA to achieve a mapping to a 4-dimensional subspace. To these 4 features we added the pitch. These 5 features were used by the bayesian classifiers to identify the current vowel.

Scenario 4: From the 16 MFCC coefficients existing in the parameter vector, we used PCA to achieve a mapping to a 4-dimensional subspace. These 4 features were used by the bayesian classifiers to identify the current vowel.

3.1 Simulation Results

The four approaches described previously were primarily evaluated using Matlab. In this environment, we created the parameter vectors corresponding to the several samples (a total of 5060 samples were used, randomly separated in training and testing sets - 3645 were used for training , 1495 for test). Next, both the mappings and the classifiers were trained and tested. A cross-validation approach was used to obtain the results, by repeating this process 50 times. Table 2 presents the recognition rates obtained for the several approaches (corresponding to the average value of the 50 trials), for the linear and quadratic classifiers, respectively. It is visible the advantage of including pitch as a feature in the dataset, particularly for the quadratic classifier: the scenarios using this feature in addition to the MFCC-derived features yield better results. Also, and as expected, the results obtained with the quadratic classifier were superior, as this allows the definition of more complex discriminating functions. The overall results show an increase in the recognition rate when comparing to the reported 85% of positively biased results (with no separation between training and testing data) obtained by the VATA system [Zahorian et al., 2002].

Table 2. Comparison of recognition rates obtained

Method	Scenario 1	Scenario 2	Scenario 3	Scenario 4
LDC	94.59%	93.40%	92.92%	92.11%
QDC	96.01%	93.75%	95.97%	95.67%

3.2   Real-Time Results

The next step consisted in observing the real-time behavior of the developed classifier. With that purpose in mind, a C++ code implementing the linear mapping together with the bayesian classifiers was created. This code produces results on a frame-by-frame basis, using only the information contained in a very small segment of sound (about 16 ms long). This approach is necessary to obtain "immediate" results, i.e. the visual display changes must be seen by the user as a direct consequence of his/her change on the articulatory positions. Our informal and preliminary results are based on series of 6 tests for each approach, with one female speaker not included in the training dataset. In each test, the 5 vowels were uttered in sequence. The results were saved in a .txt file, and later the middle samples (corresponding to a sustained vowel utterance) were selected to calculate the statistics. The recognition rates obtained are presented in Table 3.These results must be seen as a simple indication of the real-time behavior of the system. Nearly 3000 samples were obtained from each test: a total of 12000 samples were considered for calculating the statistics for the LDC classifier, and 11890 for the QDC classifier.

3.3   Comparison of Results

In Table 3, the results obtained in the several tests are presented.

The results show that, contrarily to the simulation results, the behavior when using pitch as a feature is worse. In fact, Scenario 2 is the approach showing better results in real-time. Possible reasons for this fact may be estimation errors of the real-time algorithm when detecting pitch. Additionally, it should be noted that these results were obtained only for one speaker, and thus they are merely indications of the performance of our classifier. Although in some scenarios some degradation was observed between the real-time results and the simulation results, its extent is rather small. This is in fact a fairly good indication concerning the reliability of the linear mapping methods.

Table 3. Comparison of recognition rates obtained

Method	Scenario 1	Scenario 2	Scenario 3	Scenario 4
LDC Real-Time	93.93 %	96.43 %	89.37 %	92.30 %
LDC Simulation	94.59 %	93.40 %	92.92 %	92.11 %
QDC Real-Time	91.33 %	97.08 %	92.87 %	91.04 %
QDC Simulation	96.01 %	93.75 %	95.97 %	95.67 %

4   Real-Time Interactive Game

Interactive computer games are tools that have proven success in child motivation and training. As this is the main purpose of our work concerning visual feedback in vowel recognition, a simple car race game, completely controlled by the utterance of 5 different vowels, was developed in OpenGL.

In Figure 2, a screenshot of the game is shown. The child can hence train the vowel production as he/she plays an attractive game. The purpose of the game is to complete the circuit in the shortest amount of time.

Each of the 5 vowels match to one of controls: the continuous utterance of vowel /a/ results in the progressive increase of the car speed until a maximum speed is achieved. Vowel /i/ is responsible for slowing down the car till full stop.

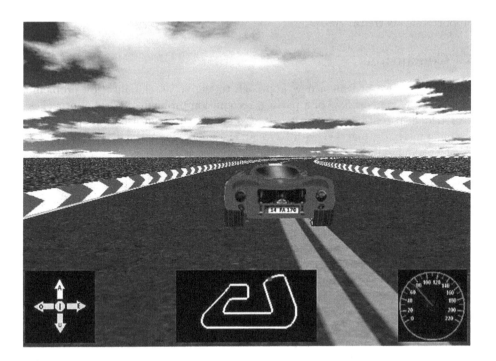

Fig. 2. Screenshot of the developed Application

Vowel /u/ allows driving the car in reverse gear, increasing the "negative" speed. However, if the car speed at this point is positive, the car will first decrease the speed until zero, and then acceleration in reverse gear starts. Vowels /o/ and /e/ allow to change the direction of the car movement (uttering /o/ makes the car turn left and /e/ makes it turn right) without changing the speed. To help the user understand the control, three auxiliary elements were added to the visual display: a graphical representation of each command (showing the effect of each utterance, as well as the currently identified vowel), a small representation of the entire circuit where the current position of the car is emphasized, and also a representation of the current car speed.

Abrupt changes in the uttered vowel may result in misclassification, but that problem is easily smoothed out with the introduction of a simple filtering step, that provides an output only if the results of the discriminant function corresponding to the identified class are significantly higher and thus more confident than the results obtained by the other discriminant functions.

The test results have shown that, after a few trials by a user, the game is easily controlled using only vowels, although some problems were identified in distinguish vowels /a/ and /o/. This problem is not unexpected, as these two vowels have very similar spectral envelopes. Also, some tests were made with speakers from different genders, and some weaknesses were revealed when male speakers tested the game. However, that is mainly due to the lack of sufficient representatives of this genre in the training set: as the purpose of this game is to serve children, we used mainly child speakers in the training database, as supported in [Ferreira, 2007].

5   Conclusions

In this paper, we present a new approach to the vowel classification problem. Following the general flow of a pattern recognition problem, several approaches were tested in real-time operation. It was shown that the use of simple linear mapping methods, together with bayesian classifiers allows the development of a satisfactory classifier. Also, the method developed is capable of being applied to other sets of characteristics extracted from the speech signal. Although MFCC are the most used state-of-the art features representing a speech signal, they also have many weaknesses. Hence, the application of the same method to alternative but more robust and representative features should yield better results.

A real-time interactive game has been designed and implemented that allows full control by means of the utterance of 5 isolated vowels. Although preliminary test results are encouraging concerning the playability and usefulness of the game, more tests are required to validate and improve user acceptance.

References

[Blandon, 1982] Blandon, R.W.: Arguments agains formants in the auditory representation of speech. The representation of Speech in the Peripheral Auditory System, 95–102 (1982) [de Lima Araújo, 2000] de Lima Araújo, A.M.: Jogos computacionais fonoarticu-latórios para crianças com deficiência auditiva. PhD thesis, Universidade Estadual de Campinas (in Portuguese) (2000)

[Duda et al., 2001] Duda, R.O., Hart, P.E., Stork, D.G.: Pattern classification, 2nd edn. Wiley Interscience, Chichester (2001)

[Escobar and Partridge, 1994] Escobar, J., Partridge, C.: Flow synchronization proto-col. IEEE/AXM Transactions on Networking 2, 111–121 (1994)

[Ferreira, 2005] Ferreira, A.J.S.: New signal features for robust identification of isolated vowels. In: InterSpeech 2005 (2005)

[Ferreira, 2007] Ferreira, A.J.S.: Static features in real-time recognition of isolated vow-els at high pitch. Journal of Acoustical Society of America 122, 2389–2404 (2007)

[Hatzis, 1999] Hatzis, A.: Optical Logo-Therapy (OLT): Computer-based audio-visual feedback using interactive visual displays for speech training. PhD thesis, Univer-sity of Sheffield (1999)

[van der Maaten, 2007] van der Maaten, L.J.P.: An introduction to dimensionality re-duction using matlab. Technical report, Universiteit Maastricht (2007)

[Wang and Paliwal, 2003] Wang, X., Paliwal, K.K.: Feature extraction and dimension-ality reduction algorithms and their applications in vowel recognition. Pattern Recognition 36, 2429–2439 (2003)

[Whalen and Levitt, 1995] Whalen, D.H., Levitt, A.G.: The universality of intrinsic f0 of vowels. Journal of Phonetics 23, 349–366 (1995)

[Zahorian and Jagharghi, 1993] Zahorian, S.A., Jagharghi, A.J.: Spectral-shape fea-tures versus formants as acoustic correlates for vowels. Journal of Acoustic Society of America 94, 1966–1982 (1993)

[Zahorian et al., 2002] Zahorian, S.A., Zimmer, A.M., Meng, F.: Vowel classification for computer-based visual feedback for speech training for the hearing impaired. International Conference on Spoken Language Processing 78, 973–976 (2002)

[Zimmer, 2002] Zimmer, A.M.: Vata: An improved personal computer based vowel articulation training aid. Master's thesis, Old Dominion University (2002)

Improving Robustness in Jacobian Adaptation for Noisy Speech Recognition

Yongjoo Jung

Department of Electronics, Keimyung University
Daegu, S. Korea

Abstract. A method to improve the robustness of the Jacobian adaptation (JA) is proposed. Although it is a usual idea that the reference hidden Markov model (HMM) in the JA is constructed by using the model composition methods like the parallel model combination (PMC), we propose to train the reference HMM directly with the noisy speech and then select the appropriate reference HMM based on the noise types and signal to noise ratio (SNR) values obtained from the input noisy speech. For the estimation of Jacobian matrices and other statistical information for the JA, a data driven method is employed during the training.

1 Introduction

In the model parameter compensation approaches based on the hidden Markov model (HMM), the HMM parameters are updated using the statistics of the noise signal in the testing speech (see [Gales, 1995], [Moreno, 1996], [Martin, 1992] and [Sagayama, Yamaguchi and Takahashi, 1997]). The Jacobian adaptation (JA) is known to be very useful when we have HMMs which have been trained in a similar condition as the target environment [Sagayama, Yamaguchi and Takahashi, 1997]. The trained (reference) HMM parameters can be easily adapted to the testing speech by using the Jacobian matrices. In the training session of JA, the reference HMM is usually constructed by the model combination methods like the PMC [Gales, 1995] or NOVO [Martin, 1992]. Those model composition approaches make it easy to associate the Jacobian matrix for each mixture component of the continuous density HMM with the mean vector of the clean speech HMM. However, it is well known that the composite HMM will not perform better than the HMM which has been trained directly with the noisy speech in the target environment. We think that the use of the composite HMM makes it difficult to for the JA method to outperform the PMC/NOVO despite its merit in the computational complexity. In a previous study, we found that the data-driven approach for the HMM parameter compensation was quite effective for the noisy speech recognition [Chung, 2005]. Motivated by the success, a data-driven JA method is proposed in this paper. In the method, the reference HMM is trained directly with the noisy speech. But, as this will make the relation between the Jacobian matrices and the clean speech HMM parameters obscure, the Jacobian matrices as well as other statistical information for the adaptation are estimated during the training along with the HMM parameters by using the Baum-Welch algorithm [Rabiner and Juang, 1993].

E. André et al. (Eds.): PIT 2008, LNAI 5078, pp. 168–175, 2008.

We also suggest to use the proposed adaptation algorithm in a multi-model structure using multiple reference HMM sets corresponding to the various Signal-to-Noise ratio (SNR) values and the noise types. By using the multiple reference HMM sets in recognition, the approximation errors occurring in the JA can be significantly reduced compared with the single reference HMM set, thus improving the recognition performance. In the next section, we explain in detail the improved JA method. And in section3, the multi-model speech recognition system combined with the model adaptation method is introduced. In section 4, the experimental results are explained and finally the conclusion is given in section 5.

2 Data-Driven Jacobian Adaptation

2.1 Data-Driven Jacobian Adaptation (D-JA)

In general, the noise-corrupted speech vector $\mathbf{y}$ in the cepstral domain is characterized by the following nonlinear equation.

$$\mathbf{y} = \mathbf{C}[\log\{\exp(\mathbf{C}^{-1}\mathbf{x}) + \exp(\mathbf{C}^{-1}\mathbf{n})\}] \tag{1}$$

$\mathbf{x}$ and $\mathbf{n}$ represents the clean speech and noise vector in the cepstral domain. $\mathbf{C}$ is the matrix representing the discrete cosine transformation (DCT).

In an HMM-based speech recognition, the HMM parameters are usually estimated by the Baum-Welch algorithm. For example, in the continuous density HMM, the re-estimation formula for the mean vector in the state j and mixture component k is as follows.

$$E(\mathbf{x}_t) = \frac{\displaystyle\sum_{t=1}^{T} \gamma_t(j,k)\mathbf{x}_t}{\displaystyle\sum_{t=1}^{T} \gamma_t(j,k)} \tag{2}$$

Here, $\gamma_t(j,k)$ is the probability of being in state j at time t with the k-th mixture component accounting for the cepstral feature vector $\mathbf{x}_t$.

When the noisy speech $\mathbf{y}_t$ is affected by the small changes in the cepstral noise vector $\mathbf{n}_t$, it can be expressed using the Jacobian matrix as follows.

$$\tilde{\mathbf{y}}_t = \mathbf{y}_t + \frac{\partial \mathbf{y}_t}{\partial \mathbf{n}_t}(\mathbf{n}_t - \tilde{\mathbf{n}}_t) \tag{3}$$

Based on Eq. (2) and (3), the mean vector of the noisy speech $\tilde{\mathbf{y}}_t$ can be written as follows.

$$E(\tilde{\mathbf{y}}_t) = \frac{\sum_{t=1}^{T} \gamma_t(j,k)(\mathbf{y}_t + \frac{\partial \mathbf{y}_t}{\partial \mathbf{n}_t}(\mathbf{n}_t - \tilde{\mathbf{n}}_t))}{\sum_{t=1}^{T} \gamma_t(j,k)} \tag{4}$$

If we make the assumption that the difference $\Delta \mathbf{n}(\equiv \mathbf{n}_t - \tilde{\mathbf{n}}_t)$ in the noise vectors can be substituted for its mean value (i.e., independent of the time), the above equation can be rewritten as follows.

$$E(\tilde{\mathbf{y}}_t) = \frac{\sum_{t=1}^{T} \gamma_t(j,k)\mathbf{y}_t}{\sum_{t=1}^{T} \gamma_t(j,k)} + \frac{\sum_{t=1}^{T} \gamma_t(j,k)\frac{\partial \mathbf{y}_t}{\partial \mathbf{n}_t}}{\sum_{t=1}^{T} \gamma_t(j,k)} \Delta \mathbf{n} \tag{5}$$

$$\boldsymbol{\mu}_{\tilde{\mathbf{y}}} = E(\mathbf{y}_t) + E(\frac{\partial \mathbf{y}_t}{\partial \mathbf{n}_t}) \Delta \mathbf{n} = \boldsymbol{\mu}_{\mathbf{y}} + \boldsymbol{\mu}_{\mathbf{J}} \Delta \mathbf{n} \tag{6}$$

$\boldsymbol{\mu}_{\mathbf{y}}$ is the mean vector of the reference HMM and $\boldsymbol{\mu}_{\mathbf{J}}$ is the estimated Jacobian matrix. $\Delta \mathbf{n}$ is obtained by finding the difference between the mean values of the reference noise and observed noise in the testing speech. After estimating $\boldsymbol{\mu}_{\mathbf{y}}$ and $\boldsymbol{\mu}_{\mathbf{J}}$ during the training, the adapted mean vector $\boldsymbol{\mu}_{\tilde{\mathbf{y}}}$ in Eq. (6) is calculated in recognition using the noise mean difference $\Delta \mathbf{n}$. The distinctive feature of the proposed method is that Jacobian matrix $\boldsymbol{\mu}_{\mathbf{J}}$ is estimated during the training along with the mean vector $\boldsymbol{\mu}_{\mathbf{y}}$ of the reference HMM. In a similar approach, the covariance matrix can be adapted by substituting Eq. (3) into the following equation.

$$\text{cov}(\tilde{\mathbf{y}}_t) = E\{(\tilde{\mathbf{y}}_t - \boldsymbol{\mu}_{\tilde{\mathbf{y}}})(\tilde{\mathbf{y}}_t - \boldsymbol{\mu}_{\tilde{\mathbf{y}}})^T\}$$

$$= \frac{\sum_{t=1}^{T} \gamma_t(j,k)((\tilde{\mathbf{y}}_t - \boldsymbol{\mu}_{\tilde{\mathbf{y}}})(\tilde{\mathbf{y}}_t - \boldsymbol{\mu}_{\tilde{\mathbf{y}}})^T}{\sum_{t=1}^{T} \gamma_t(j,k)}$$

$$= \frac{\sum_{t=1}^{T} \gamma_t(j,k)((\mathbf{y}_t + \frac{\partial \mathbf{y}_t}{\partial \mathbf{n}_t}(\mathbf{n}_t - \tilde{\mathbf{n}}_t) - \boldsymbol{\mu}_{\tilde{\mathbf{y}}}) \cdot (\mathbf{y}_t + \frac{\partial \mathbf{y}_t}{\partial \mathbf{n}_t}(\mathbf{n}_t - \tilde{\mathbf{n}}_t) - \boldsymbol{\mu}_{\tilde{\mathbf{y}}})^T)}{\sum_{t=1}^{T} \gamma_t(j,k)} \tag{7}$$

We can see from Eq. (7) that some statistical information in addition the Jacobian matrix need to be estimated for the covariance matrix adaptation and they are estimated directly with the noisy speech rather than derived analytically by assuming some statistical approximations as in the conventional JA [Sagayama, Yamaguchi and Takahashi, 1997].

The delta-cepstrum feature vector is calculated as follows.

$$\dot{\mathbf{y}}_t = \mu \sum_{k=-K}^{K} k \mathbf{y}_{t+k} \tag{8}$$

If we substitute Eq. (3) into (8), we obtain the formula for the delta-cepstrum mean vector adaptation as follows.

$$E(\tilde{\dot{\mathbf{y}}}_t) = \mu \sum_{k=-K}^{K} k E(\mathbf{y}_{t+k}) + \mu \sum_{k=-K}^{K} k E(\frac{\partial \mathbf{y}_{t+k}}{\partial \mathbf{n}_t}) \Delta \mathbf{n} \tag{9}$$

From Eq. (9), we can see that the statistical information $E(\mathbf{y}_{t+k})$, $E(\frac{\partial \mathbf{y}_{t+k}}{\partial \mathbf{n}_t})$ should be estimated during the training.

2.2 Multi-model Speech Recognition System

In the multi-model speech recognition system, multiple reference HMMs for the assumed various noise environments are constructed during training and the reference HMM which is most appropriate for the testing noisy speech is selected for recognition. To select the reference HMM, we need to estimate the SNR values of the testing noisy speech and classify its noise types. In Fig. 1, we show the architecture of the multi-model speech recognition system. The parameters of the selected reference HMM will be compensated by using the D-JA in the recognition process.

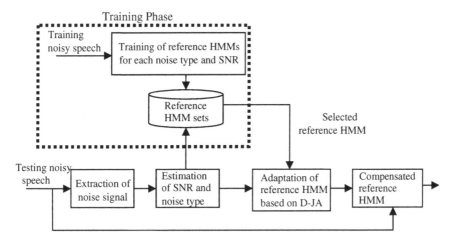

Fig. 1. The architecture of the multi-model speech recognition system

3 Experiments and Results

In this section, the performance of the proposed method of compensating the HMM parameters is evaluated on speaker-independent isolated word noisy speech recognition. The vocabulary consists of 75 phoneme-balanced Korean words and the basic recognition unit is the set of 32 phoneme-like units that are modeled by the left-to-right continuous density HMM. Utterances from 80 speakers are used in these experiments and each speaker uttered the 75 words once. A jack knife approach is used in the recognition experiment. We divided the speakers into 4 sets with 20 speakers in each set. Each set is successively used as the test set and the remaining three as the training sets. This has the effect of increasing the number of testing speakers to 80(4x20).

The noisy speech was obtained by adding the car, babble, exhibition and subway noise to the clean speech at various signal-to-noise ratios (SNRs). The noise signal was taken from the noise files contained in the AURORA 2 database. 13-th order mel-frequency cepstral coefficients (MFCC) and their time derivatives (delta-MFCC) are used as the feature vectors.

Table 1. Performance comparison in word recognition rates(%) of the proposed method (D-JA) with the conventional model compensation methods

	0dB	5dB	10dB	20dB	30dB	Clean
Baseline	10.8	28.1	54.2	90.1	96.3	98.6
Re-training	78.9	89.4	93.8	97.0	98.0	98.6
MCT	65.0	83.9	91.3	95.3	96.3	97.4
PMC	61.3	77.2	86.9	94.9	97.4	98.4
JA	63.2	78.3	87.1	95.1	97.3	98.4
D-JA	78.7	89.3	93.9	97.0	98.0	98.6

In Table 1, we show the recognition rates of the proposed method, namely the data-driven Jacobian adaptation (D-JA) in comparison with the baseline recognizer, re-training method, MCT(multi-condition training) and the conventional model compensation methods like the PMC and JA. Both the SNR and noise type of the testing speech are assumed to be known for the re-training and D-JA method. The results shown are the averaged recognition rates for the respective recognition experiments on the 4 kinds of noisy speech data (car/babble/exhibition/subway).

In the baseline recognizer, the HMM parameters are trained using only clean speech signal. As shown in the table, the recognition performance of the baseline recognizer with no compensation dropped severely at 10dB or below. In the re-training method, as we assume the same noise types and SNR values during the training and testing, the recognition performance is shown to be superior to other model compensation methods such as the PMC and JA. The MCT method was first introduced as a training method using the Aurora DB in which the training database was arranged considering all 4 noise types (car/babble/exhibition/subway) and wide range of SNR values (clean, 5~20dB). Although the MCT method has a merit that the HMM parameter can take into account the various possible acoustical environments, it may smooth too much the HMM parameters so that its performance is usually inferior to the re-training method as shown in the table.

The D-JA method has shown superior performance compared with the conventional model compensation methods because the D-JA uses the re-trained HMM as the reference HMM. So, overall, the re-trained method and the D-JA method both are shown to perform better than other methods in Table 1 if the SNR and the noise type of the testing speech are known beforehand.

Table 2. Performance comparison in word recognition rates(%) of the proposed method (D-JA) with the case of without adaptation in the multi-model structure when only the noise type is known beforehand

SNR Number of reference HMMs		0dB	5dB	10dB	20dB	30dB
D-JA	1	77.6	89.5	94.1	97.0	97.2
	2	79.5	89.9	93.9	97.1	97.8
	3	78.9	88.6	93.8	97.1	97.8
	5	79.2	89.2	93.7	97.1	98.0
	7	79.2	89.2	93.7	97.1	98.0
Without adaptation	1	55.1	84.6	93.6	96.6	95.4
	2	72.0	88.9	93.8	96.9	97.3
	3	79.0	86.7	93.4	96.9	97.3
	5	79.4	88.8	93.4	96.8	97.8
	7	79.4	88.8	93.5	96.9	97.9

In Table 1, we only used 1 reference HMM set as the SNR and noise type of the testing speech are assumed to be known in advance. However, the SNR of the testing speech in real environment is not usually known exactly. To overcome this problem, we used the D-JA method in the multi-model speech recognition system in Fig. 1 and investigated its performance as the number of reference HMM sets changes assuming that we do not know the SNR of the testing speech beforehand. Totally, 7 reference HMM sets corresponding to the SNR values (0, 5, 10, 15, 20, 25, 30 dB) are employed in the multi-model speech recognition system and they are obtained by using the re-training method. The recognition results are shown in Table 2 where the number of the reference HMM sets used is shown. From the results in Table 2, we can see that there is not much difference in performance when we use more than 2 reference HMM sets. We can see that the recognition results are not very sensitive to the number of reference HMM sets. To see if this insensitiveness comes from the adaptation effects, we also show the results when we do not adapt the reference HMMs. Without adaptation, the performance becomes a little deteriorated when the number of reference HMM sets is less than 3. However, with more than 3 reference HMM sets, we do not see any performance degradation even without adaptation. From these results, we could see that the HMM parameters are basically more or less robust to the variation of SNR values of the noisy speech.

In Table 2, we assumed that the type of noise signal is known in advance. However, in real environments, the noise type of the testing speech is also not usually given. So we employed a noise classifier based on the GMM (Gaussian mixture model). We trained the GMM for each type of noise signal and classified the noise signal in the testing speech into one of the 4 noise types considered in this paper. The performance of the GMM-based classifier was very high with average classification accuracy about 99.5%. Due to the high accuracy of the noise classifier, we could obtain similar results even if we do not assume the noise type as in Table 2.

Table 3. Performance comparison in word recognition rates(%) of the proposed method (D-JA) with the case of without adaptation in the multi-model structure when the testing speech contains an unknown type of noise signal not seen during training (STREET noise)

SNR / Number of reference HMMs		0dB	5dB	10dB	20dB	30dB
D-JA	1	80.6	90.5	94.7	96.7	95.4
	2	82.7	91.0	94.2	96.8	97.2
	3	84.1	90.8	93.7	96.8	97.2
	5	84.6	91.0	94.1	96.8	97.8
	7	84.6	90.9	94.3	97.0	97.9
Without adaptation	1	62.6	82.7	91.2	95.2	93.2
	2	72.5	86.9	92.4	96.3	96.5
	3	77.3	86.9	91.9	96.3	96.5
	5	77.9	87.6	92.0	96.3	97.3
	7	77.9	87.8	92.1	96.4	97.6

In Table 3, the performance of the multi-model speech recognition is shown when the testing input speech contains an unknown type of noise signal which is not seen during the training. The unknown type of noise used in this experiment is the STREET noise signal in the Aurora 2 DB. The recognition rates when the reference HMM parameters are adapted by the D-JA are shown in comparison with when no adaptation is applied. In contrast with the results in Table 2, the performance of the recognizer with the D-JA is much better than without adaptation. This implies that the D-JA method is very efficient in compensating the HMM parameters even when the characteristic of the noise signal in the testing speech is different from the noise signal in the training.

4 Conclusion

In this paper, we used a data-driven Jacobian adaptation method in the multi-model speech recognition system and showed that performance of the multi-model structure is quite superior to other model compensation methods.

Although the multi-model structure is basically more robust compared with using just a single reference HMM set, the recognition rate could be significantly improved with less reference HMM sets by employing the D-JA. The D-JA method could overcome quite well the differences in the SNR values and the noise types between the training and testing speech with only a few reference HMM sets for each noise type in the multi-model speech recognition system.

Acknowledgments. This work has been supported by The Advanced Medical Technology Cluster for Diagnosis and Prediction at KNU, which carries out one of the R&D Projects sponsored by the Korea Ministry Of Commerce, Industry and Energy.

References

[Gales, 1995] Gales, M.J.F.: Model Based Techniques for Noise-Robust Speech Recognition. Ph.D. Dissertation. University of Cambridge (1995)

Moreno, P.J.: Speech Recognition in Noisy Environments. Ph.D. Dissertation. Carnegie Mellon University (1996)

[Martin, 1992] Martin, F.: Recognition of Noisy Speech by Using the Composition of Hidden Markov Models. In: Proc. 1992 Autumn ASJ Conf. (1992)

[Sagayama, Yamaguchi and Takahashi, 1997] Sagayama Sagayama, S., Yamaguchi, Y., Takahashi, S.: Jacobian adaptation of noisy speech models. In: IEEE Workshop on Automatic Speech Recognition and Understanding, pp. 396–403 (1997)

[Hung, Shen and Lee, 2001] Hung, J.-W., Shen, J.-L., Lee, L.-S.: New approaches for domain transformation and parameter combination for improved accuracy in parallel model combination (PMC) techniques. IEEE Trans. Speech and Audio Processing 9(8), 842–855 (2001)

[Rabiner and Juang, 1993]Rabiner, R.L., Juang, B.-H.: Fundamentals of Speech Recognition. Prentice-Hall, Englewood Cliffs (1993)

[Chung, 2005]Chung, Y.J.: A Data-driven Model Parameter Compensation Method for Noise-Robust Speech Recognition. IEICE Trans. Info. & Syst. E-88-D(3), 432–434 (2005)

Comparing Linear Feature Space Transformations for Correlated Features

Daniel Vásquez[1,2], Rainer Gruhn[1,2], Raymond Brueckner[2],
and Wolfgang Minker[1]

[1] Department of Information Technology, University of Ulm, Ulm, Germany
{daniel.vasquez,wolfgang.minker}@uni-ulm.de
[2] Harman/Becker Automotive Systems, Speech Dialog Systems, Ulm, Germany
{rgruhn,rbrueckner}@harmanbecker.com

Abstract. In automatic speech recognition, a common method to decorrelate features and to reduce feature space dimensionality is Linear Discriminant Analysis (LDA). In this paper, the performance of LDA has been compared with other linear feature space transformation schemes, as many alternative methods have been suggested and lead to higher recognition accuracy in some cases. Different approaches such as MLLT, HLDA, SHLDA, PCA, and combined schemes were implemented and compared. Experiments show that all methods lead to similar results.

In addition, recent research has shown that the LDA algorithm is unreliable if the input features of LDA are strongly correlated. In this paper a stable solution to the correlated feature problem, consisting of a concatenation scheme with PCA and LDA, is proposed and verified. Finally, several transformation algorithms are evaluated on uncorrelated and strongly correlated features.

1 Introduction

The human preference for spoken language communication has increased the interest of many research groups over the years in developing Spoken Language Systems (SLS). An SLS consists of at least one of the following subsystems [Huang et al., 2001]: Speech recognition system, Text-to-speech system and Spoken language understanding system. In order to improve the performance of a SLS, it is necessary to build a robust speech recognition system which best maps the input speech signal into the words that the user has probably said. However, in the task of speech recognition, there are different factors in the speech signal that are difficult or impossible to control such as the variability in the acoustic environment, due to the presence of noise in diverse scenarios, and some other variabilities dependent on the user, such as dialect, gender and rate among others.

One branch of speech recognition research is seeking new types of features that more efficiently represent the relevant information of a speech signal than the commonly used Mel Frequency Cepstral Coefficients (MFCC). But having been the standard feature type for quite some time already speech recognition

E. André et al. (Eds.): PIT 2008, LNAI 5078, pp. 176–187, 2008.
© Springer-Verlag Berlin Heidelberg 2008

with MFCCs has become highly optimized. In order to achieve improvements over baseline systems one approach to overcome this limitation is to combine a new feature set with MFCCs into a larger feature vector and to apply a feature space transformation like LDA to reduce this combination to a hopefully superior feature vector of standard dimensionality.

Recent research [Schlüter et al., 2006] has cast doubts on the reliability of LDA when handling correlated features. An assumption about LDA is that recognition accuracy should at worst stay the same if new features are added to the LDA input vector, because LDA dismisses all information irrelevant for discrimination. But a decrease in recognition accuracy was reported when MFCCs were combined with strongly correlated features in a system that employs LDA for feature space transformation.

The scope of this paper is therefore:

- To verify the results in [Schlüter et al., 2006], to show that the problems of LDA lie in the algorithm, not just in its implementation, and to explain the reason for these instabilities.
- To propose a solution yielding a stable and reliable feature space transformation given correlated input features.
- To compare the performance of LDA to other feature space transformation methods such as MLLT, HLDA, SHLDA, PCA, and concateneated schemes.

This paper is divided as follows: Section 2 explains briefly all schemes that have been implemeted, Section 3 describes the experiments and results and finally, conclusions and a proposal for future work are given in Section 4.

2   Linear Feature Space Transformations

A feature space transformation performs a mapping of the parameters from an *original* feature space R^n, to a *transformed* feature space R^p, aiming to retain all information relevant and required for discrimination. A common choise is $p < n$, so that the feature transformation performs a dimensionality reduction.

2.1   Maximum Likelihood Linear Transform (MLLT)

A common problem in Automatic Speech Recognition is modeling correlation, which in the case of HMM/GMM system results to determining the covariance matrices; since these are symmetric, the number of parameters to be stored per matrix is $\frac{n(n+1)}{2}$. In practice, *diagonal* covariance matrices are widely used for reducing complexity, since the number of parameters to be stored per matrix is reduced to n, and the complexity for computing the covariance matrix inverse and the determinant decrease significantly.

MLLT aims to find a feature space transformation where a diagonal modeling is suitable in the transformed space [Gopinath, 1998]. MLLT can be seen as a model-space transfomation since it is acting on the model parameters, rather than implementing a dimensionality reduction [Gales, 1999a].

In maximum-likelihood (ML) modeling, the idea is to find that parameter set $\{\breve{\mu}_j\}$ and $\{\breve{\Sigma}_j\}$ which maximizes the likelihood of the training data $p(\mathbf{x}_1^N, \{\breve{\mu}_j\}, \{\breve{\Sigma}_j\})$ [Gopinath, 1998], where N is the number of observation vectors of the training data. In this way, the likelihood that the estimated means and covariances are close to their true value, is maximized [Alphonso, 2001].

By expressing the likelihood of the training data as a function of the matrix transform $\mathbf{A}$ and the parameters in the transformed feature space $\{\mu_j\}$ and $\{\Sigma_j\}$ i.e.,

$$p(\mathbf{x}_1^N, \{\breve{\mu}_j\}, \{\breve{\Sigma}_j\}) = f(\mathbf{A}, \mathbf{x}_1^N, \{\mu_j\}, \{\Sigma_j\}) \tag{1}$$

the likelihood function can be maximized with respect to its parameters, according to the ML criteria, hence finding the transform $\mathbf{A}$.

MLLT is also known as Semi-tied Covariance matrices [Sima and Gales, 2004] (STC) and it is commonly defined with multiple transform matrices, where each class or cluster consisting of a set of classes, has its own matrix transform.

2.2   HLDA

Heteroscedastic Linear Discriminant Analysis (HLDA) is a linear transformation trying to reduce the dimension of the original feature space while retaining a maximum amount of class discrimination information in the transformed feature space [Kumar, 1997, Demuynck et al., 1999]. In [Gopinath, 1998] it is shown that HLDA is a derivation of MLLT with the constraint of dimensionality reduction and only one matrix transform. This derivation can be observed in Figure 1 with the mapping of two classes. Under Gaussian modeling, these two classes are represented by ellipses, where each ellipse corresponds to the contour-line of a full covariance Gaussian.

MLLT projects an original feature space to a transformed feature space where a diagonal modeling is well suited. Hence, MLLT can be considered as a transformation scheme aiming to decorrelate the features. In addition to the decorrelation process, HLDA aims to remove the so-called *nuisance* dimensions, which do not carry information for discriminating between the classes, achieving a dimensionality reduction. At the same time, HLDA retains the *useful* dimensions which contain class discriminant information.

2.3   LDA

HLDA assumes that each class can be adequately modeled with a single multi-dimensional Gaussian. For this reason, a covariance matrix for each class has to be estimated. This fact can be a drawback in the case of limited training data where it may be difficult to obtain robuts covariance estimates for those classes with a reduced number of feature vectors.

A solution to this problem may be the the use of a constrained scheme of HLDA, Linear Discriminant Analysis (LDA). Here it is assumed that the covariance matrices of all classes are the same, as shown at the bottom of Figure 1.

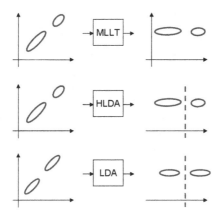

Fig. 1. Linear transformations derived from ML criteria

A ML solution for finding the LDA matrix transform can be obtained by first estimating the between covariance matrix $\mathbf{B}$ and the within covariance matrix $\mathbf{W}$. The matrix transform is obtained by taking the top p right eigenvectors of $\mathbf{W}^{-1}\mathbf{B}$ associated with the largest eigenvalues [Fukagana, 1972]. For obtaining the HLDA matrix transform, an efficient iterative algorithm given in [Gales, 1999b] has been utilized. The same algorithm was used for implementing MLLT under the condition that this scheme does not implement a dimensionality reduction.

2.4   SHLDA

By assuming all class covariance matrices to be the same in LDA transformation, the covariance matrices are more robustly estimated since for estimating a single class covariance matrix, all training data is available. But these assumptions can be far away from the real model and LDA can be wrongly selected, particularly in those application where the class distributions are heretoscedastic. In this case, HLDA would be more suitable but it has the disadvantage of poor estimates when there is a lack of training data.

For taking advantage of both LDA and HLDA schemes, a new method was proposed in [Burget, 2004a] called Smoothed HLDA (SHLDA). This method combines HLDA and LDA, where class covariance matrices are estimated more robustly, and at the same time, the major difference between covariance matrices of different classes is preserved. SHLDA consists of estimating the within covariance matrix $\hat{\Sigma}_j$ of class j as an average of the global within covariance matrix $\mathbf{W}$ and the within covariance matrix $\check{\Sigma}_j$ of class j:

$$\hat{\Sigma}_j = \alpha\check{\Sigma}_j + (1 - \alpha)\mathbf{W} \qquad (2)$$

where α is a weight factor in the range of 0 to 1. For $\alpha = 0$ SHLDA reduces to the standard LDA while $\alpha = 1$ yields HLDA.

2.5   PCA

Principal Component Analysis (PCA) is an orthogonal linear transform that transforms the input data to a new coordinate system such that the greatest variance by any projection of the data comes to lie on the first P coordinates, where P denotes the output dimension of the transform. The matrix transform can be calculated by estimating the global covariance matrix of the data set, denoted by $\mathbf{T}$, followed by finding the eigenvectors associated with the largest eigenvalues. These eigenvectors compound the matrix transform.

3   Experiments and Results

We performed a set of experiments which can be divided in two parts: The first part, described in Section 3.2 verifies the results reported in [Schlüter et al., 2006] regarding the robustness of LDA when either uncorrelated or strongly correlated features are the input to the LDA. The second part compares the performance of the LDA with other feature space transformation schemes. In addition, the robustness of all schemes towards feature correlation is examined. The results of these experiments are reported in Section 3.3.

3.1   Experimental Setup

All experiments were conducted on the AURORA2 database. The Aurora task consists of connected digit strings (from TIdigits), spoken by American English talkers [Pearce and Hirsch, 2000]. Acoustic models were trained on the clean data only. The three predefined test sets were combined into one large test set.

The input to the linear feature space transformations are 9 consecutive observation vectors concatenated into multi-feature vectors. The tested multi-feature vectors are shown in Table 1.

The output of the feature space transformation always was fixed to a 25-dimensional vector.

The Aurora2 model set consists of 10 digits, each modeled by a 10-state HMM, plus one single state silence model. Hence, there are a total of 111 states; each

Table 1. Multi-feature vectors utilized

Multi-feature vector	Dim.	Base features
Baseline	99	11 MFCC (energy + C1 .. C10)
A	198	11 MFCC + 11 random features
B	396	11 MFCC + 33 random features
C	198	11 MFCC + 11 repeated MFCC

digit state has on average 9000 samples and the silence state approximately 60000 samples.

Acoustic model training was carried out using HarmanBecker proprietary software.

3.2 Robustness of LDA

The robustness of LDA is examined by adding either irrelevant, uncorrelated features (random values) or highly correlated, relevant features (repeated fetures) to the base feature vector. To rule out that increasing the feature vector length alone impairs LDA performance, we experimented by adding 11 (setup **A**) and 33 (setup **B**) random components, respectively.

The random features were generated with MATLAB, using the *rand* routing (method *twister*).

As can be seen in Table 2, it could be verified that the addition of random features does not affect the performance of the system, which is in agreement with [Schlüter et al., 2006].

Table 2. Robustness of LDA towards random features

Multi-feature vector	Accuracy [%]
Baseline	98.89
A	98.89
B	98.91

The robustness of LDA, when strongly correlated features are added to the input feature vector, is tested in setup **C**. We observed instabilities in the algorithm when processing strongly correlated features. In contrast to [Schlüter et al., 2006] the LDA matrix could not even be computed. In the following, a rationale for this outcome will be set forth and a solution for the case of strong correlation will be presented.

As explained in Section 2.3, the LDA matrix transform can be obtained by first estimating the within covariance matrix $\mathbf{W}$ and the between covariance matrix $\mathbf{B}$ and subsequently solving the eigenvalue problem of $\mathbf{W}^{-1}\mathbf{B}$. Evidently, $\mathbf{W}$ needs to fulfill the properties of an invertible matrix. In fact, all covariance matrices, such as $\check{\Sigma}_j$, $\mathbf{W}$, $\mathbf{B}$ and $\mathbf{T}$, possess these characteristics.

Figure 2 illustrates a n-dimensional multi-feature vector next to its covariance matrix. Let us assume that one dimension generates a row vector in the covariance matrix, as depicted in Figure 2a. If there is a repeated dimension in the feature vector, the same row vector will be obtained, as shown in Figure 2b. Since the covariance matrix is symmetric it unfolds as depicted in Figure 2c . We can observe that the matrix is singular, as it has linearly dependent columns. This is in accordance with theory which states that the eigenvalue problem $\mathbf{W}^{-1}\mathbf{B}$ can not be solved if $\mathbf{W}^{-1}$ contains linearly dependent columns or rows.

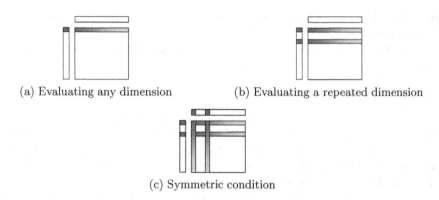

(a) Evaluating any dimension   (b) Evaluating a repeated dimension

(c) Symmetric condition

Fig. 2. Characteristics of the within covariance matrix **W** with repeated features

In similar experiments Schlüter [Schlüter et al., 2006] computed a matrix transform but found it to be instable.

We propose a solution to this problem by processing the input data by PCA transform prior to applying the LDA. This concatenation scheme is common practice in e.g. face recognition where the within covariance matrix is reported to be always singular or near singular [Belhumeur et al., 1997]. PCA has the desirable property that *all* covariance matrices become invertible in the image space. Once the within covariance matrix can be inverted, LDA transformation can be used without any problem.

In our experiments we used a variant of the PCA, referred to as PCA *stabilization* (PCAs) [Burget, 2004b], in which the criterion for choosing the final dimension is based on the eigenvalues of the PCA transform matrix **T**. The dimensionality d of the transformed feature space is given by:

$$d = \operatorname{argmin}_k \left\{ \frac{\sum_{i=1}^{k} |\lambda_i|}{\sum_{i=1}^{n} |\lambda_i|} > 1 - \frac{\varepsilon}{100} \right\} \qquad (3)$$

where n is the dimensionality of the original feature space and λ_i are the eigenvalues sorted in decreasing order. In all cases we set $\varepsilon = 0.5$ (ref. [Burget, 2004b]).

Figure 3 outlines the dimensionality reduction of this concatenation scheme with the multi-feature vectors for the **Baseline** and setup **C**. The numbers represent the dimensionality of the respective feature spaces. In the baseline the PCAs removes 43 dimensions leaving a 56-dimensional transformed feature space. In the case of the strongly correlated features PCAs removes 142 dimensions consisting of the 43 previous dimensions and the 99 repeated dimensions again leaving a 56-dimensional space. It will be shown that these two 56-dimensional transformed feature spaces are equivalent. In fact, these two experiments have exactly the same results, given in the first row of Table 2.

In general, a feature space transformation with dimensionality reduction can be seperated into two steps: first, mapping a n-dimensional space to a n-dimensional

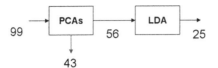

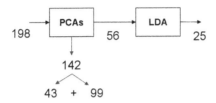

(a) **Baseline** multi-feature vector

(b) Multi-feature vector for setup **C**

Fig. 3. Dimensionality reduction with the PCAs+LDA scheme

(transformed) space and second, retaining only the first dimensions in the transformed space while discarding the rest. Hence, in order to show where the instabilities emerge the following analysis does not take into consideration the latter step [Vásquez, 2007].

For the case of the baseline, 99 different, non-zero eigenvalues were obtained by solving the eigenvalue problem for **T**. The 99 eigenvectors, corresponding to the 99 eigenvalues arranged in decreasing order, span a 99-dimensional feature space. This transformed feature space in linear algebra is termed the *image* of the linear map. Furthermore, the dimensionality of the image is equal to the *rank* of the matrix transform. Since in this case the dimensionality of the original feature space equals the dimensionality of the image the transform matrix is defined to be *full-rank*. Under the constraint that PCAs does not implement a dimensionality reduction, the projected **W** will have 99 dimensions in the transformed feature space. This projection is illustrated in Figure 4a.

For strongly correlated features, the eigenvalue problem is solved for **T** which now has 198 dimensions. The global covariance matrix has 99 repeated rows and columns as it was illustrated in Figure 2. By solving the eigenvalue problem, 99 zero and 99 non-zero eigenvalues are obtained. The 99 eigenvectors, corresponding to the 99 non-zero eigenvalues arranged in decreasing order, span a 99-dimensional feature space, i.e. the image of the linear map. As it was mentioned above, the dimensionality of the image equals the rank of the matrix transform. Since in this case, the rank of the matrix transform is less than the dimensionality of the original space, the matrix transform is defined to be *rank-deficient*.

Furthermore, the 99 non-zero eigenvalues are exactly the same as the 99 eigenvalues obtained in the baseline, but scaled by a factor of 2. This way the first 99 dimensions in the transformed feature space have essentially the same parameters in both experiments, the baseline and the strongly correlated features setups.

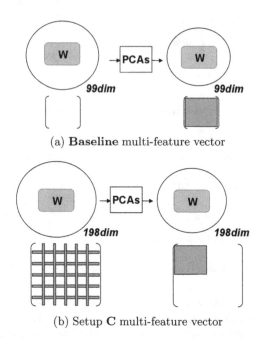

(a) **Baseline** multi-feature vector

(b) Setup **C** multi-feature vector

Fig. 4. PCA feature space transformation without dimensionality reduction

The 99 eigenvectors corresponding to the 99 zero eigenvalues span a 99-dimensional null-space, also known as the *kernel* of the linear map. Therefore, the blank space representing the last 99 dimensions of the transformed space represents the projected **W** in the null-space, as it is illustrated in Figure 4b.

Under the criteria given by Equation 3, 56 dimensions were choosen for the transformed feature space. For the case of strongly correlated features, the projection of **W** through PCAs is still singular in a 198-dimensional transformed feature space, but through the dimensionality reduction and hence removing its projection into the null-space **W** become invertible. Therefore, applying the LDA on the 56-dimensional original feature space both experiments yield the same results.

It is important to mention that under a linear mapping scaling the parameters in the original feature space is equivalent to scaling the transform matrix. Hence, the abovementioned factor of two in all parameters before the LDA does not influence the performance of the transform.

3.3 Comparing the Performance of LDA with Other Transformantion Schemes

In this section, the performance of LDA is compared to other linear feature space transformation schemes, utilizing the multi-feature vectors given in Table 1. Table 3 shows the word accuracies on the clean test data averaged over the AURORA2 test sets a, b and c. The HMM models were trained on the clean data setup.

Table 3. Average accuracy [%] for **Baseline**, **A**, **B** and **C** multi-feature vectors. Note that setup **C** can not be computed without applying the PCA.

Setup	BL	A	B	C
LDA	98.89	98.89	98.91	-
PCA	98.80	98.80	98.80	98.80
PCAs+LDA	98.91	98.92	98.90	98.91
LDA+MLLT	98.89	98.89	98.89	-
PCAs+SHLDA($\alpha = 1$)	98.87	98.86	98.87	98.87
PCAs+SHLDA($\alpha = 0.75$)	98.93	98.90	98.89	98.93
PCAs+SHLDA($\alpha = 0.5$)	98.88	98.88	98.88	98.88
PCAs+SHLDA($\alpha = 0.25$)	98.89	98.89	98.87	98.89
PCAs+SHLDA($\alpha = 0$)	98.88	98.89	98.87	98.88

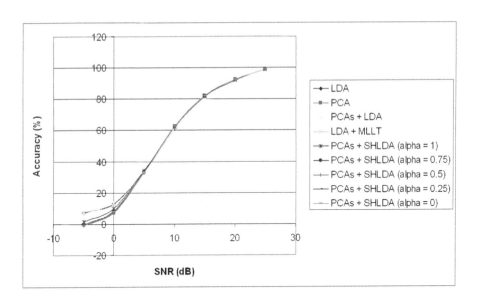

Fig. 5. Average accuracy over all test sets A, B and C of Aurora2 clean training

The results for the **Baseline** indicate that all of the feature transformation schemes show roughly the same performance. Figure 5 proves that this holds for most of the SNRs in the Aurora test set. Thus, it can be concluded that replacing LDA by another linear transformation does not significantly affect performance.

For setups **A** and **B** in Table 1, it can be observed that none of the schemes was affected by adding random features. All schemes were also tested with strongly correlated features. In fact, the same results were obtained with the **Baseline** and setup **C**. The reasons for this were exposed in Section 3.2. For the schemes LDA and LDA+MLLT no matrix transform could be computed and thus no results were obtained.

4   Summary, Conclusions and Future Work

In this paper, the results of the experiments given in [Schlüter et al., 2006] were verified, and a stable solution to the correlated feature problem was proposed and verified.

We propose an stable approach towards correlation: Instead of looking for a more general algorithm which can handle singular matrices and calculate the LDA matrix transform an additional feature space transformation is applied before LDA. The resulting feature space transformation consists of a concatenated scheme between PCA and LDA. PCA is selected as a preprocessing state of LDA, since it yields stable solutions even in the cases where singular matrices are involved. This concatenated scheme works perfectly well under the extreme correlation problem of adding repeated features to the input feature vector. In addition, it is also verified that the performance of LDA is not affected when concatenating with PCA feature transformation.

Different approaches such as MLLT, HLDA, SHLDA, PCA and concatenated schemes were implemented but no considerable improvement was achieved compared to LDA alone. The experiments performed in this work were based on the AURORA2 setup, a standard but small vocabulary speech recognition task. A suggestion for future work is to test these linear transformations on a large vocabulary speech recognition task, to verify if any of the techniques implemented in this work are more fruitful if abundant data is available for training. Future research could extend the comparison to non-linear feature transformation schemes as well.

As in this paper the feature space transformation stability problem has been solved, examinations can now be conducted to increase recognition rates by combining different types of features.

References

[Alphonso, 2001] Alphonso, I.: Heteroscedastic discriminant analysis. Critical Review Paper, ECE 8990 – Special Topics in ECE – Pattern Recognition, Institute for Signal and Information Processing (2001)

[Belhumeur et al., 1997] Belhumeur, P., Hespanha, J., Kriegman, D.: Eigenfaces vs. fisherfaces: Recognition using class specific linear projection. IEEE Transactions on Pattern Analysis and Machine Intelligence 19(7), 711–720 (1997)

[Burget, 2004a] Burget, L.: Combination of speech features using smoothed heteroscedastic linear discriminat analysis. In: Proc. ICSLP, pp. 2549–2552 (2004a)

[Burget, 2004b] Burget, L.: Complementarity of Speech Recognition Systems and System Combination. PhD thesis, Faculty of Information Technology BUT (2004b)

[Demuynck et al., 1999] Demuynck, K., Duchateau, J., Compernolle, D.V.: Optimal feature sub-pace selection based on discriminant analysis. In: Proc. EUROSPEECH, Budapest, Hungary, pp. 1311–1314 (1999)

[Fukagana, 1972] Fukagana, K.: Introduction to Statistical Pattern Recognition. Academic Press, London (1972)

[Gales, 1999a] Gales, M.: Maximum likelihood multiple projection schemes for hidden markov models.Technical Report CUED/F-INFENG/TR365 (1999a)

[Gales, 1999b] Gales, M.: Semi-tied covariance matrices for hidden markov models. IEEE Transactions Speech and Audio Processing 7, 272–281 (1999b)

[Gopinath, 1998] Gopinath, R.: Maximum likelihood modeling with gaussian distributions for classification. In: Proc. ICASSP, vol. 2, pp. 661–664 (1998)

[Huang et al., 2001] Huang, X., Acero, A., Hon, H.: Spoken Language Processing: A Guide to Theory Algorithm, and System Development. Prentice-Hall, Englewood Cliffs (2001)

[Kumar, 1997] Kumar, N.: Investigation of Silicon Auditory Models and Generalization of Linear Discriminant Analysis for Improved Speech Recognition. PhD thesis, Johns Hopkins University (1997)

[Pearce and Hirsch, 2000] Pearce, D., Hirsch, H.: The aurora experimental framework for the performance evaluation of speech recognition systems under noisy conditions. In: Proc. ICSLP, Beijing, vol. 4, pp. 29–32 (2000)

[Schlüter et al., 2006] Schlüter, R., Zolnay, A., Ney, H.: Feature combination using linear discriminant analysis and its pitfalls. In: Proc. ICSLP, Pittsburgh, pp. 345–348 (2006)

[Sima and Gales, 2004] Sima, K., Gales, M.: Basic superposition precision matrix modeling for large vocabulary continuous speech recognition. In: Proc. ICASSP (2004)

[Vásquez, 2007] Vásquez, D.: Feature space transformation for speech recognition. Master's thesis, Dept. of Information Technology, University of Ulm (2007)

EmoVoice — A Framework for Online Recognition of Emotions from Voice

Thurid Vogt, Elisabeth André, and Nikolaus Bee

Multimedia Concepts and their Applications, University of Augsburg, Germany
{vogt,andre,bee}@informatik.uni-augsburg.de

Abstract. We present EmoVoice, a framework for emotional speech corpus and classifier creation and for offline as well as real-time online speech emotion recognition. The framework is intended to be used by non-experts and therefore comes with an interface to create an own personal or application specific emotion recogniser. Furthermore, we describe some applications and prototypes that already use our framework to track online emotional user states from voice information.

1 Introduction

Research on the automatic recognition of emotions in speech has emerged in the last decade and has since then shifted from purely acted to more natural emotions. So far, most of this research has been concerned with the offline analysis of available or specifically created speech corpora. However, most applications that could make use of affective information would require an online analysis of the user's emotional state. Therefore, the consideration of real-time constraints is also important for emotion recognition. Of course, recognition rates must be expected to be lower than for offline analysis, and tasks should be limited to very few emotional states. In this paper, we present EmoVoice, our framework to building an emotion classifier and to recognising emotions online.

Among possible application scenarios for online speech emotion recognition are call center conversations, by e. g. providing call center employees with information regarding the emotions their voice might portray, or by automatically switching from computer to human operators if a caller exhibits high arousal in his voice, an indication for a problem [Burkhardt et al., 2005b]. Further examples of application scenarios include computer-enhanced learning [Ai et al., 2006] or emotionally aware in-car systems [Schuller et al., 2007a].

As already mentioned, so far only few approaches to online emotion recognition exist. One example is the Jerk-O-Meter that monitors attention (activity and stress) in a phone conversation, based on speech feature analysis, and gives the user feedback allowing her to change her manners if deemed appropriate [Madan, 2005]. Jones and colleagues have explored online emotion detection in games [Jones and Deeming, 2007] and for giving feedback in human-robot interaction [Jones and Sutherland, 2007]. Our own applications will be presented later in Sect. 4.

E. André et al. (Eds.): PIT 2008, LNAI 5078, pp. 188–199, 2008.

The rest of this paper is organised as follows: first, in Sect. 2, we give an overview of the modules of EmoVoice, and explain the individual components of the recognition process in detail. Section 3 explains our data acquisition method, while Sect. 4 describes applications and prototypes that already make use of our framework. Finally, we draw some conclusions and indicate our future steps.

2   Components of EmoVoice

The major steps in speech emotion recognition are *audio segmentation*, which means finding appropriate acoustic segments as emotion classification units, *feature extraction* to find those characteristics of the acoustic signal that best describe emotions and to represent each segmented acoustic unit as a (series of) feature vector(s), and lastly the actual *classification* of the feature vectors into emotional states.

EmoVoice, our framework for emotion recognition from speech (see Fig. 1), consists of two modules, one for the offline creation and analysis of an emotional speech corpus, and one for the online tracking of affect in voice while someone is talking. The first module is a set of tools for audio segmentation, feature extraction, feature selection and classification of an emotional speech corpus, and a graphical user interface to easily record and segment speech files, extract features and create a classifier. This classifier can then be used for the second module, the online emotion recognition. Here, classification results are obtained continuously during talking, there is no "push-to-talk".

Primarily, the online emotion recognition just outputs the recognised emotions name, so just provides the functionality of emotion recognition. However, it can easily be plugged into other applications visualising or making use of the affective information which is the topic of Sect. 4.

Now we will describe how audio segmentation, feature extraction and classification are addressed in EmoVoice, both in offline and online recognition.

2.1   Audio Segmentation

The first step in online emotion recognition is to segment the incoming speech signal into meaningful units that can serve as classification units. Commonly, these are linguistically motivated units such as words or utterances. Though the decision on which kind of unit to take is evidently important, it has not received much attention in past research on emotion recognition. Most approaches so far have dealt with the offline classification of utterances of acted emotions where the choice of unit is obviously just this utterance, a well-defined linguistic unit with no change of emotion within in this case.

However, in spontaneous speech this kind of obvious unit does not exist. Neither is the segmentation into utterances straight-forward nor can a constant emotion be expected over an utterance. On the other hand, a good unit should be long enough so that features can reliably be calculated by means of statistical functions. Words are often too short for this. Therefore, a suitable unit for spontaneous speech can e. g. be found at the phrase level.

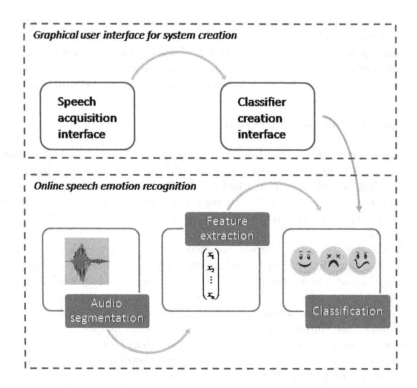

Fig. 1. Overview of the two modules of EmoVoice: The graphical user interface allows for convenient speech corpus and classifier creation. The online recognition module can be plugged into other applications and continuously tracks the emotional state of the user as expressed in his/her voice.

The task is further constrained when dealing with online recognition, as for a word/utterance/phrase segmentation, an automatic speech recogniser (ASR) is required. Though the often faulty ASR output does not necessarily degrade the performance of the emotion recogniser [Schuller et al., 2007b], it is at least time-consuming. For this reason, we use *voice activity detection* to segment by pauses into signal chunks of voice activity without pauses longer than 200 ms within. This method is very fast and comes close to a segmentation into phrases though it does not make use of any linguistic knowledge. Still, no change of emotion can be expected to occur within such a chunk. The algorithm used comes from the Esmeralda environment for speech recognition [Fink, 1999].

For spontaneous speech, voice activity detection yields a very favorable segmentation. When reading speakers usually do not make long enough pauses, even between text sections that differ in terms of content, and emotions. However, in EmoVoice, there is also the option to set a maximum interval for the output of a classification result if no pause has occurred before. For this interval, 2–3 seconds turned out to be a suitable duration.

2.2   Feature Extraction

The goal of the feature extraction is to find those properties of the acoustic signal that best characterise emotions. Common features for speech emotion recognition are based on short-term acoustic observations like pitch or signal energy. Since the specific values of these measures are usually not too expressive *per se*, but rather their change over time, the modeling of the temporal behavior is crucial to the success of the task. Basically, there are two approaches to do this, which depend on the type of classifier that is used. Learning algorithms like HMMs model temporal changes by considering sequences of feature vectors, looking especially at the transitions between the vectors. Thus, a classification unit consists of a series of feature vectors obtaining one label by the classifier. Standard classifiers, however, assign one label to each feature vector. As a result, time needs to be encoded in the features themselves, usually by (optional) transformations of the basic values and applying (statistical) functions like mean calculation, that map a series of values onto a single value. The latter approach is the one followed here.

Since an optimal feature set for speech emotion recognition is not yet established, we calculate, starting from basic acoustic observations, a multitude of statistical values for each measure. This is similar to our earlier work on feature extraction in [Vogt and André, 2005, Vogt and André, 2006]. Of course, because of online processing, we use only fully automatically in real-time extractable features which is opposed to most other approaches to speech emotion recognition that rely to some extent on manually annotated information. Our basic observations are logarithmised pitch, signal energy, Mel-frequency cepstral coefficients (MFCCs; 12 coefficients), the short-term frequency spectrum, and the harmonics-to-noise ratio (HNR). The resulting series of values are transformed to different views, and for each of the resulting series mean, maximum, minimum, range, variance, median, first quartile, third quartile and interquartile range are derived (based on [Oudeyer, 2003]). These values constitute the actual features used. The transformations into different views comprise the following:

- *logarithmised pitch:* the series of the local maxima, local minima, the difference, slope, distance between local extrema, the first and second derivation, and of course the basic series;
- *energy:* the basic series and the series of the local maxima, local minima, the difference, slope, distance between local extrema, first and second derivation as well as the series of their local maxima and local minima;
- *MFCCs:* the basic, local maxima, local minima for basic, first and second derivation for each of 12 coefficients alone;
- *frequency spectrum:* the series of the center of gravity, the distance between the 10 and 90 % frequency quantile, the slope between the strongest and the weakest frequency, the linear regression;
- *HNR:* only the basic series.

Additionally, four duration related features are used: segment length in seconds, pause as the proportion of unvoiced frames in a segment obtained from pitch calculation and as the number of voiceless frames in a segment obtained from voice activity detection and the zero-crossings rate. Duration, or speaking rate, is also encoded in the distance between local energy extrema. For pitch, also the positions of the global maximum and minimum in the segment, and the number of local maxima and minima as well as the number of falling resp. rising pitch frames are added as features. For energy, additional features include the position of the global maximum and the number of local maxima. Furthermore, we use jitter, shimmer and the number of glottal pulses of the analysed speech features as voice quality features in addition to HNR.

Our pitch and voice quality calculation are based on the Praat phonetics software [Boersma and Weenink, 2007], energy and MFCC calculation come from the Esmeralda speech recognition environment [Fink, 1999].

Overall, we thus have a feature vector containing 1302 features. Of course, this is a large number of features for fast classification, and it is very likely that some of the features in the set are redundant. We optionally employ a correlation-based feature subset selection [Hall, 1998] from the data-mining software Weka [Witten and Frank, 2005] to reduce our feature set to only uncorrelated features with respect to a specific training audio corpus. This usually means a reduction to 50–200 features, which is a tractable number of features for the classification algorithms.

2.3 Classification

Currently, two classification algorithms are integrated in EmoVoice: a naïve Bayes (NB) classifier and a support vector machine (SVM) classifier (from the LibSVM library [Chang and Lin, 2001]). The NB classifier is very fast, even for high-dimensional feature vectors, and therefore especially suitable for real-time processing. However, it yields slightly lower classification rates than the SVM classifier which is a very common algorithm used in offline emotion recognition. In combination with feature selection and thereby a reduction of the number of features to less than 100, SVM is also feasible in real-time.

3   A Training Procedure for Non-experts

Statistical classifiers, as used in EmoVoice, give better results when they are specifically trained on the situation they will be used in. Therefore, in order to facilitate the process of building an own emotion recognition system also for non-experts, we have developed an interface for recording an emotional speech corpus and training a correspondent classifier. The idea of this is also that a normal user could create his/her own speaker dependent recognition system whose accuracy can be expected to be considerably higher than that of a general recognition system. The method used for emotion elicitation is oriented at the Velten mood induction technique [Velten, 1968] as used in [Wilting et al., 2006] where subjects have to read out loud a set of emotional sentences that should set them into the desired emotional state. We have predefined a set of such sentences for the four quadrants in a two-dimensional emotional space: positive-active, positive-passive, negative-active, negative-passive which we map on the emotions joy, satisfaction, anger, frustration. However, users are encouraged to change sentences according to their own emotional experiences. Though our goal is the recognition of non-acted emotions, of course, this method does not yield truly natural emotions, we could rather call them semi-acted. For offline recognition, research has shifted just in recent years from acted to spontaneous emotions, so that for fully natural low-intensity emotions in online recognition, only low accuracies can be expected. At the current state of the art, rather applications should be considered where expressive speech comes natural, e. g. games or voice training.

We tested this method with 29 students of computer science (8 females, 21 males, aged 20 to 28). The sentence set was as described above and in German, though there were also 10 non-native speakers among them. Students could do the recordings at home, so the audio quality and equipment were not controlled, but all students were told to use a head-set microphone. Offline speaker-dependent accuracies in 10-fold cross-validation for all 4 classes varied — not surprisingly — a lot among speakers and ranged from 24 % to 74 %, with an average of 55 %. This great variation is to a good extent due to the uncontrolled audio recordings which led to very different audio and emotion qualities but this especially makes our setting very realistic with regard to how people cope with the technology on their own.

From all test persons, we selected 10 speakers (5 female, 5 male) that were German native speakers, whose speaker-dependent accuracy was not below 40 % and where audio quality was satisfactory, to train a speaker-independent classifier that could be used as general classifier in many applications responding to emotional states occuring in the recorded set. This resulted in a recognition accuracy of 41 %. All results were obtained with the NB classifier on the full feature set (no selection) and though the figures may not sound high overall, they are well above chance level. Especially in the speaker-independent evaluation, the use of different microphones is responsible to a great extent for low recognition rates. Furthermore, for good results in a realistic setting and online recognition, only 2 or 3 of these classes should be used. For example, we obtained recognition rates between 60 % and 70 % for the speaker independent system when leaving two classes out. Again note that all recognition accuracy figures were obtained offline, though speech data and recording conditions are similar to online conditions. A systematic evaluation of online recognition accuracy has not been done yet, but is empirically 10–20 % lower than the offline accuracy if applied in a scenario similar to the recording conditions. In offline analysis of emotional speech databases, we achieved in our earlier work recognition rates of about 80 % for 7 classes [Vogt and André, 2006] on an actors database [Burkhardt et al., 2005a] and about 50 % in [Vogt and André, 2005] resp. [Batliner et al., 2006] on two spontaneous emotional speech databases, the SmartKom database (3 emotion classes) [Schiel et al., 2002] and the German Aibo database (4 emotion classes) [Batliner et al., 2004].

It took each speaker about 10–20 minutes to record the 80 sentences, 20 for each emotion. For a good speaker dependent system, however, we recommend at least 40 sentences per emotion.

4   Integration into Applications

Of course, knowing the emotion expressed by one's own voice is not very useful *per se*, but only in the context of an application making use of the affective information. The integration of the online recognition tool of EmoVoice into other applications is simple, as the result of the emotion recognition can be continuously transmitted over a socket connection to that application.

EmoVoice has been also successfully integrated in a number of applications or existing architectures. So far, there exist several prototypes and applications that use EmoVoice. Two of them look at whether affective reactions make a robot or virtual agent more believable. These include a scenario of human-robot interaction where a user reads a fairy tale to Barthoc, a humanoid robot, expressing the emotions joy and fear, and the robot mimics these emotions with its facial expressions (see Fig. 4). The other is a virtual agent named Greta

Fig. 2. Emotionally telling a fairy tale to Barthoc, a humanoid robot[Hegel et al., 2006].

[de Rosis et al., 2003] which mirrors a user's emotional state in her face (see Fig. 3) and gives emotionally coloured small-talk feedback, thus showing empathy with the user [Vogt et al., 2007]. Furthermore, through the mirroring behavior, the results of the emotion recognition are made especially clear to the user. For the first scenario, Hegel et al. [Hegel et al., 2006] show in a user study a preference of the emotionally reacting robot over a robot without emotion recognition. For the second scenario, the formal proof of this is still pending but due to the more subtle emotional response by the Greta agent, we expect an even stronger effect.

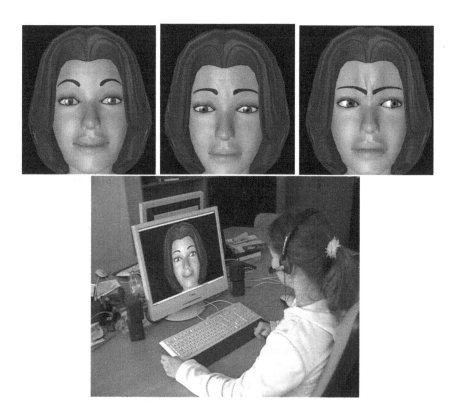

Fig. 3. Conversation with a virtual agent showing empathy by mirroring the user's emotional state in her face (upper row from left to right: joy, sadness, anger)

Other applications are of rather artistic nature having the goal of visualising emotions and allowing users to express themselves emotionally. One of them is an animated kaleidoscope that changes according to a speaker's emotions (see Fig. 4). Within the EU project Callas[1], showcases of interactive art are being developed that respond to the multimodal emotional input of spectators. Some of them are intended to be used primarily by professional actors, and it is assumed and encouraged that users express themselves with strong, possibly exaggerated and acted emotions. For this reason these scenarios are ideally suited for the current state of the art in emotion recognition technology. One of the showcases integrating EmoVoice is an Augmented Reality application with a tree whose appearance can be changed according to affective input from the user. Among others, the tree can be made grow or shrink and change its color by positive or negative emotions as expressed in the voice [Gilroy et al., 2007] (see Fig. 5). In another showcase, a virtual character watches a (horror) movie and reacts to the emotions conveyed in the scenes and by a human spectator [Charles et al., 2007].

---

[1] http://www.callas-newmedia.eu

Fig. 4. An animated kaleidoscope to visualise online recognised emotional states (examples from left to right: joy, sadness, anger)

Fig. 5. Making E-Tree [Gilroy et al., 2007] grow: influence of neutral, positive active, negative passive emotions from voice (from left to right)

Finally, — not in the context of Callas — Rehm et al. [Rehm et al., 2008] have built a virtual Karaoke dancer whose expressiveness can be controlled by expressive singing and gestures.

In the mentioned applications or prototypes, three different languages, German, English and Finnish, were used. This shows that the methodology of EmoVoice is language-independent.

5   Conclusions and Future Work

We presented EmoVoice, our framework to emotion recognition from speech which allows online tracking of the emotions expressed in a user's voice and comes with an easy-to-use audio acquisition method to quickly build a speaker- or scenario specific recogniser. The framework has been integrated successfully already in a number of applications. Regarding the recognition process, the biggest contribution of EmoVoice is not the single components used for speech emotion recognition (audio segmentation, feature extraction, classification) but the way — or even the fact that — they are plugged together. Of course, feature extraction and classification should be improved to have higher accuracy and are subject to constant improvements as also in offline emotion recognition, the real breakthrough has not yet been achieved. By combining EmoVoice with other modalities or information sources like visual attention, facial expressions, bio signals or word information, which we have partly already investigate (bio signals

[Kim et al., 2005], gender information [Vogt and André, 2006]), we plan to explore further possiblities of recognition rates improvements. Primarily, however, with EmoVoice we have a framework to explore user behavior and acceptance of affective technology. Consequently, one of our future steps will therefore include a thorough user study where we will also assess systematically the accuracy of our system in online usage.

Acknowledgements

Thanks to Stephen Gilroy from Univ. of Teesside, UK, for providing the pictures in Fig. 5.

This work was partially supported by the European Community (EC) within the Callas project IST-034800, the eCIRCUS project IST-4-027656-STP and the network of excellence Humaine IST-507422. The authors are solely responsible for the content of this publication. It does not represent the opinion of the EC, and the EC is not responsible for any use that might be made of data appearing therein.

References

[Ai et al., 2006] Ai, H., Litman, D.J., Forbes-Riley, K., Rotaru, M., Tetreault, J., Purandare, A.: Using system and user performance features to improve emotion detection in spoken tutoring dialogs. In: Proceedings of Interspeech 2006 — ICSLP, Pittsburgh, PA, USA (2006)

[Batliner et al., 2004] Batliner, A., Hacker, C., Steidl, S., Nöth, E., D'Arcy, S., Russell, M., Wong, M.: "You stupid tin box" - children interacting with the AIBO robot: A cross-linguistic emotional speech corpus. In: Proceedings of the 4th International Conference of Language Resources and Evaluation LREC 2004, Lisbon, pp. 171–174 (2004)

[Batliner et al., 2006] Batliner, A., Steidl, S., Schuller, B., Seppi, D., Laskowski, K., Vogt, T., Devillers, L., Vidrascu, L., Amir, N., Kessous, L., Aharonson, V.: Combining efforts for improving automatic classification of emotional user states. In: Proc. IS-LTC 2006, Ljubljana, Slovenia (2006)

[Boersma and Weenink, 2007] Boersma, P., Weenink, D.: Praat: doing phonetics by computer (version 4.5.15) [computer program] (2007) (Retrieved 24.02.2007) http://www.praat.org/

[Burkhardt et al., 2005a] Burkhardt, F., Paeschke, A., Rolfes, M., Sendlmeier, W.F., Weiss, B.: A database of German emotional speech. In: Proceedings of Interspeech 2005, Lisbon, Portugal (2005a)

[Burkhardt et al., 2005b] Burkhardt, F., van Ballegooy, M., Englert, R., Huber, R.: An emotion-aware voice portal. In: Electronic Speech Signal Processing Conference, Prague, Czech Republic (2005b)

[Chang and Lin, 2001] Chang, C.-C., Lin, C.-J.: LIBSVM: a library for support vector machines (2001), http://www.csie.ntu.edu.tw/~cjlin/libsvm

[Charles et al., 2007] Charles, F., Lemercier, S., Vogt, T., Bee, N., Mancini, M., Urbain, J., Price, M., André, E., Pelachaud, C., Cavazza, M.: Affective interactive narrative in the callas project. In: Demo paper in Proceedings of the 4th International Conference on Virtual Storytelling, Saint Malo, France (2007)

[de Rosis et al., 2003] de Rosis, F., Pelachaud, C., Poggi, I., Carofiglio, V., de Carolis, B.: From Greta's mind to her face: modelling the dynamics of affective states in a conversational embodied agent. International Journal of Human-Computer Studies 59, 81–118 (2003)

[Fink, 1999] Fink, G.: Developing HMM-based recognizers with ESMERALDA. In: Matoušek, V., et al. (eds.). Lecture notes in Artificial Intelligence, vol. 1962, pp. 229–234. Springer, Heidelberg (1999)

[Gilroy et al., 2007] Gilroy, S.W., Cavazza, M., Chaignon, R., Mäkelä, S.-M., Niiranen, M., André, E., Vogt, T., Billinghurst, M., Seichter, H., Benayoun, M.: An emotionally responsive AR art installation. In: Proceedings of ISMAR Workshop 2: Mixed Reality Entertainment and Art, Nara, Japan (2007)

[Hall, 1998] Hall, M.A.: Correlation-based feature subset selection for machine learning. Master's thesis, University of Waikato, New Zealand (1998)

[Hegel et al., 2006] Hegel, F., Spexard, T., Vogt, T., Horstmann, G., Wrede, B.: Playing a different imitation game: Interaction with an empathic android robot. In: Proc. 2006 IEEE-RAS International Conference on Humanoid Robots (Humanoids 2006) (2006)

[Jones and Deeming, 2007] Jones, C., Deeming, A.: Affective human-robotic interaction. In: Peter, C., Beale, R. (eds.) Affect and Emotion in Human-Computer Interaction. LNCS, vol. 4868. Springer, Heidelberg (2007)

[Jones and Sutherland, 2007] Jones, C., Sutherland, J.: Acoustic emotion recognition for affective computer gaming. In: Peter, C., Beale, R. (eds.) Affect and Emotion in Human-Computer Interaction. LNCS, vol. 4868. Springer, Heidelberg (2007)

[Kim et al., 2005] Kim, J., André, E., Rehm, M., Vogt, T., Wagner, J.: Integrating information from speech and physiological signals to achieve emotional sensitivity. In: Proceedings of Interspeech 2005, Lisbon, Portugal (2005)

[Madan, 2005] Madan, A.: Jerk-O-Meter: Speech-Feature Analysis Provides Feedback on Your Phone Interactions (2005) (retrieved: 28.06.2007),
http://www.media.mit.edu/press/jerk-o-meter/

[Oudeyer, 2003] Oudeyer, P.-Y.: The production and recognition of emotions in speech: features and algorithms. International Journal of Human-Computer Studies 59(1–2), 157–183 (2003)

[Rehm et al., 2008] Rehm, M., Vogt, T., Wissner, M., Bee, N.: Dancing the night away — controlling a virtual karaoke dancer by multimodal expressive cues. In: Proceedings of AAMAS 2008 (2008)

[Schiel et al., 2002] Schiel, F., Steininger, S., Türk, U.: The SmartKom multimodal corpus at BAS. In: Proceedings of the 3rd Language Resources & Evaluation Conference (LREC) 2002, Las Palmas, Gran Canaria, Spain, pp. 200–206 (2002)

[Schuller et al., 2007a] Schuller, B., Rigoll, G., Grimm, M., Kroschel, K., Moosmayr, T., Ruske, G.: Effects of in-car noise-conditions on the recognition of emotion within speech. In: Proc. of the DAGA 2007, Stuttgart, Germany (2007a)

[Schuller et al., 2007b] Schuller, B., Seppi, D., Batliner, A., Maier, A., Steidl, S.: Towards more reality in the recognition of emotional speech. In: IEEE (ed.) Proc. ICASSP 2007, Honolulu, Hawaii, USA, vol. 2, pp. 941–944 (2007b)

[Velten, 1968] Velten, E.: A laboratory task for induction of mood states. Behavior Research & Therapy 6, 473–482 (1968)

[Vogt and André, 2005] Vogt, T., André, E.: Comparing feature sets for acted and spontaneous speech in view of automatic emotion recognition. In: Proceedings of International Conference on Multimedia & Expo, Amsterdam, The Netherlands (2005)

[Vogt and André, 2006] Vogt, T., André, E.: Improving automatic emotion recognition from speech via gender differentiation. In: Proc. Language Resources and Evaluation Conference (LREC 2006), Genoa (2006)

[Vogt et al., 2007] Vogt, T., André, E., Wagner, J.: Automatic recognition of emotions from speech: a review of the literature and recommendations for practical realisation. In: Peter, C., Beale, R. (eds.) Affect and Emotion in Human-Computer Interaction. LNCS, vol. 4868. Springer, Heidelberg (2007)

[Wilting et al., 2006] Wilting, J., Krahmer, E., Swerts, M.: Real vs. acted emotional speech. In: Proceedings of Interspeech 2006 — ICSLP, Pittsburgh, PA, USA (2006)

[Witten and Frank, 2005] Witten, I.H., Frank, E.: Data Mining: Practical machine learning tools with Java implementations, 2nd edn. Morgan Kaufmann, San Francisco (2005)

Real-Time Emotion Recognition Using Echo State Networks

Stefan Scherer, Mohamed Oubbati, Friedhelm Schwenker, and Günther Palm

Institute of Neural Information Processing, Ulm University, 89069 Ulm, Germany
{stefan.scherer,mohamed.oubbati,friedhelm.schwenker,
guenther.palm}@uni-ulm.de

Abstract. The goal of this work is the exploration of real-time emotion recognition from speech. In this approach a novel type of recurrent neural networks called echo state networks (ESN) are utilized. Biologically motivated features representing modulations of the speech signal are used as input to the ESNs. The standard Berlin Database of Emotional Speech is used to evaluate the performance of the proposed approach. However, in this paper ongoing work is being presented and the final architecture has yet to be determined.

1 Introduction

The current aims of affective computing include the enhancement of human-computer interfaces, by improving their efficiency and usability [Cowie et al., 2001]. Recognizing emotions of fellow men plays an important role in daily conversations. For example, as it is mentioned in [Calder et al., 2000] a simple facial expression of disgust by your counterpart may prevent you from tasting your own food, in order not to experience the same unpleasant savor. In this work however, an approach towards real-time emotion recognition from speech only is introduced. The presented system describes still ongoing work and should be understood as some sort of proof of concept.

In contrast to common emotion recognition systems, a novel approach using modulation spectrum features as input for a recurrent neural network ensemble consisting of so called echo state networks (ESN) is presented. An ESN has an easy to use training algorithm, where only the output weights are to be adjusted. The basic idea of an ESN is to use a dynamic reservoir, which contains a large number of sparsely interconnected neurons with non-trainable weights. Since, the only weights that need to be adjusted in an ESN are the output weights, the training is not computationally expensive using the direct pseudo inverse calculation instead of gradient descent training. The issues being addressed using this approach comprise the necessity of noise insensitive emotion recognition and the need for fast emotion recognition, due to the nature of emotions. Emotions are a constantly changing signal as the following example found in [Picard, 2000] illustrates: A tennis player feels a piercing pain in his lower back and he first turns around clenching his fist and feeling angry, but as he sees that woman in a wheelchair hit him his feelings changed to sadness and sympathy.

E. André et al. (Eds.): PIT 2008, LNAI 5078, pp. 200–204, 2008.

The paper is organized and presented in five sections: Section 2 gives an overview of the database used for experiments, Sect. 3 describes the feature extraction and the automatic emotion recognition system, Sect. 4 presents preliminary results, and finally Sect. 5 concludes.

2   Database Description

The Berlin Database of Emotional Speech is used as a test bed for our approach. This corpus is a collection of around 800 utterances spoken in seven different emotions: anger, boredom, disgust, fear, happiness, sadness, and neutral. The database is publicly available at `http://pascal.kgw.tu-berlin.de/emodb/`. Ten professional actors (five male and five female) read the predefined utterances in an anechoic chamber, under supervised conditions. The text was taken from everyday life situations, and did not include any emotional bias. A human perception test to recognize various emotions with 20 participants resulted in a mean accuracy of around 84% [Burkhardt et al., 2005].

3   Experimental Setup

Common emotion recognition systems are utilizing short term analysis of the speech signal, e.g. extracting the fundamental frequency from frames not more than several milliseconds. In order to be able to generate decisions on the spoken emotion using this feature it is necessary to aggregate information over a whole utterance or several seconds of speech. Furthermore, computationally expensive statistics including variance, mean, and formants need to be evaluated [Scherer et al., 2007,Petrushin, 1999,Yacoub et al., 2003]. However, as mentioned before emotions are constantly changing and aggregating statistics of pitch or other similar features may not suffice [Scherer et al., 2003, Picard, 2000]. In this work this issue is being addressed by using long term modulation spectrum features extracted from larger segments of the speech signal (100ms) and novel recurrent neural networks (RNN) called echo state networks (ESN).

3.1   Feature Extraction

In contrast to common audio processing techniques, larger frames of speech are analyzed (100ms) in this work. The slow temporal evolution of the speech is used to represent the emotional status of the user [Scherer et al., 2003,Scherer et al., 2007]. Furthermore in earlier studies, these features have shown to be insensitive towards noise and robust against changing recording situations [Scherer et al., 2008]. After a lead time of 400 ms the used feature extraction algorithm extracts feature vectors with a frequency of 25 Hz, which is sufficient for emotion recognition in many applications regarding time-critical issues. The extraction is based on standard techniques such as the Fourier transform and Mel filtering, rendering a biologically inspired algorithm. The exact algorithm is described in [Scherer et al., 2008, Scherer et al., 2007].

3.2   Echo State Network Ensemble

For the real-time emotion recognition task ESNs were chosen, because of their capability to take previous information into account due to feedback connections [Jaeger, 2002]. Furthermore, ESNs are trained efficiently using the direct pseudo inverse method. The topology of an example ESN is shown in Fig. 1 (a). After thorough parameter tuning, for the experiments $K = 8$ input neurons, $N = 1500$ internal neurons and $L = 1$ output neurons were used. The connections within the internal neurons were randomly set with a probability of 50%. Additionally, the spectral width $\lambda_{\max}$ was set to 0.25. This is achieved by scaling the weight matrix W in such a way that its maximum eigenvalue is set to $\lambda_{\max}$.

For the training the following offline learning procedure was used:

1. Given I/O training sequence $(U(n), D(n))$
2. Generate randomly the matrices (W^{in}, W, W^{back}), scaling the weight matrix W such that its maximum eingenvalue $|\lambda_{max}| \leq 1$.
3. Drive the network using the training I/O training data, by computing

$$X(n+1) = f(W^{in}U(n+1) + WX(n) + W^{back}D(n)),   (1)$$

where f is the transfer function tanh of a neuron.

4. Collect at each time the state $X(n)$ as a new row into a state collecting matrix M, and collect similarly at each time the sigmoid-inverted teacher output $tanh^{-1}D(n)$ into a teacher collection matrix T.
5. Compute the pseudo inverse of M and put

$$W^{out} = (M^{-1}T)^t   (2)$$

t: indicates transpose operation.

For each possible 1vs1 combination of two emotions such a network was trained, resulting in 21 separate networks (Fig. 1 (b)) responsible for only two emotions each. Every feature frame is used as input to all networks and their outputs are combined in a decision fusion (Fig. 1 (c)) step. For the time being the outputs of the ESNs are used as votes for the possible emotions. For example, the network accountable for anger vs. neutral may output a value between -1 and 1, if the value is below zero the network votes for neutral and vice versa. In this manner the decisions of all the networks are combined to a conclusive classification result. Furthermore, an alternative decision fusion technique called decision templates proposed in [Kuncheva, 2004] was used. However, the decision fusion requires more testing in order to find an optimal way of classifying the emotional utterances. For example, it may be necessary to exclude decisions from indecisive ESNs distinguished by output values close to zero. Additionally, decision shifts from frame to frame should be detected and filtered out.

4   Preliminary Results

All the experiments were carried out on a German dataset, which is described in Sect. 2. A standard 10-fold cross validation experiment series was conducted.

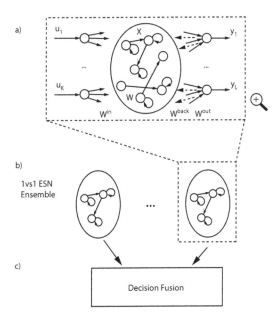

Fig. 1. (a) Basic architecture of an ESN. Dashed lines indicate optional connections. (b) ESN 1vs1 Ensemble architecture. Each ESN is trained to recognize two different emotions. (c) Single votes of the ESNs are collected and an overall decision is formed.

For each of the experiments in the series a randomly chosen tenth of the data was used for testing and the rest was used for training the 21 ESNs. Each of the ESNs was solely trained with the data it is responsible for, such as the anger vs. neutral ESN was trained with angry and neutral emotional material.

In the first experiment the outputs of the ESNs were used as supporting weights for the different emotions. The results reveal an accuracy of 53%, which is much better than chance since there are seven possible outputs, but the accuracy needs further improvement.

In the second experiment, the decision fusion (Fig. 1 (c)) was accomplished by the decision templates technique. The accuracy of 57% is comparable to earlier studies [Scherer et al., 2007], where accuracies of around 70% were achieved using three different types of features and the decisions were made on whole utterances not on single frames.

5   Conclusions and Future Work

In this work an easy to train 1vs1 ensemble architecture using ESNs was presented to recognize emotions close to real-time. As input to the networks biologically motivated modulation features from the speech signal were used. Since, this is still work in progress the results should improve over the time while experimenting with different fusion techniques. However, the results are already comparable to earlier studies that cannot recognize emotions on a frame wise basis.

Concluding it is to mention, that the ESN ensemble architecture in combination with speech modulation features revealed promising results. However, it is necessary to vary the architecture further, find the optimal fusion technique, and analyze the results in order to improve the recognition performance. Additionally, it may be interesting to test the stability of the architecture according to noisy environments as in [Scherer et al., 2008].

References

[Burkhardt et al., 2005] Burkhardt, F., Paeschke, A., Rolfes, M., Sendlmeier, W., Weiss, B.: A database of german emotional speech. In: Proceedings of Interspeech 2005 (2005)

[Calder et al., 2000] Calder, A.J., Keane, J., Manes, F., Antoun, N., Young, A.W.: Impaired recognition and experience of disgust following brain injury. Nature Neuroscience 3, 1077–1078 (2000)

[Cowie et al., 2001] Cowie, R., Douglas-Cowie, E., Tsapatsoulis, N., Votsis, G., Kollias, S., Fellenz, W., Taylor, J.: Emotion recognition in human-computer interaction. IEEE Signal Processing Magazine 18(1), 32–80 (2001)

[Jaeger, 2002] Jaeger, H.: Tutorial on training recurrent neural networks, covering bppt, rtrl, ekf and the echo state network approach. Technical Report 159, Fraunhofer-Gesellschaft, St. Augustin Germany (2002)

[Kuncheva, 2004] Kuncheva, L.: Combining pattern classifiers: methods and algorithms. Wiley, Chichester (2004)

[Petrushin, 1999] Petrushin, V.: Emotion in speech: recognition and application to call centers. In: Proceedings of Artificial Neural Networks in Engineering (1999)

[Picard, 2000] Picard, R.W.: Affective Computing. MIT Press, Cambridge (2000)

[Scherer et al., 2003] Scherer, K.R., Johnstone, T., Klasmeyer, G.: Handbook of Affective Sciences - Vocal expression of emotion, ch.23. In: Affective Science, pp. 433–456. Oxford University Press, Oxford (2003)

[Scherer et al., 2008] Scherer, S., Oubbati, M., Schwenker, F., Palm, G.: Real-time emotion recognition from speech using echo state networks. In: Proceedings of ANNPR (submission, 2008)

[Scherer et al., 2007] Scherer, S., Schwenker, F., Palm, G.: Classifier fusion for emotion recognition from speech. In: Proceedings of Intelligent Environments 2007 (2007)

[Yacoub et al., 2003] Yacoub, S., Simske, S., Lin, X., Burns, J.: Recognition of emotions in interactive voice response systems. In: Proceedings of Eurospeech 2003 (2003)

Emotion Classification of Audio Signals Using Ensemble of Support Vector Machines

Taner Danisman and Adil Alpkocak

Computer Engineering Department,
Dokuz Eylul University, 35160 Izmir, Turkey
{taner,alpkocak}@cs.deu.edu.tr

Abstract. This study presents an approach for emotion classification of speech utterances based on ensemble of support vector machines. We considered feature level fusion of the MFCC, total energy and F0 as input feature vectors, and choose bagging method for the classification. Additionally, we also present a new emotional dataset based on a popular animation film, Finding Nemo where emotions are much emphasized to attract attention of spectators. Speech utterances are directly extracted from video audio channel including all background noise. Totally 2054 utterances from 24 speakers were annotated by a group of volunteers based on seven emotion categories. We concentrated on perceived emotion. Our approach has been tested on our newly developed dataset besides publically available datasets of DES and EmoDB. Experiments showed that our approach achieved 77.5% and 66.8% overall accuracy for four and five class classification on EFN dataset respectively. In addition, we achieved 67.6% accuracy on DES (five classes) and 63.5% on EmoDB (seven classes) dataset using ensemble of SVM's with 10 fold cross-validation.

1 Introduction

Emotions have a great role in human-to-human communication. Over the last quarter century, there is increasing number of researches performed on understanding the human emotions. A variety of computer systems can use emotional speech classification including call center applications, psychology and emotion enabled Text to Speech (TTS) engines. Current studies on emotion detection mainly concentrate on visual modalities, including facial expressions, muscle movements, action units, body movements, etc. However, emotion itself is a multimodal concept and emotion detection task requires interdisciplinary studies including visual, textual, acoustic, and physiological signal domains.

Although it seems to be easy to understand for a human to detect the emotional class of an audio signal, researches showed that [Engberg and Hansen, 1996], average score of identifying five different emotional classes (neutral state, surprise, happiness, sadness and anger) is between 56-85%, (global average is 67% and kappa statistic is 0.59). Without emotional clues, it is difficult to understand exact meaning of spoken words. Words are followed by punctuation characters like "?" "!" "..." in textual domain which makes easy to understand the meaning of the text. On the other hand understanding the context from linguistic information is limited in some cases.

E. André et al. (Eds.): PIT 2008, LNAI 5078, pp. 205–216, 2008.
© Springer-Verlag Berlin Heidelberg 2008

In this case prosodic features of speech signal carries paralinguistic clues about the physical and emotional state of the human.

Emotional Speech Classification is not a trivial task, and requires a set of successive operations such as voice activity detection (VAD), feature extraction, training and finally classification. Previous works on this area use Mel Frequency Cepstral Coefficients (MFCC) [Shami and Verhelst, 2007], [Altun and Polat, 2007], [Le et al., 2004], pitch frequencies as formants [Zervas et al., 2006], [Ververidis et al., 2004], [Hammal et al., 2005], [Datcu and Rothkrantz, 2005], [Shami and Verhelst, 2007], [Teodorescu and Feraru, 2007], [Lugger and Yang, 2006], [Sedaaghi et al., 2007], [Altun and Polat, 2007], [Lugger and Yang, 2007], [Zhongzhe et al., 2006], [Sedaaghi et al., 2007], [Pasechke and Sendlmeier, 2000] speech rate [Hammal et al., 2005], zero crossing rate [Lugger and Yang, 2007], Fujisaki parameters [Fujisaki and Hirose, 1984], [Zervas et al., 2006], energy [Zhongzhe et al., 2006], [Ververidis et al., 2004], [Hammal et al., 2005], [Altun and Polat, 2007], [Sedaaghi et al., 2007], [Lugger and Yang, 2007], linear predictive coding (LPC) [Altun and Polat, 2007], [Le et al., 2004] for feature extraction purposes. In addition, [Zhongzhe et al., 2006], [Ververidis et al., 2004], [Sedaaghi et al., 2007] and [Lugger and Yang, 2007] used sequential floating forward selection (SFFS) method to discover the best feature set for the classification. Classification techniques used in emotion classification task includes Support Vector Machines (SVM) [Hammal et al., 2005], [Shami and Verhelst, 2007], [Altun and Polat, 2007], Neural Networks (NN) [Zhongzhe et al., 2006], Hidden Markov Models (HMM) [Le et al., 2004], Linear Discriminant Analysis (LDA) [Hammal et al., 2005], [Lugger and Yang, 2006], Instance Based Learning [Zervas et al., 2006], Vector Quantification (VQ) [Le et al., 2004], C4.5 ([Zervas et al., 2006], [Shami and Verhelst, 2007]), GentleBoost [Datcu and Rothkrantz, 2005], Bayes Classifiers [Ververidis et al., 2004], [Hammal et al., 2005], [Lugger and Yang, 2007] and K-Nearest Neighbor (K-NN) [Ververidis et al., 2004], [Hammal et al., 2005], [Shami and Verhelst, 2007] classifiers.

Main contribution of this paper is two fold. First, we present an approach for emotion classification of speech utterances based on ensemble of support vector machines. It considers feature level fusion of the MFCC, total energy and F0 as input feature vectors, and uses bagging method to ensemble of SVM classifiers. The second, we present a new emotional dataset based on a popular animation film, Finding Nemo where emotions are much emphasized to attract attention of spectators. In this dataset, speech utterances are directly extracted from video audio channel including all background noise and music to fulfill the real world requirements, properly. We concentrated on perceived emotion in video therefore a total of 2054 utterances from 24 speakers were annotated by a group of volunteers based on seven emotion categories, and we selected 250 utterances each for training and test sets. Our approach is tested on both newly developed dataset as well as two publically available data sets, and the results are promising with respect to current state-of-the-art.

The rest of the paper is organized as follows. In section two, structures and detailed properties of publicly available data collections and related works on these collections are explained. In section three, our approach to feature extraction and ensemble classification technique used in this study is presented. Section four shows the results of the experiments performed on the test sets and explain the details of the multimodal emotion dataset EFN. Finally, section five concludes the study, provides a general discussion, and gives a look at the future studies on this subject.

2   Background and Related Works

Before starting on a research on emotion classification, there are two important questions exist: The first question is "Which emotions should be addressed?" and the latter is "is there any training set available for this research?" Of course there are many different emotion sets exist in literature covering basic emotions, universal emotions, primary and secondary emotions, and neutral vs. emotional. According to the latest review by [Ververidis and Kotropoulos, 2006], 64 emotion related datasets exists. Many of the datasets (54%) are simulated, 51% are in English and 20% are in German Language. In addition, 73% of the datasets are compiled for emotion recognition purposes whereas 25% is for speech synthesis.

In this study, we focused two publicly available and commonly used datasets, and provide a comparison of studies based on two of them.

2.1   Danish Emotional Speech Database (DES)

Danish Emotional Speech Database DES [Engberg and Hansen, 1996] is in Danish Language, and it consists of 260 emotional utterances, including 2 single words ('Yes',' No'), 9 sentences and 2 long passages, recorded from two female and two male actors. Each actor speaks under five different emotional states including anger, happiness, neutral state, sadness, and surprise. Utterances were recorded under silent condition in mono channel, sampled at 20 KHz with 16-bit, and only one person speaks at a time. Average length of the utterances in DES dataset is about 3.9 seconds, 1.08 seconds when long passages ignored. Table 1 shows the details of DES, such as the number of utterances and total length per emotion for both training and test set.

Table 1. Properties of DES dataset, where #U and #FN indicates, number of utterances and number of feature vectors, respectively

Emotion	Positive Samples			Negative Samples		Number of Subsets
	#U	Length(sec.)	#FV	#U	#FV	
Anger	52	192.9	2222	208	9423	4
Happiness	52	207.4	2494	208	9151	3
Neutral	52	207.3	2370	208	9275	3
Sadness	52	223.3	2196	208	9449	4
Surprise	52	205.1	2363	208	9282	3
TOTAL	260	1036	11645	1040	46580	17

To date, many of studies on this subject employed on DES dataset, and Table 2 provides a quick snapshot of them. [Zervas et al., 2006] and [Datcu and Rothkrantz, 2005] achieved better accuracy than human based evaluation [Engberg and Hansen, 1996] using Instance Based Learning and GentleBoost algorithms respectively. Baseline accuracy is computed by classifying all the utterances as the major emotional class in test set. According to [Engberg and Hansen, 1996], 67% of the emotions are correctly identified by humans on average on DES dataset. [Sedaaghi et al., 2007] used sequential floating feature selection (SFFS) for optimizing correct classification rate of Bayes Classifier on DES dataset and get 48.91% accuracy, in average. [Le et al., 2004] achieved 55% accuracy for speaker independent study. Their speaker dependent result is between 70% and 80%.

Table 2. Performance of past studies on DES dataset in terms of accuracy

Study	Classifier	# of Classes	Accuracy %
Baseline		5	20.0
[Datcu and Rothkrantz, 2005]	GentleBoost	5	72.0
[Hammal et al., 2005]	Bayes Classifier	5	53.8
Human Eval. [Engberg and Hansen,1996]		5	67
[Le et al., 2004]	Vector Quantification	5	55.0
[Sedaaghi et al., 2007]	Bayes + SFFS + Genetic Alg.	5	48.9
[Shami and Verhelst,2007]	ADA-C4.5+ AIBO approach	5	64.1
[Shami and Verhelst,2007]	ADA-C4.5+ SBA approach	5	59.7
[Ververidis et al., 2004]	Bayes+SFS	5	51.6
[Zervas et al., 2006]	C4.5	5	66.0
[Zervas et al., 2006]	Instance Based Learning	5	72.9

2.2 Berlin Database of Emotional Speech (EmoDB)

EmoDB [Burkhardt et al., 2005] dataset is another popular and publically available emotional dataset. It is in German Language, and consists of 535 emotional utterances recorded from 5 female and 5 male actors. Each actor speaks at most 10 different sentences in 7 different emotions anger, happiness, neutral, sadness, boredom, disgust, and fear. Files are 16-bit PCM, mono channel; sampled at 16Khz. Total length of the 535 utterances in the dataset is 1487 seconds and average utterance length is about 2.77 seconds. Table 3 shows its properties of EmoDB for both training and test set, in detail.

Table 3. Properties of EmoDB dataset, where #U and #FN indicates, number of utterances and number of feature vectors and number of subsets, respectively

Emotion	Positive Samples			Negative Samples		Number of Subsets
	#U	Length (sec.)	#FV	#U	#FV	
Angry	127	335.3	6076	408	22178	3
Happiness	71	154.2	3385	464	24869	7
Neutral	79	154.1	3613	456	24641	6
Sadness	62	186.3	4896	473	23358	4
Boredom	81	180.6	4348	454	23906	5
Disgust	46	251.2	3013	489	25241	8
Fear	69	225.0	2923	466	25331	8
TOTAL	535	1487	28254	3210	169524	41

Table 4 presents squeezed comparison of studies held on EmoDB dataset in terms of classifier type, number of classes and accuracy. As in studies on DES, [Datcu and Rothkrantz, 2005] again used GentleBoost algorithm on EmoDB dataset for six emotion classes out of seven, and achieved 86.3% accuracy. [Altun and Polat, 2007] used SVM for four class emotion classification, [Lugger and Yang, 2007] used linear discriminant analyses for anger, happiness, sadness, and neutral emotions and they reported 81.8% accuracy. Additionally, they have tested Bayes classifier, and achieved 74.4% accuracy for six classes using leave-one-speaker-out method on short utterances. Gender dependent study from [Zhongzhe et al., 2006] achieved 77.3% accuracy for female subjects considering seven classes.

Table 4. Previous studies on EmoDB dataset in terms of accuracy %

Study	Classifier	# of Classes	Accuracy %
[Altun and Polat,2007]	SVM	4	85.5
Baseline		7	23.7
[Datcu and Rothkrantz, 2005]	GentleBoost	6	86.3
Human Eval.[Burkhardt et al.,2005]		7	86.0
[Lugger and Yang, 2007]	Bayes Classifier	6	74.4
[Lugger and Yang, 2007]	Linear Discriminant Analyses	4	81.8
[Shami and Verhelst,2007]	SVM+ AIBO approach	7	75.5
[Shami and Verhelst,2007]	SVM+ SBA Approach	7	65.5
[Zhongzhe et al., 2006]	Two-Stage NN	7	77.3

3 Our Approach to Emotion Classification

The feature vector we used to represent the emotional speech in our approach, aims to preserve the information needed to determine the emotional content of such a signal. First, each speech utterance was segmented into ~46ms frames (512samples) with a ~23ms overlap area (256 samples) with next frame. As a feature vector, we have used 30 MFCC, total energy, and F0 formant values calculated from each frame and combined them as seen in equation (1). We assume that each frame from an utterance represents the same emotional state.

In order to calculate MFCC coefficients, we have used Matlab Audio Toolbox [Pampalk, 2004], with 30-bin Mel Filter Bank. Then, a set of MFCC vectors, K_{MFCC} shown in (1), is prepared for each utterance.

$$K_{MFCC} = \begin{bmatrix} C_{1,1} & C_{2,1} & \cdot & \cdot & \cdot & C_{n-1,1} & C_{n,1} \\ C_{1,2} & C_{2,2} & \cdot & \cdot & \cdot & C_{n-1,2} & C_{n,1} \\ \cdot & \cdot & \cdot & \cdot & \cdot & \cdot & \cdot \\ C_{1,m} & C_{2,m} & \cdot & \cdot & \cdot & C_{n-1,m} & C_{n,m} \end{bmatrix} \quad (1)$$

Similarly, F0 and total energy values are computed. At the end of the feature extraction phase, each speech frame was represented with 32-bin feature vector, containing *MFCC*, total energy and F0 value.

In training phase, we used support vector machines (SVM), which is a supervised learning algorithm that tries to map the input feature space having known positive and negative samples into high dimensional space where a hyperplane maximizes the data separation. Since SVM is primarily a dichotomy classifier, we have used one-vs-all method where the numbers of positive and negative samples are not equal. However, having such a distribution made the classifier biasing to negative class, as expected. Moreover, for an m-class classifier, it is a general problem since there exist m-1 negative samples for each positive sample. Consequently, the results biased toward to the majority class.

To overcome the biasing problem, first, we divided the negative samples into smaller parts equal to the size of the positive samples. However this fragmentations arises another problem of ensemble of classifiers. On the other hand, literature [Zhou et al., 2002] shows that generalization ability of ensemble of classifiers has a better performance than a single learner. In literature, many solutions have been suggested for this problem, such as boosting, bagging, or k-fold partitioning. We choose bagging [Breiman, 1996] (Bootstrap aggregating) method to overcome aforementioned difficulties. Bagging is useful especially when the classifier gives unstable results in response to small changes such as speaker changes in the training data. In order to do this, we first manipulate our training samples, where we have provided a non-overlapping set of negative examples for each positive set, as seen in Fig. 1.

Let us assume that we have equal size of samples in our training set for m classes. For a given positive class, C_i^+, normally there exist m-1 negative classes. In order to create sub-training sets including equal positive and negative samples, we have divided each negative class samples, C_i^-, into sub sets ($S_{i,j}$, where $\forall i,j, 1 \le i \le m, S_{i,j} = m$-1 for balanced sets) from $C_{i,1}^-$ to $C_{i,m-1}^-$. For each negative emotion class, C_i^-, there is a corresponding negative subsets, $C_{i,j}^-$, that need to be merged to create C_i^- with the same size as positive samples. This finalizes the creation of final training sets, as seen in Fig. 1. These sets are then used for the creation of emotion model $\underline{EM_{ij}}$ where i represent emotion and j represents the sub model of respective emotional class. Therefore total number of emotion models EM_{ij} in this approach is $m \times (m\text{-}1)$ for balanced sets.

If the number of samples for each emotion class is not equal then, the value of $S_{i,j}$ depends on the size of the C_i^+ and C_i^- and can be computed by (2).

$$S_{i,j} = \left(\sum_{i=1, i \in C^-}^{m} size(C_i^-) \right) / size(C_i^+) \tag{2}$$

After preparing a set of Emotional Model, EM_{ij}, we performed a cumulative addition on the floating SVM predictions as shown in (3). In other words, we sum up the classification results (i.e., prediction values) of the frame belonging to a specific utterance.

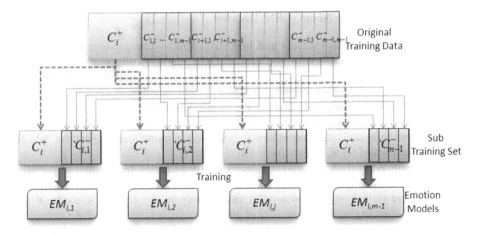

Fig. 1. Partitioning data into equal positive and negative subsets for $m=5$

Considering a supervised learning algorithm, it receives a set of training samples, TS=$\{(x_1,y_1),\ldots,(x_n,y_n)\}$ where n is the number of samples in the training set and each x_i represents the feature vector in a form of $\langle x_{i,1},x_{i,2},\ldots,x_{i,k}\rangle$, where each $x_{i,j}$ is a real valued component of x_i. Similarly, our training set at utterance level is represented by a set of samples, TSU=$\{(U_1, y_x), (U_2, y_z),\ldots,(U_n,y_s)\}$ where $y_i \in y=\{1,2,\ldots,m\}$ is its multiclass emotion label.

As the original implementation of SVM proposes a dichotomy classifier, we defined a function $f : U \rightarrow Y$ which maps an utterance U to an emotion label $f(U)$. Each utterance U_i consists of a set of features vectors x_i, represented by $U_{i,j}$, the number of feature vectors for a given utterance U_i is represented by size(U_i) and the number of models for a given emotion, and EM_i is represented by size(EM_i). Each EM_i has equal weights and for a given test sample U, the binary SVM classifier outputs an m-vector $f(U)=(f_1(U), f_2(U),\ldots, f_m(U))$ as shown in (3).

$$f_i(U) = \sum_{j=1}^{size(EM_i)} \sum_{k=1}^{size(U_i)} EM_{ij}(U_{i,k}) \tag{3}$$

Finally, classifier selects the maximum of $f_i(U)$ as result, and assigns the corresponding class label using (4).

$$f(U) = \arg\max_i f_i(U) \tag{4}$$

4   Experimentations

In this section we discuss the details and experiences on constructing a new emotional dataset activity and the details of experimentations we conducted in order to evaluate our approach.

4.1 Emotional Finding Nemo (EFN) Dataset

Publically available datasets, DES and EmoDB, includes utterances recorded under silent conditions, and only one person speaks at a time. This is mostly not a case for a real world application. For example, for a given video fragment, speech utterances rarely come with a silent background. Additionally, the number of utterance samples in both DES and EmoDB is not enough for an efficient training and testing. Because of the lack of the small sized dataset, studies on those datasets usually measured using cross validation technique. Consequently, we need a more realistic dataset which fulfils the real world requirements for video.

We have developed an emotional dataset directly extracted from video of popular animation film of Finding Nemo, and called EFN. Main reason for selecting an animation movie is that, animation movies usually targets the children's attention by using music, dancing and high intensity of emotions which makes them help to understand the content. Firstly, EFN dataset is in English, and the utterances were extracted directly from video audio channel including all background music, noise etc, which make it closer to meet real world situations in terms of perceived emotions. It contains 2054 utterances from 24 speakers.

Boundaries of the utterances were extracted using the timestamp information exists in subtitles and voice activity detection (VAD) is used to find presence of speech signal as described in [Danisman and Alpkocak, 2007]. Boundaries of utterances are determined considering continuous speech. The dataset is constructed using "Emotional Speech Annotator" application developed in MatLab. Fig. 2 shows a snapshot of respective application.

A total of seven persons, from our department, whose ages are between 24-59 and secondary language is English were participated in the experiment. Participants were

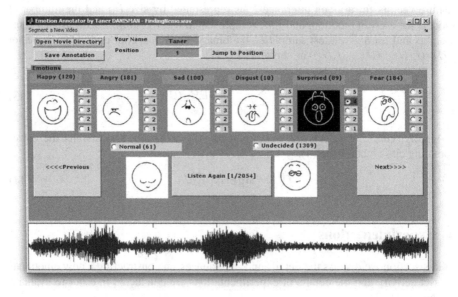

Fig. 2. Emotional Speech Annotator

instructed first to classify each of 2054 utterance of length 3802 seconds (63.38 minutes) in a forced choice procedure choosing one among the seven emotion classes in addition to undecided class using the Emotional Speech Annotator. Default choice is set to the undecided class. For each utterance except normal and undecided classes there are five different intensity levels exist. Level 1 represents the least intensity and level 5 represents the highest intensity for the emotion. Participants are able to listen to any utterance at any time. Correction in previous decisions is also possible. The average, minimum and maximum speech utterance length in EFN is 1.85, 0.5 and 6.1 seconds, respectively.

Classifying utterances into a number of emotion classes is alone difficult task, as there is no clear cut between emotional classes. Assigning an emotion label to the utterances may change from annotator to annotator. In order to overcome this problem, we have selected best representative and consistent annotations having high intensity values. After that top ranked emotions for each emotion class are selected for training and testing. For experimental studies we selected utterances having more than 71.4% accuracy only. In other words, we have chosen utterances, where at least five out of seven participants agreed. We did not include disgust emotion since there are too few samples in this class.

Table 5 shows the details of EFN dataset, including feature vectors in each emotion model used in training process. The total number of samples for both training and test set contains 250 different speech utterances. Table 5 also includes training and testing times of our experimentations.

Table 5. Number of utterances, subsets and corresponding feature vectors in EFN training and test set. #U=Number of Utterances, #FV=Number of feature vectors, #SS=Number of subsets

Emotion	Training Set					Test Set	
	(+) Samples		(-) Samples		#SS	Samples	
	#U	#FV	#U	#FV		#U	#FV
Angry	50	2009	200	7070	3	50	1964
Happiness	50	2178	200	6901	3	50	2342
Neutral	50	1174	200	7905	4	50	1728
Sadness	50	1877	200	7202	4	50	1952
Surprise	50	1841	200	7238	4	50	1603
TOTAL	250	9079	200	36316	18	250	9589

4.2 Experimental Results

For all experimentations, we assumed that the smallest measurement unit is utterance and sampling rate of the all audio files is converted to 11025Hz and mono channel. Since the number of emotion classes is not equal in DES, EmoDB and EFN datasets, we have performed different experimentations in terms of number of classes. We made several experimentation using SVM^{Light} [Joachims, 1999] with linear and RBF kernels. For linear kernel we have choose the cost factor *Cost*=0.001 and for the RBF kernel the *gamma* and *Cost* values are 9.0-e005 and 6.0, respectively.

Table 6 shows the results we obtained from our experimentations using EFN dataset. Overall accuracy we achieved is 66.8% with kappa=0.58 for five emotional classes (i.e., anger, happiness, neutral state, sadness, and fear). For four emotional classes (i.e., anger, happiness, sadness, and fear) emotion classification using RBF kernel we get 77.5% accuracy with kappa value of 0.67 substantial agreements. For six classes (i.e., anger, happiness, neutral state, sadness, fear, and surprise) we get 61.3% (kappa=0.53) and 52.3% (kappa=0.42) accuracy for RBF kernel and linear kernel, respectively.

Table 6. Confusion matrix using EFN trained linear and RBF kernels on EFN test set, Cost=1.0e-3 for linear kernel, gamma=9.0-e005, Cost=6 for RBF kernel

Predicted⇒ ⇓Actual	Accuracy in %, Overall=66.8% with RBF kernel									
	Anger		Happiness		Neutral		Sadness		Fear	
	Lin.	RBF	Lin.	RBF	Lin.	RBF	Lin.	RBF	Lin.	RBF
Anger	**56**	**58**	22	14	14	18	4	8	4	2
Happiness	10	12	**58**	**72**	12	8	12	2	8	6
Neutral	2	4	18	14	**58**	**68**	22	14	0	0
Sadness	4	4	12	8	18	14	**66**	**74**	0	0
Fear	22	18	12	18	0	0	2	2	**64**	**62**

Experiments show that Surprise-Happiness and Neutral-Sadness couples are most confused emotion classes as seen in Table 7, as in previous studies. For the DES and EmoDB, we achieved 67.6% and 63.5% accuracy using RBF kernel as seen in Table 7 and Table 8, where reported human based evaluations are 67% [Engberg and Hansen, 1996] and 86% [Burkhardt et al., 2005] respectively. In terms of computation time, RBF kernel method is more expensive as than linear kernel. However, its performance is better than the linear kernel.

Table 7. Confusion matrix using ensembles of SVM RBF kernel on DES, gamma=9.0e-5, Cost=6 vs. Human based evaluation [Engberg and Hansen,1996], H=Human

Predicted⇒ ⇓Actual	Accuracy in %, Overall=67.6% using ensembles									
	Anger		Happiness		Neutral		Sadness		Surprise	
	RBF	H.	RBF	H.	RBF	H.	RBF	H.	RBF	H.
Anger	**82**	**60.8**	12	2.6	0	0.1	2	31.7	4	4.8
Happiness	20	10.0	**70**	**59.1**	0	28.7	2	1.0	8	1.3
Neutral	14	8.3	2	29.8	**58**	**56.4**	24	1.7	2	3.8
Sadness	4	12.6	0	1.8	16	0.1	**78**	**85.2**	2	0.3
Surprise	12	10.2	36	8.5	0	4.5	2	1.7	**50**	**75.1**

Table 8. Confusion matrix using ensembles of SVM on EmoDB, gamma=9.0e-5, C=6

Predicted⇒ ⇓Actual	Accuracy in %, Overall=63.5% using ensembles						
	Anger	Happiness	Neutral	Sadness	Boredom	Disgust	Fear
Anger	**90.0**	5.8	0.0	0.0	0.0	0.8	3.3
Happiness	30.0	**47.1**	1.4	0.0	0.0	12.9	8.6
Neutral	0.0	0.0	**60.0**	1.4	32.9	0.0	5.7
Sadness	0.0	0.0	16.7	**71.7**	11.7	0.0	0.0
Boredom	1.3	0.0	43.8	8.8	**40.0**	3.8	2.5
Disgust	5.0	0.0	12.5	0.0	5.0	**72.5**	5.0
Fear	5.0	6.7	15.0	1.7	1.7	6.7	**63.3**

5 Conclusion

In this study, we present an approach to emotion recognition of speech utterances that is based on ensembles of SVM classifiers. Since generalization ability of ensemble of classifiers has a better performance than a single learner, we considered feature level fusion of the MFCC, total energy and F0 as input feature vectors, and choose bagging method to ensemble of SVM classifiers.

Additionally, we also present a new emotional dataset based on a popular animation film, Finding Nemo. We choose this film because of utterances in cartoon films are especially exaggerated. Speech utterances are directly extracted from video audio channel including all background noise. Then, total of 2054 utterances from 24 speakers were annotated by a group of volunteers based on seven emotion categories, and we selected 250 utterances each for training and test sets. We used original English version of film. However, annotated dataset can be easily transformed into other languages since many dubbed version of this film is available.

We tested our approach on our newly developed dataset EFN as well as publically available datasets of DES and EmoDB. Experiments showed that our approach 77.5% and 66.8% overall accuracy for four and five class emotional speech classification on EFN dataset respectively. In addition, we achieved an overall accuracy of 67.6% on DES with five classes and 63.5% on EmoDB with seven classes dataset using ensemble of SVM's with 10 fold cross-validation.

Our study showed that, different emotion sets have different classification results. Some emotions have higher detection rates like anger, sadness and fear. On the other hand, surprise is the least detected emotion. Furthermore, experiments on EFN which is based on video audio channel also showed that background and multi-speaker voices did not affect the performance of the classifiers. We reached up to 77.5% accuracy on four-class emotion classification in EFN dataset. The results we obtained will lead us to new studies on emotional classification of video fragments and can be further improved by using multimodality such as visual, musical and textual attributes.

Acknowledgments. This study was supported by the Scientific and Technological Research Council of Turkey (TUBITAK) Project No: 107E002.

References

[Altun and Polat, 2007] Altun, H., Polat, G.: New Frameworks to Boost Feature Selection Algorithms in Emotion Detection for Improved Human-Computer Interaction. In: Mele, F., Ramella, G., Santillo, S., Ventriglia, F. (eds.) BVAI 2007. LNCS, vol. 4729, pp. 533–541. Springer, Heidelberg (2007)

[Breiman, 1996]Breiman, L.: Bagging predictors. Machine Learning 24(2), 123–140 (1996)

[Burkhardt et al., 2005]Burkhardt, F., Paeschke, A., Rolfes, M., Sendlmeier, W., Weiss, B.: A Database of German Emotional Speech. In: Proc. INTERSPEECH 2005, ISCA, Lisbon, Portugal, pp. 1517–1520 (2005)

[Danisman and Alpkocak, 2007] Danisman, T., Alpkocak, A.: Speech vs. Nonspeech Segmentation of Audio Signals Using Support Vector Machines. In: Signal Processing and Communication Applications Conference, Eskisehir, Turkey (2007)

[Datcu and Rothkrantz, 2005] Datcu, D., Rothkrantz, L.J.M.: Facial expression recognition with Relevance Vector Machines. In: IEEE International Conference on Multimedia & Expo (ICME 2005) (2005) ISBN 0-7803-9332-5

[Engberg and Hansen, 1996] Engberg, I.S., Hansen, A.V.: Documentation of the Danish Emotional Speech Database (DES). Internal AAU report, Center for Person Kommunikation, Denmark (1996)

[Fujisaki and Hirose, 1984] Fujisaki, H., Hirose, K.: Analysis of voice fundamental frequency contours for declarative sentences of Japanese. Journal of the Acoustical Society of Japan 5(4), 233–242 (1984)

[Hammal et al., 2005] Hammal, Z., Bozkurt, B., Couvreur, L., Unay, U., Caplier, A., Dutoit, T.: Passive versus active: Vocal classification system. In: Proc. XIII European Signal Processing Conf., Antalya, Turkey (2005)

[Joachims, 1999] Joachims, T.: Making Large-Scale SVM Learning Practical. In: Schölkopf, B., Burges, C., Smola, A. (eds.) Advances in Kernel Methods - Support Vector Learning. MIT-Press, Cambridge (1999)

[Le et al., 2004] Le, X.H., Quenot, G., Castelli, E.: Speaker-Dependent Emotion Recognition for Audio Document Indexing. In: International Conference on Electronics, Information, and Communications (ICEIC 2004) (2004)

[Lugger and Yang, 2006] Lugger, M., Yang, B.: Classification of different speaking groups by means of voice quality parameters. ITG-Sprach-Kommunikation (2006)

[Lugger and Yang, 2007] Lugger, M., Yang, B.: An Incremental Analysis of Different Feature Groups In Speaker Independent Emotion Recognition. In: 16th Int. Congress of Phonetic Sciences (2007)

[Pampalk, 2004] Pampalk, E.: A Matlab Toolbox to Compute Music Similarity from Audio. In: Proc. of the 5th Int. Conferance on Music Information Retrieval, pp. 254–257 (2004)

[Pasechke and Sendlmeier, 2000] Pasechke, A., Sendlmeier, W.F.: Prosodic Characteristics of Emotional Speech: Measurements of Fundamental Frequency Movements. In: Proceedings of ISCA Workshop on Speech and Emotion, Northern Ireland, pp. 75–80 (2000)

[Sedaaghi et al., 2007] Sedaaghi, M.H., Kotropoulos, C., Ververidis, D.: Using Adaptive Genetic Algorithms to Improve Speech Emotion Recognition. In: IEEE 9th Workshop on Multimedia Signal Processing, MMSP 2007, pp. 461–464 (2007)

[Shami and Verhelst, 2007] Shami, M., Verhelst, W.: An evaluation of the robustness of existing supervised machine learning approaches to the classification of emotions in speech. Speech Communication 49(3), 201–212 (2007)

[Teodorescu and Feraru, 2007] Teodorescu, H.-N., Feraru, S.M.: A Study on Speech with Manifest Emotions. In: Matoušek, V., Mautner, P. (eds.) TSD 2007. LNCS (LNAI), vol. 4629, pp. 254–261. Springer, Heidelberg (2007)

[Ververidis and Kotropoulos, 2006] Ververidis, D., Kotropoulos, C.: Emotional speech recognition: Resources, features, and methods. Speech Communication 48(9), 1162–1181 (2006)

[Ververidis et al., 2004] Ververidis, D., Kotropoulos, C., Pitas, I.: Automatic Emotional Speech Classification. In: Proceedings of International Conference on Acoustics, Speech, and Signal Processing, Montreal, Canada, pp. 593–596 (2004)

[Zervas et al., 2006] Zervas, P., Mporas, I., Fakotakis, N., Kokkinakis, G.: Employing Fujisaki's Intonation Model Parameters for Emotion Recognition. In: Antoniou, G., Potamias, G., Spyropoulos, C., Plexousakis, D. (eds.) SETN 2006. LNCS (LNAI), vol. 3955, pp. 443–453. Springer, Heidelberg (2006)

[Zhongzhe et al., 2006] Zhongzhe, X., Dellandrea, E., Dou, W., Chen, L.: Two-stage Classification of Emotional Speech. In: Int. Conference on Digital Telecommunications, p. 32 (2006)

[Zhou et al., 2002] Zhou, Z.H., Wu, J., Tang, W.: Ensembling Neural Networks: Many Could Be Better Than All. Artificial Intelligence 137(1-2), 239–263 (2002)

On the Influence of Phonetic Content Variation for Acoustic Emotion Recognition

Bogdan Vlasenko[1], Björn Schuller[2], Andreas Wendemuth[1], and Gerhard Rigoll[2]

[1] Cognitive Systems, IESK, Otto-von-Guericke University, Magdeburg, Germany
{Bogdan.Vlasenko,Andreas.Wendemuth}@ovgu.de
[2] Institute for Human-Machine Communication, Technische Universität München, Germany
{Schuller,Rigoll}@tum.de

Abstract. Acoustic Modeling in today's emotion recognition engines employs general models independent of the spoken phonetic content. This seems to work well enough given sufficient instances to cover for a broad variety of phonetic structures and emotions at the same time. However, data is usually sparse in the field and the question arises whether unit specific models as word emotion models could outperform the typical general models. In this respect this paper tries to answer the question how strongly acoustic emotion models depend on the textual and phonetic content. We investigate the influence on the turn and word level by use of state-of-the-art techniques for frame and word modeling on the well-known public Berlin Emotional Speech and Speech Under Simulated and Actual Stress databases. In the result it is clearly shown that the phonetic structure does strongly influence the accuracy of emotion recognition.

1 Introduction

Today's approaches to the acoustic recognition of emotion ignore the spoken textual content by using one general model per emotion (see [Batliner, 2006]). Considering that many features highly depend on phonetic structure, such as spectral and cepstral features which have become very popular recently [Batliner, 2006], the question arises if this is the optimal way of acoustic modeling. We therefore aim at answering the question how strongly spoken content variance influences emotion recognition performance, herein. Models trained specifically on the unit at hand could then be considered in future engines to improve on accuracies. This would require a combination with an Automatic Speech Recognition (ASR) engine to pick the right unit-specific emotion models at a time. However, several works already demand for ASR inclusion, e.g. for word-boundary detection (see [Schuller, 2006]). In this context we report results considering specific models vs. general models to demonstrate the amount of dependence of acoustic emotion recognition on phonetic transcription of utterence.

The paper is structured as follows: in sect. 2 we introduce the databases, in sect. 3 and 4 spoken content influence on the turn and on the word level.

2 Acted and Spontaneous Data

To demonstrate the influence of spoken content variation on acted and spontaneous data, we decided first for the popular studio recorded Berlin Emotional Speech

E. André et al. (Eds.): PIT 2008, LNAI 5078, pp. 217–220, 2008.
© Springer-Verlag Berlin Heidelberg 2008

Database (EMODB) [Burkhardt, 2005], which covers the 'big six' emotion set (MPEG-4) besides boredom instead of surprise, and added neutrality. 10 (5f) professional actors speak 10 German emotionally undefined sentences. 494 phrases are marked as min. 60% natural and min. 80% assignable by 20 subjects. 84.3% accuracy are reported for a human perception test.

Secondly, we selected the Speech Under Simulated and Actual Stress (SUSAS) database [Hansen, 1997] as a reference for spontaneous recordings. Here, speech is partly masked by field noise. It consists of five domains, encompassing a wide variety of stresses and emotions. We decided for the 3,663 actual stress speech samples recorded in subject motion fear and stress tasks. 7 speakers, 3 of them female, in roller coaster and free fall actual stress situations are contained in this set. Two different stress conditions have been collected: medium stress, and high stress. Within the further samples also neutral samples, fear during freefall and screaming are contained as classes. SUSAS samples are constrained to a 35 words vocabulary.

3   Text Dependence on the Turn Level

We first investigate the influence of spoken content variation on the turn level. At this level we use frame-level features: speech input is processed using a 25ms Hamming window, with a frame rate of 10ms. Next, we employ a 39 dimensional feature vector per each frame consisting of 12 MFCC and log frame energy plus speed and acceleration coefficients. Cepstral Mean Subtraction (CMS) and variance normalization are applied to better cope with channel characteristics. Classification is carried out with GMM as described in [Schuller 2007b]. The priors are chosen as an equal distribution among emotion classes.

Test runs on EMODB and SUSAS for utterance models are carried out speaker independently by Leave-One-Speaker-Out (LOSO) evaluation. Table 1 reports average among all speakers and all utterances accuracies for three cases to address text independent (TI) evaluation. A total of 10 different utterances are found in EMODB and 35 in SUSAS, respectively. We included all utterances from training set for general model training. In other cases we left out all samples with target or non-target utterance from tarining set.

Table 1. Mean Accuracies for turn-level modeling on EMODB and SUSAS. Frame-level features with GMM, LOSO evaluation.

Accuracy [%]	EMODB	SUSAS
General model	**77.1**	**46.0**
Non-target utterance left out	**75.9**	**45.4**
Target utterance left out	72.7	44.2

From Table 1. it is clear that removal of target utterance from training set fundamentally reduce accuracy of emotion recognition in comparison with removal non-target utterance. Random removal non-target utterances preserves the context, which results in higher accuracy than removing the target utterance, which makes the training data context-independent.

4 Text Dependence on the Word Level

Second, we investigate the influence of spoken content variation on the word level. Therefore we use a different strategy to cover another typical approach to acoustic modeling in emotion recognition from speech: a state-of-the-art brute-force feature generation by projection of a typical prosodic, spectral and voice quality low-level-descriptors (LLD) onto a static feature vector by statistical functionals (see [Schuller, 2006]). The obtained 1,406 dimensional feature vector is classified by SVM with polynomial Kernel and SMO learning [Witten, 2000].

73 different words are found in EMO-DB of which we select only those that have a minimum frequency of occurrence of 3 within each emotion. This comprises a total of 41 words with roughly 200 instances per word. Within an equivalent selection process we picked the according 11 highest frequency terms from SUSAS out of a total of 35.

Table 3. Accuracies for word-level modeling in matched and mismatched condition compared to general models at diverse relative sizes of training corpora on EMODB and SUSAS. tsf *abbreviate training size factor*. Static features with SVM, LOSO.

Accuracy [%]	EMODB	SUSAS
matched	**48.9**	**60.7**
mismatched	37.4	54.2
tsf 1%	43.1	50.6
tsf 2%	44.8	56.1
tsf 5%	49.1	60.7
tsf 10%	51.7	61.5
tsf 100%	**55.5**	**64.7**

Table 3 visualizes the results obtained on these two corpora: first, matched vs. mismatched conditions are analyzed, whereby mismatching is an average of the accuracy of all selected words in a corpus was computed, when the emotion models were taken from all other words. Spoken content clearly does influence accuracy throughout word-model comparison, as can be seen by the mean accuracy in table 1.

We next address the question how a general model trained on any word in the corpus – the common state-of-the-art –performs in relation to the amount of training data available by the relative training size factor (tsf). Random down-sampling preserving class-balance is used. Noting that every word will occur with an average frequency of 2.5% in the corpora, it can be seen that a general model *with that tsf* will perform between matched and mismatched models. The general model will outperform the matched case already at *tsf=10%*.

5 Discussion

The results presented in this work clearly demonstrate dependence of emotion models on the spoken phonetic content for both, acted and spontaneous emotions, and employing the two typical types of emotion recognition engines (1.4k large-feature-space turn-level SVM and MFCC space frame-level HMM/GMM) (see [Vlasenko, 2007]).. In future works we therefore aim at investigation how this could be exploited by use of unit-specific models.

Acknowledgements

The work has been conducted in the framework of the NIMITEK project (Sachsen-Anhalt Federal State funding) FKZ XN3621H/1005. This project is associated and supported by the Magdeburg Center for Behavioral Brain Sciences (Neuroscience Excellence Cluster). Bogdan Vlasenko acknowledges support by a graduate grant of the Federal State of Sachsen-Anhalt.

References

[Batliner, 2006] Batliner, A., Steidl, S., Schuller, B., Seppi, D., Laskowski, K., Vogt, T., Devillers, L., Vidrascu, L., Amir, N., Kessous, L., Aharonson, V.: Combining Efforts for Improving Automatic Classification of Emotional User States. In: Proc. 1st Int. Language Technologies Conference IS-LTC 2006, Ljubljana, Slovenia (2006)

[Burkhardt, 2005] Burkhardt, F., Paeschke, A., Rolfes, M., Sendlmeier, W., Weiss, B.: A Database of German Emotional Speech. In: Proc. INTERSPEECH 2005, pp. 1517–1520 (2005)

[Hansen, 1997] Hansen, J.H.L., Bou-Ghazale, S.: Getting Started with SUSAS: A Speech Under Simulated and Actual Stress Database. In: Proc. EUROSPEECH 1997, Rhodes, Greece, vol. 4, pp. 1743–1746 (1997)

[Schuller, 2006] Schuller, B., Rigoll, G.: Timing Levels in Segment-Based Speech Emotion Recognition. In: Proc. INTERSPEECH 2006, pp. 1818–1821 (2006)

[Schuller, 2007] Schuller, B., Vlasenko, B., Minguez, R., Rigoll, G., Wendemuth, A.: Comparing One and Two-Stage Acoustic Modeling in the Recognition of Emotion in Speech IEEE ASRU 2007, pp. 596–600 (2007)

[Vlasenko, 2007] Vlasenko, B., Schuller, B., Wendemuth, A., Rigoll, G.: Combining Frame and Turn-Level Information for Robust Recognition of Emotions within Speech 2007. In: Proc. INTERSPEECH 2007, pp. 2225–2228 (2007)

[Witten, 2000] Witten, I.H., Frank, E.: Data Mining: Practical machine learning tools with Java implementations, p. 133. Morgan Kaufmann, San Francisco (2000)

[Young, 2002] Young, S., Evermann, G., Kershaw, D., Moore, G., Odell, J., Ollason, D., Povey, D., Valtchev, V., Woodland, P.: The HTK-Book 3.2. Cambridge University Press, Cambridge (2002)

On the Use of Kappa Coefficients to Measure the Reliability of the Annotation of Non-acted Emotions

Zoraida Callejas and Ramón López-Cózar

Dept. of Languages and Computer Systems, 18071 Granada, Spain
{zoraida,rlopezc}@ugr.es

Abstract. In this paper we study the impact of three main factors on measuring the reliability of the annotation of non-acted emotions: the annotator biases, the similarity between the classified emotions, and the usage of contextual information during the annotation. We employed a corpus collected from real interactions between users and a spoken dialogue system. The user utterances were classified by nine non-expert annotators into four categories. We discuss the problems that the nature of non-acted emotional corpora impose in evaluating the reliability of the annotations using Kappa coefficients. Although deeply affected by the so-called paradoxes of Kappa coefficients, our study shows how taking into account context information and similarity between emotions helps to obtain values closer to the maximum agreement rates attainable, and allow the detection of emotions which are expressed more subtly by the users.

1 Introduction

One of the difficulties of non-acted emotion recognition is that in most application domains the corpora obtained are very unbalanced, because there is usually a higher proportion of neutral than emotional utterances [Morrison et al., 2007]. Thus, the Kappa coefficients indicate very low inter-annotator agreement even when the actual observed agreement between the annotators is high. This is called the *prevalence* phenomena, which is caused by the high probability of agreeing by chance in the neutral category. Hence, interpretation approaches based uniquely on already established values of acceptability such as the ones proposed by [Landis and Koch, 1977] and [Krippendorff, 2003] are not suitable for this application domain, as they would consider most of the annotation results not reliable.

As prevalence appears as an unavoidable consequence of the natural skewness of non-acted emotional corpora, some authors report additional measures to complement the information provided with the Kappa coefficients. For example, [Forbes-Riley and Litman, 2004] report on both observed agreement and Kappa, whereas [Lee and Narayanan, 2005] report on Kappa along with an hypothesis test. Although reported Kappa values in emotion recognition employing unbalanced corpora are usually low, e.g. from 0.32 to 0.42 in [Shafran et al., 2003]

E. André et al. (Eds.): PIT 2008, LNAI 5078, pp. 221–232, 2008.
© Springer-Verlag Berlin Heidelberg 2008

and below 0.48 in [Lee and Narayanan, 2005] and [Ang et al., 2002], there is not a deep discussion about the problematic of Kappa values in the area, not even in papers explicitly devoted to challenges in emotion annotation (for instance, [Devillers et al., 2005]). Furthermore, even when other agreement measures are reported along with Kappa, e.g. [Forbes-Riley and Litman, 2004] and [Lee and Narayanan, 2005], there is only one Kappa coefficient calculated (usually multi-π) and no discussion about why there is such a big difference between the Kappa values and the other measures reported.

In this paper, we report experimental results on the annotation of the recordings of real interactions of users with a spoken dialogue system. The procedure was carried out by nine non-expert annotators following two strategies: in the former the annotators had information about the dialogue context and the users' speaking style; in the latter, their decision was based only on the acoustics of the utterances. With the recorded emotional corpora, we address three main issues related to the use and interpretation of kappa coefficients in the annotation of real emotions: i) the impact of annotator bias, that is, given a fixed number of agreements, the effect that the distribution of disagreements between categories has in the Kappa value; ii) the level of importance of all possible disagreements in our task, i.e. disagreements between emotions which are easily distinguishable should have a more negative impact in the Kappa coefficient than disagreements in more similar categories; and iii) the benefits yielded by the use of contextual information on the obtained agreement values and the emotions annotated.

2   Experimental Set-Up

The UAH (Universidad al Habla - University On the Line) dialogue system was developed in our laboratory to provide telephone-based spoken access to the information in our Department web page [Callejas and López-Cózar, 2005]. The corpus used for the experiments described in this paper is comprised of 85 dialogues of 60 different users interacting with the system. The corpus contains 422 user turns, with an average of 5 user turns per dialogue. The recorded material has a duration of 150 minutes. The users were mainly students and professors at the University of Granada, which is in South Eastern Spain. The way the users expressed themselves was influenced by the Eastern Andalusian accent, which although similar to Spanish Castilian has several differences, for example a faster rhythm and lower expiratory strength.

To get the best possible annotation employing non-expert annotators, the labelling process must be rigorously designed. We have followed some of the ideas suggested by [Vidrascu and Devillers, 2005] to decide the list of labels and annotation scheme. The first step is to decide the labels to be used for annotation. Our goal was to annotate negative emotional states of the user during the interaction with the UAH system in order to obtain an emotional corpus to train an emotion recognizer for the system. We have used four categories in the annotation of the corpus: *angry, bored, doubtful* and *neutral*. The first three categories represented the major negative emotions encountered in the UAH corpus; whereas *neutral* represented a non-negative state[1].

We decided to use an odd, high number of annotators (nine) which is more than is typically reported in previous studies [Forbes-Riley and Litman, 2004] [Lee and Narayanan, 2005]. In our group of annotators, six were used to the Andalusian accent and three were not. Regarding the "segment length", in our study this is the whole utterance because our goal was to analyze the emotion as a whole response to a system prompt, without considering the possible emotional changes within the response. The utterances were annotated twice by every annotator following both annotation schemes, the annotations were carried out in different sessions separated by a long period of time to avoid obtaining a biased second annotation. In the first case the annotators had information about the dialogue context and the users' speaking style. In the second case, the annotators did not have this information, so their annotations were based only on acoustic information.

The final emotion category assigned to each utterance in the ordered and unordered schemes was the one annotated by the majority of annotators. Global emotions for the whole corpus were then computed from the results of each of the schemes. In situations where there was no majority emotion (e.g. 4 *neutral*, 4 *bored* and 1 *doubtful*), priority was given to non-neutrals (*bored* in the example). If this conflict was between two non-neutral emotions (e.g. 4 *doubtful*, 4 *bored* and 1 *neutral*), the results were compared between both annotation schemes to choose the emotion annotated by majority among the 18 annotations (the 9 of the ordered and the 9 of the unordered schemes).

On average, among the nine annotators, more than 85% of the utterances were annotated as *neutral*. We have also observed that this proportion is affected in 3.4% of the cases by the annotation style. Concretely, for the ordered annotation, 87.28% were tagged as *neutral*, whereas for the unordered annotation the corpus was even more unbalanced: 90.68% of the utterances were annotated as *neutral*.

3   Calculation of the Agreement between Annotators

Several Kappa coefficients were used to study the degree of inter-annotator agreement for both annotation styles (ordered and unordered). Kappa coefficients are based on the idea of rating the proportion of pairs of annotators in agreement (P_o) with the expected proportion of pairs of annotators that agree by chance (P_c). The result is a proportion between the agreement actually achieved beyond chance $(P_o - P_c)$ and all the possible agreements that are not by chance $(1 - P_c)$:

$$\kappa = \frac{P_o - P_c}{1 - P_c} \tag{1}$$

For our study we used five different Kappa coefficients with which we studied two main issues: i) the impact of annotator bias, i.e. given a fixed number of

---

[1] Positive emotions were treated as neutral because our interest was only on those emotions that could lead to user frustration and interaction failure.

agreements, the effect that the distribution of disagreements between categories has in the Kappa value; and ii) the level of importance of all the possible disagreements, i.e. disagreement between emotions which are easily distinguishable should have a more negative impact on the Kappa coefficient than disagreements in very different categories.

[Artstein and Poesio, 2005] made a considerable effort to clarify the definitions of the different Kappa coefficients. In order to avoid inconsistencies, we follow their notation for all the Kappa coefficients employed in this paper. The simplest Kappa coefficient used was proposed by [Fleiss, 1971], which we have noted as **multi-π**. The calculation of multi-π is based on Equation 1, where the observed agreement (P_o) is computed as the number of cases in which two different annotators agreed to annotate a particular utterance with the same emotion category:

$$P_o = \frac{1}{UA(A-1)} \sum_{u=1}^{U} \sum_{e=1}^{E} n_{ue}(n_{ue} - 1) \tag{2}$$

In Equation 2, U is the number of utterances to be annotated, A the number of annotators, E the number of emotions, and n_{ue} the number of times the utterance 'u' was annotated with the emotion category 'e'.

Fleiss assumed that all the annotators share the same probability distribution. In our experiments, this means that the probability that an annotator classifies an utterance 'u' with a particular emotion category 'e', can be computed as the overall probability of annotating 'u' as 'e'. This global probability was computed as the total number of assignments to emotion category 'e' made by all annotators (n_e in Equation 3) divided by the total number of assignments ($U \cdot A$). Chance agreement (Equation 3) was then computed as the probability that any pair of labellers annotated the same utterance with the same category, which was assumed to be the joint probability of each of them making such assignment independently, as they judged all the utterances independently from each others.

$$P_c^{\pi} = \sum_{e=1}^{E} \left(\frac{1}{UA} n_e \right)^2 \tag{3}$$

The calculation of multi-π assumes that each annotator follows the same overall distribution of utterances into emotion categories. However, such a simplification may not be plausible in all domains due to the effect of th so-called *annotator bias* in the Kappa value. In our experiments, the annotator bias can be defined as the extent to which annotators disagree on the proportion of emotions, given a particular number of agreements. With the rest of the parameters fixed, the Kappa value increases as the bias value gets higher, that is, when disagreement proportions are not equal for all emotions and there is a high skew among them. This is the so-called *Kappa second paradox*. Different studies of the impact of this paradox can be found in the literature, e.g. [Feinstein and Cicchetti, 1990], [Lantz and Nebenzahl, 1996], and [Artstein and Poesio, 2005].

To study whether the inclusion of the different annotating behaviours could improve the Kappa values, we calculated the Kappa value that is proposed by [Davies and Fleiss, 1982], which we have noted as **multi-κ**. As happens with multi-π, the calculation of multi-κ also relies on Equation 1, and has the same observed agreement (Equation 2). However, for the chance agreement, it includes a separate distribution for each annotator. Thus, in this case the probability that an annotator 'a' classifies an utterance 'u' with an emotion category 'e' is computed with the observed number of utterances assigned to 'e' by that annotator (n_{ae}), divided by the total number of utterances (U). The probability that two annotators agree in annotating an utterance 'u' with the emotion category 'e' is again the joint probability of each annotator doing the annotation independently:

$$P_c^\kappa = \frac{1}{\binom{A}{2}} \sum_{e=1}^{E} \sum_{j=1}^{A-1} \sum_{k=j+1}^{A} \frac{n_{a_j e}}{U} \frac{n_{a_k e}}{U} \tag{4}$$

Despite of including differences between annotators, multi-κ gives all disagreements the same importance. In practice, all disagreements are not equally probable and do not have the same impact on the quality of the annotation results. For example, in our experiments, a disagreement between *neutral* and *angry* is stronger than between *neutral* and *doubtful*, because the first two categories are more easily distinguishable.

To take all this information into account we have used weighted Kappa coefficients, which put the emphasis on disagreements instead of agreements. The calculation of these coefficients is based on Equation 5 (equivalent to Equation 1):

$$\kappa_w = 1 - \frac{\overline{P}_o}{\overline{P}_c} \tag{5}$$

where $\overline{P}_o$ indicates observed disagreement, and $\overline{P}_c$ disagreement by chance. For all the coefficients used, the observed disagreement has been calculated as the number of times each utterance 'u' was annotated with two different emotion categories e_j and e_k by every pair of annotators, weighted by the distance between the categories:

$$\overline{P}_o = \frac{1}{UA(A-1)} \sum_{u=1}^{U} \sum_{j=1}^{E-1} \sum_{k=j+1}^{E} n_{ue_j} n_{ue_k} distance(e_j, e_k) \tag{6}$$

Consequently, the computation of the weighted coefficients implies employing distance metrics between the four emotions used for annotation (*neutral, angry, bored* and *doubtful*). To do so, we have arranged our discrete list of emotions within a continuous space, using the bidimensional activation-evaluation space [Russell, 1980]. In the horizontal axis, evaluation deals with the "valence" of emotions, i.e. positive or negative evaluations of people, things or events. In the vertical axis, activation measures the user disposition to take some action rather than none. Emotions form a circular pattern in this space. This is why other authors proposed a representation based on angles and distance to the centre. Taking advantage of this circular disposition, we have used angular distances between our emotions for the calculation of the weighted Kappa coefficients. Instead of establishing our own placement of the emotions in the space, we employed an already established angular disposition to avoid introducing measurement errors. We used the list of 40 emotions with their respective angles proposed by [Plutchik, 1980], which has been widely accepted and used by the scientific community. In this list, *bored* (136.0) and *angry* (212.0) were explicitly considered, but this was not the case for *doubtful*. The most similar emotions found were "uncertain", "bewildered" and "confused", which only differentiated in 2 in the circle. We chose "uncertain" (139.3) which was the one that better reflected the emotion we wanted to annotate. [Plutchik, 1980] did not reflect neutral in his list as it really is not an emotion but the absence of emotion. Instead, he used a state called "accepting" as the starting point of the circle (0), which we used as *neutral* in our experiments.

With the angle that each of the four emotions forms in the space we calculated the distance between them in degrees. We chose always the smallest angle between the emotions being considered (x or 360-x). This way, the distance between every two angles was always between 0 and 180 degrees. For the calculation of the Kappa coefficients, distances were converted into weights with values between 0 and 1. A 0 weight (which corresponds to 0 distance in our approach) implies annotating the same emotion, and thus having no disagreement. On the contrary, *weight* = 1 (180 distance) corresponds to completely opposite annotations and thus maximum disagreement. The resulting distances and weights are listed in Table 1.

Table 1. Distance between emotions

Angle/ Weight	Neutral	Angry	Bored	Doubtful
Neutral	0.00 / 0.00	148.00 / 0.82	136.00 / 0.75	139.30 / 0.77
Angry	148.00 / 0.82	0.00 / 0.00	76.00 / 0.42	72.70 / 0.40
Bored	136.00 / 0.75	76.00 / 0.42	0.00 / 0.00	3.30 / 0.02
Doubtful	139.30 / 0.77	72.70 / 0.40	3.30 / 0.02	0 / 0.00

There is not a consensus in the scientific community about the properties of the distance measures. However, [Artstein and Poesio, 2005] have proposed some constraints: the distance between a category and itself should be minimal and the distance between two categories should not depend on the order (i.e. the distance from A to B should be equal to distance from B to A). As can be observed by the symmetry of the table, our distance measures and weights follow these restrictions as the angle an emotion forms with itself is 0 and, as we established to choose the minimal angle, the distance between two emotions is the same regardless of the order.

As can be observed in the table, the highest distances were between non-neutrals and neutral. Thus, when calculating weighted Kappa coefficients, disagreements in which an annotator judged an utterance as neutral and the other as non-neutral were given more importance than, for example, a disagreement between the *angry* and *bored* categories.

We calculated three weighted Kappa coefficients. The first one was α, proposed by [Krippendorff, 2003]. The second was a variant called α' proposed by Artstein and Poesio, and the third coefficient was the β that is proposed by [Artstein and Poesio, 2005]. All of them shared the same observed disagreement calculation (Equation 5). Disagreement by chance for α and α' was calculated as:

$$\overline{P_c^\alpha} = \frac{1}{UA(UA-1)} \sum_{j=1}^{E-1} \sum_{k=j+1}^{E} n_{e_j} n_{e_k} distance(e_j, e_k) \tag{7}$$

$$\overline{P_c^{\alpha'}} = \frac{1}{(UA)^2} \sum_{j=1}^{E-1} \sum_{k=j+1}^{E} n_{e_j} n_{e_k} distance(e_j, e_k) \tag{8}$$

As can be observed in Equations 7 and 8, these coefficients do not consider annotator bias. This was addressed by employing the β coefficient, with which we have measured also the observed behaviour of each annotator:

$$\overline{P_c^\beta} = \sum_{j=1}^{E-1} \sum_{k=j+1}^{E} \left[\frac{1}{U^2 \binom{A}{2}} \sum_{m=1}^{A-1} \sum_{n=m+1}^{A} n_{a_m e_j} n_{a_n e_k} distance(e_j, e_k) \right] \tag{9}$$

4   Discussion of the Results

The results for each described coefficient are listed in Table 2. A plausible reason for these results is that the incorporation of context in the ordered case influences the annotators in assigning the utterances belonging to the same dialogues to the same emotional categories. This way, there were no very noticeable transitions between consecutive utterances. For example, if anger was detected in one utterance, then the next one was probably also annotated as *angry*. Besides, the context allowed the annotators to have information about the user's speaking style and the interaction history. In contrast, in the unordered case the annotators only had information about the current utterance. Hence, sometimes they could not decide whether the user was either angry or he normally spoke loudly and fast.

In addition, when listening to the corpus in the ordered scheme, the annotators had information about the position of the current user turn within the whole dialogue, which also gave a reliable clue to the user's state. For example, a user was more likely to get bored after a long dialogue, or to become angry after many confirmation prompts generated by the system.

As can be observed in Table 2, the values of the different Kappa coefficients also vary slightly depending on the annotating scheme used. In the unordered

Table 2. Values of the Kappa coefficients for unordered and ordered annotation schemes

Coefficient	Unordered	Ordered
multi-π	0.3256	0.3241
multi-κ	0.3355	0.3256
α	0.3382	0.3220
α'	0.3381	0.3218
β	0.3393	0.3237

case, both taking into account annotator bias (multi-κ vs. multi-π, and β vs. α), and weighting disagreements (β and α vs. multi-κ) improves the agreement values. However, in the ordered case only taking into account annotator bias enhances the agreement values, whereas weighting the disagreements reduces Kappa. This is a consequence of the increment of non-neutral annotations in the ordered case. Taking into account that the great majority of agreements occur when annotators tag the same utterance as neutral, an increment in the number of emotions annotated as non-neutral provokes more discrepancies among the annotators and thus reduces the Kappa value. Furthermore, most of the disagreements occur between neutral and non-neutral categories, which are the emotions with higher distances according to our weighting scheme (Table 1), thus provoking weighted agreements to be lower in the case of the ordered scheme.

When we examined the annotation results, we found that there were remarkable differences between the annotators who were used to the Andalusian accent. From the non-neutral emotions encountered by the nine annotators, most of them were annotated by the ones that were not used to the Andalusian accent. This was probably caused by the confusion of characteristics of the accent with emotional cues, for example, confusing the Andalusian fast rhythm with an indication of anger. We studied the effect on the annotation schemes for both kinds of annotator and obtained the results shown in Table 3.

As can be observed in the table, the annotators used to the Andalusian accent obtained Kappa values for both annotation schemes which were more similar (ranging between 0.3234 to 0.3621). For these annotators, the Kappa values were smaller for the ordered scheme because there were fewer utterances annotated as neutral.

On the contrary, annotators not used to the Andalusian accent had very different Kappa values depending on the annotating scheme used: in the ordered case, values ranged from 0.5593 to 0.5697, whereas in the unordered the values ranged from 0.3639 to 0.3746. This is due to the big decrement of the chance agreement. The most likely reason for this is the lower number of neutrals annotated by annotators not used to Andalusian. This happens for both annotation schemes, but the number of neutrals annotated is higher in the unordered one, and this is why the results are more similar to those obtained by Andalusian annotators with the unordered annotation scheme. Even though the number of non-neutral annotations increased proportionally with the decrement of neutrals, the unbalancement of the corpus made the probability of agreeing

Table 3. Kappa values for the different annotator types

	Andalusian annotators		Non-andalusian annotators	
	Unordered	Ordered	Unordered	Ordered
multi-π	0.3608	0.3234	0.3734	0.5593
multi-κ	0.3621	0.3275	0.3746	0.5598
α	0.3595	0.3248	0.3644	0.5691
α	0.3592	0.3245	0.3639	0.5688
β	0.3607	0.3265	0.3703	0.5697

by chance in the neutral emotion more important in the computation of the overall agreement by chance. For example, in the case of multi-κ, the agreement by chance (P_c) was calculated as the sum of agreeing by chance in each emotion $(P_c = P_c^{neutral} + P_c^{bored} + P_c^{angry} + P_c^{doubtful})$. The values for agreeing by chance when annotators not used to Andalusian used the ordered scheme were $P_c^{neutral} = 0.6645$, $P_c^{bored} = 0.0052$, $P_c^{angry} = 0.0069$ and $P_c^{doubtful} = 0.0008$. For the rest of annotators these values were: $P_c^{neutral} = 0.8137$, $P_c^{bored} = 0.0010$, $P_c^{angry} = 0.0014$ and $P_c^{doubtful} = 0.0008$. Thus, $P_c^{neutral}$ was the determining factor in obtaining the global P_c.

The situation in which although having almost identical number of agreements, the distribution of these across the different annotation categories deeply affects Kappa, is typically known as the *first Kappa paradox*. This phenomenon establishes that other things being equal, Kappa increases with more symmetrical distributions of agreement. That is, if the prevalence of a category compared to the others is very high, then the agreement by chance (P_c) is also high and the Kappa is considerably decremented [Feinstein and Cicchetti, 1990].

As already reported by other authors, e.g. [Feinstein and Cicchetti, 1990], the first Kappa paradox can drastically affect Kappa values and thus must be considered in its interpretation. There is not an unique and generally accepted interpretation of the Kappa values. One of the most widely used is the one presented by [Landis and Koch, 1977], which makes a correspondence between intervals for Kappa values and interpretations of agreement. Following this approach, our experimental results indicate fair agreement for both annotating schemes and with the four different Kappa coefficients. Alternatively, [Krippendorff, 2003] established 0.65 as a threshold for acceptability of agreement results. Hence, considering this value, our 0.3393 highest Kappa would not be acceptable. However, most authors seem to agree in that using a fixed benchmark of Kappa intervals does not provide enough information to make a justified interpretation of acceptability of the agreement results. In order to provide a more complete framework, a number of authors, e.g. [Dunn, 1989], propose to place Kappa into perspective by reporting *maximum*, *minimum* and *normal* values of Kappa, which can be calculated from the observed agreement (P_o) as follows [Lantz and Nebenzahl, 1996]:

$$kappa_{max} = \frac{P_o^2}{(1 - P_o)^2 + 1}; \quad kappa_{min} = \frac{P_o - 1}{P_o + 1}; \quad kappa_{nor} = 2P_o - 1 \quad (10)$$

For the same observed agreement, the possible values of Kappa can deeply vary from $kappa_{min}$ to $kappa_{max}$ depending on the balancement of the corpus. $Kappa_{max}$ is obtained when maximally skewing disagreements while maintaining balanced agreements, whereas $kappa_{min}$ is obtained when agreements are skewed and disagreements balanced. $Kappa_{nor}$ does not correspond to an ideal value of Kappa, but rather to symmetrical distributions of both agreements and disagreements. As observed in Table 4, the displacement between actual and normal values was smaller in the ordered scheme. Thus, contextual information does not only allow recognizing more non-neutral emotions, but also obtaining Kappa values which, although smaller than in the unordered scheme in absolute value, are much closer to the *normal* and *maximum* agreement values attainable and further from the *minimum*.

Table 4. Kappa minimal, observed, normal and maximal values in the ordered and unordered schemes

	multi-π		multi-κ		α		α'		β	
	Unord.	Ord.	Unord.	Ord.	Unord.	Ord.	Unord.	Ord.	Unord.	Ord.
κ_{min}	-0.062	-0.086	-0.069	-0.085	-0.046	-0.064	-0.046	-0.064	-0.046	-0.064
κ_o	0.326	0.324	0.335	0.326	0.338	0.322	0.338	0.329	0.339	0.324
κ_{nor}	0.767	0.686	0.767	0.686	0.823	0.759	0.823	0.759	0.823	0.759
κ_{max}	0.770	0.693	0.770	0.693	0.825	0.763	0.825	0.763	0.825	0.763

As stated in [Lantz and Nebenzahl, 1996], departures from the $kappa_{nor}$ value indicate asymmetry in agreements or disagreements depending on whether they are closer to the minimum or maximum value respectively. Our results corroborate that reporting Kappa values is more informative when they are put into context, as we obtain a valuable indicative of possible unbalancements that has to be considered to reach appropriate conclusions about reliability of the annotations. For example, in our case there were significant departures from $kappa_{nor}$ in all cases, which corroborates that there was a big asymmetry in the categories. This is due to the prevalence phenomena discussed in Section 1 (first Kappa paradox).

Finally, to obtain a more approximate idea about the real level of agreement reached by the nine annotators, we report the values of the observed agreement

Table 5. Observed agreement for all annotation schemes and annotator types

		Observed agreement	Weighted observed agreement
Unordered	Total	0.8836	0.9117
	Andalusian	0.8950	0.9197
	Non-andalusian	0.8767	0.9050
Ordered	Total	0.8429	0.8800
	Andalusian	0.8761	0.9049
	Non-andalusian	0.8578	0.895

in Table 5, which has been used along with Kappa by other authors in different areas of study, e.g. [Ang et al., 2002] [Forbes-Riley and Litman, 2004]. As can be observed in the table, in all cases the observed agreement was above 0.85. This measure does not take into account the high probability of agreeing by chance in the neutral category, and thus values were not higher for the annotators not used to the Andalusian accent in the ordered case.

5   Conclusions

We have shown that when evaluating the reliability of the annotation of non-acted emotions corpora, very low Kappas can be obtained (Table 2) which are usually much lower than the agreement values observed (Table 5). This is due to the unavoidable natural skewness of such corpora, in which there is usually a noticeable prevalence of the neutral categories. We have discussed other coefficients that can be reported along with Kappa, such as observed agreement and minimal, maximal and normal Kappa values, in order to obtain meaningful interpretations about the reliability of the annotations.

Additionally, our experimental results show that employing contextual information about the users' speaking style and the history of the interaction allowed the annotation of more non-neutral emotions in our speech database. Unfortunately, this translates into lower Kappa coefficients as most of the agreements occur for neutrals. However, although the Kappa value and the observed agreement percentages were lower when using contextual information, we found that it can be useful to obtain results which are closer to the maximum Kappa values achievable. Besides, as shown in Table 5, giving a weight to the different disagreement types considerably incremented the observed agreement between annotators. We have presented a method to compute distances between such disagreements.

Our results indicate that multiple annotators should be used for annotating natural emotions to obtain reliable emotional corpora. One possible way to overcome the problem of high chance agreements, is maximizing the observed agreement. For example, [Litman and Forbes-Riley, 2006] propose the usage of "consensus labelling", i.e. to reach a consensus between annotators until a 100% observed agreement is obtained.

References

[Ang et al., 2002] Ang, J., Dhillon, R., Krupski, A., Shriberg, E., Stolcke, A.: Prosody-based automatic detection of annoyance and frustration in human-computer dialog. In: Proc. of Interspeech'02 - ICSLP, Denver, USA, pp. 2037–2040 (2002)

[Artstein and Poesio, 2005] Artstein, R., Poesio, M.: $kappa_3$ = alpha (or beta). Technical report, University of Essex (2005)

[Callejas and López-Cózar, 2005] Callejas, Z., López-Cózar, R.: Implementing modular dialogue systems: a case study. In: Proc. of ASIDE 2005 (2005)

[Davies and Fleiss, 1982] Davies, M., Fleiss, J.L.: Measuring agreement for multinomial data. Biometrics 38(4), 1047–1051 (1982)

[Devillers et al., 2005] Devillers, L., Vidrascu, L., Lamel, L.: Challenges in real-life emotion annotation and machine learning based detection. Neural Networks 18(4), 407–422 (2005)

[Dunn, 1989] Dunn, G.: Design and analysis of reliability studies: the statistical evaluation of measurement errors. Edward Arnold (1989)

[Feinstein and Cicchetti, 1990] Feinstein, A.R., Cicchetti, D.V.: High agreement but low Kappa: I. The problems of two paradoxes. Journal of Clinical Epidemiology 43(6), 543–549 (1990)

[Fleiss, 1971] Fleiss, J.L.: Measuring nominal scale agreement among many raters. Psychological Bulletin 76(5), 378–382 (1971)

[Forbes-Riley and Litman, 2004] Forbes-Riley, K., Litman, D.J.: Predicting emotion in spoken dialogue from multiple knowledge sources. In: Proc. of HLT-NAACL 2004, pp. 201–208 (2004)

[Krippendorff, 2003] Krippendorff, K.: Content Analysis: An Introduction to its Methodology. Sage Publications, Inc., Thousand Oaks (2003)

[Landis and Koch, 1977] Landis, J.R., Koch, G.G.: The measurement of observer agreement for categorical data. Biometrics 33, 159–174 (1977)

[Lantz and Nebenzahl, 1996] Lantz, C.A., Nebenzahl, E.: Behavior and interpretation of the κ statistic: Resolution of the two paradoxes. Journal of Clinical Epidemiology 49(4), 431–434 (1996)

[Lee and Narayanan, 2005] Lee, C.M., Narayanan, S.S.: Toward detecting emotions in spoken dialogs. IEEE Transactions on Speech and Audio Processing 13(2), 293–303 (2005)

[Litman and Forbes-Riley, 2006] Litman, D.J., Forbes-Riley, K.: Recognizing student emotions and attitudes on the basis of utterances in spoken tutoring dialogues with both human and computer tutors. Speech Communication 48(5), 559–590 (2006)

[Morrison et al., 2007] Morrison, D., Wang, R., Silva, L.C.D.: Ensemble methods for spoken emotion recognition in call-centers. Speech Communication 49, 98–112 (2007)

[Plutchik, 1980] Plutchik, R.: EMOTION: A psychoevolutionary synthesis. Harper and Row publishers (1980)

[Russell, 1980] Russell, J.A.: A circumplex model of affect. Journal of Personality and Social Psychology 39, 1161–1178 (1980)

[Shafran et al., 2003] Shafran, I., Riley, M., Mohri, M.: Voice signatures. In: Proc. of IEEE ASRU 2003 Workhop, pp. 31–36 (2003)

[Vidrascu and Devillers, 2005] Vidrascu, L., Devillers, L.: Real-Life Emotion Representation and Detection in Call Centers Data. In: Tao, J., Tan, T., Picard, R.W. (eds.) ACII 2005. LNCS, vol. 3784, pp. 739–746. Springer, Heidelberg (2005)

Annotation of Emotion in Dialogue: The Emotion in Cooperation Project

Federica Cavicchio and Massimo Poesio

CIMeC, Università degli Studi di Trento
Palazzo Fedrigotti, Corso Bettini 31, 38068 Rovereto (Tn) Italy
{federica.cavicchio,massimo.poesio}@unitn.it

Abstract. In this research we investigate the relationship between emotion and cooperation in dialogue tasks. It is an area were still many unsolved questions are present. One of the main open issues is the labeling of "blended" emotions and their recognition. Usually there is a low agreement among raters in labeling and naming emotions and surprisingly emotion recognition is higher in a condition of modality deprivation (only acoustic or only visual vs. bimodal). Because of this previous results we don't ask raters to directly label emotions, but to use a small set of features (as lips or eyebrows shape) to annotate our corpus. The analyzed materials come from an audiovisual corpus of Map Task dialogues elicited with a script. We point out the "emotive" tokens by simultaneous recordings of the phsychophysiological indexes (ElectroCardioGram ECG, Galvanic Skin Conductance GSC, ElectroMyoGraphy EMG). After this selection we annotate each token with our multimodal annotation scheme. Each annotation will lead to a cluster of signals identifying the emotion corresponding to a cooperative/non cooperative level; the last step involves agreement among coders and reliability of the emotion description. Future research will deal with brain imaging experiment on the effect of putting emotions into words and the role of context in emotion recognition.

1 Task and Material: Map Task Revisited

Map Task is a cooperative task involving two participants used for the first time by the HCRC group at Edinburg University [Anderson et al., 1991]. In this task two speakers sit opposite one another and each of them has a map that the other cannot see. One speaker, designated the Instruction Giver, has a route marked on her map; the other speaker, the Instruction Follower, has no route. The speakers are told that their goal is to reproduce the Instruction Giver's route on the Instruction Follower's map. The maps are not identical and the speakers are told this explicitly at the beginning of their session. However, it is up to them to discover how the two maps differ. In our Map Task the two participants sitting one in front of the other are separated by a short barrier or a full screen. They both have a map with some objects. Some of them are in the same position and with the same name, but most of them are in different positions or have names that sound similar to each other. One participant (the giver) must drive the other participant (the follower) from a starting point (the bus station) to the finish point (Rovereto Castle). They are both native Italian speakers. A

E. André et al. (Eds.): PIT 2008, LNAI 5078, pp. 233–239, 2008.
© Springer-Verlag Berlin Heidelberg 2008

further condition is added: the follower or the giver could be alternatively a confederate with the aim of getting the giver angry. It is said to the participants that the whole task should end in no more than 15 minutes. The confederate at minutes 4, 9 and 13 acts the following script [Anderson et al., 2005]:

- *"You driving me in the wrong direction, try to be more accurate!"*
- *"It's still wrong, this can't be your best, try harder! So, again, from where you stop"*
- *"You're obviously not good enough in giving instruction"*

During this dialogue the giver psychophysiological state is recorded and synchronized with video and audio recordings. This elicitation and collection method allow us pointing out that at that moment something is happening at the peripheral nervous system level, an emotive state is felt by the participant as her heart rate and skin conductance are significantly different from the resting state and the task state. At the same time it is a quite impossible recognizing which is the felt emotion on the basis of these data [Cacioppo et al., 2000]. Thus, it is up to our coding scheme to label multimodal aspects of the emotive tokens, recognizing which is the emotion display and the correlation with cooperative behavior performed at the same time.

2   Method

The emotion annotation coding scheme used to analyze our map task chunks partially follows [Craggs and Wood, 2004] and [Martin et al., 2006] annotation schemes of blended emotions. As for the emotions analyzed by those authors, our corpus emotions are expressed at different blending levels (i. e. blending of different emotion and emotive levels). In Craggs and Wood opinions' annotators have to label the given emotion with a main emotive term (e. g. anger, sadness, joy etc.) correcting the emotional state with a score ranging from 1 (low) to 5 (very high).

From a cognitive and neuroscience point of view several studies have shown how emotional words and their connected concepts influence emotion judgments and, as a consequence, emotion labeling (for a review see [Feldman Barrett et al., 2007]). Moreover research on yemotion recognition by face display found out that some emotions as anger or fear are discriminated only by mouth or eyes/eyebrows configuration. Face seems to be evolved to transmit orthogonal signals, with a lower correlation each other, which are deconstruct by the human filtering functions as optimized inputs [Smith et al., 2005], [Susskind et al., 2007]. On the basis of these findings, we decide not to label emotions directly. We attribute valence and activation to verbal and nonverbal signals "deconstructing" them in simpler signs with implicit emotive dimensions. Thus, in our coding scheme a smile would be annotate as ")" and a large smile as "+)", meaning a higher valence and activation (see Fig. 1.). One of the aims of this coding scheme is to separately annotate expressions of upper and lower part of face to find out if these two indexes suffice to label blended emotions as well as "prototypical" emotions, as suggested by PCA analysis of emotion expressions.

As our corpus is multimodal, we analyze and annotate different communication modalities: nonverbal (ranging from face to gesture and posture), verbal (speech) and pragmatics (cooperation and turn management) as it is shown in Table 1.

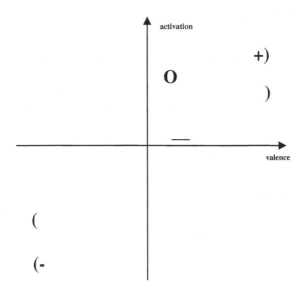

Fig. 1. Example of representation of mouth data from annotation scheme into an emotional space

Table 1. Modalities involved in the multimodal analysis

Modality	Expression type
Facial displays	Eyebrows
	Eyes
	Gaze
	Mouth
	Head
Gestures	Hand gestures
	Body posture
Speech	Segmental
	Suprasegmental
Pragmatics/ Conversation Analysis	Cooperation
	Turn management

3 The Coding Scheme

Selected audio and video clips are orthographically transcribed. For orthographic transcription we adopted a subset of the conventions applied to LUNA project corpus transcription [Rodríguez et al., 2007].

As regards cooperative behavior we listed different types of cooperative or not cooperative utterances disrupting or following Gricean cooperative maxims (see Table 2. [Davies, 2006] adapted):

Table 2. Cooperation types implemented in our coding scheme and corresponding levels

No answer to question: cooperation level -2
No information add when required: cooperation level -2
Inappropriate reply (no giving info): cooperation level -1
Giving instruction: cooperation level 0
Question answering y/n: cooperation level +1
Repeating instruction: cooperation level +1
Question answering y/n + adding info: cooperation level +2
Checking the other understands (*ok? Are you there?*): cooperation level +2
Spontaneous info/description adding: cooperation level +2

We also analyze turn management: we annotate turn taking of giver and follower, if one of them give the turn to the other (even when speaker is offering the speaking turn to the interlocutor), the kept or hold of the conversation turn.

As regards facial expressions we analyze upper and lower part of the face. Thus an analysis of emotive labial configurations as well as eyebrows patterns and forehead wrinkles are implemented in our annotation system. The annotation is based on a little amount of signs similar to emoticons. We sign two levels of arousal using the plus and minus signs. In particular, as regard mouth movements:

- **Closed lips:** when the mouth is closed choose **closed** label.
- **Corners up:** e.g. when smiling,); +) very happy .
- **Corners down:** e.g. in a sad expression, (, +(very sad.
- **Protruded:** when the lips are rounded, O.
- **Lip biting:** when one of the lips is bite, usually lower lip.
- **1 corner up:** for asymmetric smiles.

As regard *Gesture,* the categories used to annotate hand movements are taken mainly from McNeill's work [McNeill, 2005]. Hand gesture annotation presupposes the so-called gesture phrases identification as a markable. In fact to simplify the annotators work we do not try to capture the internal structure of a gesture phrase (i. e. preparation, stroke and retraction phases). In other words, annotators find the gestures she have to annotate marked, and can go on with emotive aspects tagging. The tagging of the shape of hand gestures is very simplified in comparison with the coding scheme used at the McNeill Lab. We only take into account the two dimensions *Handedness* and *Trajectory,* without analyzing orientation and shape of the various parts of the hand(s), and we define trajectory in a very simple manner, similar to what is commonly done for gaze movements. The semantic-pragmatic analysis consists of the categorization of the gesture type in semiotic terms, the second concerns the communicative functions of gestures. We also score the emotive aspects of gesture inspiring to the annotation scheme used for the emoTv database [Martin et al., 2006]. Speed and temporal expansion of gesture are both calculated in frame per second.

Coding scheme is implemented in AnViL, a well known software allowing us to analyze audio and video features (see Fig. 2).

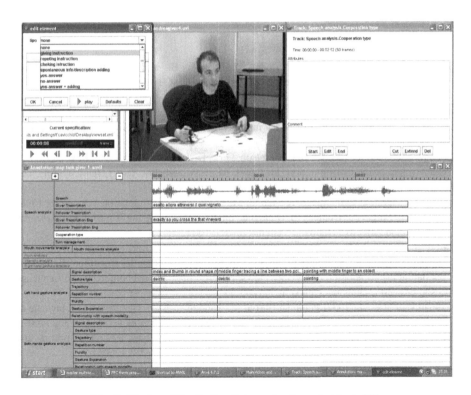

Fig. 2. Display of the Coding Scheme Implemented in AnViL

4 Conclusions and Future Works

Cooperative behavior and its relationship with emotions is a topic of great interest in the field of dialogue annotation. Even emotion annotation in dialogue is an open issue. Usually emotion annotation achieves a low agreement among raters and surprisingly the emotion recognition is higher in a condition of modality deprivation (only acoustic or only visual vs. bimodal). Cognitive and neuroscience research on emotion shows that emotion recognition is a process performed firstly by sight and processed by limbic system, but the awareness and the consequently labeling of emotions are mediated by prefrontal cortex. Moreover a predefined set of emotion labels can influence the perception of emotive facial expressions. Thus we decide to deconstruct each signal without attributing directly an emotive label. Even if we don't have final results we considerate promising the implementation of neuroscience evidences on transmitting and decoding facial expression of emotions in computational annotation schemes. Further research will carry out an fMRI experiment to investigate the influence of task and context on labeling emotions expressed by the face.

References

[Anderson et al., 1991] Anderson, A., Bader, M., Bard, E., Boyle, E., Doherty, G.M., Garrod, S., Isard, S., Kowtko, J., McAllister, J., Miller, J., Sotillo, C., Thompson, H.S., Weinert, R.: The HCRC Map Task Corpus. Language and Speech 34, 351–366 (1991)

[Anderson et al., 2005] Anderson, J.C., Linden, W., Habra, M.E.: The importance of examining blood pressure reactivity and recovery in anger provocation research. International Journal of Psychophysiology 57, 159–163 (2005)

[Cacioppo et al., 2000] Cacioppo, J.T., Berntson, G.G., Larsen, J.T., Poehlmann, K.M., Ito, T.A.: The psychophysiology of emotion. In: Lewis, M., Haviland, J.M. (eds.) Handbook of emotions 2nd, pp. 173–191. The Guilford Press, New York (2000)

[Craggs and Wood, 2004)] Craggs, R., Wood, M.: A Categorical Annotation Scheme for Emotion in the Linguistic Content of Dialogue. In: Proceedings of the Tutorial and Research Workshop on Affective Dialogue Systems, pp. 89–100 (2004)

[Martin et al., 2006] Martin, J.-C., Caridakis, G., Devillers, L., Karpouzis, K., Abrilian, S.: Manual Annotation and Automatic Image Processing of Multimodal Emotional Behaviors: Validating the Annotation of TV Interviews. In: Fifth international conference on Language Resources and Evaluation, Genoa, Italy (2006)

[Feldman Barrett et al., 2007] Feldman Barrett, L., Lindquist, K.A., Gendron, M.: Language as Context for the Perception of Emotion. Trends in Cognitive Sciences 11(8), 327–332 (2007)

[Smith et al., 2005] Smith, M.L., Cottrell, G.W., Gosselin, F., Schyns, P.G.: Transmitting and Decoding Facial Expressions. Psychological Science 16(3), 184–189 (2005)

[Susskind et al., 2007] Susskind, J.M., Littlewort, G., Bartlett, M.S., Movellan, J., Anderson, A.K.: Human and computer recognition of facial expressions of emotion. Neuropsychologia 45, 152–162 (2007)

[Rodríguez et al., 2007] Rodríguez, K., Stefan, K.J., Dipper, S., Götze, M., Poesio, M., Riccardi, G., Raymond, C., Wisniewska, J.: Standoff Coordination for Multi-Tool Annotation in a Dialogue Corpus. In: Proceedings of the Linguistic Annotation Workshop at the ACL 2007, Prague, Czech Republic (2007)

[Davies, 2006] Davies, B.L.: Testing dialogue principles in task-oriented dialogues: An exploration of cooperation, collaboration, effort and risk. Leeds Working Papers in Linguistics and Phonetics, 11 (2006)

[McNeill, 2005] McNeill, D.: Gesture and thought. University of Chicago Press, Chicago (2005)

Potential Benefits of Human-Like Dialogue Behaviour in the Call Routing Domain

Joakim Gustafson, Mattias Heldner, and Jens Edlund

KTH Speech Music and Hearing
{jocke,mattias,edlund}@speech.kth.se

Abstract. This paper presents a Wizard-of-Oz (Woz) experiment in the call routing domain that took place during the development of a call routing system for the TeliaSonera residential customer care in Sweden. A corpus of 42,000 calls was used as a basis for identifying problematic dialogues and the strategies used by operators to overcome the problems. A new Woz recording was made, implementing some of these strategies. The collected data is described and discussed with a view to explore the possible benefits of more human-like dialogue behaviour in call routing applications.

1 Introduction

This paper discusses the possibility of making the interaction with *natural-language call routing systems* more human-like through different dialogue strategies, improved interaction control and utterance unit segmentation, and explores possible benefits of such dialogue behaviour in call-routing and similar applications. We use a large corpus of 42,000 Woz dialogues, where wizards were given the possibility to route problematic calls back to themselves and to act as operators. Based on an analysis of 82 such human-human intervention dialogues, we re-designed the system prompts in the Woz setup to capture the operators' behaviour in the intervention dialogues. We collected 188 new calls with the modified Woz setup in order to study the effect of adding more human-like dialogue behaviour to a call routing dialogue system. Specifically, we wanted to investigate if the new behaviour would elicit longer and semantically richer user utterances, and whether it would affect the quality of service.

2 Natural Language Call Routing Systems

The goal of customer care centres in large companies is to direct callers to the appropriate human operator or self-service application. In simpler cases, this can be automated using a voice controlled menu system, in which callers should ideally be presented with no more than four to six choices at each dialogue step. This is a limitation which makes voice controlled menu systems and system directed dialogues in general unsuitable for call centres where the number of possible reasons for calling is large, since it is difficult and time consuming to navigate large menu trees. Another problem is that the design of menu trees typically reflect the solution to the problem,

E. André et al. (Eds.): PIT 2008, LNAI 5078, pp. 240–251, 2008.

while the callers usually only know the effects of the problem – the symptoms – and call to find the solution [Acomb et al., 2007]. Making callers navigate a menu tree that reflects, from the point of view of the callers, an unknown problem solving structure is not likely to be optimal. Another possibility is to ask callers to describe their symptoms and let an automatic classifier decide to which tree node they should be directed. Systems automatically directing callers based on their verbal description of their concern are called *natural language call-routing systems*. Callers are either routed to the appropriate human operator or self-service application, or taken through additional dialogue steps allowing the system to obtain more information. This kind of call-routing is becoming increasingly more common in commercial settings. Well-known examples include the AT&T How May I Help You (HMIHY) [Gorin et al., 1997], Bell Canada's 310-BELL customer service line, and more recently the entrance to TeliaSonera residential customer care in Sweden [Wirén et al., 2007]. A related application is that of *automated technical support* [Acomb et al., 2007].

3 Human-Like Dialogues

In this paper we explore the possible benefits of adding more human-like conversational behaviour to commercial call routing systems, under the hypothesis that when confronted with more human-like system behaviour, callers are more likely to behave as if they were speaking to a human operator. This hypothesis is supported by other studies. For example, users of spoken dialogue systems generally produce shorter utterances than when they speak to human beings [e.g. Zoltan-Ford, 1991]. A finding from early data collections in the HMIHY project [Gorin et al., 1997] provides a relevant example. Gorin and colleagues noted a unimodal distribution and a very long tail in the histogram of utterance length. On closer inspection, the long utterances turned out to be interspersed with backchannel feedback by the operator. When similar interactions were recorded with pre-recorded prompts (and no backchannel feedback), the long tail disappeared, and a bimodal distribution appeared, with the extra mode on very short utterances. Gorin and colleagues call this particular computer-directed manner of talking *menu-speak*. Others have used other terms for this type of talk, for example *computerese* [Gustafson et al., 1997], *machine talk* [Martinovsky and Traum, 2003], and *computer talk* [Fischer, 2006]. The hypothesis that human-like system behaviour elicits user behaviour that is more like human-human dialogue and less menu-speak is also supported by a large number of studies on entrainment, showing generally that people adapt their speaking behaviour to the behaviour of their interlocutor, even if that happens to be a computer [Bell, 2000, Brennan, 1996, Garrod and Pickering, 2004]. Finally, the hypothesis is in effect revisited and put to the test in the experiments reported here.

As noted above, people generally produce longer and more semantically rich utterances when speaking to humans than when speaking to computers, and a principal reason for wanting callers to behave more like when speaking to humans in call routing applications is to elicit longer, richer utterances. As a call routing system analyses callers' verbal descriptions to automatically route the call, short menu-speak may force the system to prompt callers for many pieces of information, making it very similar to traditional menu based customer care systems. Longer and semantically richer descriptions stand a better chance of containing sufficient information for appropriate routing. That this information can be utilised by human operators is evident, but whether current call-routing technology can make as much use of it is an open question. The technology used by Gorin and colleagues in the 90s was not helped by the longer human-human data (A. Gorin, personal communication, February 2nd 2006), and to the extent that the necessary information is present in the utterances, this represents a challenging task for the data miners.

4   Wizard of Oz Collections

Wizard-of-Oz (Woz) simulation is often used for collection of human-computer data when building a fully functional system is impractical or too expensive. In a Woz simulation, a human (the wizard) performs (part of) the system's functions unbeknownst to the subject, who is led to believe the system is fully automated and operational. As a typical example, Woz data collections are used in the early stages of a spoken dialogue system project to gather the first set of data on which the various models used by the system are based [Wooffitt et al., 1997]. Traditionally, wizards have been asked to produce output that resembles what can be expected from a talking computer, rather than from a person, so that the collected data will be representative for such interactions [Dahlbäck et al., 1993], and in many Woz collections, the wizard is the system designer and the subjects are friends or students that are given scenarios with tasks to solve with the system. Allwood & Haglund argue that the wizard and the subjects play roles at several possibly conflicting levels in Woz collections [Allwood and Haglund, 1992]. At the same time, the wizard has the role of the researcher and is playing the role of the system. Similarly, the user has the role of a subject in a scientific study whilst playing the role of a customer.

In a paper describing the development of the TeliaSonera call routing system [Wirén et al., 2007], Wirén et al. argue that the role playing aspects of traditional Woz collections make them unsuitable for use in the initial steps of developing a call routing system, since "we want to learn not just *how* callers express themselves, but also *what kind of tasks they have*, which obviously rules out prewritten scenarios." To overcome the lack of realism in traditional Woz collections they conducted what they coined an *in-service Wizard-of-Oz data collection*, where real customer care operators acted as wizards handling calls from real customers with real problems. Using actual customer care operators as wizards provided valuable feedback on dialogue and prompt design. Furthermore, by allowing the wizards to route complicated calls to themselves, the in-service Woz setup yielded follow-up dialogues representative of how a human operator would sort out the problem at hand. These human-human dialogues are the basis for the present study. Porzel has proposed a similar variation of Woz simulations, which he called WOT (Wizard and Operator Test) [Porzel, 2006]. WOT involves a human operator acting as wizard. At a predefined moment, an obvious system breakdown is simulated, after which the operator stops acting as a wizard and takes the call in person, telling the caller that the system broke down and that (s)he will have to handle the remaining tasks. The result is that human-computer (wizard) and human-human (operator) data is collected within the same dialogue. In this paper, a combination of the in-service Woz and WOT methods is used to explore possible benefits of adding human-like conversational behaviour in a call routing system. The method is summarised in the following steps:

1. Perform an in-service Woz collection, in which the wizards are encouraged to intervene when the pre-defined prompt set is insufficient and causes communication problems.
2. Analyse the intervention dialogues to gain information about how the problem was solved and what linguistic and/or conversational resources were used.
3. Re-design the system prompts, adding dialogue features identified in the step 2.
4. Perform a second round of in-service Woz collections.
5. Compare relevant aspects of the interaction with the first collection.

Steps 2-5 can be iterated using all available intervention dialogues as a source of information when seeking more dialogue features to investigate. In this method, the wizards themselves decide when it is necessary to resort to intervention dialogues, making it more labour intensive than the WOT method, which always results in two types of dialogue for each recording. However, in an in-service Woz, the WOT method is not feasible, since deliberately causing system failure would annoy paying customers. More importantly, the wizards' decisions on when to intervene give valuable information about the limitations of the current set of system prompts. Finally, the method clearly identifies callers who have problems describing their errand in menu-speak, and allows us to investigate whether they also have problems describing it with human-directed talk.

5   Three Call Routing Dialogue Collections

The call routing data collections and corpora described here are all in Swedish. The examples given are all translated from Swedish to English by the authors. The general statistics of the corpora are as follows:

Label	# dialogues	mean # turns/dialogue
ISWoz-I	2228	4.6
Intervent	82	10.2
ISWoz-II	188	6.4

All corpora have been labelled on the utterance level with a small label set: INITIAL HMIHY was used for the first open prompt, DESCRIPTION for the callers' description of the nature of their requests, HMIHY for a general request for more details, FOLLOW-UP QUESTION for requests for specific information, ANSWER for the callers' responses to FOLLOW-UP QUESTIONS, GREETING for greetings on both sides, CHANNEL for channel checks verifying that parties could hear each other, FEEDBACK for feedback, META for turns that discussed the dialogue itself (What did you say?) or the nature of the speaker (Are you a human or machine?). ROUTING was used when callers were informed that they were being directed to an operator. The corpora and their collection are described in detail in the following.

5.1   In-Service Woz I (ISWoz-I)

In 2005, the Swedish telecom operator TeliaSonera developed a Swedish natural language call routing system for their main customer care line, a service which handles 14 million calls per year since its deployment in 2006. During the development, 42,000 calls were collected in an in-service Woz, in which the wizards were ten real customer care operators that handled real incoming calls [Wirén et al., 2007]. The initial open prompt was designed to inform callers that they were talking to a machine, but that they could express themselves freely. The wording was: "Welcome to Telia. Here you describe the nature of your request in your own words instead of pressing buttons on your phone. If you say what you need help with I can direct you to the correct place in the customer care centre. What are you calling about?" After this initial open prompt, the system engaged in a system-driven, menu-based dialogue in those cases additional pieces of information was needed to route the call. In case the dialogue got stuck, the wizards had the option to let the system say "You are now being directed to an operator" (the same utterance that was used when routing was successfully achieved), whilst routing the call to themselves, effectively taking over the call in the role of the operator (done in about 5% of the calls). The design decision in this collection was to use system prompts that would signal that it was a machine talking, in order to limit the callers' expectations on the system's understanding capabilities [see also Boyce, 1999]. In particular, the aim was to achieve consistency between the initial open prompt and the subsequent system-driven disambiguation prompts. We will call the corpus collected in this design *in-service Woz I* (ISWoz-I), to contrast with the second in-service Woz described in this paper (ISWoz-II).

5.2   The Operator Intervention Dialogues (INTERVENT)

The second data set (INTERVENT) was obtained as an effect of the design of the in-service Woz. It consists of 82 of the ISWoz-I dialogues that lead to a communication breakdown. As a result of the breakdown, these dialogues have two parts: the first part is the Woz dialogue leading to the breakdown, and the second is the human-human dialogue taking place afterwards, as operators routed the calls to themselves. The dialogues are of particular interest since they give access to callers that had a hard time describing their reason for calling to a machine. It is worth noting that the problems leading to interventions were not insurmountable. The operators succeeded, without exception, in collecting the information needed to route these calls in the human-human dialogue. Furthermore, a small number of specific reasons causing the Woz dialogues to get stuck were discernible: (1) many dialogues never got started, as the caller was unsure whether the system was listening when they said "Hello?", although the system responded "This is a voice controlled system where you describe the nature of your request in your own words. You can for example say..."; (2) callers found it hard to match their problem to the multiple-choice voice menus; (3) callers would occasionally answer "yes" to multiple choices given by the system; and (4) callers began by providing background information, either personal, as in *"This is Lars, calling from Stockholm"*, or task-related: *"I ordered broadband from you three weeks ago"*, for which the system had no response. After taking over the calls, operators solved all these issues with ease: for (1), they simply responded with *"Hello, what's your problem?"*; (2) did not reappear, callers were perfectly able to describe their concerns to the operator; (3) was avoided by asking a yes/no question instead, such as *"Does it concern your land line?"*, using the most probable choice in that context, to which the caller typically responded *"Yes"* or *"No, my cell phone"* (there was not one instance of operators presenting multiple choices to get information in the 82 calls); and (4), finally, was typically handled with short utterances like "ok", "hi", "uh-huh" or "yes" encouraging the caller to continue describing their concerns (these feedback utterances constitute 24% of all operator utterances in these dialogues). To conclude, the operators made use of basic conversational skills by responding promptly to channel checks and greetings and encouraging callers to keep talking by providing feedback.

5.3 In-Service Woz II (ISWoz-II)

The analysis of the INTERVENT data led us to make a second in-service Woz collection (ISWoz-II) to investigate how well the wizards would perform their task if given a redesigned prompt piano with which they could generate the behaviour they displayed in the intervention dialogues. Furthermore, we wanted to see how callers would react when faced with a dialogue system displaying such dialogue strategies. The setup with real customer care operators acting as wizards was kept and used to collect 188 new calls. The new collection was explicitly designed to make the system more human-like. In order to avoid moral indignation in the callers by pretending to be a real human operator, the calls began with a different voice announcing that "You are now being directed to an automatic voice controlled operator" followed by a 7 second silence. Then the newly designed initial open prompt "Welcome to Telia how may I help you?", read in a casual manner, was presented. The multiple-choice voice menus were replaced by the kind of yes/no-questions the operators had used. In addition, there was a prompt to be used to follow up no-answers: "So what is it about?" "Yes, hello?" and "Hello, what is you reason for calling?" were added as responses to channel checks and greetings; Finally, we added generic requests for more information such as "Could you tell me more" and a repertoire of feedback utterances (e.g. "uh-huh", "ok", and "yes") to be used to encourage callers to continue speaking. The wizards were only given 15 minutes to get acquainted with the new layout of the prompt piano before starting to handle real calls from the customer care line. Table 1 contains a typical ISWoz-II dialogue, showing that the wizards frequently used the feedback options that had been added to the prompt piano.

Table 1. Labelled dialogue example from ISWoz-II

	Utterance	Label
Wizard	Welcome to Telia how may I help you!	INITIAL HMIHY
Caller	Yes hello?	CHANNEL?
Wizard	Hello!	CHANNEL!
Caller	Oh sorry, the thing is that I got a bill from you...	DESCRIPTION
Wizard	Mm...	FEEDBACK
Caller	Amounting to 800 something...	DESCRIPTION
Wizard	Okay...	FEEDBACK
Caller	But the thing is that I have moved my subscription to X, and my subscription with you should have ended in Jan.	DESCRIPTION
Wizard	Yes...	FEEDBACK
Caller	So I don't understand why I got a bill from you and it is on 800 kr!	DESCRIPTION
Wizard	Is it for your phone at home?	FOLLOW-UP QUESTION
Caller	Yes.	ANSWER
Wizard	Okay, wait while I connect you...	ROUTING

6   Effects of Human-Like Dialogue Behaviour

An analysis of ISWOz-II showed a rate of 94% successful calls; 3% where callers hung up prematurely; and 3% in which the human operator intervened – in all cases either because the caller did not speak Swedish or because they had to inform the caller to call another phone number to get help. This can be compared with 89% successful calls in ISWOz-I, where 9% hung up during or immediately after the initial open prompt, while 2% lead to intervention.

6.1   Effects on Caller Talkativity

Another effect of human-like dialogue strategy is reflected by differences in turn lengths in the three collections (see Fig. 1). For example, whereas the callers' descriptions were considerably longer in ISWOz-II than in ISWOz-I, were equally long in ISWOz-II and in the human-human dialogues (INTERVENT). Also, it seems that one to two-word turns were more frequent in ISWOz-I than in the other datasets. The cumulative distributions of turn length were furthermore very similar for ISWOz-II and INTERVENT, but quite different from that of ISWOz-I (see Fig. 2). The fact that one and two word utterances were common in the descriptions, suggest that many speakers use *menu-speak* in ISWOz-I.

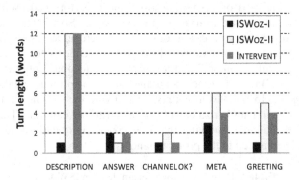

Fig. 1. Median caller turn length (in number of words) for different turn types

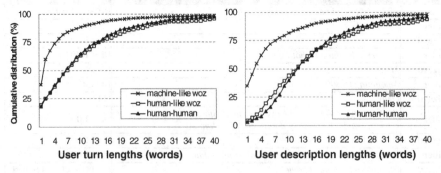

Fig. 2. Cumulative distribution of turn lengthsin the two Woz collections and in the human-human intervention dialogues for all turn types and for the description type separately

6.2 Effects on Turn Type

The effects of human-like dialogue is also reflected by differences in the distribution of turn types in the corpora (see Figure 3). Figure 3 suggests that the dialogue strategies in ISWoz-II resulted in dialogues that were more like those in INTERVENT than those in ISWoz-I. It is worth noting that the amount of FOLLOW-UP QUESTION from the wizard/operator and the corresponding ANSWER from callers were considerably higher in ISWoz-I than in the other corpora, although the dialogues in these corpora were as successful as the ones in ISWoz-I. This suggests that the FEEDBACK utterances used in ISWoz-II and INTERVENT is a successful strategy to elicit the required information. Finally, the dialogue strategies in ISWoz-II elicited more greetings, channel checks and questions about the nature of the speaker, which the wizards were able to respond to using the new prompts added for this purpose.

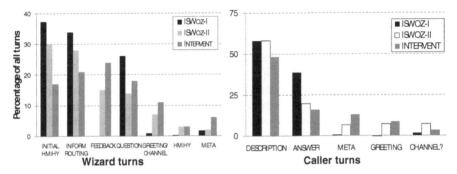

Fig. 3. Distribution of turn types (%) in the three corpora for the wizard/operator side of the conversations and the caller side

In order to examine in more detail how the wizards handled the calls, the flow of turn types (including both participants) in ISWoz-II was analysed. Figure 4 shows a dialogue flow chart that covers 90% of all caller/wizard turns in ISWoz-II. Arrows representing less than 5% of the utterance have been excluded to avoid cluttering. Most callers (65%) described their reason for calling immediately after the initial open prompt. After such descriptions, the wizards did one of three things: if they had enough information they routed the call (34%); if they lacked a certain piece of information they posed a follow-up question (32%); and if the description contained too little information they used feedback like "ok" (28%). The distribution of these choices is approximately an even three-way split. Figure 4 also shows that feedback proved to be a very efficient way of getting callers to provide further descriptions (92%). Responding appropriately to greetings, channel checks and meta questions had a similar effect and also proved efficient for making callers describe their reason for calling.

6.3 Effects of Turn-Taking Behaviour

Wizards often refrained from responding when a caller stopped talking, so there is a number of *pauses* within caller turns in the corpora. In the following we compare ISWoz-II and INTERVENT with respect to such pauses, and any speaker internal silence of more than 200ms is considered a pause. We also discuss the duration of *gaps*, that

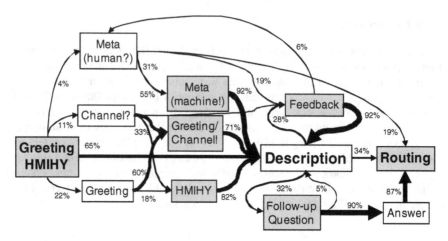

Fig 4. Flow chart of the dialogues in ISWoz-II. System turns are marked with shaded boxes

is silences at speaker changes. 40% of all caller utterances in ISWoz-II contain one or more pauses, which can be compared with 25% in INTERVENT. The median gap duration in INTERVENT is about 200ms in both directions, whereas the median pause duration is almost 500ms. In ISWoz-II, the median gap duration in speaker changes from caller to wizard increases to 950ms, which seemingly influences the callers to some degree, as the median gap duration from wizard to caller is almost 500ms. The median pause duration in ISWoz-II is almost 700ms. Figure 5 shows the cumulative distribution of pauses and gaps in ISWoz-II and INTERVENT. Note that in INTERVENT, the distribution of gap duration (right panel) is quite similar for speaker changes in both directions.

Although the distribution of gap durations in caller-wizard speaker changes in IS-Woz-II is different to that in wizard-caller speaker changes and both are slower than the same changes in INTERVENT, the distributions seem to lend support to the notion that gap duration is a feature that interlocutors mimic from each other, as the callers' turn-taking is much slower when speaking to the slower system (Figure 5, right panel). Figure 5 corroborates earlier findings that silence duration thresholds are insufficient to create good turn-taking in dialogue systems, as pauses are as long or longer than gaps [e.g. Edlund et al., 2005].

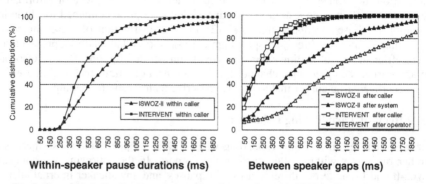

Fig 5. Cumulative distribution of pause durations and gaps in ISWoz-II and INTERVENT

As we are aiming for a more human-like system in ISWOZ-II, we want that the increase in gap length in speaker shifts should appear at places where one would expect longer gaps from human interlocutors. To test this, we analysed the effect of the discourse context on gaps in INTERVENT and ISWOZ-II. The flow-chart in Figure 4 illustrates the shifts described in the following. Regarding the behaviour of the wizard/operator, both corpora have more long gaps between DESCRIPTION and FOLLOW-UP QUESTION or ROUTING. Conversely, short gaps are more common between DESCRIPTION from the callers and FEEDBACK from the wizard, as well as after channel checks from the caller. The effect on the callers is also similar in the two corpora. In both corpora, the callers have more long gaps after requests for information from the wizard/operator, and before channel checks. In ISWOZ-II callers often made long gaps before inquiring whether it was a human or machine talking. These inquiries were often followed by a very swift reply from the wizard stating that it indeed was a machine, which again was often followed by a long gap. Finally, short gaps are more common between FEEDBACK from wizard/operator and further DESCRIPTION from the caller.

7 Discussion

In the data collections discussed here, the wizards did things current call-routing technology generally cannot handle. In both in-service Woz collections, wizards did not base their turn-taking behaviour strictly on silence duration thresholds, like spoken dialogue systems commonly do. In particular, they did not barge into hesitation pauses. Refraining from barging in when speakers hesitate or pause can be achieved in several ways. The problem has been approached using combinations of semantic and dialogue state information, as in [Bell et al., 2001, Nakano et al., 1999, Skantze and Edlund, 2004]. These approaches require that input be processed incrementally, in chunks much smaller than turns, as recognised by Allen et al., who argue that incremental interpretation of user input is necessary for the interaction with spoken dialogue systems to become more natural [Allen et al., 2001]. An alternative or complementary approach that distinguishes pauses (in speech) from gaps between speakers is using prosodic information [Edlund et al., 2005]. Such approaches can avoid violating in-speech pauses, while at the same time making it possible for the system to respond considerably faster when appropriate.

In ISWOZ-II, wizards frequently used the feedback options (e.g. "uh-huh", "ok") to encourage the callers to continue their description, and such feedback can indeed be viewed as a fast way of saying "tell me more". In order to use feedback in the manner of the wizards, the system needs to know when to respond with ROUTE, FOLLOW-UP QUESTION, and FEEDBACK. The contents of the calls collected give a clear impression that the operators utilised prosody, semantics, and pragmatics in making this three-way decision. A preliminary analysis of the content in caller descriptions preceding each of these choices suggests that in excess of 50% of the FEEDBACK choices were preceded by descriptions that can be classified as background information, such as "*I called you before*". Conversely, less than 5% of the FEEDBACK decisions were preceded by ellipses and other condensed utterances, although these were not uncommon in the material, giving rise to 30% of both ROUTE and FOLLOW-UP QUESTION decisions.

250 J. Gustafson, M. Heldner, and J. Edlund

The use of feedback after background information makes sense, since it is not possible for the wizards to route and it would be hard to know which follow up question to choose without more information. This problem faces fully automatic systems as well, and brief feedback utterances could help matters considerably. Deciding when the system should provide brief feedback could be done by other means as well. If the categoriser used for the routing provides confidence measures, one could use feedback responses until a certain confidence is reached or until some time-out is exceeded. Feedback could also be used until the caller has spoken a certain preset number of words, given that we have statistics of how many words it usually takes to get good categorisation results.

We may also note that the whole idea of using brief feedback responses is associated with increasing callers' trust in the system. By creating dialogue that appears more human-like, callers' talkatively is increased, and we occasionally need callers to talk more than they generally do when faced with a machine. Note, however, that we are not suggesting we build spoken dialogue systems that behave as human operators in every respect. It is sufficient that the system exhibits behaviour that *elicits the same kind of descriptions* as those found in *caller-human operator calls*, or to quote Cassell: "a machine that acts human enough that we respond to it as we respond to another human" [Cassell, 2007]. We have shown similarities between caller behaviour in INTERVENT, the human-human dialogue corpus, and ISWOZ-II, the second in-service Woz data collection in which we aimed for more human-like dialogue. If these similarities are anything to judge by, we might say that we at least in part succeeded with this ambition.

Acknowledgement

This had not been possible if it wasn't for the ASR 90 200 pilot team at TeliaSonera that provided us with the data collection tools, and for the skilled Wizards that showed us how to do human-like dialogue. Finally, Anders Lindström at TeliaSonera also participated in the design and collection of ISWOZ-II.

References

[Acomb et al., 2007] Acomb, K., Bloom, J., Dayanidhi, K., Hunter, P., Krogh, P., Levin, E., Pieraccini, R.: Technical support dialog systems: Issues, problems, and solutions. In: Proc. Bridging the Gap: Acad. and Ind. Res. in Dialog Tech., Rochester, USA (2007)
[Allen et al., 2001] Allen, J., Ferguson, G., Stent, A.: An architecture for more realistic conversational systems. In: Proc. IUI 2001, Santa Fe, USA (2001)
[Allwood and Haglund, 1992] Allwood, J., Haglund, B.: Communicative activity analysis of a Wizard of Oz experiment. Technical Report, Göteborg Univ., Gothenburg (1992)
[Bell, 2000] Bell, L.: Linguistic adaptations in spoken and multimodal dialogue systems. Licentiate thesis, KTH, Stockholm (2000)
[Bell et al., 2001] Bell, L., Boye, J., Gustafson, J.: Real-time handling of fragmented utterances. In: Proc. Adaptation in Dialogue Systems, Pittsburgh, USA (2001)

[Boyce, 1999] Boyce, S.J.: Spoken natural language dialogue systems: User interface issues for the future. In: Gardner-Bonneau, D. (ed.) Human factors and voice interactive systems. Kluwer, Boston (1999)

[Brennan, 1996] Brennan, S.: Lexical entrainment in spontaneous dialog. In: Proc. ISSD, Philadelphia, USA (1996)

[Cassell, 2007] Cassell, J.: Body language: Lessons from the near-human. In: Genesis Redux. University of Chicago Press, Chicago (2007)

[Dahlbäck et al., 1993] Dahlbäck, N., Jönsson, A., Ahrenberg, L.: Wizard of Oz studies – why and how. In: Proc. Intelligent User Interfaces (1993)

[Edlund et al., 2005] Edlund, J., Heldner, M., Gustafson, J.: Utterance segmentation and turn-taking in spoken dialogue systems. In: Computer Studies in Language and Speech, Peter Lang, Frankfurt am Main (2005)

[Fischer, 2006] Fischer, K.: The role of users' preconceptions in talking to computers and robots. In: Proc. How People Talk To Computers Robots And Other Artificial Communication Partners, Delmenhorst, Germany (2006)

[Garrod and Pickering, 2004] Garrod, S., Pickering, M.J.: Why is conversation so easy? Trends Cogn. Sci. 8, 8–11 (2004)

[Gorin et al., 1997] Gorin, A.L., Riccardi, G., Wright, J.H.: How I help you. Speech Commun. 23, 113–127 (1997)

[Gustafson et al., 1997] Gustafson, J., Larsson, A., Carlson, R., Hellman, K.: How do system questions influence lexical choices in user answers? In: Proc. Eurospeech, Rhodes (1997)

[Martinovsky and Traum, 2003] Martinovsky, B., Traum, D.: The error is the clue: Breakdown in human-machine interaction. In: Proc. Error Handling in Spoken Dialogue Systems, Château d'Oex-Vaud, Switzerland (2003)

[Nakano et al., 1999] Nakano, M., Miyazaki, N., Hirasawa, J., Dohsaka, K., Kawabata, T.: Understanding unsegmented user utterances in real-time spoken dialogue systems. In: Proc. ACL (1999)

[Porzel, 2006] Porzel, R.: How computers (should) talk to humans. In: Proc. How People Talk To Computers Robots And Other Artificial Communication Partners, Delmenhorst, Germany (2006)

[Skantze and Edlund, 2004] Skantze, G., Edlund, J.: Robust interpretation in the Higgins spoken dialogue system. In: Proc. Robust, Norwich, UK (2004)

[Wirén et al., 2007] Wirén, M., Eklund, R., Engberg, F., Westermark, J.: Experiences of an in-service Wizard-of-Oz data collection for the deployment of a call-routing application. In: Proc. Bridging the Gap: Acad. and Ind. Res. in Dialog Tech., Rochester, USA (2007)

[Wooffitt et al., 1997] Wooffitt, R., Fraser, N.M., Gilber, N., McGlashan, S.: Humans, computers and wizards. Routledge, London (1997)

[Zoltan-Ford, 1991] Zoltan-Ford, E.: How to get people to say and type what computers can understand. Int. J Man-Mach Stud. 34, 527–547 (1991)

Human-Likeness in Utterance Generation: Effects of Variability

Anna Hjalmarsson and Jens Edlund

Centre for Speech Technology, KTH, Stockholm, Sweden
{annah,edlund}@speech.kth.se

Abstract. There are compelling reasons to endow dialogue systems with human-like conversational abilities, which require modelling of aspects of human
behaviour. This paper examines the value of using human behaviour as a target
for system behaviour through a study making use of a simulation method. Two
versions of system behaviour are compared: a replica of a human speaker's behaviour and a constrained version with less variability. The version based on
human behaviour is rated more human-like, polite and intelligent.

1 Introduction

Content, form and timing shape our interpretation of utterances as well as their speakers, and the phrasing of utterances in spoken dialogue systems (SDSs) affects how the
systems are received. [Norman, 1988] states that we should provide a good conceptual model, allowing users to predict the effects of their actions. A plausible model for
spoken language is human conversation, in which we express complex meaning;
engage in social relationships; and solve problems. However, many human manners
(e.g. hesitations; false starts and repetitions; fragmental utterances; and brief feedback) are not in the repertoire of current SDSs, yet research shows that their variation
brings information beyond the literal meanings of words and affect our comprehen-
sion [Brennan, 2000; Arnold, Fagano and Tanenhaus, 2003]. To make SDSs more
human-like, we need output that is coherent with human behaviour. This paper introduces a method to test the effects of human behaviour in SDSs: to simulate an SDS
behaving much like a human by replacing one of the parties in a recording of human-
human conversation with a synthetic voice. A first study is presented: non-
participating listeners were asked to compare two different versions of SDS behaviour
in dialogue.

2 Data Collection and Stimuli Preparation

The human-human dialogues used for this study were collected during the development of the KTH Connector [Edlund and Hjalmarsson, 2005], an SDS acting as a
personal secretary. 10 subjects were used: 2 posing as secretaries and 8 as callers. The
secretaries took calls over VoIP. They were given a fictional employer's personal
agenda, and asked to act as personal secretaries. The callers were asked to book a
meeting. The dialogues are about 10 minutes long and in English. All dialogues were

E. André et al. (Eds.): PIT 2008, LNAI 5078, pp. 252–255, 2008.

transcribed orthographically, including repetitions, hesitations and false starts. Two dialogues were chosen as stimuli for this experiment. In these, the secretary's voice was replaced with a synthetic voice, creating the illusion of a human interacting with an SDS. Two versions were created from each dialogue: a word-by-word replica of the human speaker (UNCONSTRAINED) and a version based on the same set of transcriptions, but constrained lexically through transformations to obtain more limited variability (CONSTRAINED). Similar transformations are suggested in [Jönsson and Dahlbäck, 2000]. These transformations were applied: (a) remove filled pauses, repetitions and false starts; (b) remove any information not directly relevant for the task (banter); (c) reduce lexical variation to one word per meaning only; (d) make brief feedback more explicit – "Ok", for example, was transformed to a full confirmation such as "ok a Chinese restaurant"; (e) replace pronouns unless referring to an entity in the same utterance with the nouns to which they refer; and (f) remove system (secretary) barge-ins. The resulting dialogues differ in presentation, while preserving the literal meaning in the context of the conversation: (UNCONSTRAINED) *mm she she has a dinner on Friday mm but she is available on Saturday and Sunday and on Thursday as well*; (CONSTRAINED) *Anna is available for dinner on Thursday Saturday and Sunday*. Both versions were produced using Mbrola synthesis [Dutoit, Pagel, Pierret, Bataille and Van der Vreken, 1996]. Apart from minor edits to transcriptions, no acoustical adjustments were done. Note that the choice of voice is not principally important in this study: the same voice was used in both cases and the focus of the study was on the lexical content of the utterances rather than on acoustic characteristics.

3 Method

23 subjects (15 male and 8 female) between 23 and 65 years of age acted as judges. None had professional experience of speech technology. The test was web-based, with a form and sound clips. Subjects where led to believe the clips were of people interacting with a fully operational SDS. The test contained the two stimuli dialogues, divided into units of about 2-3 utterances each. Each such unit was presented with two sound clips: UNCONSTRAINED and CONSTRAINED, in random order, and subjects were not told how the versions differed. They were asked to compare the two versions on five dimensions, four of which were chosen as they describe characteristics closely associated with human behaviour, the fifth because it is frequently used in SDS evaluations: (1) HUMAN-LIKENESS: the system behaves like a human would do in a similar situation; (2) POLITENESS: the system acts polite towards the caller; (3) INTELLIGENCE: in the context of this dialogue the system behaves intelligently; (4) Display of UNDERSTANDING: the system behaves as if it understands the caller well; and (5) EFFICIENCY: the system tries to help the user in an efficient way. The subjects were further asked to state which version they would prefer, were they to interact with a similar type of system. The subjects chose one of the clips for each dimension, or *no difference* if they considered the clips equal on some dimension. After completion, they were asked to provide their rating of the importance of the dimensions, on a scale between 1, *not important at all*, and 5, *very important*.

4 Results

A McNemar test showed significant differences for HUMAN-LIKENESS, POLITENESS and INTELLIGENCE (p=0.05), but no significant differences for EFFICIENCY and UNDERSTANDING, neither was there any preference for a particular version (Fig.1.).

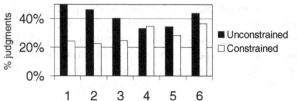

Fig. 1. Judgments (%) distributed over strategies and dimensions

Efficiency in SDSs is traditionally measured quantitatively (e.g. number of words, syllables or utterances to complete a task; see e.g. [Walker, Kamm and Litman, 2000]). To see how such metrics relate to EFFICIENCY, the qualitative metric, the number of syllables in each system utterance was calculated. The difference in syllables between versions was calculated as a percentage and checked for correlation with EFFICIENCY, but no support for such a correlation was found. EFFICIENCY was also checked for correlations with the other dimensions. A strong correlation (Pearson's correlation coefficient = 0.93) was found between EFFICIENCY and UNDERSTANDING (Fig. 2). EFFICIENCY appears to be rated subjectively rather than by the relative length of the dialogues.

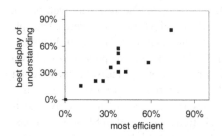

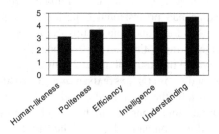

Fig. 2. Correlation between % EFFICIENCY and % UNDERSTANDING

Fig. 3. Mean importance ratings (1-not important at all and 5- very important)

Figure 3 shows the subjects' ratings of the importance of each dimension. All dimensions yield averages > 3. POLITENESS and HUMAN-LIKENESS, both of which were more frequently associated with UNCONSTRAINED, receive the lowest ratings. However, these dimensions were highly correlated with the preferred version (POLITENESS p=0.93; HUMAN-LIKENESS p=0.72), suggesting that subjects were unaware of what type of behaviour they prefer. This is in line with findings that respondents are often unaware of the processes underlying their decision (see [Nisbett and Wilson, 1977] for an overview).

5 Discussion

The results of this study suggest that people have no problems accepting SDSs based on more human behaviour, at least not when judging the interactions of others. The results also support that utterances retaining a larger part of the full spectra of human conversational behaviour are considered more human-like, more intelligent and more polite, compared to utterances with more constrained variability, and that no negative effect on the perception of efficiency and level of understanding can be found. This is interesting since the features removed in the CONSTRAINED version – *disfluencies* in many accounts – are often regarded as flaws of language. Interestingly, efficiency was not correlated with the utterance length, yet length measures are often used as efficiency measures in SDS evaluations. This may be less of a contradiction than it seems: in task-oriented SDSs, there is often a near-linear relationship between dialogue length and mis- or non-understandings, since there are typically fixed strategies for error handling and utterance generation, and requests for confirmations or repair sequences are only produced when problems occur. Human-human dialogue shows no linear relationship between errors and dialogue length – humans are economic speakers, but not in the same sense as SDSs. Non-task related information, hesitations and repetitions do not necessarily arise as a result of communicative problems.

Acknowledgments

This research was supported by the Swedish research council project #2006-2172 (Vad gör tal till samtal/What makes speech special) and project #2007-6431, GEN-DIAL. Many thanks to Rolf Carlson and Joakim Gustafson.

References

[Arnold, Fagano and Tanenhaus, 2003] Arnold, J.E., Fagano, M., Tanenhaus, M.K.: Disfluencies signal theee, um, new information. J. of Psycholinguistic Research 32, 25–36 (2003)

[Brennan, 2000] Brennan, S.E.: Processes that shape conversation and their implications for computational linguistics. In: Proceedings of the 38th Annual Meeting of the ACL, Hong Kong (2000)

[Dutoit, Pagel, Pierret, Bataille and Van der Vreken, 1996] Dutoit, T., Pagel, V., Pierret, N., Bataille, F., Van der Vreken, O.: The MBROLA project: Towards a set of high-quality speech synthesizers free of use for non-commercial purposes. In: Proceedings of ICSLIP 1996, pp. 1393–1396 (1996)

[Edlund and Hjalmarsson, 2005] Edlund, J., Hjalmarsson, A.: Applications of Dis-tributed Dialogue Systems: the KTH Connector. In: Proc. of ASIDE 2005, Aalborg, Denmark (2005)

[Jönsson and Dahlbäck, 2000] Jönsson, A., Dahlbäck, N.: Distilling dialogues - a method using natural dialogue corpora for dialogue systems development. In: Proceedings of the 6th Applied Natural Language Processing Conference, Seattle (2000)

[Norman, 1988] Norman, D.A.: The design of everyday things. MIT Press, Cambridge (1988)

[Walker, Kamm and Litman, 2000] Walker, M., Kamm, C., Litman, D.: Towards developing general models of usability with PARADISE. Natural Language Engineering: Special Issue on Best Practice in Spoken Dialogue Systems (September 2000)

[Nisbett and Wilson, 1977] Nisbett, R.E., Wilson, T.D.: Telling More Than We Know: Verbal Reports on Mental Processes. Psychological Review 84(3), 231–259 (1977)

Designing Socially Aware Conversational Agents

Koen van Turnhout, Jacques Terken, and Berry Eggen

Technische Universiteit Eindhoven, Faculteit Industrial Design,
Postbus 513, 5600 MB Eindhoven, The Netherlands
{k.g.v.turnhout,j.m.b.terken,j.h.eggen}@tue.nl

Abstract. In this paper we address the problem of how to make conversational agents socially aware. State-of-the-art conversational agents cannot deal with multi-user situations where the user-system dialog is interleaved with discussions between users. We describe the development of an algorithm for determining addressee-hood of user utterances. The algorithm makes errors in determining addressee-hood for individual utterances, classifying utterances intended for the system as utterances intended for the other user and the other way around, creating unexpected situations in the agent's behaviour. This raises the question of how to design the conversational agent so that the users understand why the agent behaves in particular ways. We describe a study aimed at obtaining guidelines for the design of a socially aware conversational agent. We conclude that principles for modelling the behaviour of the agent are to be derived from theories about human communication rather than from theories about human-computer interaction.

1 Introduction

Imagine a scenario in which a user interacts with a multimodal interface to book a flight or plan a vacation. The system may ask questions by speech and display results of queries on the screen, and the user may enter query parameters by speech and activate fields on the screen. There are many demonstrators showing that this can be done with reasonable success. That is to say, as long as the user is alone. This is because most research on speech-based interfaces implicitly assume a 'single user - single system' scenario. However, many applications involving speech concern situations where the presence of several people is highly likely and interaction with the application is interleaved with interaction between humans. Thus, people may be interacting with a speech-based database query system such as an integrated trip planner or an automated real estate agent, and the interaction with the system is interleaved with discussions between the users about search parameters or intermediary results.

Current systems, lacking contextual awareness, assume that all the speech that arrives at the microphone is intended for the system, and will in many cases react to a user utterance with "I'm sorry, I didn't understand, could you please repeat". For utterances that are not addressed at the system this is not only incorrect, it is also socially inappropriate since it is likely to interrupt the ongoing human-human conversation. In order to deal with this problem, we need to make systems aware of the communicative context so that they understand who is being addressed and may display

E. André et al. (Eds.): PIT 2008, LNAI 5078, pp. 256–267, 2008.

socially appropriate behaviour. Of course, we could apply solutions such as Push-to-talk buttons, enabling the user to indicate explicitly when speech is intended for the system. However, such solutions bring their own problems. In addition, we want to explore solutions that enable the users to interact in a more natural way, i.e., to exploit information that is provided implicitly rather than only relying on explicit information. In other words, we need to teach these systems the rules for appropriate turn-taking behaviour. However, most research on and computational models of turn-taking behaviour have concentrated on two-party dialogues (e.g. [Cassell et al., 1999] [Thórisson, 2002]), whereas the current situation concerns three-party dialogue, for which much less research has been conducted (notable exceptions are [Takemae et al., 2003] [Vertegaal et al., 2001]).

In previous papers [[Bakx et al., 2003] [Terken et al., 2007] [van Turnhout et al., 2005] we studied the behaviour of users in such triadic conversations, both when interacting with an automated information retrieval service and when interacting with a human agent, in order to determine what features could be used to enable automatic determination of addressee-hood by means of perceptual technologies. It was found that both visual, auditory and contextual information contributed to determination of addressee-hood. In the visual modality the primary cue for addressee-hood was eye gaze: speakers have a tendency to look at the person or agent they are addressing. In the auditory modality, the content of the utterance contained information about addressee-hood. However, it was also found that utterance length might contribute to determination of addressee-hood, since utterances directed at the system differed in length from utterances directed at the fellow user. Finally, dialogue context might contribute to determination of addressee-hood; for instance, user utterances following a question by the system had a higher likelihood of being directed at the system than utterances following a user utterance.

A naïve Bayes classifier was constructed to determine to what extent addressee-hood may be determined automatically (this is further elaborated in section 2). Feature combination resulted in a classification accuracy of .84 (recall .80, precision .33, corresponding to a relatively low miss rate but a high false alarm rate, the imbalance being due to the fact that users often watched the screen when talking to the other user, a finding that is in line with findings reported in [Argyle and Graham, 1977]). For offline recognition and classification tasks such a performance is not too bad and in fact poses interesting challenges to engineers to improve the classification performance. However, when we want to include automatic determination of addressee-hood in an actual system, this performance means that the system will make frequent mistakes in determining the addressee of an utterance. Thus, it may erroneously classify a user utterance that was intended for the fellow user as an utterance intended for the system and produce a response (false alarm), which means interrupting the conversation between the users. Or it may erroneously classify a user utterance that was intended for the system as one that was intended for the other user (miss) and thus not react, resulting in a disruption of the dialog.

In human-human communication, mis-interpretations of addressee-hood may occur but are relatively rare and are usually repaired easily once they have occurred (by statements such as "no, I was not talking to you" or "hey, I was talking to you"). However, given the current Precision and Recall figures, corresponding to a relatively high incidence of cases where the system mis-interprets the addressee-hood of user utterances, we reasoned that it might help if the interface provided information about its inferences concerning the addressee-hood of user utterances, in order to make the interaction more transparent. In the current paper we address the question of how to achieve such transparency. In section 2 we describe the development of an algorithm for determining addressee-hood. In section 3 we describe a study with iterative interface design and small-scale evaluations of interface concepts for conveying information about the system's inferences about addressee-hood. We conclude by discussing the present findings and issues for further research.

2 Determining Addressee-Hood

The studies described in [Bakx et al. 2003] and [van Turnhout et al., 2005] involved pairs of two users planning a trip and asking a travel information system about train departure and arrival times. The users were provided with information about interesting places to visit, and the two users were given different priorities concerning their interests and return times, in order to elicit negotiation about the places to visit and travel times. Analyses of the materials that were collected in the studies showed that user utterances directed at the other user and utterances directed at the system could be differentiated on the basis of visual, auditory and context features. (In the studies of triadic human-human communication reported in [Terken et al., 2007] user utterances could also be directed both at the other customer and the travel agent, but such utterances did not occur in the studies of mixed human-human-computer interaction.)

A naïve Bayes classifier was constructed by which user utterances could be classified as intended for the system or intended for the other user on the basis of information about eye gaze, utterance duration and dialogue context. Eye gaze was estimated from head orientation; in the experiments people and system were arranged physically such that a shift in eye gaze from the system to the partner or the other way around required a shift in head orientation, and head orientation could be measured in an unobtrusive way more easily than eye gaze. More information on the feature definitions and the classifier may be found in [van Turnhout et al., 2005].

Inspection of classification performance (accuracy .84, recall .80, precision .33) showed that head orientation was the most effective cue: leaving it out had the strongest effect on classification performance. The dialogue context feature (denoting the preceding dialog event) was next most effective, but almost all utterances belonged to one particular class so that this feature had little differentiating power. Utterance length had relatively little impact on classification performance, but since the dialogue context feature had little differentiating power, it still made sense to include utterance length as a feature as well.

Given the fact that researchers have used different data sets, different sets of features, different feature definitions, different tasks and different evaluation metrics, it is difficult to compare performance across different studies. However, one study that is worth mentioning is [Katzenmaier et al., 2004], who studied addressee-hood determination in mixed human-human-robot communication and included a feature representing the fit of the incoming utterance into the language model of the system. They found that head orientation was the most powerful cue to addressee-hood and that adding the fit into the language model gave only a slight improvement.

In sum, user utterances can be classified with reasonable success as being intended for the other user or the system on the basis of information about head orientation, utterance length and dialogue context, and the system may then take appropriate action (either responding or withholding a response) accordingly.

2.1 Predicting Addressee-Hood

While the classification task described in the previous section concerned the classification of the current utterance, in the context of a working system we would rather have predictions about the upcoming utterance. In the former case, information about the addressee-hood of the utterance becomes available *after* the utterance. However, if the user knows that the system is likely to classify the *upcoming* utterance as intended for the system of for the other user, s/he is already able to predict whether the system will respond or not to the upcoming utterance, and s/he may alter his/her behaviour in order to increase the likelihood of a correct classification. For example, while talking to the other user, s/he may be looking at the screen, therewith increasing the likelihood that the system will classify the next utterance as being intended for the system. Now, getting feedback about this from the system, the user may look away from the system, therewith informing the system that the utterance is in fact intended for the other user.

On the basis of this reasoning, we also investigated whether the addressee-hood of the *upcoming* utterance could be decided on the basis of feature values for the previous utterance. Whereas the accuracy for the earlier classification task was .84, the accuracy for predicting the addressee of the upcoming utterance was .69 (Precision .37, Recall .65), on the basis of the head orientation and dialogue context of the previous utterance (utterance length gave a result at chance level).

So we conclude that the previous utterance already contains information about the addressee-hood of the upcoming utterance, and this information can be used to provide the user with advance information about the system's current assumptions about whether it will be addressed in the next utterance and whether it is likely to respond after that utterance. This information may then be used by the user to adjust his/her behaviour in order to communicate more effectively and avoid disruptions of the dialogue flow. In the next section we describe a study aimed at investigating how to visualize information about the system's inferences about addressee-hood in order to create a transparent interface.

3 Visualizing the System State

As outlined in the previous section, the algorithm that we devised will make mistakes leading to two types of unexpected and undesirable events. Given a particular user utterance, either the system will assume that it is addressed while in fact it is not. In this case the system will respond while it should not, therewith interrupting the conversation between the users. Or the system will assume that it is not addressed while in fact it is. In this case the system will not respond while it should, leaving the dialogue in a waiting state. So, the fact that the system makes such addressee-hood mistakes will create uncertainty in the users, and they may wonder "if I speak to the system, will it understand that I'm addressing it?" and "if I speak to my partner, will the system understand that I'm not addressing it?". In order to enable the users to answer such questions, the system might provide information to the users about its inferences about addressee-hood, according to Nielsen' design heuristic concerning Visibility of system status: "The system should always keep users informed about what is going on, through appropriate feedback within reasonable time" [Nielsen, 1994].

Therefore, a question to be addressed is how to visualize such information. We generated interface concepts based on two different philosophies. One philosophy, derived from Schneiderman [Shneiderman, 1992], holds that Human-Computer Interaction is a field in its own right and that there is no *a priori* reason to devise interface concepts that emulate strategies from human-human communication. Inspired by this philosophy, we devised interface concepts in which the system visualized its inference that the user was or was not going to address the system by indicating whether information could be entered into the system or not. More details of the interface concepts will be presented below.

A second philosophy holds that, certainly in the area of conversational interfaces, it *does* make sense to emulate strategies from human-human communication, precisely because the users are already familiar with them. A good source of strategies in human-human communication is provided by Clark's analysis of language use [Clark, 1996]. Arguing that communication is cooperative action and the addressee needs to play an active role in the communication, Clark analyses language use in terms of four levels of action, as follows.

Level	Speaker A's actions	Addressee B's actions
4	A is proposing joint project w to B	B is considering A's proposal of w
3	A is signalling that p for B	B is recognizing that p from A
2	A is presenting signal s to B	B is identifying signal s from A
1	A is executing behaviour t for B	B is attending to behaviour t from A

In order for communication to be successful, B needs to provide feedback to A about the state of the communication, and A needs to look for evidence at all levels. In the context of addressee-hood, level 1 is of special interest. As Clark notes and as has been shown in a number of studies of communicative behaviour, eye gaze of the listener is the primary evidence that the addressee is attending to the speaker. Of course, appropriate responses by the addressee to the speaker's utterance are another type of evidence that the communication is successful, but this information becomes available only after the utterance. This brings us to the dimension of time, and we see that evidence of successful communication at lower levels becomes available earlier than evidence at higher levels. In fact, for successful communication to be possible, the speaker should verify that s/he has the listener's attention already before the start of the utterance.

Inspired by Clarks' analysis of language use, we formulated a design principle for conversational systems, stating that the system should display active listening behaviour. In particular, it should provide adequate feedback to the speaker at different levels of action at appropriate times. Concretely, this means that, for the speaker to address the system successfully, the system should already display signals of attention before the start of the utterance.

We may now reformulate our question and ask what philosophy is most productive for generating concepts by which we can communicate the system's assumptions about addressee-hood of user utterances. In the next sections we describe the approach [section 3.1], and the concepts generated under the two design principles and the setup of the tests and the results [section 3.2].

3.1 Approach

Given the complexity of the design space, we opted for a research-by-design approach rather than an experimental approach in which a few versions are evaluated in factorial experiments. In a research-by-design approach, interface concepts are realized and subjected to tests, often with small numbers of subjects, in order to elicit user comments. The user comments serve to inform the design of new or modified concepts, which are then in turn subjected to tests with users. In this way, an iterative approach provides qualitative information about whether the concepts achieve their goals.

In each iteration, two concepts were designed and tested, derived from the two philosophies discussed above. One concept always included typical GUI elements, appropriate for Human Computer Interaction. We will refer to concepts instantiating this philosophy as the HCI concept. The other concept was always grafted on human-human communication and aiming to realize convincing behaviour for a Conversational Agent. We will refer to this series of concepts as the CA concept.

A last element of the approach was the use of a bionic Wizard of Oz approach, meaning that simulated components are combined with automated components. Since we were interested in exploring concepts for providing information to users about the system's assumption about addressee-hood of user utterances, we did not care too much about implementing a fully automated dialogue system. Instead, a Wizard of Oz environment was set up containing the following elements: a) a module for automatic addressee-hood determination taking input from b) a module determining the head orientation of the user and an accompanying person and c) a module for speech diarization, providing information about who is speaking when; d) a dialogue manager; e) an output module visualizing the assumptions of the system about the addressee-hood of the user utterances (the visualizations are described below) and displaying relevant information on a screen. In earlier studies it had been found that the user's task was facilitated if the system showed a form displaying the values for search parameters that had already been fixed and that were under discussion, and the parameters that had still to be fixed [Sturm et al., 2002] [Sturm et al., 2005]. Therefore such a form was included in the current interface as well. The dialogue manager and the speech recognition and natural language processing components, were replaced by a Wizard of Oz module. In the current context, one particular dialogue strategy needs to be mentioned. In cases where the system assumed that utterances were intended for the system, the wizard extracted relevant information from the user utterance and displayed it in the corresponding field of the form (e.g. a station name or a departure or arrival time; in case no relevant information could be extracted, the next open field in the form was filled by question marks) and a prompt was started asking for the next parameter, except when the users were involved in further discussion. Concretely, this means that in the case of false alarms the system gave only visual output but did not interfere in the user conversation through spoken prompts. A more complete description of the test environment can be found in [van Turnhout, 2007].

The tests had always the same structure. Two people planned a joint trip to a place of interest (museum or zoo) and had to find out the train schedule for an outward trip and a return trip. The two participants were provided with tourist information and were given different interest profiles to make them discuss options concerning places to visit and time to travel. In all cases participants first went through a practice session in which they planned two trips, but no information about the system's assumptions about addressee-hood was provided. The practice session was intended to familiarize the users with the task and the nature of the dialogue.

3.2 Design Iterations and Tests

Iteration 1
Concepts. In first instance we chose rather abstract ways to visualize the system's assumptions about addressee-hood. The rationale was as follows. As indicated above, the interface included a form displayed on the screen, showing the search parameters that had been fixed and the ones under discussion and still open. Now, if we would have included an Embodied Conversational Agent, the form and the ECA would have competed for the user's visual attention. For that reason we decided to opt for a more abstract visualization, so that the visualization of the system's assumptions about addressee-hood could be integrated into the form.

HCI concept: In situations where the system assumed that the upcoming utterance was intended for the system, the elements of the form retained their default colour (yellow for the logo of the Dutch railroad company), while in situations where the system assumed that the upcoming user utterance was intended for the partner the logo would turn red (analogous to greying out inaccessible options in a menu), meaning that the system would not respond to the utterance (see Fig. 1a).

(a)   (b)

Fig. 1. Visualizations for Iteration 1: (a) HCI concept. Left panel: utterance intended for system - the logo retains its standard colour. Right panel: utterance intended for partner – the logo turns red. (b) CA concept – the form rotates in the horizontal plane towards the speaker or partner.

CA concept: In this case the form could rotate in a horizontal plane, analogous to shifts in eye gaze or head orientation (see Fig. 1b). In situations where the system assumed that the upcoming utterance was intended for the system, the form turned towards the speaker, while in situations where the system assumed that the upcoming user utterance was intended for the partner the form turned towards the partner. (The underlying idea for employing a gaze-following strategy rather than a speaker-follower strategy was that the system was considered as a kind of assistant of the user, and assistants often have the tendency to look at the person the "boss" is speaking at).

Test. Four pairs of participants ran two scenarios and were interviewed afterwards.

Results. None of the participants noted a difference between the interface concepts. Also, they were not aware of the fact that the system might not react to some of the user utterances directed at the system.

Iteration 2

Concepts. Since participants in Iteration 1 turned out not to be aware of differences between the two versions, we opted for more conspicuous visualizations, making use of eyes, which makes the visualizations more anthropomorphic (see Fig. 2).

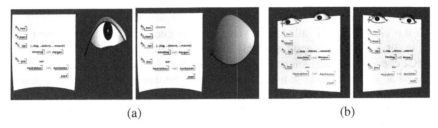

(a)   (b)

Fig. 2. Visualizations for Iteration 2: (a) HCI concept. Left panel: utterance intended for system – eye open. Right panel: utterance intended for partner – eye closed. (b) CA concept – the form and the eyes rotate in the horizontal plane towards the speaker or partner.

HCI concept: A single large eye was shown next to the form, either open or closed to signal the interpretations "utterance intended for the system" and "utterance intended for the partner", respectively (Fig. 2a).

CA concept: A pair of eyes was added on top of the rotating form of Iteration 1 (Fig. 2b).

Test. Four pairs of participants ran two scenarios and were interviewed afterwards.

Results. Some participants did not note a difference between the interface concepts. Other participants noted a difference, but did not attach meaning to the concepts. None of the participants was aware of the fact that the system might not react to some of the user utterances directed at the system.

Iteration 3

Concepts. Since the visualizations in Iteration 2 were still not effective, we explored still more obvious visualizations (see Fig. 3).

(a)   (b)

Fig. 3. Visualizations for Iteration 3: (a) HCI concept. Left panel: utterance intended for system. Right panel: utterance intended for partner. (b) CA concept – rotating bear face: when the utterance is assumed to be intended for the system, the face is turned towards the speaker; when the utterance is assumed to be intended for the partner, the face is also turned towards the partner.

HCI concept: A bear's face with an arrow pointing towards the ear or a stop sign.

CA concept: A rotating bear's face replacing the rotating eyes of Iteration 2.

Test. Four pairs of participants ran two scenarios and were interviewed afterwards.

Results. Three out of four pairs of participants noted some or all of the differences, and for the HCI concept they were able to come up with the right interpretation, in particular for the stop sign, which was interpreted as "the system is not listening". No pair was able to attach the right interpretation to the CA concept.

Intermediate Discussion
So far it is clear that only rather brute visualizations manage to convey the meaning of the concept, and still this applies mainly to the HCI concept. However, a drawback of the HCI concept is that it suggests that the system is not listening, which is not precisely what we want to communicate. In human-human communication, conversational participants may still be listening without being addressed. This is known as overhearing, and during such situations over-hearers may pick up relevant information. For instance a travel agent may overhear a dialogue between the customers leading to the conclusion that they do not favour a particular country, and s/he may take the initiative to propose alternative destinations. Since we believed that the CA concept could be extended more naturally to cover this situation as well, we decided to explore further visualizations.

Iterations 4 and 5
Concepts. In Iterations 4 and 5 the visualizations were the same as in Iteration 3 (see Fig. 3). However, for the CA concept, both in Iterations 4 and 5 a speaker-following strategy was applied instead of a gaze-following strategy, as a speaker-following strategy is more in accordance with human behaviour (see [Terken et al., 2007]). Also, for the CA concept a rotating camera was added, for which also a speaker-following strategy was applied, meaning that the camera would "look" at the speaker (both Iterations 4 and 5). Finally, the incidence of false alarms was increased, meaning that the system would more often respond to user utterances that were in fact intended for the partner (Iteration 5 only).

Test. In both iterations four pairs of participants ran two scenarios and were interviewed afterwards.

Results. The CA concept was interpreted correctly by seven out of eight pairs, in the sense that they noted that the camera applied a speaker-following strategy. In addition, they noted that the camera signalled attention of the system to the speaker, and one pair explicitly mentioned that they thought they could not address the system if the camera was not pointed towards the speaker. Finally, situations where false alarms led to a disruption of the dialogue were noticed by the users.

Discussion
In Iterations 4 and 5 the users noticed that the camera followed the speaker and they found it quite natural. The display of information on the screen in case the system incorrectly assumed the utterance was intended for the system was not perceived as an intrusion. Finally, users found false alarms that led to a disruption of the dialogue irritating. So we need to make sure that the dialogue strategy is devised such that the disruptive effect of a false alarm is minimized.

4   Conclusions and Discussion

We have shown that addressee-hood of current and upcoming user utterances produced in the context of mixed human-human-system interaction can be automatically determined with reasonable success on the basis of fairly low-level information, although the system produces a considerable number of false alarms (meaning that it assumes it is being addressed while in fact it is not). Therefore we developed interface concepts to convey the assumptions that the system makes to the users in order to make the interaction transparent. We have presented an iterative research-by-design approach testing several visualization concepts. The study gave the following results. (1) Applying an HCI design philosophy, we were able to develop a convincing visualization informing the users that the system was not always listening. (2) Applying a design philosophy inspired by theories about human-human communication, we were able to develop a visualization that convincingly signals that the system is attending to the speaker. The signalling function is amplified by physical elements such as a rotating camera.

Concerning the first finding, the problem is that we do not so much want to convey that the system is not listening, but rather that the system may sometimes erroneously conclude that it is not addressed. We conclude that we have not been able to develop a concept derived from HCI design principles to convey this message to the user in a convincing manner.

Concerning the second finding, the positive outcome is that we have developed a convincing way to visualize attention to the speaker in a multi-user situation, derived from a design principle based on theories of human communication. A rotating camera following the speaker made clear that the system was aware of the social context, and the users found this very natural. The negative outcome is that, within this line of thinking, we were not able to convey the inferences of the system concerning the addressee-hood of user utterances in a convincing way either. On the other hand, we devised a dialogue strategy that is tolerant against addressee-hood errors by exhibiting unobtrusive behaviour in the case of false alarms. The system responded by means of spoken prompts only if the users did not continue their conversation. When the user conversation was continuing, spoken interruptions were suppressed and the system displayed information that it picked up from the user conversation on the screen, mimicking overhearing behaviour in human communication. As a result, the number of spoken interruptions was minimal, while the system still exhibited contextual awareness. The results of intervention 5 confirmed that this is an acceptable strategy for dealing with multi-user situations. Thus, we may formulate the following rules for dealing with addressee-hood and turn-taking for a multimodal socially aware conversational agent:

1. Display information that was extracted from user utterances on the screen.
2. Don't start talking when someone else is talking.
3. If you think you are not addressed and no one else starts talking, don't start talking.
4. If you think you are addressed and no one else starts talking, start talking.

Given the high incidence of false alarms (where the system believes it is addressed while in fact it is not) and the low incidence of false rejections (where the system believes it is not addressed while in fact it is), these rules result in dialogues with few noticeable addressee-hood mistakes. And those that occur relate to situations where the user need to remind the system that it was being addressed ("hey, I'm talking to you"), a situation which can also be observed in human-human communication.

Next steps are to conduct more rigorous testing with this concept, to refine the system's signalling of attention according to the findings in [Terken et al., 2007] and to improve the technology for overhearing, to make sure that the system picks up the appropriate information from the user conversation and reacts to it in an adequate way.

Acknowledgements

The research reported in this study was made possible by a grant of the Dutch Ministry of Economic Affairs through the Innovation Oriented Programme Man-Machine Interaction (IOP-MMI). We thank two anonymous reviewers for recommendations for improvement.

References

[Argyle and Graham, 1977] Argyle, M., Graham, J.: The Central Europe experiment - looking at persons and looking at things. Journal of Environmental Psychology and Non-verbal Behaviour 1, 6–16 (1977)

[Bakx et al., 2003] Bakx, I.H.M., Van Turnhout, K.G., Terken, J.M.B.: Facial orientation during multi-party interaction with information kiosks. In: Proceedings of Interact 2003, pp. 701–704. IOS Press, Amsterdam (2003)

[Clark, 1996] Clark, H.H.: Using Language. Cambridge University Press, Cambridge (1996)

[Cassell et al., 1999] Cassell, J., Torres, O., Prevost, S.: Turn Taking vs. Discourse Structure: How Best to Model Multimodal Conversation. In: Wilks (ed.) Machine Conversations, pp. 143–154. Kluwer, The Hague (1999)

[Katzenmaier et al., 2004] Katzenmaier, M., Stiefelhagen, R., Schultz, T.: Identifying the addressee in human-human-robot interactions based on head pose and speech. In: Sharma, R., Darrell, T., Harper, M.P., Lazzari, G., Turk, M. (eds.) Proceedings of the International Conference on Multimodal Interfaces ICMI 2004, State College, PA, USA, pp. 144–151 (2004)

[Nielsen, 1994] Nielsen, J.: Heuristic evaluation. In: Nielsen, J., Mack, R.L. (eds.) Usability Inspection Methods, pp. 25–62. John Wiley & Sons, New York (1994)

[Shneiderman, 1992] Shneiderman, B.: Designing the User Interface: Strategies for Effective Human-Computer Interaction, 2nd edn. Addison-Wesley, Reading (1992)

[Sturm et al., 2002] Sturm, J.A., Bakx, I.H.M., Cranen, B., Terken, J.M.B., Wang, F.: Usability evaluation of a Dutch multimodal system for railway information. In: Conference on Language Resources and Evaluation, May 29-30. LREC, Las Palmas (2002)

[Sturm et al., 2005] Sturm, J.A., Cranen, B., Terken, J.M.B., Bakx, I.: Effects of prolonged use on the usability of a multimodal form-filling interface. In: Minker, W., Bühler, D., Dybkjaer, L. (eds.) Spoken Multimodal Human-Computer Dialogue in Mobile Environments, pp. 329–348. Springer, Dordrecht (2005)

[Takemae et al., 2003] Takemae, Y., Otsuka, K., Mukawa, N.: Video cut editing rule based on participants' gaze in multiparty conversation. In: Proceedings of the 11th ACM International Conference on Multimedia, November 2-8, pp. 303–306. ACM Press, New York (2003)

[Terken et al., 2007] Terken, J., Joris, I., De Valk, L.: Multimodal cues for addressee-hood in triadic communication with a human information retrieval agent. In: Proceedings of the 9th international Conference on Multimodal interfaces, ICMI 2007, Nagoya, Aichi, Japan, November 12 - 15, pp. 94–101. ACM Press, New York (2007)

[Thórisson, 2002] Thórisson, K.R.: Natural Turn-Taking Needs No Manual: Computational Theory and Model, from Perception to Action. In: Granström, B., House, D., Karlsson, I. (eds.) Multimodality in Language and Speech Systems, pp. 173–207. Kluwer Academic Publishers, Dordrecht (2002)

[van Turnhout, 2007] van Turnhout, K.G.: Socially Aware Conversational Agents. Unpublished Doct. Dissertation, Eindhoven (NL): Technische Universiteit Eindhoven (2007)

[van Turnhout et al., 2005] van Turnhout, K., Terken, J., Bakx, I., Eggen, B.: Identifying the intended addressee in mixed human-human and human-computer interaction from non-verbal features. In: Proceedings of the 7th international Conference on Multimodal interfaces, ICMI 2005, Trento, Italy, October 04-06, pp. 175–182. ACM Press, New York (2005)

[Vertegaal et al., 2001] Vertegaal, R., Slagter, R., Van der Veer, G., Nijholt, A.: Eye gaze patterns in conversations: There is more to conversational agents than meets the eye. In: Proceedings of Human Factors in Computing Systems (CHI 2001), pp. 301–308. ACM Press, New York (2001)

A Prototype for Future Spoken Dialog Systems Using an Embodied Conversational Agent

Marcel Dausend and Ute Ehrlich

Daimler AG, System Components and Peripherals, Infotainment and Telematics,
D-89081 Ulm, Germany
marcel.dausend@daimler.com
ute.ehrlich@daimler.com

Abstract. Mercedes Benz presented its prototype F700 at the IAA 2007 automotive fair. This paper describes the multimodal dialog component as part of the Human Machine Interaction concept in this car. An Embodied Conversational Agent (ECA) was integrated into the dialog system based on concepts from human cognitive perception. The ECA supports a more natural dialog, e.g. spontaneous speech or mixed-initiative. This required the implementation of an advanced confirmation and correction strategy taking into account both safety and driver comfort. We set the focus of this demonstration on the navigation service.

1 Introduction

Avatars, human-controlled virtual representatives, play a central role in today's interconnected computer world as counterparts to human users. Whether in Skype (Klonies) or the "World of Warcraft" computer game, avatars are becoming ever more popular and lend a personal, human-like touch to an otherwise cold on-line world. According to Oviatt [Oviatt, 1999] "in the future, more balanced systems will be needed in which powerful input and output capabilities are better matched with one another." She suggests using avatars to enhance multimodal output interfaces. "Embodied Conversational Agents" (ECA) [Cassell, 2001] are in effect computer-controlled avatars and serve the same purpose.

We introduced an ECA as a new concept into the car. It is used as part of the bridge between state-of-the-art command-and-control input to freely formulated spoken dialogs of the future. The virtual female character in this dialog system puts the user at ease, thus encouraging him to speak more freely and naturally, and explicitly assists the user in carrying out more complex tasks such as specifying a destination for navigation. The outward appearance of the ECA was adapted to reflect both the company image and human cognitive aspects. Speech input is analyzed semantically with respect to an enhanced dialog strategy to enable the ECA to react appropriately. This new Human Machine Interaction (HMI) concept was successfully demonstrated with the Mercedes Benz prototype car at the IAA 2007 automotive fair in Frankfurt/Main.

E. André et al. (Eds.): PIT 2008, LNAI 5078, pp. 268–271, 2008.

2 The Prototype

The HMI concept of the prototype provides manual operation for the basic functions, whereas interactive spoken dialogs are used to deal with complex self-contained tasks. The manual operations are performed using the Central Control Element (CCE), which can be turned, slid and pressed. The initial choice of application and navigation within menus must be performed manually. However, once the spoken dialog is active, no manual operations are allowed except for interrupting the on-going dialog. Three speech-activated applications were realized in this prototype: radio, telephone, and navigation. This paper focuses on the navigation application. Every speech application is accessible by at most three manual steps at any time. That guarantees a very fast access to the speech applications.

Fig. 1. The GUI of the HMI prototype of the Mercedes Benz F700 – The navigation interface

The screen (see Fig. 1) provides a status bar at the bottom and soft keys on the left side for switching to another application (telephone, radio, or navigation). The main area shows the relevant information of the currently activated application. The soft keys "Abbruch" (cancel) and "Manuell" (manual) are provided for canceling the spoken dialog or switching to manual operation.

Unlike conventional speech systems in cars, this new prototype offers an implicit invitation to speak. Whenever the ECA appears, the system is prepared for a speech input. The user may speak to the system as long it remains present. Also, he may interrupt system prompts or take the initiative.

The technical basis for this prototype is the system architecture described in [Mann et al., 2007]. The main system components, the graphic/manual interface and the spoken dialog, communicate via a synchronization module (Sync). The central component of the spoken dialog is the task-driven dialog manager (TDDM) that controls and manages the ongoing dialog interaction with the natural language understanding unit (NLU), the automatic speech recognizer (ASR), and the text-to-speech engine (TTS). The TTS was extended with the Charamel Avatar Software (CAS) in order to synchronize the speech and animation of the ECA, e.g. lip and head movements. These animations are defined as control characters within the prompt. So the XML dialog specification described in [Ehrlich and Jersak, 2006] must only be extended by the ECA commands and in general need not to be changed.

3   ECA-Guided Spoken Dialog Strategy

The motivations for using an ECA can be summarized from the recent research on cognition [Rüggenberg, 2007]: The use of ECA and thus the effect on human perception should ease user reservations, provide a more user-friendly natural operation, increase the user's appreciation, and give pleasure using such a system.

To support a more natural interaction, the explicit request for speech input by a signal tone has been replaced with the appearance of the ECA, which implicitly indicates a request for speech input. Its presence and design improves personalization and use of natural speech towards the system [Krämer, 2005]. Our ECA appears as a female assistant. Assigning a social role to the ECA in context of an interactive spoken dialog leads the user to personify the system [Jensen, 2005]. This in turn helps to overcome restraints and makes the user feel the tasks were easier. The degree of life-likeness of the ECA influences the user's expectations and acceptance of the system, and, consequently, the basic trust in it [Rüggenberg, 2007], [Krämer, 2005], [Krämer and Bente, 2002]. On this basis a medium degree of reality was chosen to balance expectations and acceptance.

Badler recognized that speech is particularly suited for communicating with ECAs because it does not require any additional resources of the user [Badler, 1997]. Seeing the ECA from the corner of one's eye and getting voice feedback is sufficient to conduct the conversation without any further visual aid. Furthermore, this improves driving safety. In order to further increase the naturalness of the dialog, the phonetics of the TTS output were carefully scrutinized and modified where appropriate.

System output		User utterances
What is your destination?		I want to go to the Amselweg in Frankfurt.
The city Frankfurt is ambiguous.		
Do you want to go to Frankfurt (Oder)?		*<no response>*
Frankfurt am Main?		Yes, that's right.
Frankfurt am Main, Amselweg?		
Please start navigation or add house number.	Please start the navigation.

Fig. 2. Example of a spoken dialog with ambiguous city input

Taking into account the above described requirements and features a dialog strategy was designed which supports mixed-initiative dialog and spontaneous speech, e.g. dealing with sentence breaks and ungrammatical phrases. Recognition alternatives, e.g. for cities, are not shown to the driver as a list as it is done in current in car spoken dialog systems, but the best alternative is assumed to be the correct choice. Picklists are only shown if the given information is ambiguous or contradictory, e.g. if street and city do not fit. This requires an advanced confirmation and correction strategy: confirmations usually are given implicitly as in the above example (e.g. "The city Frankfurt is ambiguous ...") adding an additional question to continue the dialog properly. Only in case of understanding problems, e.g. rejections or corrections, explicit confirmation is requested, e.g. "Frankfurt am Main?" A positive answer would prevent any further correction of the given value. Otherwise the driver is free to correct all input at each time.

4 Conclusion

The HMI prototype of the Mercedes Benz demonstrator using an embodied conversational agent (ECA) for multimodal dialog systems was very successful. We accomplished our goals: ease user reservations in using the dialog system, provide more user-friendly natural operations, increase the user's appreciation, and comfort using the system. To achieve these goals we extended the dialog concept and improved the dialog strategy taking into account cognitive aspects and perceptive concepts.

We adapted our system architecture and dialog specification to support natural output of the ECA, i.e. lip-synchronization and specific prompt reactions. This prototype was received favorably by the press and visitors at the IAA 2007 automotive fair in Frankfurt am Main. Overall this HMI has the potential for satisfying the requirements for intuitive use and user friendliness. An evaluation of the system is planned to verify the success of the prototype and detect ways for improvement.

For the sake of driving safety, we have deliberately separated manual and speech input. Future research concerning ECA-guided dialog systems in the car could deal with real multimodal interactive dialogs, merging our already existing concepts for multimodal dialogs with the above concepts regarding ECAs.

References

[Badler, 1997] Badler, N.I.: Real-time virtual humans. In: PG 1997: Proceedings of the 5th Pacific Conference on Computer Graphics and Applications, p. 4. IEEE Computer Society, Washington, DC (1997)

[Cassell, 2001] Cassell, J.: Embodied Conversational Agents: Representation and intelligence in user interfaces. AI Magazine 22(4), 67–84 (2001)

[Ehrlich and Jersak, 2006] Ehrlich, U., Jersak, T.: Definition und Konfiguration der Wissensbasen und Schnittstellen von Sprachdialogapplikationen mit XML. In: XMLT2006 (2006)

[Jensen et al., 2000] Jensen, C., Farnham, S., Drucker, S., Kollock, P.: The effect of communication modality on cooperation in online environments. In: Proceedings of the SIGCHI conference on Human factors in computing systems, pp. 470–477 (2000)

[Krämer, 2005] Krämer, N.: Social Communicative Effects of a Virtual Program Guide. In: Panayiotopoulos, T., Gratch, J., Aylett, R.S., Ballin, D., Olivier, P., Rist, T. (eds.) IVA 2005. LNCS (LNAI), vol. 3661, pp. 442–453. Springer, Heidelberg (2005)

[Krämer and Bente, 2002] Krämer, N., Bente, G.: Virtuelle Helfer: Embodied Con-versational Agents in der Mensch-Computer-Interaktion. In: Bente, G., Krmer, N., Petersen, A. (eds.) Virtuelle Realitäten, pp. 203–225. Hofgrefe Verlag (2002)

[Mann et al., 2007] Mann, S., Berton, A., Ehrlich, U.: A multimodal dialogue system for interacting with large audio databases in the car. In: Fellbaum, K. (ed.) Elektronische Sprachsignalverarbeitung Studientexte zur Sprachkommunikation, vol. 46, pp. 202–209. TUDpress (2007)

[Oviatt, 1999] Oviatt, S.: Ten myths of multimodal interaction. Communications of the ACM 42(11), 74–81 (1999)

[Rüggenberg, 2007] Rüggenberg, S.: So nah und doch so fern. Soziale Prasenz und Vertrauen in der computervermittelten Kommunikation. PhD thesis, Universität Köln (2007)

Innovative Interfaces in MonAMI:
The Reminder

Jonas Beskow, Jens Edlund, Björn Granström, Joakim Gustafson,
and Gabriel Skantze

KTH Speech Music and Hearing
{beskow,edlund,bjorn,jocke,gabriel}@speech.kth.se

Abstract. This demo paper presents the first version of *the Reminder*, a prototype ECA developed in the European project MonAMI, which aims at "main-
streaming accessibility in consumer goods and services, using advanced
technologies to ensure equal access, independent living and participation for
all". The Reminder helps users to plan activities and to remember what to do.
The prototype merges ECA technology with other, existing technologies:
Google Calendar and a *digital pen and paper.* This innovative combination of
modalities allows users to continue using a paper calendar in the manner they
are used to, whilst the ECA provides verbal notifications on what has been written in the calendar. Users may also ask questions such as *"When was I supposed
to meet Sara?"* or *"What's on my schedule today?"*

1 Introduction

This demo paper presents the first version of a multimodal spoken dialogue system
developed within the European project MonAMI (http://www.monami.info/). The
objective of the MonAMI project is to demonstrate that accessible, useful services for
elderly and disabled persons living at home can be delivered in mainstream systems
and platforms. The technology platforms delivering the services are largely derived
from standard technology, and integrate elements such as wearable devices, user interaction technology, and service infrastructures to ensure quality of service, reliability and privacy. The services are delivered on mainstream devices and services such
as digital-TV, cell telephones and broadband Internet.

As traditional human-machine interfaces often assume a degree of computer liter-
acy and are unintuitive to those unfamiliar with technology, development of innovative interfaces is also a part of the MonAMI project. The overall goal is to relieve
human-computer interaction from some of the demands posed on the cognitive, visual
and motor skills of the user, especially for elderly and disabled persons. Conversational interfaces are a radically different approach to human-machine interaction
where the interaction metaphor is shifted from desktop manipulation to spoken dialogue, modelled on communication we are intrinsically familiar with: human-human
face-to-face spoken dialogue. The result is an ECA – an *embodied conversational
agent*, communicating with speech, facial expression, gaze and gesture. The innovative interfaces effort within MonAMI aims to develop interface technology based on
the ECA; to implement a prototype that will be evaluated with users in the target

E. André et al. (Eds.): PIT 2008, LNAI 5078, pp. 272–275, 2008.

group; and to adapt and use existing design and evaluation methods, based on end user involvement, for gaining understanding of IT functions and services that are considered meaningful by people with disabilities and people close to them. This demo paper presents the first version of *the Reminder*, the prototype ECA developed in the project in order to reach these goals.

2 Domain

The choice of target application for an ECA prototype was informed by the services allocated for the Swedish FU centre (a *Feasibility and Usability centre* where user tests are held in lab-like conditions) in MonAMI, and in particular by meetings held with two potential users, both of whom have had a brain tumour and have cognitive disability, to identify potential areas addressing real key problems in their daily life. Based on these interviews, the choice fell on an application helping users plan activities and remember what to do. The overall application design is largely based on requirements from the interviews with the potential users, both of whom used a range of reminder applications and devices: paper calendars, paper notes, PDA calendars, electronic whiteboards, and SMS notifications, and both of whom expressed interest in using an ECA for getting notifications. The reminder addresses this by supporting pen input as well as speech, as illustrated by the following scenario:

December 14
10:00   *When speaking to Sara on the phone, Peter and Sara agree on a meeting at 12:00 the next day. Peter writes this down in his calendar.*

December 15
8:00	Peter:	What happens today?
	System:	At 12 o'clock you have written "meeting with Sara".
	Peter:	Ok, remind me 1 hour ahead.
	System:	OK, I will remind you att 11 o'clock.
10:00	Peter:	When is my meeting with Sara?
	System:	You have written "meeting with Sara" at 12 o'clock. I will remind you at 11 o'clock.
	Peter:	Ok, thank you

The domain presents hard challenges for ECAs. For example, the things a person may want to be reminded varies indefinitely, which is a problem for speech recognition.

3 System

The Reminder application architecture is based on the Higgins architecture [Edlund, Skantze and Carlson, 2004]. The architecture is chiefly designed to cater to development and research needs, such as flexibility and ease of use, and places few constraints on components, which can be implemented in any language and run on any platform. Figure 1 shows the components and the message flow in the Reminder application. From the ASR, the top hypothesis with word confidence scores (2) is forwarded for natural language understanding components. First it is sent to the robust interpreter Pickering [Skantze and Edlund, 2004], which makes a robust interpretation of this

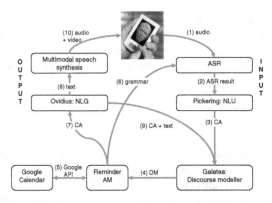

Fig. 1. The Reminder architecture

hypothesis and creates context-independent semantic representations of communicative acts (CAs). The results from Pickering (3) are forwarded to the discourse modeller Galatea [Skantze, in press], which may be regarded as a further interpretation step taking dialogue context into account. Galatea adds these to a discourse model (DM). The discourse model (4) is passed to the Reminder Action Manager, which initiates systems actions. The Reminder uses Google Calendar as its backend. When the discourse model is updated by a user request for calendar information, the action manager searches Google Calendar (5) to generate a system response in the form of a CA (7), which is passed to a component called Ovidius [Skantze, 2007]. Ovidius generates a textual representation of the system utterance (8) that forwarded to a multimodal speech synthesiser for rendering (10). (The CA and the textual representation are both passed to Galatea (9) for inclusion in the discourse model.) The text-to-speech synthesis and facial animation is responsible of producing verbal as well as non-verbal responses from the system. The animated character is based on a 3D parameterised talking head that can be controlled by a text-to-speech system to provide accurate lip-synchronised audio-visual synthetic speech [Beskow, 1997]. The facial model includes control parameters for articulatory gestures as well as non-verbal expressions, which can be derived from motion recordings or developed using an interactive parameter editor (see [Beskow, Edlund and Nordstrand, 2005] for details).

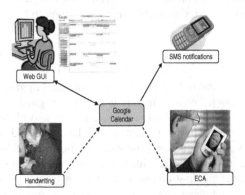

Fig. 2. Calendar interfaces. Dotted lines added interfaces.

Each time the system initiates or if the Google Calendar entries are updated, the action manager also parses the calendar entries to build new speech recognition grammars and send them to the ASR (6). A schematic of Google Calendar can be seen in Figure 2, in which the original service interfaces are represented by solid lines and the extensions implemented in MonAMI by dotted lines. Utilising Google Calendar brings the obvious advantage of not having to provide hardware, software and connectivity for the calendar backbone, but there are several other benefits as well. Some of the more noteworthy come from the fact that the Google Calendar already provides user APIs in the form of a Web GUI for input and output, and SMS notifications as a form of output.

To meet the requirements from the potential users we interviewed, and partly in order to address the large and unknown vocabulary problem, we designed a solution based on a mix of speech technology and a *digital pen and paper*. To the user, the effect of the pen input is that of writing down events in a seemingly ordinary paper calendar. The text written by the user is transferred to a computer which performs handwriting recognition and transfers the information to a calendar backbone. The information may then be accessed by the ECA. This innovative combination of modalities allows the users to use a paper calendar like they are used to, and furthermore addresses the ASR vocabulary problem: users may write anything they like in the calendar, but vocabulary can be limited to a base vocabulary the contents of calendar entries, which is used to update the vocabulary so that the user may speak about events in the calendar.

Acknowledgements

This research was carried out at the Centre for Speech Technology, a competence centre at KTH, supported by MonAMI, an Integrated Project under the European Commission's Sixth Framework Program (IP-035147).

References

[Edlund, Skantze and Carlson, 2004] Edlund, J., Skantze, G., Carlson, R.: Higgins - a spoken dialogue system for investigating error handling techniques. In: Proc. of the International Conference on Spoken Language Processing, ICSLP 2004, Jeju, Korea, pp. 229–231 (2004)

[Skantze and Edlund, 2004] Skantze, G., Edlund, J.: Robust interpretation in the Higgins spoken dialogue system. In: ISCA Tutorial and Research Workshop (ITRW) on Robustness Issues in Conversational Interaction, Norwich, UK (2004)

[Skantze, in press] Skantze, G.: Galatea: A discourse modeller supporting concept-level error handling in spoken dialogue systems. In: Dybkjær, L., Minker, W. (eds.) Recent Trends in Discourse and Dialogue. Springer, Heidelberg (in press)

[Skantze, 2007] Skantze, G.: Error Handling in Spoken Dialogue Systems - Managing Uncertainty, Grounding and Miscommunication. Doctoral dissertation, KTH, Department of Speech, Music and Hearing (2007)

[Beskow, 1997] Beskow, J.: Animation of talking agents. In: Proc. of ESCA Workshop on Audio-Visual Speech Processing, Rhodes, Greece, pp. 149–152 (1997)

[Beskow, Edlund and Nordstrand, 2005] Beskow, J., Edlund, J., Nordstrand, M.: A model for multi-modal dialogue system output applied to an animated talking head. In: Minker, W., Bühler, D., Dybkjaer, L. (eds.) Spoken Multimodal Human-Computer Dialogue in Mobile Environments (2005)

Evaluation Methods for Multimodal Systems:
A Comparison of Standardized Usability Questionnaires

Ina Wechsung and Anja B. Naumann

Deutsche Telekom Laboratories, TU Berlin, 10587 Berlin, Germany
ina.wechsung@telekom.de
http://www.qu.tlabs.tu-berlin.de

Abstract. Different questionnaires assessing the usability of two multimodal systems and one unimodal system were compared. Each participant (N=21) performed several tasks with each device and was afterwards asked to rate the system by filling out different questionnaires. The results show that standardized questionnaires are applicable only to a limited extent. Despite some concordance, the results differ considerably and thus indicate the need for the development of a valid and reliable questionnaire covering the usability and quality of multimodal systems.

1 Introduction

Up to now a wide range of established usability evaluation methods is available, most of them designed for the evaluation of unimodal systems. Thus it is not clear if these established methods are applicable to multimodal systems (see [Bernsen and Dybkjær, 2004], [Sturm, 2005] and [Petersen, 1998]. The probably most common technique applied in subject-based evaluations are questionnaires, but a standardized and validated questionnaire addressing the evaluation of multimodal systems is still not available. Even for speech-based systems the probably most common questionnaire, the Subjective Assessment of Speech Interfaces questionnaire (SASSI) [Hone and Graham, 2000], still lacks psychometric validation [Larsen, 2003].

In the current study, we used several established questionnaires to assess the users' opinion about multimodal systems. The results were compared with each other. The general objective is to investigate to which extent well known and widely used scales for the evaluation of graphical user interfaces and speech-based systems are appropriate for the evaluation of multimodal systems. Therefore it was analyzed in which aspects different established questionnaires lead to the same result and where there are inconsistencies across different questionnaires.

2 Method

Twenty-one German-speaking individuals (11 male, 10 female) between the age of 19 and 69 (M = 31.24) took part in the study. All users participated in return for a book token.

E. André et al. (Eds.): PIT 2008, LNAI 5078, pp. 276–284, 2008.
© Springer-Verlag Berlin Heidelberg 2008

The multimodal devices adopted for the test were a PDA (Fujitsu-Siemens Pocket LOOX T830) and a tablet PC (Samsung Q1-Pro 900 Casomii). Both devices could be operated via voice control as well as via graphical user interface with touch screen. Additionally, the PDA could be operated via motion control. Furthermore, a unimodal device (a conventional PC controllable with mouse and keyboard) was used as control condition. The application, a media recommender system, was the same for all devices.

The users performed five different types of tasks: seven navigation tasks, six tasks where checkboxes had to be marked or unmarked, four tasks where an option from a drop-down list had to be selected, three tasks where a button had to be pressed, and one task where a phone number had to be entered. The questionnaires used were the AttrakDiff questionnaire [Hassenzahl et al., 2003], the System Usability Scale (SUS) [Brooke, 1996], the Software Usability Measurement Inventory (SUMI) [Kirakowski and Corbett, 1993], the SASSI questionnaire [Hone and Graham, 2000] and a self-constructed questionnaire covering overall ratings and preferences. SUMI, SASSI and AttrakDiff were used in their original form. The SUS was adapted for voice control by exchanging the word "system" with "voice control". The order of the question-naires was randomized.

Each test session took approximately three hours. Each participant performed a series of tasks with each device. Participants were verbally instructed to perform the tasks with a given modality. This was repeated for every modality supported by that specific device. After that, the tasks were presented again and the participants could freely choose the interaction modality. Finally, they were asked to fill out the SUMI, the AttrakDiff, the SUS and the SASSI questionnaire to rate the previously tested device. This procedure was repeated for each of the three devices. The order of the devices was randomized for each subject. After the third device, a final question-naire regarding the overall impressions and preferences had to be filled out by the participants.

3 Results

3.1 SUMI Ratings

All negatively poled SUMI items were recoded, so that higher values indicate better ratings. The scales were calculated according to the SUMI handbook [Porteous et al., 1998]. The SUMI raw data (results were not transformed to the T-Scale) of the global scale showed significant differences between the devices, $F(2,40) = 6.56$, $p = .003$; partial $eta^2 = .247$. The PDA, the device with the most modalities, was rated best ($M = 45.29$, $SD = 10.14$), the Tablet PC was rated second ($M = 40.19$, $SD = 7.87$), and the unimodal PC got the worst rating ($M = 38.04$, $SD = 7.06$).

For the subscales, significant differences between devices were found for affect, efficiency, control and learnability. The unimodal PC was rated worst on all subscales, except the learnability scale. No effect was found for helpfulness. The detailed results are shown in Table 1.

Table 1. Ratings on SUMI Subscales (Min.=10/ Max.=30)

Scale	System	Mean	SD	F (2,40)	p (part. eta²)
Efficiency	Tablet PC	19.00	3.39		
	PDA	19.90	3.48	6.19	.005 (.236)
	Unimodal	16.67	3.15		
Affect	Tablet PC	19.33	2.13		
	PDA	19.95	2.13	10.02	.000 (.334)
	Unimodal	17.38	2.73		
Helpfulness	Tablet PC	22.05	1.96		
	PDA	22.19	2.09	1.46	.244 (.068)
	Unimodal	21.48	1.89		
Control	Tablet PC	22.67	2.27		
	PDA	22.24	2.21	3.33	.046 (.143)
	Unimodal	21.38	2.22		
Learnability	Tablet PC	15.57	3.23		
	PDA	14.57	3.47	5.98	.005 (.230)
	Unimodal	16.90	4.40		

3.2 AttrakDiff Ratings

The results of the AttrakDiff show that the unimodal system got the best ratings regarding the pragmatic qualities whereas the PDA, $F(2,38)=16.80$, p=.000, part.eta²=.469, got the worst (s. Figure 1). The new modalities had obviously an impact on the users' impression of the hedonic qualities (s. Figure 1). The unimodal system got the worst ratings on the scale hedonic qualities – stimulation, $F(2,38)=3.59$, p=.037, part.eta²=.159, and on the scale hedonic qualities – identity, $F(2,38)=23.03$, p=.000, part.eta²=.548.

The tablet PC was rated best on both scales. Regarding the overall attractiveness further differences could be found, $F(2,38)=4.04$, p=.026, part.eta²=.175. The tablet PC was rated most attractive. The least attractive system was the PDA.

3.3 SASSI Ratings

Since the questionnaire was designed to cover speech based applications, SASSI ratings were only collected for both multimodal systems (PDA and tablet PC). All negatively poled items were recoded, so that higher values indicate better ratings.

Major differences between the devices could only be shown for cognitive demand: The PDA was rated as more cognitive demanding than the tablet PC. Minor differences could be found for the global scale, the likeability scale and the annoyance

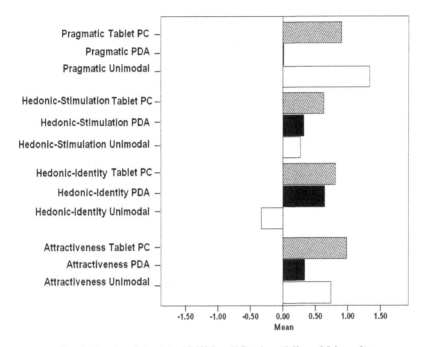

Fig. 1. Results of the AttrakDiff for all Devices (Min.=-3/Max.=3)

scale: The tablet PC got better ratings on all of these scales. The detailed results are shown in Table 2.

Table 2. Ratings on SASSI Subscales (Min.=0/Max.=4)

Scale	System	Mean	SD	t (20)	p
Global	Tablet PC	2.24	.52	1.95	.059
	PDA	1.96	.48		
Speed	Tablet PC	1.64	.50	.40	.693
	PDA	1.59	.46		
Accuracy	Tablet PC	2.11	.69	1.20	.166
	PDA	1.90	.58		
Likeability	Tablet PC	2.60	.62	1.79	.065
	PDA	2.23	.61		
Habituality	Tablet PC	1.69	.74	2.00	.246
	PDA	1.52	.52		
Cognitive Demand	Tablet PC	2.30	.59	1.95	.036
	PDA	1.86	.68		
Annoyance	Tablet PC	2.49	.59	2.25	.089
	PDA	2.18	.64		

3.4 SUS Ratings

The SUS items were adapted for voice control and were thus only collected for the tablet PC and the PDA. All items were poled in one direction. Higher values indicate better ratings. Since the SUS does not include any subscale, the global scale and the single items were compared. The global scale was calculated according to the instructions given in [Brooke, 1996].

Major differences could only be shown for one item regarding the consistency: The tablet PC was rated as more consistent than the PDA. Furthermore the participants tended to rate the tablet PC better regarding the learnability. The detailed results are displayed in Table 3.

Table 3. Ratings on SUS (Global Scale: Min. = 0/Max. = 100; Items: Min.=0/Max.= 4)

	Device	Mean	SD	t (20)	p
Global Scale	Tablet PC	53.93	16.59	1.32	.232
	PDA	50.12	13.38		
Would use voice control frequently	Tablet PC	2.00	1.18	1.45	.162
	PDA	1.74	1.05		
Voice control unnecessarily complex	Tablet PC	2.19	.93	.72	.480
	PDA	1.74	1.05		
Voice control easy to use	Tablet PC	2.10	.94	1.24	.229
	PDA	1.80	.98		
Need support to use voice control	Tablet PC	2.33	.86	.70	.493
	PDA	2.42	.93		
Various functions in voice control well integrated	Tablet PC	2.00	.84	.44	.666
	PDA	2.10	.70		
Too much inconsistency in voice control	Tablet PC	2.04	1.02	2.36	.029
	PDA	1.67	.66		
Most people would learn to use voice control very quickly	Tablet PC	2.48	.98	.75	.463
	PDA	2.29	1.01		
Found voice control very cumbersome	Tablet PC	2.14	1.01	.55	.590
	PDA	2.00	.89		
Felt very confident using voice control	Tablet PC	1.76	1.00	.78	.446
	PDA	1.57	.87		
Need to learn a lot before going with voice control	Tablet PC	2.52	.68	1.9	.072
	PDA	2.14	.96		

3.5 Comparison of Questionnaire Results

For a general overview of the different results, the raw scores of the global or overall scales of SUMI, SASSI and SUS were transformed into ranks. For the AttrakDiff

Table 4. Ranks Based on Raw Data of Global Scales

	Ranks			
	SUMI Global Scale	AttrakDiff Attractiveness Scale	SASSI Global Scale	SUS Overall Scale
Tablet PC	2	1	1	1
PDA	1	3	2	2
Unimodal System	3	2	n.a.	n.a.

results of the attractiveness scale were transformed into ranks, since this scale is reflecting the overall attractiveness of the system. The device with the highest value got rank one, the one with lowest score rank three or if data was available for only two devices rank two. Table 4 shows the rankings for each device and each question-naire. The comparison make obvious that the results of different questionnaires are inconsistent. There is no agreement between the questionnaires: No device got the same ranking on all questionnaires. Especially the SUMI-Ratings are not supported from any of the other questionnaires. On the other questionnaires the tablet PC was ranked best and the PDA least. But since the ranks are based on the raw scores and do therefore not show significant differences the ranks only show trends.

Table 5. Pearson Correlations of Global Scales (** $p<.01$; * $p<.05$)

		AttrakDiff Attractiveness Scale	SASSI Global Scale	SUS Overall Scale
Tablet PC	SUMI Global Scale	-.714**	-.817**	-.486*
	AttrakDiff Attractiveness Scale		.664**	.185
	SASSI Global Scale			.583**
PDA	SUMI Global Scale	-.766**	-.771**	.081
	AttrakDiff Attractiveness Scale		.521*	-,335
	SASSI Global Scale			.190
Unimodal System	SUMI Global Scale	-.496*	n.a.	n.a.

In a further step the global or overall scales of the different questionnaires were correlated (s. Table 5). As indicated from the ranking, the SUMI results are least consistent with the results of all other questionnaires: For all devices the SUMI global scale correlates negatively with all other scales, except the PDA's SUS scale. This means that the SUMI global scale results are contradictory to the results of the most other global scales. Regarding the tablet PC the SASSI is highly correlated with AttrakDiff and the SUS. Also for the PDA a significant correlation could be found between SASSI and AttrakDiff.

Additionally to the global scales, scales measuring similar constructs were correlated. The scales efficiency of the SUMI, pragmatic qualities of the AttrakDiff and speed of the SASSI were correlated with each other. Furthermore the scales affect of the SUMI, the hedonic scales of the AttrakDiff and the annoyance scale of the SASSI were correlated.

Significant negative correlations were found for the tablet PC and the PDA between the SUMI scale efficiency and the AttrakDiff's pragmatic qualities scale (s. Table 6). For all devices the SASSI speed scale was neither correlated with the AttrakDiff scale covering pragmatic qualities nor with the SUMI efficiency scale. Thus these scales seem not to provide measures of the same construct.

The scales measuring emotional aspects support the results reported above. Regarding the tablet PC no correlations were found between the SUMI affect scale and all other scales. Both hedonic scales of the AttrakDiff and the SASSI annoyance scale (recoded so that higher values indicate better ratings) correlate positively with each other. This means these scales measure a similar construct. The results for the PDA show significant positive correlation only between both AttrakDiff scales. The ratings of the unimodal system show significant positive correlations between the both hedonic scales of the AttrakDiff and the SUMI affect scale. Only for this measurement the SUMI scales are in strong agreement with results from other questionnaires.

Compared to the scales measuring other constructs, the scales measuring emotional aspects show the highest agreement across all different questionnaires.

Table 6. Pearson Correlations between Scales Measuring Efficiency (** p<.01)

		AttrakDiff Pragmatic Scale	SASSI Speed Scale
Tablet PC	SUMI Efficiency Scale	-.562**	-.220
	AttrakDiff Pragmatic Scale		.307
PDA	SUMI Efficiency Scale	-.655**	.051
	AttrakDiff Pragmatic Scale		-.118
Unimodal System	SUMI Efficiency Scale	-.382	n.a.

Table 7. Pearson Correlations between Scales Measuring Emotional Aspects (** p<.01; *p<.05)

		AttrakDiff Hedonic Stimulation Scale	AttrakDiff Hedonic Identity Scale	Sassi Annoyance Scale
Tablet PC	SUMI Affect Scale	.117	.015	-.48
	AttrakDiff Hedonic-Stimulation Scale		.735**	.624**
	AttrakDiff Hedonic Identity Scale			.674**
PDA	SUMI Affect Scale	.204	.054	-.118
	AttrakDiff Hedonic-Stimulation Scale		.683**	.133
	AttrakDiff Hedonic-Identity Scale			.306
Unimodal System	SUMI Affect Scale	.312	.485*	n.a.
	AttrakDiff Hedonic Stimulation Scale		.638**	n.a.

4 Discussion

The ratings most inconsistent to the results of all other questionnaire are the ratings of the SUMI. The best system according to the SUMI is the PDA. On the AttrakDiff's overall scale attractiveness as well as on the SASSI's global scale the tablet PC got the highest ratings. The SUS reveals no significant difference between the systems.

Further differences where shown for the subscales: Solely on the SUMI the PDA was rated best regarding efficiency. The results of the AttrakDiff's pragmatic quality scale, which is associated with efficiency and with the speed scale of the SASSI, are in sharp contrast to the SUMI results. Both, AttrakDiff as well as SASSI, indicate that the tablet PC is most efficient and the PDA least efficient.

Also, concerning the SUMI affect scale where the PDA was rated best too, the results are inconsistent with similar scales of the other questionnaires. The AttrakDiff implies that the tablet PC has more hedonic qualities than the other systems. The SASSI scales likeability and annoyance also point to the tablet PC as the system most fun to use. Only regarding the unimodal system consistency between AttrakDiff and SUMI could be shown.

Considering these results it remains unclear which system is the one with the best usability. It is rather shown that questionnaires designed for unimodal systems are not very applicable for usability evaluation of multimodal systems, since they seem to measure different constructs. The questionnaires with the most concordance were the AttrakDiff and the SASSI. A possible explanation for that could be that the kind of rating scale, the semantic differential, used in the AttrakDiff is applicable to all systems. The semantic differential uses no direct questions but pairs of bipolar adjectives, which are not linked to special functions of a system. The SASSI uses direct questions but was specifically developed for the evaluation of voice control systems and may therefore be more suitable for multimodal systems including voice control than questionnaires developed for GUI based systems.

Overall further studies are needed to see if these two questionnaires show matching results also for other multimodal systems. Moreover, in a next step these subjective ratings will be validated with more objective and continuous parameters like log data and psychophysiological data recorded during the experiment.

References

[Bernsen and Dybkjær, 2004] Bernsen, N.O., Dybkjær, L.: Evaluation of Spoken Multimodal Conversation. In: Proceedings of the Sixth International Conference on Multimodal Interfaces (ICMI 2004), Penn State University, USA, pp. 38–45 (2004)

[Brooke, 1996] Brooke, J.: SUS: A 'quick and dirty' usability scale. In: Jordan, P.W., Thomas, B., Weerdmeester, B.A., McClelland, I.L. (eds.) Usability Evaluation in Industry, pp. 189–194. Taylor & Francis, London (1996)

[Hassenzahl et al., 2003] Hassenzahl, M., Burmester, M., Koller, F.: AttrakDiff: Ein Fragebogen zur Messung wahrgenommener hedonischer und pragmatischer Qualität. In: Ziegler, J., Szwillus, G. (eds.) Mensch & Computer 2003. Interaktion in Bewegung, pp. 187–196. B.G. Teubner, Stuttgart (2003)

[Hone and Graham, 2000] Hone, K.S., Graham, R.: Towards a tool for the subjective assessment of speech system interfaces (SASSI). Natural Language Engineering 6(3/4), 287–305 (2000)

[Kirakowski and Corbett, 1993] Kirakowski, J., Corbett, M.: SUMI: The software usability measurement inventory. British Journal of Educational Technology 24(3), 210–212 (1993)

[Larsen, 2003] Larsen, L.B.: Assessment of spoken dialogue system usability - what are we really measuring? In: Proceedings of Eurospeech 2003, pp. 1945–1948 (2003)

[Petersen, 1998] Petersen, M.G.: Towards Usability Evaluation of Multimedia Applications. Crossroads 4(4), 3–7 (1998)

[Porteous et al., 1993] Porteous, M., Jurek, K., Corbett, M.: SUMI: User Handbook. Human Factors Research Group, University of Cork, Ireland (1993)

[Sturm, 2005] Sturm, J.: On the usability of multimodal interaction for mobile access to information services. PhD thesis, Radboud University Nijmegen, Nijmegen, The Netherlands (2005)

Subjective Evaluation Method for Speech-Based Uni- and Multimodal Applications

Benjamin Weiss, Ina Wechsung, Anja Naumann, and Sebastian Möller

Deutsche Telekom Laboratories, TU Berlin, 10587 Berlin, Germany
BWeiss@telekom.de,
http://www.qu.tlabs.tu-berlin.de

Abstract. Questionnaires are a widespread method for subjective usability evaluation. Concerning speech-based systems the SASSI questionnaire is probably the most common one. This paper examines SASSI results obtained by different studies in order to evaluate its reliability and validity. Furthermore, it is investigated if SASSI is appropriate also for multimodal systems. The results indicate that some SASSI sub-scales need a revision.

1 Introduction

Services supporting multimodal interaction have attracted increasing interest in the last years. As more of such systems become available, the attention is consequently directed at suitable methods assessing the quality of users experience during interaction. In particular, subjective evaluation can provide useful information to verify the proper choice of modalities and their fission for information output, as well as their fusion for users' input. A typical way to evaluate interactive systems is to carry out (semi-)formal interaction experiments and assess users' judgments with standardized questionnaires. One of the most common questionnaires for speech-based dialog systems is SASSI [Hone and Graham, 2000]. After evaluation with data from eight experiments, the final version of SASSI consists of 34 items on six factors, named *systems response accuracy, likeability, cognitive demand, annoyance, habitability*, and *speed*. However, further research is necessary to confirm the factor structure identified during the development and evaluation of SASSI, as stated by its developers, as well as to evaluate its usage for multimodal systems [Larsen, 2003]. In this paper, the factor structure presented by [Hone and Graham, 2000] is compared to results of three different studies with two distinct scenarios (one unimodal, one multimodal). Possible implications for adjustments of SASSI are discussed.

2 Method

Two different applications were used to collect subjective judgments of spoken interaction in different scenarios, namely a smart home environment and a mobile device for multimedia entertainment.

E. André et al. (Eds.): PIT 2008, LNAI 5078, pp. 285–288, 2008.

2.1   Scenario 1: Smart Home

The smart home environment used in two studies has been developed in the EU-funded IST project INSPIRE (IST-2001-32764). With the help of the IN-SPIRE system, users can operate various devices in the test room by voice [Möller et al., 2007]. The system uses pre-recorded speech as main output modality, although the electronic program guide presents its output visually (search results as lists). The input modality is spoken language only. During the experiments, participants had to operate all devices successively. To do so, they were instructed to fulfil series of six to eleven tasks specified on cards and embedded in everyday situations. After each series, they had to fill out a questionnaire, that includes 20 of the 34 SASSI items and 17 additional items. For the first experiment, each participant had to perform three different series of interactions. 28 subjects participated in this experiment. They were paid for their service. See [Möller et al., 2008] for a more detailed description. In the second experiment, two different series of interactions had to be performed. 32 individuals took part in this experiment (cf. [Gödde et al., 2008] for further information).

2.2   Scenario 2: Mobile Media Service

The application used in this scenario runs on mobile devices (PDA: Fujitsu-Siemens Pocket LOOX T830 / tablet PC: Samsung Q1-Pro 900 Casomii) and provides a service to find, watch and share music clips and television shows, and to watch trailers. Both devices can be operated via voice control as well as via a graphical user interface with touch screen. Additionally, the PDA can be operated via motion control. The users performed five different types of tasks: seven navigation tasks, six tasks where checkboxes had to be marked or unmarked, four tasks were an option from a drop-down list had to be selected, three tasks where a button had to be pressed, and one task where a phone number had to be entered. The participants were verbally instructed to perform the tasks with a given modality. This was repeated for every modality supported by that specific device. After that, the tasks were presented again and the participants could freely choose the interaction modality. Finally, they were asked to fill out different questionnaires to rate the previously tested device. For the SASSI questionnaire, they were told to evaluate the interaction with regard to spoken language. Only these results will be considered here. Each participant tested both devices resulting in two different data sets. 21 individuals participated.

3   Results

3.1   Smart Home

For this analysis, only those 20 items identical to the original SASSI are considered. To test the reliability of the SASSI factors, Cronbach's α was computed for the factors proposed by [Hone and Graham, 2000]. Because only one of these 20 items is assigned to *annoyance* and *habitability* in each case, these sub-scales

Table 1. Results of the reliability analysis of both Scenarios (Cronbach's α)

Sub-Scale	Scenario 1		Scenario 2	
	Experiment 1	Experiment 2	PDA	Tablet PC
Accuracy	.845	.819	.842	.904
Likeability	.848	.840	.883	.836
Cognitive Demand	.745	.748	.836	.814
Speed	.587	.404	.507	.401
Annoyance	—	—	.751	.758
Habitability	—	—	.466	.850

could not be tested. The analysis confirms the reliability of *accuracy*, *likeability*, and *cognitive demand* (see Table 1). By removing some of the items, the sub-scale's reliability (Cronbach's α) could be improved further for *accuracy* and *likeability*. The sub-scale *speed* did not show sufficient reliability. The Kaiser-Meyer-Olkin measure of sampling adequacy (KMO) shows that both data sets are appropriate to be used for a factor analysis ($KMO_{exp1} = .869$, $KMO_{exp2} = .827$). Four principal components are revealed for the first experiment (total variance explained: 63.93%) and five for the second (total variance explained: 67.58%, Varimax rotation, Kaiser normalization, Eigenvalues over one). In both experiments, the first factor contains the majority of items of the SASSI sub-scales *accuracy* and *likeability*. So, these two different sub-scales cannot be seperated in our experiments. However, the sub-scale *cogitive demand* could be confirmed. The remaining factors do not correspond to SASSI sub-scales.

3.2 Mobile Media Service

As for the first scenario, the reliability (Cronbach's α) was computed for all SASSI sub-scales. Regarding the tablet PC all sub-scales except *speed* are consistent. The PDA results are similar: As for the tablet PC the sub-scale *speed* lacks reliability. Furthermore, the sub-scale *habitability* could not be confirmed. As for the first scenario, removing some of the items would improve the sub-scale's reliability further. Detailed results for each device are shown in Table 1.

For both systems a factor analysis was conducted. The number of factors to be extracted was pre-assigned to six according to [Hone and Graham, 2000]. The KMO measure could not be calculated for neither device since the correlation matrix was not positively definite. Furthermore, the determinant is not greater than 0.00001. Thus, it can be concluded that both data sets collected with the mobile media service are not appropriate for a factor analysis because of multicollinearity. The following results should consequently regarded as tentative ones. Regarding the tablet PC this six factors explained 77.74% of the total variance. For the PDA 74.92% of the total variance was explained. The PDA's results show that *likeability* can be confirmed. *Accuracy* and *speed* can not be separated. For *annoyance* the results are sufficient, but not as good as reported from [Hone and Graham, 2000]. Items related to the sub-scales *cognitive demand*

and *habitability* load on several factors. Regarding the tablet PC the factor analysis revealed that the items of the sub-scales *likeability, cognitive demand* and *annoyance* load on one single factor and thus built no independent sub-scales. Items for *accuracy, habitability* and *speed* are distributed over different factors.

4 Conclusion

Despite the limited amount of data examined, some interesting results on the SASSI items and dimensions could be obtained. In all of the four available data sets, the sub-scale *speed* lacks reliability. Moreover, those items building this sub-scale load on different factors for our data and therefore have to be examined closer. In particular, more items are needed to evaluate this sub-scale. It should be reconsidered, if a system's reaction time is perceived akin to the interaction duration at all. We assume that the latter affects subjects in a much more complex way, e.g. interacts heavily with other factors and therefore belongs to a different dimension of quality (cf. also [Möller et al., 2007]).

As expected, results of the factor analysis do not show the well-defined factor structure found in [Hone and Graham, 2000]. To summarize, the sub-scale *likeability* could be confirmed, but mostly overlaps with other predefined scales. For the first (unimodal) scenario, *accuracy* could be confirmed as well. Although items related to *cognitive demand* or *annoyance* display high α-values, these sub-scales cannot be confirmed as independent factors. For the first scenario, this general examination reveals an additional interpretable factor that covers questions regarding *appropriateness of system's reaction, clarity of information* and *clarity of system's expectations* and could be called "communication efficiency" with reference to [Möller et al., 2007]. However, additional studies have to be conducted to obtain a more appropriate data basis for modifying SASSI in order to cover also multimodal systems.

References

[Gödde et al., 2008] Gödde, F., Möller, S., Engelbrecht, K.-P., Kühnel, C., Schleicher, R., Naumann, A., Wolters, M.: Study of a speech-based smart home system with older users. In: IUI4AAL 2008, pp. 287–305 (2008)
[Hone and Graham, 2000] Hone, K.S., Graham, R.: Towards a tool for the subjective assessment of speech system interfaces (SASSI). Natural Language Engineering 6(3/4), 287–305 (2000)
[Larsen, 2003] Larsen, L.B.: Issues in the evaluation of spoken dialogue systems using objective and subjective measures. In: ASRU 2003, pp. 209–214 (2003)
[Möller et al., 2008] Möller, S., Engelbrecht, K.-P., Schleicher, R.: Predicting the quality and usability of spoken dialogue services. Speech Communication (submitted, 2008)
[Möller et al., 2007] Möller, S., Smeele, P., Boland, H., Krebber, J.: Evaluating spoken dialogue systems according to de-facto standards: A case study. Computer Speech and Language 21, 26–53 (2007)

Weighting the Coefficients in PARADISE Models to Increase Their Generalizability

Klaus-Peter Engelbrecht, Christine Kühnel, and Sebastian Möller

Deutsche Telekom Laboratories, TU Berlin, 10587 Berlin, Germany
klaus-peter.engelbrecht@telekom.de

Abstract. For spoken dialog systems, PARADISE [Walker et al. 1997] provides a framework to train a user satisfaction prediction model on given data. The approach weights and sums interaction parameters to predict a satisfaction metric calculated from a questionnaire. In this paper, we try to tackle a major problem of these models, namely their weak generalizability. We show, that the weights associated with interaction parameters in the model change in dependence of the system's major problems by examining correlations under different quantities of understanding errors in the dialogs.

1 Introduction

As spoken dialog systems (SDS) are more widely applied to different tasks and services, we witness an increasing need of evaluation techniques facilitating usability tests. [Walker et al., 1997] proposed the PARADISE framework which allows the prediction of user satisfaction from interaction parameters measured during dialogs. A considerable advantage of this approach is, among others, that real-life data can be considered for evaluation, which can increase the validity of test results drastically. A precondition to such evaluations is, however, that the model trained on experimental data generalizes to the field data.

PARADISE utilizes linear regression (LR) to form a weighted sum of interaction parameters to ideally predict a satisfaction metric acquired on a questionnaire in an experiment. The LR algorithm selects from a set of parameters those which contribute most to the variance of the target and sets the optimal weights to minimize the prediction error. As parameters are z-transformed before the training, the coefficients indicate the relative importance of the parameter to user satisfaction. [Nielsen, 1993] noted that new problems can become visible in user tests once a major problem of the interface has been eliminated. Similarly, the importance of individual predictors in the model can change in dependence of the most prominent interface problems [Hajdinjak and Mihelič, 2006]. This contributes to the low generalizability which is observed for PARADISE models.

In order to gain insight in and quantify the relation between the severity of problems and importance of individual predictors, we analyzed a database acquired with the Wizard-of-Oz (WOZ) technique, in which various speech recognition rates have been simulated. We computed correlations between interaction parameters and a satisfaction metric and observed their change across three categories with varying number

E. André et al. (Eds.): PIT 2008, LNAI 5078, pp. 289–292, 2008.
© Springer-Verlag Berlin Heidelberg 2008

of understanding errors. Then, we analyzed how the perception of individual quality aspects (i.e. questionnaire items) correlates with users' overall satisfaction in the categories. Some of these aspects (hedonic and output-related) are not covered by the interaction parameters. We hypothesized, that these aspects would relate closer to the user satisfaction in the categories with higher understanding accuracies. We also analyzed judgments related to the interaction parameters and compared the results. Before we report our results in Section 3, we will briefly discuss our method.

2 Method

Our database stems from an experiment which was carried out in the EU-funded IN-SPIRE project (IST 2001-32746). The SDS tested in the experiment is capable of controlling domestic devices such as lamps and a video recorder, leading a mixed-initiative dialog with the user. The aim of the experiment was to test the impact of ASR accuracy on user satisfaction by adding different degrees of word substitutions, deletions and insertions to the WOZ's transcription [Trutnev et al., 2004]. 28 users took part in the experiment. Test participants were required to carry out three scenarios, each with 9-11 tasks and covering all devices which can be operated with the system. This results in 84 dialogs in this database. Further details can be found in [Möller et al., 2007].

We chose to divide the data into three equally sized groups by the measured concept accuracy (CA) of the dialogs to ensure that the groups show clearly distinguishable quantities of speech understanding problems. To measure the relation of parameters, we used Spearman's ρ, although LR models demand a linear relationship between the target and predictors. However, our aim was to find any relationships, assuming that predictors could be transformed appropriately if a relation would be detected. Furthermore, our hypothesis implies an uncommon interpretation of significance of correlations. Our aim was to show that a correlation's significance can depend on the CA-groups, i.e., a non-significant correlation can perfectly confirm this hypothesis. Therefore, in this study we report a number of insignificant correlations (asterisks mark significance on the .05(*) or .01(**) level).

Interaction parameters and user judgments in the database can be assigned to six quality aspects, namely effectiveness, efficiency, error frequency, interaction quality, output quality and hedonic aspects. The interaction parameters, which follow a recommendation by the ITU [ITU-T, 2005], can be assigned to the first four aspects. The judgments were acquired with a modified SASSI [Hone and Graham, 2000] questionnaire and cover all mentioned aspects. We assigned them to the aspects by their meaning instead of mutual correlation or factor analysis and examined them individually. However, whenever we were not sure which aspect a judgment belongs to, we decided depending on its correlation with other judgments of the aspects in question.

With respect to the target variable, it has been observed that mean values of several correlated judgments can be predicted better than single judgments. Therefore, we calculated the mean of our judgments on user satisfaction and overall quality ($r=0.87$, $p<0.001$) and used it as the target variable describing the perceived overall quality of the system.

3 Results

We do not report detailed results for all individual parameters or judgments, but present the results quality-aspect-wise. In this, we follow our assumption that parameters as well as individual judgments are *indicators* of the users' perception of the system and the interaction, with perception integrating several parameters or judgments into quality aspects. We analyzed user judgments mainly to access aspects not observable in the interaction parameters, but we also analyzed ratings resembling the parameters to double-check our findings. We first report on the results for interaction parameters.

For EFFECTIVENESS, we analyzed different parameters, including *kappa* [Walker et al., 1997]. Only one parameter – a task success measure derived from hand annotations - shows the expected effect: that it would have more impact on the target variable in the groups with lower CA (correlations from lowest to highest CA group: $\rho = .63^{(**)}/.26/-.21$). The same effect was expected for ERROR FREQUENCY, and confirmed by a number of error related parameters, including *#ASR-rejections* ($-.46^{(*)}/-.28/-.02$), *#PA:IC* (incorrectly parsed sentences; $-.48^{(*)}/-.08/-.19$), *word accuracy* ($.48^{(*)}/-.36/.14$), and *user correction rate* (av. number of utterances concerned with correcting errors; $-.23/ -.14/-.01$). Correlations clearly decreased in the groups with higher CA. Consequently, coefficients of error and task-success-related parameters in a PARADISE model have to be increased if the system tested has a lower average CA value than the system the model was trained on.

EFFICIENCY-related parameters showed the opposite effect and became more important predictors of overall quality in the groups with higher CA (e.g. *#turns* $-.18/-.26/-.31$). Apparently, users become interested in efficiency only if some degree of speech recognition performance is reached.

Parameters assigned to the INTERACTION QUALITY show different effects. E.g., *#barge-in* becomes more important if CA increases ($.06/-.01/.28$), which corresponds to our findings concerning efficiency. We observed the same development for *#help-messages* ($-.26/-.29/-.38$), which describes an aspect of the system's cooperativeness. In turn, *system correction rate*, describing the elegance of the system in coping with understanding errors, is more important in the lower-CA-groups where more such errors occurred ($-.39/-.14/-.07$).

We hypothesized that the quality of the OUTPUT and HEDONIC aspects of the system's usage would show an increased impact on the users' overall impression in the higher-CA-groups. And in fact, an analysis of the corresponding questionnaire items confirmed this. Judgments of the OUTPUT quality correlating less in the low CA groups dealt with *clarity of the information* ($.24/.30/.42^{(*)}$), the *friendliness of the system* ($-.16/.40/.48^{(*)}$) and *naturalness of its voice* ($-.06/.29/.23$). HEDONIC aspects gaining significance as predictors dealt with *pleasantness* ($.70^{(**)}/.74^{(**)}/.87^{(**)}$) and *comfort* ($.73^{(**)}/.71^{(**)}/.84^{(**)}$) of the interaction, while *fun in interaction* was most significant in the group with lowest CA ($.90^{(**)}/.66^{(**)}/.79^{(**)}$).

Unfortunately, when we analyzed the user judgments about EFFECTIVENESS and ERROR FREQUENCIES, we found the opposite effect as for the related interaction parameters. This is especially strange as findings for both, parameters and judgments, are confirmed by several parameters or judgments respectively. Correlations between parameters and judgments range from $0.17 < \rho < 0.72^{(**)}$, thus, no argument can be made that the questionnaire measures different concepts than the parameters.

Question associated with EFFICIENCY consistently correlated highest in the mid CA-group (*efficient handling* $.71^{(**)}/.83^{(**)}/.78^{(**)}$; *dialog short* $.18/.54^{(**)}/.19$; *dialog fast* $.71^{(**)}/.71^{(**)}/.67^{(**)}$). This indicates that the perception of efficiency becomes more important as the system makes less errors, but is relieved by other aspects (one would hypothesize, the hedonic and appearance related) if the dialog runs basically smooth. In comparison, the efficiency parameters still became more important in the highest-CA-group.

Judgments related to INTERACTION QUALITY were consistent with the parameters. The judgment on *error recovery* showed lower correlations for higher CA $(.72^{(**)}/.74^{(**)}/.68^{(**)})$, as did the parameter *system correction rate*, while questions about the system's *flexibility* $(.27/.51^{(*)}/.77^{(**)})$ and *cooperativity* $(.49^{(*)}/.49^{(*)}/.62^{(**)})$ became increasingly important, as did the parameters *# barge-in* and *# help messages*.

4 Conclusion

We analyzed how the impact of interaction parameters on the overall judgment of an SDS changes in relation to the amount of speech understanding problems. Our motivation to do so originates from the wish to improve the generalizability of usability prediction models. We could show how hedonic and output-related aspects replace those related to speech understanding as the latter improves, although the comparison of user judgments and interaction parameters was controversial. We will continue examining such changes in other databases available to us and hope to find confirmation of our results, which eventually will lead to quantified observations. These will be the precondition of a new approach to predict users' satisfaction with SDS.

References

[Walker et al., 1997] Walker, M.A., Litman, D.J., Kamm, C.A., Abella, A.: PARADISE: A Framework for Evaluating Spoken Dialog Agents. In: Proc. Of the ACL/EACL 35th Ann. Meeting of the Assoc. for Computational Linguistics, pp. 271–280 (1997)

[Nielsen, 1993] Nielsen, J.: Usability Engineering. Morgan Kaufmann, Amsterdam (1993)

[Hajdinjak and Mihelič, 2006] Hajdinjak, M., Mihelič, F.: The PARADISE Evaluation Framework: Issues and Findings. Computational Linguistics 32, 263–272 (2006)

[Trutnev et al., 2004] Trutnev, A., Ronzenknop, A., Rajman, M.: Speech Recognition Simulation and its Application for Wizard-of-Oz Experiments. In: Proc. of 4th LREC, pp. 611–614 (2004)

[Möller et al., 2007] Möller, S., Smeele, P., Boland, H., Krebber, J.: Evaluating Spoken Dialog Systems According to De-facto Standards: A Case Study. Computer Speech and Language 21, 26–53 (2007)

[ITU-T, 2005] ITU-T Suppl. 24 to P-Series Rec. Parameters Describing the Interaction with Spoken Dialogue Systems. International Telecommunication Union, Geneva (2005)

[Hone and Graham, 2000] Hone, K.S., Graham, R.: Towards a Tool for the Subjective Assessment of Speech System Interfaces (SASSI). Natural Lang. Engineering 6, 287–303 (2000)

EXPROS: A Toolkit for Exploratory Experimentation with Prosody in Customized Diphone Voices

Joakim Gustafson and Jens Edlund

KTH Speech Music and Hearing
{jocke,edlund}@speech.kth.se

Abstract. This paper presents a toolkit for experimentation with prosody in diphone voices. Prosodic features play an important role for aspects of human-human spoken dialogue that are largely unexploited in current spoken dialogue systems. The toolkit contains tools for recording utterances for a number of purposes. Examples include extraction of prosodic features such as pitch, intensity and duration for transplantation onto synthetic utterances, and creation of purpose-built customized MBROLA mini-voices.

1 Introduction

Prosodic features, such as pitch, intensity and duration, play an important role for many of the aspects of spoken dialogue that are prolific in and central to human-human dialogue, yet to date rarely exploited in human-computer dialogues. Examples include interaction control, the management of turn-taking, interruptions, and back-channels; attitude towards what is said, such as the signalling of uncertainty or certainty; prominence, such as contrastive focus and stress; and grounding, as in brief feedback utterances for verification and clarification. There is a fair body of research into these matters from the spoken dialogue system point of view on the perception side, and some of which has been taken as far as to implementation and experimentation in full-blown spoken dialogue systems. On the production side, there are fewer examples where our knowledge of prosody has made it all the way to full-blown systems. In current spoken dialogue systems, pre-recorded prompts or unit selection synthesis are often chosen for the voice quality. The drawback is that these techniques make it difficult to vary prosody and to control this variation in any detail, so few examples of experimentation with such variations exist (see [Raux and Black, 2003], however, for an example and an overview]. Although there is a large body of studies of prosodic features using re-synthesis with modified prosody (using e.g. Praat[1]) and with HMM synthesis, the results have proven difficult to implement in real on-line systems. Other synthesis methods providing greater control over prosodic features are formant synthesis and diphone synthesis. The relatively low voice quality of formant synthesis makes it unsuitable for many user studies, however, and diphone synthesis suffers from the relatively large cost of recording the required diphones, as well as from less-than-perfect voice quality.

---

[1] http://www.fon.hum.uva.nl/praat/

E. André et al. (Eds.): PIT 2008, LNAI 5078, pp. 293–296, 2008.
© Springer-Verlag Berlin Heidelberg 2008

This paper presents EXPROS, a graphical toolkit that allows us to experiment with prosodic variation in diphone synthesis in a more efficient manner. Before going into the functionality currently built into the toolkit, lets discuss a few of its applications. Our main reason to experiment with prosodic variation is to make spoken dialogue systems that more closely mimic human-human dialogue, in order to better exploit its strengths. This need not be the case for all spoken dialogue system design, but it is our motivation here. The following are three examples of increasing complexity of dialogue needs that EXPROS aim to meet. Each of the examples is illustrated in the demonstration.

(1) A key area where humans excel over current spoken dialogue systems is interaction control, the management of the flow of the dialogue, for example turn-taking and interruptions. An oft-mentioned problem is that of user barge-ins, but we would also want our systems to be able to deal with system barge-ins and self-interrupts in a better manner. The following dialogue excerpts exemplify this:

```
U    What's the weather like in Stockton?
S    The weather in Stockholm? Wait a mo* [*ment, I'll look it up]
U                              No, I said Stockton

U    Any news on fashion /SIL/ in Tibet?
S                    OK, le* [*t me see what I can do]
S                         Ah, let me see what I can do

U    Are there any news about Camden market?
S    Let me see... no, there's no* [*thing new at the moment]
                         /fresh news arrive/
S                    Oh, hang on, there's a fire in Camden!
```

In order for a spoken dialogue system to produce the behaviours listed above, the system's processing in its entirety needs to be incremental, as noted in [Allen et al., 2001] and [Aist et al., 2006]. Here, however, we are only concerned with being able to control the rendering of the speech sounds sufficiently to produce utterances like the ones above.

(2) In order to achieve this kind of dialogue, we need to be able to test variations in perception tests as well as in real human-computer dialogue situations. To do this, we need to be able to record the required prompts with different prosody, at the very least. In many cases, we may want to record new diphones – in the example above, for example, we could record P*_SIL diphones, that go from a phoneme P to silence SIL abruptly, to make the interruptions sound more realistic. Recording extra sets of diphones for hypo- and hyper-articulated speech may also be useful, as well as affective speech, for example angry or despondent. Testing out new voices can be very time consuming, however, as a Swedish diphone voice typically contains some 5000 diphones. This is far too expensive for exploratory studies into the effects of prosodic and voice quality variations. Instead we can create mini-voices – voices with few diphones, that are able to produce only a limited number of utterances, but that are easy to record and to modify.

(3) Finally, pre-recorded prompts, unit selection synthesis, and diphone synthesis all suffer from the need to enrol the original speaker each time the voice is to be extended or changed. A diphone voice production is furthermore often created in one go, and rarely updated or changed after its completion. We attempt to make it possible

for speakers who are not the original speaker to do as many extensions as possible – particularly to record new prosodic patterns, and also for the voice creation to be done incrementally, by making it simple to add new diphones and diphone sets *when they are needed.*

Prompts and voices developed in EXPROS can be used in perception tests, either of standalone prompts or of re-synthesised dialogue utterances, but most importantly they are intended for use in interactive experiments, where the pragmatics – the actual effect prosodic variation has on the interaction – can be measured.

2 The EXPROS Toolkit

The toolkit uses the Snack sound toolkit[2] as its backbone, and integrates functions from a number of existing tools, such as the Mbrola engine and database builder[3], a PC-KIMMO[4] morphological dictionary, NALIGN forced alignment [Sjölander and Heldner, 2005], **/nailon/** prosodic extraction and normalisation [Edlund and Heldner, 2005], etc.

Text processing: Reading and management of (prosodic) labels in the orthographic input. These labels could be used to generate prosodic patterns automatically, such as increased stress or prolonged syllables.

Grapheme to phoneme conversion: The toolkit currently incorporates automatic transcription using PC-KIMMO and a Swedish dictionary with transcribed morphs, an NALIGN CART tree built on Centlex, a Swedish pronunciation dictionary developed at the Centre of Speech Technology, as well as a set of cooarticulation rules (over word boundaries) built into NALIGN. In addition, user lexica can be defined and used.

Automatic speech alignment: The toolkit uses the forced aligner NALIGN to extract phone start and end times from recordings.

Automatic prosody parameter extraction: For prosodic analysis, the toolkit can currently use the methods built into the Snack sound toolkit (ESPS get_f0 and AMDF pitch extraction as well as power analysis, which can be used to estimate spectral tilt). The normalization methods built into **/nailon/** are also available.

Modification of prosodic parameters: The toolkit provides a number of methods for modification of prosodic parameter curves as well as creation of new curves. These include direct manipulation in a GUI, stylisation, normalisation and transformation to another speakers speaking style, model generated prosodic curves, and transplantation of curves from recordings.

Diphone synthesis: The toolkit uses an extended MBROLA synthesis engine [Drioli et al., 2005] which adds control of for example gain, spectral tilt, shimmer and jitter to render audio. Using a combination of the components listed above, the toolkit also gives the possibility to automatically generate the data needed to build new

---

[2] http://www.speech.kth.se/snack/
[3] http://tcts.fpms.ac.be/synthesis/mbrola.html
[4] http://www.sil.org/pckimmo/

MBROLA diphone databases, and some scripts to make on-the-fly modifications to how the MBROLA engine select diphones.

3 Conclusions

Preliminary listening tests suggest that transplanting durations, intensity and pitch from human recordings onto the diphone synthesis makes diphone voices sound considerably better as a whole, which is promising. We have for example used the EX-PROS tool to improve the subjective ratings of a bad speaker, by re-synthesizing 30 seconds of his speech with increased pitch variation and speaking rate [Strangert and Gustafson, Submitted]. Examples are included in the demonstration.

The toolkit has also proven valuable for verifying the quality of automatic prosodic analysis – pitch and intensity extraction as well as phone durations – by listening to the original recording and its resynthesis in parallel – a method inspired by Malfrere & Dutoit [Malfrere and Dutiot, 1997].

Acknowledgements

Thanks to everyone who has put hard work on developing the publically available tools that are used in this toolkit. Special thanks to Thierry Dutoit and MBROLA and Kåre Sjölander (Snack/NALIGN). This work was supported by the Swedish research council project #2006-2172 (Vad gör tal till samtal/What makes speech special) and MonAMI, an Integrated Project under the EC's Sixth Framework Program (IP-035147).

References

[Aist et al., 2006] Aist, G., Allen, J.F., Campana, E., Galescu, L., Gómez Gallo, C.A., Stoness, S.C., Swift, M., Tanenhaus, M.: Software Architectures for Incremental Understanding of Human Speech. In: Proceedings of Interspeech, Pittsburgh PA, USA (2006)
[Allen et al., 2001] Allen, J.F., Ferguson, G., Stent, A.: An architecture for more realistic conversational systems. In: Proceedings of the 6th international conference on Intelligent user interfaces, pp. 1–8 (2001)
[Drioli et al., 2005] Drioli, C., Tesser, F., Tisato, G., Cosi, P.: Control of voice quality for emotional speech synthesis. In: Proceedings of AISV 2004, Padova, pp. 789–798 (2005)
[Edlund and Heldner, 2005] Edlund, J., Heldner, M.: Exploring prosody in interaction control. Phonetica 62(2-4), 215–226 (2005)
[Malfrere and Dutiot, 1997] Malfrere, F., Dutiot, T.: Speech synthesis for text-to-speech alignment and prosodic feature extraction. In: Circuits and Systems: Proc. of ISCAS (1997)
[Raux and Black, 2003] Raux, A., Black, A.: A Unit Selection Approach to F0 Modeling and its Application to Emphasis. In: Proceedings of ASRU 2003, St Thomas, US (2003)
[Strangert and Gustafson, Submitted] Strangert, E., Gustafson, J.: Subject ratings, acoustic measurements and synthesis of good-speaker characteristics, Interspeech 2008, Brisbane (submitted, 2008)
[Sjölander and Heldner, 2005] Sjölander, K., Heldner, M.: Word level precision of the NALIGN automatic segmentation algorithm. In: Proc of The XVIIth Swedish Phonetics Conference, Fonetik 2004, pp. 116–119. Stockholm University (2004)

Automatic Evaluation Tool for Multimodal Dialogue Systems

Hugo Wesseling[1,2], Matthias Bezold[1,2], and Nicole Beringer[1]

[1] Elektrobit Automotive GmbH, Am Wolfsmantel 46, 91058 Erlangen, Germany
[2] University of Ulm, Institute of Information Technology, Albert-Einstein-Allee 43, 89081 Ulm, Germany
hugo.wesseling@uni-ulm.de, matthias.bezold@uni-ulm.de,
nicole.beringer@elektrobit.com

Abstract. This paper presents a system built for improving the evaluation process of multimodal dialogue systems by providing a graphical representation of event-based recording data. Low-level information from recordings can visually be combined to form higher-level actions using pattern definitions to create a hierarchy of actions. Actions are visually represented by a multitrack player-like view where all modalities of the recording can be watched and manipulated. But besides tagging and derivation of higher-level actions, further help is provided by a correlation analysis and an export of charts and tables to Microsoft Excel. The tool is tested on recording data and questionnaire answers obtained from Wizard of Oz (WOZ) experiments performed within the DICIT project.

1 Introduction

One of the last stages in the development of interactive systems is normally the usability test. During this test, a number of people are asked to perform typical tasks that the system supports while they are being recorded. Moreover, they are asked to fill in a questionnaire. The recordings and questionnaire answers will then be analyzed to extract helpful quantitative and qualitative information (metrics). This process involves combining and analyzing large amounts of data, which can be a very complex task without proper tool support. In this paper, a tool is presented to ease the manipulation of recorded data and support the process of extracting the needed metrics. It generates a common format for all evaluation information in different modalities and converts recording data into so-called actions. Based on these actions, a hierarchy of higher-level actions containing task-related information can be created and metrics can be extracted. The tool is tested on recording data obtained from a Wizard of Oz (WOZ) evaluation performed within the DICIT (Distant-talking Interfaces for Control of Interactive TV) project [DICIT, 2007]. Besides improving distant-talking speech recognition, a goal of the DICIT project is to develop a multimodal interface for an interactive TV system, which can be controlled by voice and remote control.

While there are several tools that facilitate the annotation or tagging of speech-based and multimodal recording data, their focus is mostly on creating an annotation corpus, but not on providing specific evaluation support. For

E. André et al. (Eds.): PIT 2008, LNAI 5078, pp. 297–305, 2008.

example, ANVIL [Kipp, 2001] or the TASX-environment [Milde and Gut, 2002] are time-based annotation frameworks, which can export the annotated data for further processing, but do not offer evaluation facilities themselves. The graphical approach of PROMISE [Beringer et al., 2002a] integrates annotated multimodal data and spoken dialogue evaluation metrics and provides means for automatically clustering and relating data to corresponding answers out of a questionnaire. The tool presented in this paper provides additional facilities for the evaluation process.

This paper is organized as follows. In Section 2, a description of the general design goals is given and the realization of each goal is explained. Section 3 then contains future work that can be done to improve and expand the tool.

2   Tool Support for the Evaluation of Multimodal Systems

The main goal of this project is to create a tool that can assist and process automatically many of the tasks involved in the evaluation process of a multimodal dialogue system. This goal can be subdivided by looking into a typical evaluation procedure, which very roughly follows the following steps.

1. Preparing the evaluation: Setting up a usability test including a questionnaire, determining the goals of the evaluation and creating the questionnaire, specifying the tasks that are to be evaluated, and providing the accompanying descriptions for the users of the system.
2. Performing the usability test on a number of users, recording all relevant data, and storing questionnaire answers.
3. Preprocessing the data (e.g. annotation of captured audio, synchronization of different streams).
4. Evaluating the data: Converting the recorded data into a format that can be handled easily by a human, deriving metrics from the different types, and presenting the calculated metrics for further evaluation.

This evaluation tool focuses on item 4. After the user tests are performed and the data is stored in a formalized way, the tool should be able to assist in obtaining well-presented metric data and providing objective reasons for subjective assumptions. In the following sections, we present how the evaluation tool can support the single steps in the evaluation of the recording data.

2.1   Aggregating Data

Two kinds of data are produced by an evaluation of an interactive system: Time-based data such as log data or annotations of audio and video data, which are usually derived from automatically recorded data, and non time-based data such as questionnaires.

Time-based data can be specified by a type, a start time, a duration, and additional optional parameters. For example, a button press on a remote control could be seen as an action of type "pressKey" with the time specified since the beginning of the recording and the pressed key as a parameter. This is from now on referred to as an *action*. To convert a log file of a recording into a set of actions, *conversion rules* can be specified. These rules consist of a pattern to be identified in the log file (from now on referred to as *log pattern*) and *executions* that fire upon finding such a log pattern. Log patterns contain variable parts that are used to fill in the parameters of the actions, e.g. the name of the pressed button. The most common execution is that of generating an action. For instance, a rule can define the pattern and an execution to convert all "pressKey" actions into a general action format. The tool supports log files in text line format and object oriented text (for instance XML). Text-based log data can for example be data created by the dialogue manager's logging facilities, whereas object-oriented text can for instance be created by other tools such as annotation tools (e.g. Praat[1]).

Data that is not time-based (e.g. questionnaire data) is converted into a different type of format and can later be used for a correlation analysis. In order to process questionnaire data, it has to be formalized by describing each question as a label, a description, and an answer type. If the answer type is multiple choice, the possible answers should also be given labels and descriptions. When filling in the questionnaire, the answers are stored connected to the question labels. Questions asking for an answer in a one dimensional scale (such as a 7 point scale question) should be stored as a single number.

2.2   Deriving Metrics from Low-level Actions

This section discusses the presentation of the low-level data and the derivation of higher-level information from it by means of action patterns that can be specified graphically.

The low-level data that was aggregated by conversion rules is presented in the main window (Fig. 1), which is designed to look like a multi-track audio player with a track for each action type. In the figure, nine different action types have been created out of the log files. These action types can be found at the left side of the top frame of Fig. 1 and each type is represented by a time line. Moreover, additional viewing components can be created to better visualize certain log types, e.g. a Screenshot View (bottom right) or a Hard Key Events View (bottom left) for visualizing the remote control interaction. All actions including recorded audio can be played back in a synchronized way using the "Play" button and all positions of the recording can be selected using a slider.

The displayed information is, although readable, still in a low-level format. The next step is to build higher-level actions out of the low-level actions in a hierarchical way to get more expressive actions that can be connected to task information. An example of such a hierarchy is given in Fig. 2. Starting from low-level actions like key presses or a recognized speech input, the hierarchy builds up toward actions like selecting an actor and from there on to specifying a certain show. The process of building a higher-level action out of underlying (and previously defined) actions works with a pattern-based specification.

---

[1] Praat: http://www.praat.org/

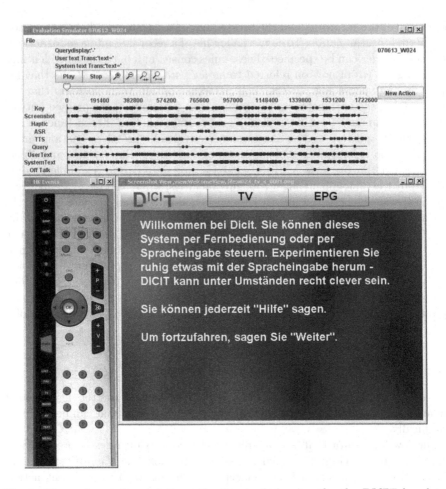

Fig. 1. The main windows of the evaluation tool showing the the DICIT log data, including a screenshot of the current view and a remote control visualization

A nondeterministic finite automaton is used to specify a *pattern matcher*, which can detect the specified pattern in action time lines based on the name of the action, the parameters, and global condition variables. Patterns are composed of sequences, repeats, and conditional clauses, like regular expressions. Actions that do not occur in the definition are skipped, if not specified otherwise. Moreover, a comparison operator is declared for matching the pattern action with the low-level actions, e.g. "equals". For each matched pattern, a higher-level action is created starting at the first match time and ending at the last match time. Moreover, a maximum time difference between two subsequent actions can be specified to limit the distance in time between two actions.

In order to illustrate the definition of patterns, a visual definition of a pattern for a volume change event, which is defined by a sequence of key presses of volume-up or volume-down keys, is given in Fig. 3. When an action of the

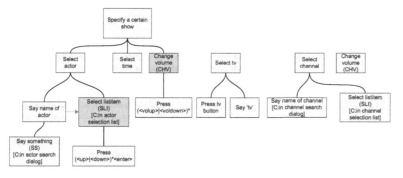

Fig. 2. The hierarchical task tree showing the composition of tasks out of actions

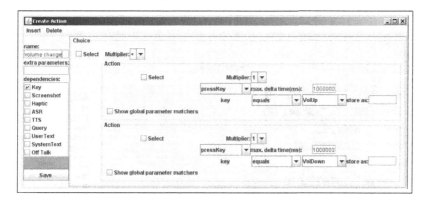

Fig. 3. Visual creation of a pattern to create a higher-level event out of lower-level events

"pressKey" type is encountered, the matcher compares the key parameter of the matcher with that of the action based on the selected "equals" condition and adds a higher-level event, if they match. In this example, an action is created from the time of the first occurrence of the action until the last time a volume up or down key is pressed. Using this pattern matcher, multiple higher-level actions are created over the length of one recording (see bottom time line "volume change" in Fig. 4), some being only single key presses and some intervals.

Moreover, conditions with global values can be attached to the pattern definitions to be able to differentiate between different contexts. For instance, the current screen of the dialogue as the context definition can be used to differentiate between a selection in a result list and a television channel list. The global condition values are loaded by a conversion rule that creates a global variable change. An example of two conditional patterns is shown in the "Select listitem" actions in Fig. 2.

Using these kinds of action matchers, a pattern is capable of calculating the number of volume changes a user performs during a session and the amount of

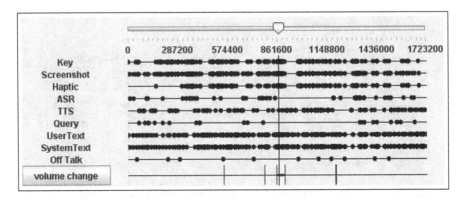

Fig. 4. A part of the main window of the tool showing the time based actions and one higher-level action called "volume change"

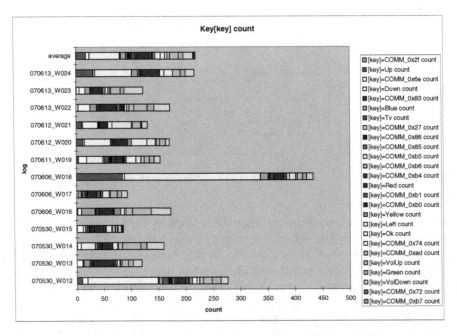

Fig. 5. Generation of a chart in Excel containing a breakdown of the different kinds key presses per user

time each volume change takes, which can be stored as possible metrics. In this way, large amounts of metrics can be generated, for instance the instrumental metrics specified in [Möller, 2005], speech metrics from [Walker et al., 2000] or [Dybkjær and Bernsen, 2001], or multimodal ones from [Beringer et al., 2002b].

2.3   Presenting the Results

The last step of the evaluation supported by the tool is presenting the data. Two data representations are available, the generation of charts and tables for Microsoft Excel and a correlation analysis.

First, charts and tables for Microsoft Excel can be generated for selected actions. The number of actions per user and the average amount of time this action takes is displayed in a graph. Moreover, it is possible to first break up the actions according to parameter values and to display the counts and averages for each parameter. For instance, separate graphs can be generated for each value of the "key" parameter of the keypress action to indicate key usage per person and per key as shown in Fig. 5.

Second, a correlation analysis is available for any action-based information (counts, average lengths and total length of an action per person) and questionnaire point scale question answers. This type of analysis enables the evaluator to determine positive or negative correlations between a subjective idea of the user and the objectively measured times and counts of actions. Correlations can be computed for all data out of the recorded data and questionnaire data that is available in a formalized format. For data mining purposes, thousands of metrics can be compared with each other to reveal expected and unexpected correlations. For instance, a negative correlation was found between the question if the users liked the voice and the amount of off-talk the user produced in the DICIT WOZ system.

3   Future Work

In this section, directions of future improvements are presented.

Evaluation Based on Subgroups of the User Base

An examination of only a part of the user group can be revealing, for instance by dividing the evaluation up into different age groups. This split-up of data can be performed based on the personal information obtained by the questionnaire, such as gender, expertise level, education, or age.

Automatic Action Generation

A start has been made in automatically detecting interesting patterns in user behavior, whereas interestingness is defined by the length of the pattern and the user reactions to the system. If the user tends to do the same action in a certain menu all the time, this pattern can be identified. Common long sequences of user input could imply a badly designed interface and point towards redesigning it to shorten the input sequence needed for frequently used functions.

EB GUIDE Studio Connection

By connecting the evaluation tool to the modeling software used in designing the system, the problem areas of the evaluated system can be traced directly in the system design. EB GUIDE Studio [Fleischmann, 2007, Goronzy et al., 2006], which is a multimodal modeling tool for statechart based multimodal dialogue systems, was employed for the DICIT prototype and work has been done in connecting these tools by showing how much time is spent in certain parts of the system and following the execution of state machines inside the dialogue.

Evaluation of Visual Data

On top of the above mentioned connection with EB GUIDE Studio, an analyzer can be built that extracts dialogue interface information and correlates this with associated metrics. User test recordings of different designs but comparable functionality can then be used to determine which design delivers better user experience. This can be accomplished by connecting interface components to low-level actions, which through the hierarchy determines the affected higher-level actions and metrics.

4   Conclusion

The current prototype version of the evaluation tool provides a structured overview of recorded user test data and assists in the manipulation to calculate a wide array of metrics. When comparing the graphical evaluation process using the tool with a standard approach like writing scripts for each metric, this method is more intuitive and supports the use by a non-programmer. Also, if more than one person is involved in the same evaluation, the tool ensures a uniform definition of the separate metrics. Moreover, the action hierarchy can be expanded easily to add a large amount of different measurements about the dialogue. The tool was applied to recording data of a Wizard of Oz evaluation performed for the DICIT project.

Acknowledgements

This work has been partly funded by the European Commission under the Framework Programme FP6 IST-034624.

References

[Beringer et al., 2002a] Beringer, N., Hans, S., Louka, K., Tang, J.: How to relate User Satisfaction and System Performance in Multimodal Dialogue Situations - a Graphical Approach. In: International CLASS Workshop on Natural, Intelligent and Effective Interaction in Multimodal Dialogue Systems, pp. 8–14 (2002a)

[Beringer et al., 2002b] Beringer, N., Kartal, U., Louka, K., Schiel, F., Türk, U.: PROMISE - A Procedure for Multimodal Interactive System Evaluation. In: 3rd International Conference on Language Resources and Evaluation (LREC), pp. 77–80 (2002b)

[DICIT, 2007] DICIT (2007), http://dicit.fbk.eu/

[Dybkjær and Bernsen, 2001] Dybkjær, L., Bernsen, N.: Usability Evaluation in Spoken Language Dialogue Systems. In: Workshop on Evaluation for Language and Dialogue Systems, pp. 1–10 (2001)

[Fleischmann, 2007] Fleischmann, T.: Model Based HMI Specification in an Automotive Context. In: Smith, M.J., Salvendy, G. (eds.) HCII 2007. LNCS, vol. 4557, pp. 31–39. Springer, Heidelberg (2007)

[Goronzy et al., 2006] Goronzy, S., Mochales, R., Beringer, N.: Developing speech dialogs for multimodal HMIs using finite state machines. In: 9th International Conference on Spoken Language Processing (Interspeech), CD-ROM (2006)

[Kipp, 2001] Kipp, M.: ANVIL - A Generic Annotation Tool for Multimodal Dialogue. In: 7th European Conference on Speech Communication and Technology (Eurospeech), pp. 1367–1370 (2001)

[Milde and Gut, 2002] Milde, J.-T., Gut, U.: The TASX-environment: an XML-based Toolset for Time Aligned Speech Corpora. In: 3rd International Conference on Language Resources and Evaluation (LREC), pp. 1922–1927 (2002)

[Möller, 2005] Möller, S.: Parameters for Quantifying the Interaction with Spoken Dialogue Telephone Services. In: 6th SIGdial Workshop on Discourse and Dialogue, pp. 166–177 (2005)

[Walker et al., 2000] Walker, M., Kamm, C., Litman, D.: Towards Developing General Models of Usability with PARADISE. Nat. Lang. Eng. 6(3-4), 363–377 (2000)

Towards a Perception-Based Evaluation Model for Spoken Dialogue Systems

Sebastian Möller and Klaus-Peter Engelbrecht

Deutsche Telekom Laboratories, TU Berlin, 10587 Berlin, Germany
sebastian.moeller@telekom.de
http://www.qu.tlabs.tu-berlin.de

Abstract. In order to facilitate the evaluation of advanced spoken dialogue systems (SDSs), we present the architecture for a new quality prediction model. The architecture follows the perception, judgment and action processes which are assumed to take place in a user interacting with a dialogue system. It is pointed out which components of the model are already available, and how they may be improved in the future.

1 Introduction

Current evaluation of SDSs is based on experiments where real or test users interact with the system and provide ratings of their impression in an appropriate questionnaire [ITU-T Rec. P.851, 2003]. The interactions are logged, and from the log files interaction parameters quantifying user and system behavior are derived [ITU-T Suppl. 24 to P-Series Rec., 2005]. On the basis of such parameters, linear regression models like PARADISE [Walker et al., 1997] are able to estimate mean overall quality judgments, as they could be obtained by asking users. Although PARADISE usually covers only around 40-50% of the variance in the individual judgments, it has been shown to lead to adequate predictions of *mean* ratings of different users for different system configurations [Engelbrecht and Möller, 2007], with correlations above 90%. In this way, it supports system development by predicting the effect of system changes on the overall quality and usability of the system.

However, for a detailed system evaluation and for identifying problematic usage situations, a better prediction of judgments reflecting individual dialogs – rather than mean values of groups of cases – is necessary. So far, it is not completely clear why prediction of mean values is so much more accurate than prediction of single judgments. Obviously, there is a more immediate relationship between measured interaction parameters and perceived quality of the system, but individual cases of judgment involve some variation induced by internal processes of the user, which are hidden from our observation. In order to be able to predict individual judgments, we review work related to quality perception and judgment and propose a new architecture for a general quality prediction model for SDSs in Section 2. Following this, we present some initial thoughts on how parts of this architecture can be implemented in Section 3, and topics for future work in Section 4.

E. André et al. (Eds.): PIT 2008, LNAI 5078, pp. 306–309, 2008.

2   Quality Perception and Judgment Model

We build on previous research in the field of auditory quality [Raake, 2006]. Here, the quality judgment process is modeled as the result of a comparison between a *perceptual event* and an *internal reference*, happening in a specific temporal and spatial context (thus the notion of "event"). The perceptual event results from a *physical event* presented to the human listener. All three, the physical and the perceptual event and the internal reference, can be described in terms of a parametric profile, e.g. an energy profile for the physical event, or a factor-loading profile of the perceptual event. By comparing the perceptual event to the internal reference, a *quality event* is triggered. Perceptual and quality events are hidden from observers, but can be described by the listener, e.g. using a rating scale.

Models for predicting auditory quality on the basis of physical signals often try to transform the physical sound event into a psycho-acoustic representation of the perceptual event, e.g. in terms of loudness or other perceptual dimensions. A reference signal is generated and represented in the same way, so that a simple comparison can be performed as a distance between the two representations. This distance is integrated over time and considered to be an estimation of the quality event. It is quantified by mapping it to an appropriate rating scale.

We can assume that the processes involved in judging SDS quality are more complex, because users actively participate in the interaction, and by this in the generation of the stimulus to be judged upon. As a consequence, our architecture includes components describing the process of taking actions in the interaction. Such components have been proposed e.g. for the MeMo workbench [Möller et al., 2006], in terms of probabilistic rule-based simulations of assumed user behavior. We postpone a detailed discussion of this part of the model to future papers.

Fig. 1 shows our proposed architecture for a general model predicting SDS quality. The upper part shows the four components involved in processing a judgment on the auditory perception, as described in the previous section. While we consider the same four components to be necessary in our model, they certainly differ in their details from the corresponding parts of a model predicting

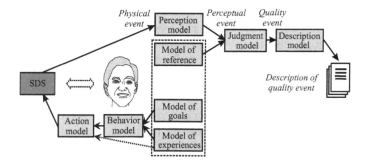

Fig. 1. General architecture of a perception-based evaluation model

auditory quality alone. The lower part shows internal processes of the user which are involved in taking actions in the interaction with the SDS. Here, the user's goals and experiences have to be considered as determinants of a user behavior model. User behavior has to be translated into actions, namely user utterances generated by the action model.

If we consider the user interacting with the SDS, the physical, the perceptual and the quality event will be largely influenced by the actions taken by the user, and consequently by the reactions of the system. Note that immediate user goals may depend on the quality event of the past interaction experience. In turn, the user's goals and experience will have an impact on the quality event, by influencing the internal reference.

3   Description of Model Components

Since we feel that we are far from understanding the perception, judgment and action process as a whole, we will focus on the detailed description of the upper components of our architecture following the physical event.

Perception model: This model describes the peripheral and cognitive processes transforming the physical event into a perceptual event. Measuring this transformation is more complicated than for an audio stimulus, as the dimensions underlying interactions are not as clear and cannot be separated easily. For the description of the physical event, we propose a parametric profile on different levels, namely a surface level (e.g. number of utterances, durations), a semantic level (e.g. number of concepts), and a pragmatic level (e.g. number of meta-communication events, appropriateness of system utterances) [ITU-T Suppl. 24 to P-Series Rec., 2005]. For the description of the perceptual dimensions, we propose to use factor analyses of questionnaire ratings, which have shown to yield some generalizability [Hone and Graham, 2000, Möller, 2005].

Reference: The reference includes all individual and functional aspects of the quality-formation process, e.g. the individual preferences of the user, habituation, emotions, task specific aspects, etc. Parts of this reference fix the "ideal points" on each dimension of the perceptual event. Other parts of the reference are triggered by the user and system interaction behavior, or by the model components in the lower part of our architecture. For example, an emotion like frustration might be modeled in dependance of negative events, such as repetitive system behavior in response to user actions. Individual preferences are predefined as user characteristics; these characteristics will be linked to the experiences in the lower part of our model.

Judgment model: The judgment model compares the perceptual event to a similar representation which is part of the reference, e.g. using a distance or similarity metric. Provided that the reference can be described in the same way as the perceptual event, a simple distance can be computed. More sophisticated models weight each dimension according to its impact on overall quality.

Description model: The description model transforms the distance or similarity measure of the judgment model into an interpretable index of quality, e.g. expressed on a rating scale of a standard questionnaire. It should reflect scale usage for the target user group and context. Either the judgment or the description model include aspects of the temporal development of the quality judgment process during the interaction, e.g. in terms of an accumulation of "bad events".

4 Future Work

The modules of our architecture are still incomplete, but we foresee that considerable advances can be made in the near future. We think that an in-depth analysis of the relations between the events is necessary to define appropriate transformation models. This analysis can be supported by simulations of the lower parts of the architecture [Möller et al., 2006]. The transformations are not necessarily linear like PARADISE, as non-linear models can better predict ideal points of individual perceptual and quality dimensions. The profiles and transformations have to be verified for a range of systems and user groups. We think that the final establishment of our complete model will make evaluation far more efficient, and will ultimately foster advances in spoken dialogue technology.

References

[Engelbrecht and Möller, 2007] Engelbrecht, K.-P., Möller, S.: Pragmatic usage of linear regression models for the prediction of user judgments. In: Proc. 8th SIGdial Workshop on Discourse and Dialogue, Antwerp, pp. 291–294 (2007)

[Hone and Graham, 2000] Hone, K.S., Graham, R.: Towards a tool for the subjective assessment of speech system interfaces (SASSI). Natural Language Engineering 6(3-4), 287–303 (2000)

[ITU-T Rec. P.851, 2003] ITU-T Rec. P.851 Subjective Quality Evaluation of Telephone Services Based on Spoken Dialogue Systems. International Telecommunication Union, Geneva (2003)

[ITU-T Suppl. 24 to P-Series Rec., 2005] ITU-T Suppl. 24 to P-Series Rec. Parameters Describing the Interaction with Spoken Dialogue Systems. International Telecommunication Union, Geneva (2005)

[Möller, 2005] Möller, S.: Perceptual quality dimensions of spoken dialogue systems: A review and new experimental results. In: Proc. 4th European Congress on Acoustics (Forum Acusticum), Budapest, pp. 2681–2686 (2005)

[Möller et al., 2006] Möller, S., Englert, R., Engelbrecht, K., Hafner, V., Jameson, A., Oulasvirta, A., Raake, A., Reithinger, N.: MeMo: Towards automatic usability evaluation of spoken dialogue services by user error simulations. In: Proc. Interspeech, Pittsburgh PA, pp. 1786–1789 (2006)

[Raake, 2006] Raake, A.: Speech Quality of VoIP: Assessment and Prediction. John Wiley & Sons Ltd., Chichester (2006)

[Walker et al., 1997] Walker, M.A., Litman, D.J., Kamm, C.A., Abella, A.: PARADISE: A framework for evaluating spoken dialogue agents. In: Proc. of the 35th ACL/EACL Ann. Meeting, pp. 271–280 (1997)

Author Index

Lecture Notes in Artificial Intelligence (LNAI)